I0816296

GOLDEN DAWN RITUALS

Chic Cicero

Charles "Chic" Cicero was born in Buffalo, New York. An early love of music, particularly of the saxophone, resulted in Chic's many years of experience as a lead musician in several jazz, blues, and rock ensembles, working with many famous performers in the music industry. Chic's interest in Freemasonry and the Western Esoteric Tradition resulted in research articles on Rosicrucianism and the Knights Templar, printed in such publications as *Ars Quatuor Coronatorum* and the *1996-2000 Transactions of the Metropolitan College of the SRIA*. Chic is a member of several Masonic, Martinist, and Rosicrucian organizations. He is a Past Grand Commander of the Grand Commandery of Knights Templar in Florida (2010–11) and is a past Chief Adept of the Florida College of the Societas Rosicruciana in Civitatibus Foederati (2016–23). He was also a close personal friend and confidant of Dr. Israel Regardie. Having established a Golden Dawn temple in 1977, Chic was one of the key people who helped Regardie resurrect a legitimate, initiatory branch of the Hermetic Order of the Golden Dawn in the United States in the early 1980s. He met his wife and coauthor, Sandra Tabatha Cicero, shortly thereafter.

Chic is an author and a skilled craftsman who has constructed all the ritual implements of the Golden Dawn. He is particularly fond of ritual, skrying, and the tarot.

Sandra Tabatha Cicero

Sandra "Tabatha" Cicero was born in rural Wisconsin. Her areas of interest include drawing, painting, poetry, theater, dance, and printmaking. A lifelong fascination with the creative arts has served to inspire her work in the magical world. After graduating from the University of Wisconsin–Milwaukee with a bachelor's degree in fine arts in 1982, Tabatha worked as an entertainer, typesetter, editor, commercial artist, and computer graphics illustrator. In 2009 she obtained an associate in science degree in paralegal studies. She is a member of several Martinist and Rosicrucian organizations.

Tabatha met her husband and coauthor, Charles "Chic" Cicero, in the early 1980s, and the Golden Dawn system of magic has been her primary spiritual focus ever since. Tabatha spent five years working on the paintings for the *Golden Dawn Magical Tarot*, which she began at the encouragement of Israel Regardie.

Both Chic and Tabatha are Chief Adepts of the Hermetic Order of the Golden Dawn as reestablished by Israel Regardie (www.hermeticgoldendawn.org). The Hermetic Order of the Golden Dawn, of which Chic is the G.H. Imperator Emeritus and Tabatha is the G.H. Imperatrix, is an international Order with temples in several countries. Tabatha is also the Imperatrix of the Societas Rosicruciana in America (www.sria.org).

GOLDEN DAWN RITUALS

Rites and Ceremonies for Groups and Solo Magicians

CHIC CICERO &
SANDRA TABATHA CICERO

LLEWELLYN
WOODBURY, MINNESOTA

FIRST EDITION
First Printing, 2025

Cover design by Shira Atakpu
Interior illustration credits on page 455

Llewellyn Publications is a registered trademark of Llewellyn Worldwide Ltd.

Library of Congress Cataloging-in-Publication Data (Pending)
ISBN: 978-0-7387-7926-3

Llewellyn Publications
A Division of Llewellyn Worldwide Ltd.
2143 Wooddale Drive
Woodbury, MN 55125-2989
www.llewellyn.com

Printed in the United States of America

GPSR Representation:
UPI-2M PLUS d.o.o., Medulićeva 20, 10000 Zagreb, Croatia
matt.parsons@upi2mbooks.hr

Other Books by Chic Cicero & Sandra Tabatha Cicero

Golden Dawn Magic

The Babylonian Tarot

Tarot Talismans

The Essential Golden Dawn: An Introduction to High Magic

Self-Initiation into the Golden Dawn Tradition

The Enochian Skrying Tarot (coauthored with Bill and Judi Genaw)

The Golden Dawn Magical Tarot (tarot kit)

Creating Magical Tools: The Magician's Craft

Ritual Use of Magical Tools

Experiencing the Kabbalah

Secrets of a Golden Dawn Temple: The Alchemy and Crafting of Magical Implements

Llewellyn's Golden Dawn series:

- *Book I: Divination*
- *Book II: Qabalah: Theory and Magic*
- *Book III: The Art of Hermes*
- *The Magical Pantheons: A Golden Dawn Journal*

Secrets of a Golden Dawn Temple: Book I: Creating Magical Tools (Thoth Publications)

Basics of Magic: The Best of the Golden Dawn Journal: Book I: Divination (H.O.G.D. Books)

The Book of Concourse of the Watchtowers (H.O.G.D. Books)

Regardie Books Edited and Annotated by Chic Cicero & Sandra Tabatha Cicero

The Middle Pillar: The Balance Between Mind and Magic
By Israel Regardie (3rd edition, edited and annotated with new material by the Ciceros)

A Garden of Pomegranates: Skrying on the Tree of Life
By Israel Regardie (3rd edition, edited and annotated with new material by the Ciceros)

The Tree of Life: An Illustrated Study in Magic
By Israel Regardie (3rd edition, edited and annotated with new material by the Ciceros)

The Philosopher's Stone: Spiritual Alchemy, Psychology, and Ritual Magic
By Israel Regardie (3rd edition, edited and annotated with new material by the Ciceros)

Gold: Israel Regardie's Lost Book of Alchemy
By Israel Regardie (1st edition, edited and annotated by the Ciceros)

To Adam and Isidora,
our good friends and companions
who have walked with us
on the path of the
Magic of Light
for forty-plus years now
and have contributed to our progress
in ways too numerous to mention.
There are no finer magicians
anywhere.

CONTENTS

FIGURES

TABLES

INTRODUCTION

Golden Dawn magic is worked through the practice of ritual magic, a structured spiritual practice that utilizes symbols, actions, and repetition to bring about a specific goal. Ritual is both action and idea: A well-crafted ritual is a compass that gives us direction and purpose. It allows us to achieve ever higher states of awareness and gauge our progress because it provides an external marker of an inner process of spiritual evolution. Within the Golden Dawn tradition, the transforming power of ritual is a powerful psychopompic tool for both individual and communal growth. Whether we perform ritual privately in the confines of our personal temple space or collectively with our magical companions, ritual magic establishes an inner sanctum where we can hone our skills in the magical arts, cultivate our often latent psychic abilities, and construct a framework for exploring the mysteries of the divine realm and our relationship to it.

One constant is that ritual magic is experiential. It must be experienced in order to bring forth the fruits that magicians past and present have promised. Reading about ritual magic is not enough. Owning a library full of occult books is insufficient. Endless pontification about magical minutiae will not cut it. Ritual magic is a physical, mental, and psychic exercise routine. It is a workout for the body, soul, and spirit. This is why magicians refer to the *practice* of magic. And Golden Dawn magicians in particular have a rich tradition of magic to draw upon.

This is not a book for beginners. Our previous book *Golden Dawn Magic* was an introductory guide to the high magical arts within our tradition. It provided readers with a foundation in the language, symbolism, exercises, and techniques that are essential for understanding and practicing the Golden Dawn's system of magic. *Golden Dawn Rituals* picks up where *Golden Dawn Magic* left off. It takes a further step, delving into the multifaceted art of ritual and equipping readers with a series of rites and ceremonies that can greatly enhance the work of any aspiring Golden Dawn magician.

It is not our wish to cover material that is readily available elsewhere. Readers who desire more information on the fundamental teachings, theoretical underpinnings, magical ethics, principles, and structure of the Golden Dawn system should consult our previous books *Golden Dawn Magic* and *The Essential Golden Dawn*. The initiation rituals of the system can be found in Israel Regardie's text *The Golden Dawn: The Original Account of the Teachings, Rites, and Ceremonies of the Hermetic Order.* If you prefer the route of the solo practitioner, consult our book *Self-Initiation into the Golden Dawn Tradition*.

Golden Dawn Rituals focuses on practical working rites that can be used or adapted by adherents of our tradition. It presents students with various types of ritual magic contained within our system and guides them through the details of ritual architecture and rationale.

Readers of this book should already know and have experience performing the basic exercises and rituals of our tradition. Outer Order students should be familiar with the magical techniques of rhythmic breathing, meditation, visualization, the Qabalistic Cross, the Lesser Ritual of the Pentagram, and the Exercise of the Middle Pillar. They will also need to know the arrangement of the Neophyte Hall and its symbolism, as well as the attributes and duties of the Officers who function within it. At a minimum, they will need to have assimilated basic Order teachings on magical correspondences such as the elements, the planets, the Zodiacal signs, the Hebrew alphabet, and the Qabalistic Tree of Life.

Advanced students and Golden Dawn Adepts will need to have expertise in the Supreme Ritual of the Pentagram, the Lesser Ritual of the Hexagram, the Greater Ritual of the Hexagram, the Analysis of the Keyword, the Rose Cross Ritual, the Opening by Watchtower, godform assumption, and skrying or spirit vision work. They should also have a firm working knowledge of the Golden Dawn's Enochian Watchtowers and the symbolism involved in the Vault of the Adepti. All this material can be found in the texts mentioned above. If you are not familiar with any of these topics or rituals, we suggest you put this book aside for the time being and consult *Golden Dawn Magic* and other suggested texts first.

Ritual magic in our tradition employs several methods for building a magical landscape, including prayer and invocation, the vibration of divine names and words of power, symbolic postures or gestures, purifications, consecrations, the raising of power, the movement of energy, focused concentration, psychic sensitivity, intuitive understanding, perceptive judgment, discernment, a certain degree of emotional intensity, and the visualization of specific images and goals. These are the skills that every magician must hone to build the physical and psychological changes needed to accomplish the goal of the ritual, for all these faculties are needed to pursue the Great Work.

In *Golden Dawn Rituals* we cover the traditional consecration rituals for the Elemental Tools, the Magic Sword, Rose Cross Lamen, and Lotus Wand of the Zelator Adeptus Minor, implements that we call the Working Tools of the Adept. These rites are excellent examples of the mechanics involved in standard Golden Dawn magic. The versions we provide have clear stage directions and are designed to be reader-friendly.

We also accommodate both solo and group workings within our tradition. For those who prefer solitary practice, we offer a selection of rites that can be performed independently, allowing you to deepen your personal connection to the magical currents on your own terms and at your own pace. For those who thrive in a communal setting, we present a range of ceremonies designed for group workings in both the Outer and Inner Orders of the Golden Dawn system.

Many of the group ceremonies provided in *Golden Dawn Rituals* presuppose that readers will already be members of a working Golden Dawn Order or temple and be well-versed in the symbolism, etiquette, customs, and expectations of their respective organizations. A group of magicians working together as a ritual team provides a sense of common cause, fellowship, and mutual support that will boost the power and potential of any magical practice.

One of our goals in writing this book is to honor the principles and teachings of the Golden Dawn tradition while encouraging students to explore their creative strengths, spiritual vision, and magical expression within the four corners of the system. *Golden Dawn Rituals* is a manual for those who wish to learn how effective rituals are designed. From solitary rites to group ceremonies, this book will examine the many facets of ritual magic and teach you the tools of our trade.

Ritual magic fills the space between the worldly and the heavenly, the secular and the sacred. Through the creation and performance of ritual, we can unlock our intrinsic capacity for personal and collective growth and construct a framework for understanding our role within the greater universe.

So mote it be.

SECTION ONE

The Basics of Magic and Outer Order Rituals

chapter 1

THE BASICS OF GOLDEN DAWN RITUAL MAGIC

The art of magic is practiced through the mechanism of formalized ritual that provides a specialized infrastructure wherein the work of magic can be effectively performed. It is a buttress of support and an organized, systematic mode for interacting with the sacred. This infrastructure uses an assortment of symbolic elements and methods that, when artfully combined, can build a liminal space for transformational magic. From the simplest rite of a solitary magician to the most elaborate group ceremony, ritual provides the essential pattern and organization needed for successful magical work. Ritual magic provides us with an orderly framework that incorporates a sequence of symbolic actions that define a relationship of meaning between the symbol and that which it symbolizes, directing magical force toward fulfilling a particular goal.

A few lucky individuals might be able to perform magic with little or no preparation or form, letting the ritual take whatever form it may. But even if their magic is successful, it will be hard to teach their methods to others, especially those who are not automatically gifted with easy access to the mental and psychic facilities needed in magical work. For most of us, having a structured ritual that can be studied, rehearsed, and performed is essential to becoming proficient in magical work.

The objectives for which magic is performed in the Golden Dawn often have a twofold application: (1) an immediate practical purpose and (2) a greater theurgic or higher spiritual purpose. The system contains rituals used for a wide variety of practical applications: invocations, evocations, the consecration of talismans, spiritual development, healing, skrying and other forms of spirit vision work, and divination rituals, as well as Qabalistic, elemental, planetary, and Zodiacal workings.

While the goal of a specific magical ritual might not seem entirely spiritual to the outside observer (such as consecrating a Jupiter talisman designed to attract financial assistance or a ritual invocation of Libra to aid in a legal matter), it is still vital to the magician's understanding of the theurgic arts. All such rites, exercises, and ceremonies are designed to give the Golden Dawn student a broad working knowledge of the magical process and provide safeguards and guidelines for what to do and what not to do in magic. However, the only way to learn magic is through practice, aided with advice from experienced authors, teachers, and peers. The real objective of all these procedures, as utilized by Golden Dawn magicians, is to gain esoteric knowledge, connect with the sacred, and complete the Great Work.

Categories of Ritual and Ritual Drama

Ritual magic often employs many of the trappings of a theatrical production. Ritual drama, or ritual enactment, is a potent tool for expressing inner mystical experiences. Using costumes and regalia, props and symbolism, and artful choreography, a simple ritual can become a rich, immersive experience. In addition to captivating our senses, dramatic ritual engages us on many levels: physical, emotional, intellectual, and spiritual. It amplifies the connection between the ritualist and their goal and strengthens the general efficiency of the rite.

Rituals fall under different broad classifications according to the intention for which they are performed. First among these are initiation ceremonies, which we discuss later in this section. There are also seasonal rituals, restorative rituals, and exploratory rituals. Some rituals don't fall neatly into these categories and may overlap in many cases.

Seasonal Rituals. Traditionally, the Golden Dawn system includes only one seasonal ritual, the Ceremony of the Equinox, which is performed on the Vernal and Autumnal Equinoxes, the only times of the year when day and night are of equal length.[1] The importance of the equinoxes was paramount to expressing the system's essential princi-

1. See the Ceremony of the Equinox, in Regardie, *The Golden Dawn*, 321–33. In the Second Order, the consecration ceremony of the Vault of the Adepti is celebrated around the time of the Summer Solstice, but its timing is based upon the feast day of Corpus Christi, which can fall anywhere from the end of May to the end of June.

ple of balance. Nevertheless, some temples and solo practitioners have also created powerful rituals for solstices and other sacred times of the year.

Restorative Rituals. Restorative rituals aim to balance some perceived defect or imbalance. Examples include healing rituals, spiritual development rituals, and talisman consecrations (as talismans are often created to obtain something lacking, such as knowledge or protection). These usually include a formalized opening and closing that bracket a middle section where the boundaries of the Work have been defined and prepared for.

Exploratory Rituals. Exploratory rites involve methods of magic generally known as spirit vision work, such as skrying, astral traveling, and rising on planes. These rituals are meant to explore other realms and levels of consciousness. They can also include opening and closing sections, but the Work can often take on a more spontaneous and somewhat free-form approach.

Initiation ceremonies are the best examples of ritual enactment, wherein participants reenact an important myth or legend in an artful blending of theatrical drama and magical technique. An initiation ritual is a kind of self-definition, the most prominent feature of which is the search for the Divine.[2] These sacred ceremonies are the truest rites of passage in magical work because initiation symbolizes a new beginning—a spiritual new birth or baptism. Initiation signals the dawning of a new life dedicated to a higher set of goals and principles than that of a previous materialistic or mundane-centered existence.

Since the initiation ceremonies of the Golden Dawn are readily available in Regardie's *The Golden Dawn*, we will not present them here. But it is important to point out that a great many other rituals also incorporate ritual drama, mythology, historical legends, and spiritual allegories into their structure. In a sense, *all* magical rituals are a type of initiation. By performing these rites regularly, we are continually reinitiating ourselves, restating our values, and recommitting ourselves to our spiritual work.

Elements of Ritual Magic

Several components go into an act of ritual magic. These can be divided into two categories: tools and methods. The tools of magic include any objects that magicians use to aid their practice. Methods are the skills needed to activate different aspects of magical energy.

---

2. Graf, *Magic in the Ancient World*, 116.

Tools can range from the simplest things needed to enhance the atmosphere of the ritual space to the most sacred symbols used to represent the goal of the rite. Some tools are purely practical, such as barbecue lighters for lighting charcoal or candles and music players and speakers that provide ambient music. Even these low-level tools have a basic symbolism in relation to the temple. Other items are both practical and symbolic, such as robes, regalia, and other types of ritual clothing.

But a good many of the items used in ritual are employed specifically for their magical symbolism, for the precise purpose of creating an active magical link between the symbol and that which it represents. These include:

1. *Sacred Space.*[3] Items that are used to define the limits of the temple and the primary points, directions, or centers of energy located within that space, such as:
    - The central altar
    - Side altars (and their placement)
    - Pillars (with red triangular capitals on their summits)
    - Thrones or chairs (sometimes called stations)
    - Banners (of East and West) on banner stands
2. *Officer's Emblems.* Active participants in group rituals use symbols such as lamens, wands, or other implements to represent their specific authority or functions. These also act as symbols of energy and protection.
3. *Universal Energies.* Items that are used to symbolize the universe's basic divisions and fundamental magical forces. The energies most often represented are elemental in nature and are affiliated with various spiritual and angelic beings:
    - Fire (red candles, wands, Fire Wand)
    - Water (chalice, Water Cup)
    - Air (fan, incense,[4] Air Dagger)
    - Earth (paten of salt, Earth Pentacle)

3. The area used as sacred space should be a private space, or at least be private for the duration of the ritual working.

4. Incense is sometimes used to represent Air, but other times it is used to represent Fire.

- Spirit (white candle, Hebrew letter Shin)
- Enochian Watchtower Tablets (four elements and Spirit)

Depending on the nature of the Working, other universal energies can also be symbolized within the temple. For example, we could set up a circle of planetary, Zodiacal, or Sephirotic symbols or banners to represent these forces. Each of these universal symbol sets is meant to provide a magical pattern or blueprint of the divine realm wherein the magician works.

4. *Specific Energies.* Items that are used to represent a particular energy invoked or the goal of the Working and are also connected to specific spiritual entities and angelic beings. We usually think of the consecration of talismans in this regard. However, virtually anything can be consecrated as a talisman or sanctified as a magical object, including candles, wands, daggers, swords, pentacles, images, Tarot cards, lamens, rings, offerings, a Mystic Repast of blessed food and drink, and symbols drawn on paper, just to name a few.
5. *Prayers and Invocations.* Over the centuries magicians have crafted invocations, spells, and rituals for every purpose imaginable. Ancient mages also looked to spiritual literature, scriptures, and scrolls for sacred names, potent words of power, and poetic incantations for connecting with deity. As a result, modern practitioners have access to an extensive collection of texts containing ritual techniques, mystical prayers, and invocations. This material is a valuable source of inspiration for rites and ceremonies. The founders of the Golden Dawn certainly took advantage of this ancient wisdom in the crafting of their ritual methods. Speeches, prayers, and invocations found in Golden Dawn rituals incorporate passages from the Egyptian *Book of the Dead* and the *Pyramid Texts*, Hebrew and Christian scriptures, Gnostic texts, Qabalistic works, the *Græco-Egyptian Magical Papyri*, the *Chaldæan Oracles*, the various books of the *Hermetica*, alchemical manuscripts, and numerous other works. Primary texts of this sort continue to provide a bounty of information and ingenuity that we can incorporate into our modern practice.

Sacred Space

The temple space used by Golden Dawn magicians embodies two things. First, it is an extension of the internal spiritual energies embodied in the magician's aura, or "magical mirror of the universe." Second, it is a projection of the external divine forces that infuse the universe. The physical temple wherein the magician makes the gestures, intones the words of power, and moves energy acts as a liminal space where macrocosmic and microcosmic forces interact to effect magic. By its very nature, ritual magic does not occur solely within the confines of the external temple space, utilizing physical objects such as wands and pentacles. Instead, it unfolds within the sacred realm of the personal universe, which encompasses both the inner and outer landscapes seamlessly and without any division.

The temple is meant to be a sacred space that is rendered holy ground—a hallowed area where the forces of the Divine may be effectively invoked. Whether the room is set up for ritual permanently or simply for the duration of any given rite, preparation of the sacred space is an important step in laying a firm foundation for successful work. This is done by cleansing the area both physically and astrally. A disorganized temple reflects a disorganized mind, something that will not help your magic. Clearing the "astral clutter" is done through ritual purification and consecration.

All the outer trappings of ritual—the specific symbolism, the arrangement of the furniture, altar, banners, and pillars—are physical representations of the divine macrocosm in which we live and effect change. In the Golden Dawn system, one of the most important temple arrangements is that of the Hall of the Neophytes, which is why Golden Dawn magicians often refer to the temple as "the Hall." In this setup, the temple symbolizes a portion of the Qabalistic Tree of Life: The altar is placed within the upper quarter of Malkuth and the black and white pillars represent the two columns of Mercy and Severity. Another popular arrangement, particularly in personal work, emphasizes the "four winds" arrangement of the elements, with Air symbols in the east, Fire symbols in the south, Water emblems in the west, and Earth emblems in the north. Some rituals call for the temple to be arranged in accordance with the twelve signs of the Zodiacal wheel or the circle of the seven ancient planets. The variations are endless, and we have just begun to scratch the surface.

YOU WANT TO DO *WHAT*??

We never cease to be amazed whenever someone asks us to instruct them on how to do black magic. "Teach me a spell to get a love slave! How can I curse my neighbor? How about soul-selling for money?" YIKES!

Anyone who knows the Golden Dawn system will already be aware of the importance that Golden Dawn magicians place on magical ethics. Initiates swear numerous oaths not to commit acts of harmful magic. Nevertheless, it bears repeating. In the Neophyte Oath, the candidate swears, "I will not debase my mystical knowledge in the labor of Evil Magic at any time tried or under any temptation." In the Adeptus Minor ceremony, the Initiate again swears "not to debase my knowledge of Practical Magic to purposes of evil and self-seeking.... and if I do this, notwithstanding this my oath, I invoke the Avenging Angel HUA, that the evil and material *may react on me*." It is difficult to imagine how anyone could mistake the meaning and intent of such important pledges. You cannot be on the side of the angels if your magical work aims to hurt or control another.

Group Ritual Versus Solo Rites

Magicians are sometimes presented with the choice of participating in group ceremonies or undertaking solitary ritual work. Both options have advantages and drawbacks geared toward different facets of the magical quest. Fortunately, many Golden Dawn rituals can be performed individually and collectively, depending on the nature of the Work.

Group Ritual. Traditionally, members of Golden Dawn temples gather at stated meetings to perform rituals of initiation and advancement, install new officers and new passwords during equinox ceremonies, and give lectures and other forms of instruction to the members. However, much of the practical work of ritual magic is expected to be performed by students at home in their own personal temple space.

Within the setting of a group ritual, participants can take on certain roles and responsibilities in accordance with their individual strengths and specialties. This can result in a powerful and well-organized ritual presentation where each ritualist lends their personal skills to the shared experience.

Working within a group allows for unified focus, mutual purpose, and coordinated action on the part of the ritualists. This can boost the magical current and increase the effectiveness of the rite. It can create more opportunities for heightened states of awareness and enable participants to access celestial worlds that could be more difficult to explore alone. The group's collective work comprises a common magical ecosystem where the shared energies merge to produce a compelling force and where all participants set their sights on the same goal.

Members of a temple also have an increased ability to tap into the egregore of the Golden Dawn. *Egregore* comes from a Greek word meaning "wakeful" or "watcher." It is sometimes described as an angelic being or thoughtform created and sustained by a group of people collectively involved in a specific activity. When we speak of a *group egregore*, we are talking about the distinctive energy of a group of magicians working together for a common set of goals. The egregore serves as a spiritual reservoir for the group's mutual actions and collective intentions. When concentrated into an egregore, the communal energy of the group is magnified. Everyone involved in a group receives the influences of the egregore, the astral counterpart of the group, in their psyche.[5]

Individual temples can also have their own distinctive egregore. If the temple has been true to its teachings, principles, and values, the group egregore will benefit the individual in various ways by providing communal wisdom and direction. But while the group egregore can bestow certain advantages, magicians must continue cultivating their own personal work and strengthening their separate relationship with the Divine.

Group work allows students to learn from the experiences of others, both positive *and* negative. They can compare notes and talk through problems. In addition to shared rituals, there are many opportunities for discussions, insights, and interactions. Members of a group can gain new perspectives on magical theories and methods. Students can increase their understanding and hone their own skills by watching the practices and techniques of their more advanced magical companions. More experienced magicians can teach students what works and what doesn't, as well as how to avoid pitfalls such as an overstimulated ego, self-delusions, and the danger of becoming unmoored from the physical world. Finally, the fellowship nurtured within a group setting can offer a bounty of motivation and support.

Solo Ritual Work. For the Outer Order student, the work of the Golden Dawn is focused on studying the Knowledge Lectures and committing the language of magic to memory. Solitary work involves meditations and exercises designed to relax and focus the mind, glean insights from symbolism, and learn the basic techniques of visualization, concentration, and vibration. Beyond the Lesser Ritual of the Pentagram, there are few traditional avenues for solo ritual work in the First Order (although contemporary authors have added to the modern corpus of Outer Order rituals in books such as our own *Self-Initiation into the Golden Dawn Tradition*). The same cannot be said for the Second Order, for much of the practical ritual magic of the Golden Dawn system is

5. Stavish, *Egregores*, 24.

designed for the Inner Order, where magicians are expected to work in private at their own pace with their own creativity, albeit with periodic guidance from their instructors.

For many of us, group ritual work is very appealing. However, some magicians prefer the independent path of the solo practitioner. The solitary magician can focus on their own unique style of magical work, free of the external influences and distractions that sometimes accompany group work.

We have found that the best method is to follow the path of the Middle Pillar and balance solo work with group ritual. Developing an equilibrium between these two lines of approach ensures a holistic practice that embraces the well-being of both the individual and the group, resulting in a well-functioning temple that values personal revelation and communal effort.

Memorization in Ritual

For some fraternal and magical groups, memorization of one's speeches for *all* rites and ceremonies is the whole ball game when it comes to ritual performance. This might be fine for groups whose rituals do not depend on inner work such as visualization and energy movement, which requires mental focus on the part of ritualists. Realistically, how many people in the modern world have the time or capacity to memorize all parts of all the initiation ceremonies of the Golden Dawn from Neophyte through all the elemental grades and beyond? The prospect of making this a requirement would scare off more potential students than it would attract. This is also true for the rituals in this book. Memorization of *some* aspects of the rituals is necessary, but certainly not for the whole of them. The most important rituals that need to be committed to memory have already been presented in our book *Golden Dawn Magic*. They include the Qabalistic Cross, the Adoration, the Lesser Ritual of the Pentagram, the Exercise of the Middle Pillar, the Supreme Ritual of the Pentagram, the Analysis of the Keyword, the Lesser Ritual of the Hexagram, the Greater Ritual of the Hexagram, the Ritual of the Rose Cross, and the Opening by Watchtower. These rituals are relatively brief and are often used as self-contained components of more complex rituals such as talisman consecrations and the like. In addition to these rituals, it would be a good idea to memorize the commencement and conclusions of group rituals that are performed regularly, such as the Opening and the Closing of the Neophyte Hall. It would also be helpful to the ritual if *certain* important and often used passages could be memorized, such as the Prayer of Osiris[6] at

6. See the Closing of the Hall of the Neophytes on page 33.

the beginning of the Mystic Repast, or the Prayer of the Redeemer[7] from the Ceremony of the Adeptus Minor. But this is not necessary. It is far more important to get the internal magical work right than to worry about whether your mind will go blank trying to recall the wording of a long speech. The rituals presented here do not require memorization. We recommend that practitioners refer to this book while performing the rituals. For some of the shorter rites, ritualists may use outlines or bullet points on note cards for reference.

Temple Etiquette and Work-Arounds

All of us wish we could have access to the perfect temple space, have the exact number of officers needed for a specific ritual, and have all rituals performed without a hitch. In reality, this is rarely the case.

Solitary magicians have an advantage in that they can perform rituals at their own pace and with their own priorities in mind. As a solo practitioner, you do not have to address issues concerning other members, such as speaking loud enough so that other participants can hear you. However, one possible disadvantage is that many people do not have a dedicated temple space in their home: You might have to rearrange furniture and use whatever dresser, tabletop, or fireplace mantel is available as a makeshift altar. You might have to keep your vibrations quiet in a shared household. Group ceremonies come with their own set of considerations: Will the temple space accommodate a large number of participants, including *sideliners*—members who do not have an active role in the ritual but who sit along the sides of the temple to observe, joining in only for group vibrations and shared gestures? Are there accessibility issues for some members? Are candles allowed? Are some participants allergic to incense or gluten bread, as used in the Mystic Repast? For some of these issues there are easy fixes, like using gluten-free bread and grape juice or water for members who cannot drink the ceremonial wine. Additionally, there might be members who are allergic to incense, essential oils, or perfumes. Make certain all participants are aware of this before they come to temple. You could try using the least amount of stick incense that a person can tolerate, or you could forgo incense altogether and use a standard symbol for Air or Fire instead, such as a rose, a handheld fan, or an unscented candle.

Some groups hold their ceremonies in public or semipublic spaces belonging to Masonic lodges, banquet halls, or even hotel convention rooms. Naturally, the group

7. "For I know that my Redeemer liveth ..." See Regardie, *The Golden Dawn*, 312.

will have to comply with whatever restrictions or insurance requirements go hand in hand with renting a room for a period of time. Most public spaces are wheelchair accessible. However, most will not allow candles or open flames, so you may have to use LED candles. If an excessive amount of incense is used, you might set off a fire alarm. If you spill red wine on the carpet, you may have to pay for it. Just be aware of all of this ahead of time.

Here are a few pointers to remember when dealing with aspects of group ritual.

Entering the Neophyte Hall: The temple is set up, candles are lit, and the Lesser Ritual of the Pentagram (LRP) is performed. The Hierophant and those seated with him/her on the Dais enter first; the Hierophant (assisted by the Dais Officers) activates the god-forms of the Hall. The rest of the Officers enter, followed by any sideliners. They are let in by the Phylax, who receives the grip, step, passwords, and grade signs from each member. The outer door is then closed and guarded by the Phylax. If a member has to leave the temple for whatever reason, they should knock on the outer door to alert the Phylax, then give the appropriate grade sign toward the east when exiting and again upon their return.

Walking Around the Temple: When moving from one point to another in temple, always try to walk in a clockwise manner, unless the script says otherwise. In a tight space where it may be impossible to walk clockwise, a compromise would be to turn partially clockwise in place and then go straight to where you need to go. Whenever passing the east, a member should give the Neophyte Signs toward the Banner of the East as a salute to the Divine Light. Finally, in the Mystic Circumambulation, as well as the Reverse Circumambulation, sideliners do not participate.

Group Vibration of Godnames: Have someone with a strong, clear voice set the vibratory "note" for the group just before everyone begins vibrating; otherwise you may end up with a cacophony of different notes that grates on the nerves and works against the magic. Make sure the starting note is in the midrange, neither too high in pitch nor too low.

Ritual Rehearsal: It is always a good idea for Officers to rehearse ceremonies beforehand. This is when confusing stage directions and possible typos can be worked out ahead of time. A ritual walk-through will give participants confidence in their ability to perform a powerful and successful ritual.

PRAXIS MAKES PERFECT!

Visualize a student learning to play the piano. The student painstakingly studies an intricate piece of classical music by Beethoven. Their ability to read music is second to none, but if they don't practice for many hours or improve the skill of their fingers to move nimbly over the piano keys, they will fail at their assigned task. It is no different for an armchair occultist who collects all manner of magical documents and books but doesn't perform any meditations, exercises, or rituals that accompany effective magical work. Ancient Greek magicians referred to the performance of their rituals as the *praxis*. And in magic, praxis makes perfect!

Some Helpful Advice

While we normally think of ritual magic as mental work, it can also be quite physically taxing, especially ceremonies that are long and involved. Magicians will often tell you that a successful ritual leaves them elated, tired, and ravenous. Therefore, maintaining good health with exercise and a balanced diet is important. If we truly want our rituals to honor the Divine within us, we should try to take care of the physical temple that houses the Spirit.

Ritualists must learn how to reach and preserve a sense of inner balance and maintain a dual position of psychic receptivity (to beneficial influences and higher wisdom) and psychic protection (from illusions, deceptions, and harmful influences). Obviously, this cannot happen overnight, with little preparation, or by simply opening a book and reading a ritual and uttering a few inscrutable words and phrases. It will take time.

No matter how well-designed a ritual is, it will fall well short of ensuring successful magic if the proverbial house has been built upon sand. The key lies in training the mind, for it is only through such groundwork that the inner dimensions of ritual can be fully realized. Mere knowledge of magical techniques is insufficient; the ritualist must cultivate their skills, multitasking their talents so that magical techniques and ritual structure are seamlessly blended. Regular practice of the basic techniques used in ritual must be maintained. Without it, don't expect any of the rituals given here to have any meaningful effect. Magic takes work—we all must work at it. And this is why we often refer to our performance of any given ritual as the Working or the Work. Ritual is the nexus between sacred symbols and symbolic action. It is a fundamental tool of the magician's trade. But as with all tools, one has to pick it up and use it to accomplish something with it.

If you take the suggestions we offer here to heart, then you will discover the many reasons why Golden Dawn ritual magic is unique and continues to attract people, namely:

1. The system is well organized. Every section of a Golden Dawn ritual is planned out with architectural precision. Nothing happens in a Golden Dawn ritual without planning for it.
2. The tradition is syncretic. It incorporates knowledge, principles, and practices from a variety of sources within the Western Esoteric Tradition.
3. The Golden Dawn system is not a religion. Deities and wisdom teachings from many different pantheons are embraced in our ceremonies. Also, there is no one true guru that we look to for the last word in our spiritual teachings or progress.
4. While all ceremonies are enacted on the physical plane, the most important part of ritual takes place on an astral and psychospiritual level.
5. Golden Dawn ritual is creative. Advanced students are expected to create their own rituals as part of their gradework. Many rituals involve the creation of specialized lamens, talismans, or other implements. This sparks the magician's imagination and ingenuity.
6. Above all else, balance is paramount to every aspect of our Work. Balanced rituals are reflections of a balanced mind.

Golden Dawn ritual magic offers us liminal areas of connection between the seen and unseen realms. Such rites afford us moments in and out of time and sacred spaces within parallel spiritual dimensions, thresholds in every sense of the word where we are free to interact with all manner of spiritual beings. Within the structure of ritual, we find a profound opportunity to reconnect with the divine spark within us and bridge the seemingly insurmountable gap between external and internal realms of existence.

chapter 2

GROUP RITUALS FOR THE OUTER ORDER

Group ritual is the lifeblood of a Golden Dawn Temple. Members come together at regularly scheduled meetings in order to carry out specific rituals and magical work. Sometimes the gathering is for the purpose of initiating new candidates as Neophytes into the Temple. At other times, meetings are held to advance existing members into higher grades or levels of teaching. Twice a year, the Temple is opened in order to commemorate the Vernal and Autumnal Equinoxes. During the Equinox Ritual, a new password is instituted and new Officers are installed in their roles. At those times when initiations and equinoxes are not on the schedule, the Temple may perform any number of different rituals designed for group work in our tradition, including invocations and consecrations. There is only one grade that is common to all Golden Dawn Initiates: the grade of Neophyte. This is because the grades are accumulative, not subtractive. Therefore, the baseline for all ceremonial workings of the Golden Dawn is the Hall of the Neophytes, because we are *all* Neophytes.

The Neophyte Hall holds a central position in the entire ritual framework of the Golden Dawn and is the most important temple arrangement in the Outer Order. It encompasses patterns and methods that mold and define space and time. The Hall is elegantly designed to be a magical model of the universe and can accommodate a wide array of ritual work characterized by powerful imagery.

During the process of initiation, the Neophyte encounters a temple filled with symbolism in the form of ritual implements and regalia used by Officers who are the living personifications of the gods and goddesses of Egypt—the initiators into the higher mysteries. Within the Neophyte Ritual itself are hidden many formulae of magic. Everything contained within the Neophyte Hall is important not only for theatrics and effect but also because each symbol is a visible emblem of invisible forces within the Hall that are directed and orchestrated by the Hierophant and other Officers.

The full symbolism of the Neophyte Hall, as well as the robes, regalia, and duties of the various Officers, are described at length in Israel Regardie's book *The Golden Dawn*. They are also described in a more abbreviated fashion in our books *The Essential Golden Dawn* and *Golden Dawn Magic*, so we will not cover the same ground here, nor will we present the initiation ceremonies or the Equinox Ritual of the Outer Order, which are also found in Regardie's text. What we will provide is a series of rituals that are appropriate for group workings in the Outer Order, where some members may be Neophytes and others may be more experienced magicians.

The rituals given in chapters 2 and 3 are designed in such a way that Neophytes and other First Order members are not expected to perform Adept-level magic. Any higher magic called for in these ceremonies are strictly performed by the Hierophant or other skilled Adepts. All other participants may be called upon to trace lineal figures such as Zodiacal symbols or lamen emblems, but they will not be asked to perform magic that is beyond their grade level. Nevertheless, all participants will gain practice in the basic magical methods of visualization, meditation, vibration, movement of energy, and energized willpower—skills that every Golden Dawn student must learn and abilities that will enhance the magician's work in future, more complex workings.

The first ritual supplied is the Opening (and Closing) of the Neophyte Hall.[8] All the rituals in chapters 2 and 3 utilize this basic rite of commencement to set the stage for group work in the Outer Order. Between the Opening and the Closing is the Work, the specific magical working that is the focus of the ceremony.

We assume that readers will already be familiar with the symbolism and duties of the Outer Order Officers.[9] Table 1 merely provides a quick reference. (NOTE: The following Officers are stationed on the Dais in the East alongside the Hierophant: Praemonstrator,

---

8. Adapted from the Ceremony of the Neophyte 0=0 Grade from Regardie's *The Golden Dawn*, 141–63.

9. See Ciceros, *Golden Dawn Magic,* 113–18. The Hierophant and Imperator wear the exact same Lamen. The Past Hierophant wears a similar but smaller Lamen, in the form of a pin.

Imperator, Cancellarius, and Past Hierophant. They don't always have active roles in the rituals in this section. If there are not enough Adepts to fill these roles, the Hierophant will have to carry out their duties, while their symbols and implements can be placed at their stations.)

Officer	*Function*	*Lamen Symbol*	*Implement*
Praemonstrator	Teacher	Circle and Cross, orange on blue	Pyramidal Cross Wand
Imperator	Governor	Circle and Cross, green on red	Red Sword
Cancellarius	Recorder	Circle and Cross, violet on yellow	Hexagram Wand
Past Hierophant	Supporter[10]	Past Hierophant Pin	Crown-Headed Wand
Hierophant	High Priest/ess	Circle and Cross, green on red	Crown-Headed Wand
Hiereus	Guardian	Triangle, white on black	Sword
Hegemon	Guide	Cross, black on white	Mitre-Headed Wand
Keryx	Herald	Caduceus, white on black	Caduceus Wand, Lamp
Stolistes	Purifier	Cup, white on black	Cup of Water
Dadouchos	Consecrator	Fylfot Cross, white on black	Censer of Incense
Phylax	Sentinel	Eye, white on black	Sword

Table 1: Outer Order Officers

Most of the rituals that follow were created by ourselves or by members of our Order for use by our temples. We expect that many readers will want to adapt these rites for their own personal use or for group work in their respective temples or Orders. Therefore, in certain introductory speeches we have left blank spaces where specific temple and Order names can be slotted into the script.

Readers should also be aware that while many of the prayers, invocations and speeches given in the various rituals are original work by us or our contributors, a good many others come straight out of Regardie's *The Golden Dawn* and are adapted from the

10. Past Hierophant steps in for Hierophant when needed.

initiation ceremonies, elemental prayers, grade lectures, and sections of original rituals written by Regardie himself.[11] It is one of the strengths of our system that these classic snippets can be easily repurposed for an endless supply of different rituals.

Opening of the Hall of the Neophytes

Items Needed: Officers' lamens and implements as given in table 1. Officers' stations as shown in diagram (see figure 1): black and white pillars, Banners of the East and West on Banner stands, and central black Altar, upon which are a rose, red candle, chalice of wine, platter of bread and salt, cross and triangle. Adept Officers on the Dais wear a white robe, as well as a *nemyss*, or Egyptian-style headdress,[12] and a mantle (cloak, tabard, or stole)[13] in their respective colors. All other Officers and members wear a black robe with a black-and-white-striped nemyss.[14]

Preparation: When the members are ready, the ceremony may proceed.[15]

HIEROPHANT: (One knock ו[16]) All except Dais Officers RISE.

KERYX, upon hearing the Hierophant's knock, stands and gives the Projection Sign toward the East, then goes to the Northeast of the Hall, faces West, raising the Lamp and Wand, and says:

KERYX: **Hekas! Hekas! Este Bebeloi!**

---

11. Regardie also recycled many of the same speeches for his own rituals provided in book six of *The Golden Dawn*, 511–74.
12. See Ciceros, *Golden Dawn Magic,* 188.
13. The mantle is an outer covering worn over the robe.
14. There is some difference in opinion on this point. In some temples the Hierophant wears a black robe to emphasize their role as an Outer Order Officer, while in other temples they wear a white robe, just as the other Dais Officers do.
15. It is assumed here that the Hierophant and the Dais officers will have performed any necessary astral work prior to the Outer Order members being admitted into the temple. See "Godform Assumption" in Ciceros, *Golden Dawn Magic,* 324–26.
16. The Hebrew letter Vav (ו) is commonly used to indicate a knock.

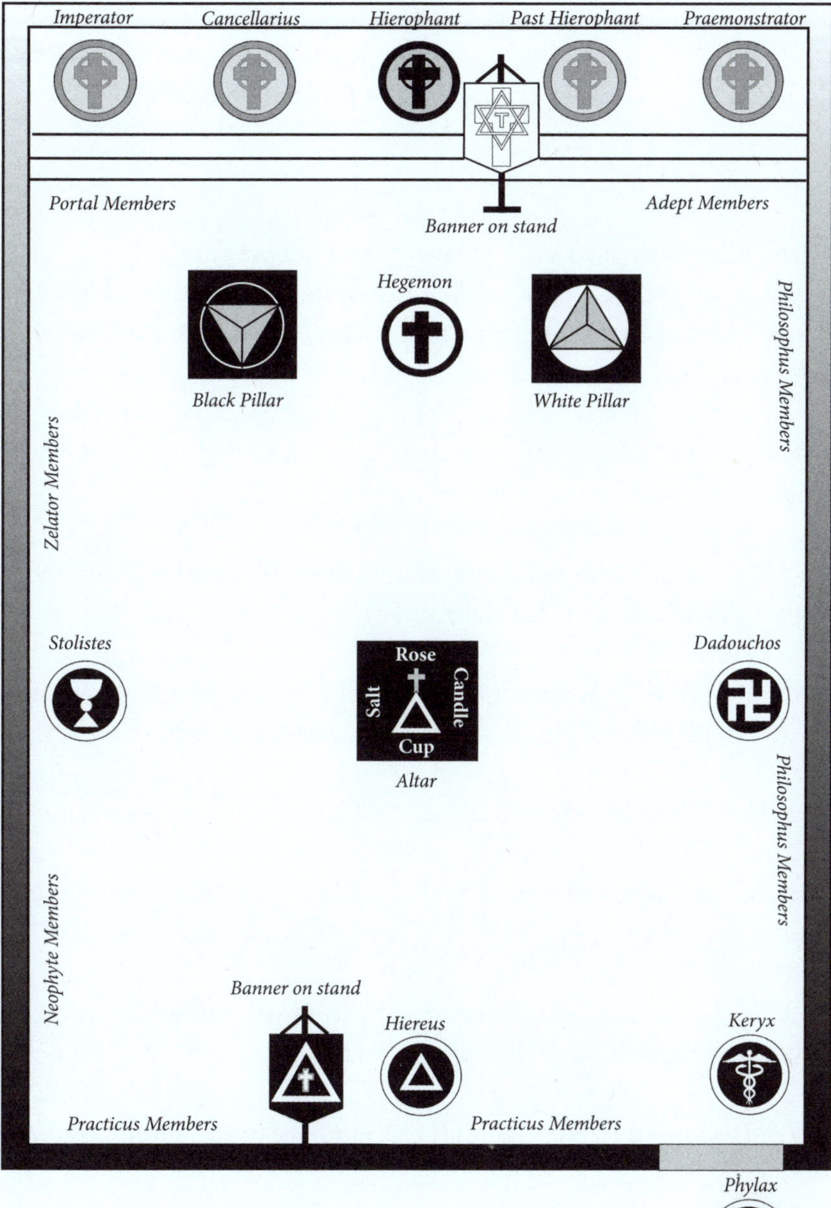

Figure 1: The Neophyte Hall

Keryx returns to place and gives the Sign of Silence.

Hierophant: **(Frater/Soror) Hiereus, perform the Lesser Banishing Ritual of the Pentagram.**[17]

Hiereus performs the LBRP.

Hierophant: (Rises with one knock ׀) **Fratres and Sorores of the (______) Temple of the (________) Order of the Golden Dawn in the Outer, assist me to open the Hall of the Neophytes. (Frater/Soror) Keryx, see that the Hall is properly guarded.**

Keryx goes to the door and gives one knock ׀.
On the outside of the door, Phylax replies with one knock ׀.

Keryx: **Very Honoured Hierophant, the Hall is properly guarded.** (Keryx salutes the Hierophant's Throne and remains by door.)

Hierophant: **Honoured Hiereus, guard the hither side of the portal and assure yourself that all present have witnessed the Golden Dawn.**

Hiereus goes to the door, stands before it with Sword. (Keryx stands to Hiereus's right.)

Hiereus: **Fratres and Sorores of the (________) Order of the Golden Dawn, give the Signs of a Neophyte.**

All except Officers on Dais and Hiereus give the Signs toward the Altar. This done, Hiereus gives Signs toward Hierophant, and says:

Hiereus: **Very Honoured Hierophant, all present have been so honoured.**

---

17. See Ciceros, *Golden Dawn Magic,* 145–46. Some temples prefer to have the Hiereus banish before the Hall is opened and members admitted. We prefer to do it at the beginning of ceremony, so that all present can lend energy and visualization to the cleansing of the Hall.

HIEREUS and KERYX return to their places. ALL are seated.

HIEROPHANT rises and gives the Sign of the Enterer toward the West, but NOT the Sign of Silence.

HIEROPHANT: **Let the number of Officers in this degree and the nature of their Offices be proclaimed once again, that the Powers whose images they are may be reawakened in the spheres of those present and in the Sphere of this Order—for by Names and Images are all Powers awakened and reawakened.** (HIEROPHANT makes the Sign of Silence and resumes his seat.)

HIEROPHANT: **Honoured Hiereus, how many Chief Officers are there in this Grade?**

HIEREUS: (Rises and projects toward the East) **There are three Chief Officers: the Hierophant, the Hiereus, and the Hegemon.**

HIEROPHANT: **Is there any peculiarity in these Names?**

HIEREUS: **They all commence with the letter *H*.**

HIEROPHANT: **Of what is this letter a symbol?**

HIEREUS: **Of life, because the letter *H* is our mode of representing the ancient Greek aspirate or breathing, and Breath is the evidence of Life.**

HIEROPHANT: **How many lesser Officers are there?**

HIEREUS: **There are three besides the Phylax: the Keryx, the Stolistes, and the Dadouchos. The Phylax is without the Portal of the Hall and has a Sword in his hand to keep out intruders. It is his duty to prepare the Candidate.** (Gives Sign of Silence and takes seat.)

HIEROPHANT: **(Frater/Soror) Dadouchos, your station and duties?**

DADOUCHOS: (Rises and projects toward the East) **My station is in the South to symbolize Heat and Dryness, and my duty is to see that the Lamps and Fires of the Temple are ready at the opening, to watch over the Censer** (elevates Censer) **and the Incense and to consecrate the Hall and the Fratres and Sorores and the Candidate with Fire.** (Gives Sign of Silence and takes seat.)

HIEROPHANT: **(Frater/Soror) Stolistes, your station and duties?**

STOLISTES: (Rises and projects toward the East) **My station is in the North to symbolize Cold and Moisture, and my duties are to see that Robes and Collars and Insignia of the Officers are ready at the Opening, to watch over the Cup of Lustral Water** (elevates Cup) **and to purify the Hall and the Fratres and Sorores and the Candidate with Water.** (Gives Sign of Silence and sits.)

HIEROPHANT: **(Frater/Soror) Keryx, your station and duties?**

KERYX: (Rises and projects toward the East) **My place is within the portal. My duties are to see that the furniture of the Hall is properly arranged at the Opening, to guard the inner side of the portal, to admit the Fratres and Sorores, and to watch over the reception of the Candidate; to lead all Mystic Circumambulations carrying the Lamp of my Office, and to make all reports and announcements.** (Elevates Lamp and Wand) **My Lamp is the symbol of the Hidden Knowledge, and my Wand is the symbol of its directing power.** (Gives Sign of Silence and sits.)

HIEROPHANT: **Honoured Hegemon, your station and duties?**

HEGEMON: (Rises and projects toward the East, then turns to face the Altar) **My station is between the Two Pillars of Hermes and Solomon and my face is toward the cubical Altar of the Universe. My duty is to watch over the Gateway of the Hidden Knowledge, for I am the reconciler between Light and Darkness. I watch over the preparation of the Candidate and assist in his reception and I lead him in the Path that conducts from Darkness to Light.**[18] **The White Color of my**

18. Underlined pronouns in the script are meant to be adapted to circumstances.

(cloak/tabard/stole)[19] **is the color of Purity, my ensign of office is a Mitre-headed Scepter** (elevates Wand) **to symbolize religion which guides and regulates life, and my Office symbolizes those higher aspirations of the soul which should guide its action.** (Gives Sign of Silence and sits.)

HIEROPHANT: **Honoured Hiereus, your station and duties?**

HIEREUS: (Rising with Sword and Banner, projects toward the East) **My station is on the Throne of the West and is a symbol of increase of Darkness and decrease of Light and I am the Master of Darkness. I keep the Gateway of the West and watch over the reception of the Candidate and over the lesser officers in the doing of their work. My black (cloak/tabard/stole) is an image of the Darkness that was upon the Face of the Waters.** (Elevates Sword and Banner) **I carry the Sword of Judgment and the Banner of the Evening Twilight, which is the Banner of the West, and I am called Fortitude by the Unhappy.** (Gives Sign of Silence and takes seat.)

HIEROPHANT: (Hierophant rises, holding Scepter and Banner of the East) **My station is on the Throne of the East in the place where the Sun rises, and I am the Master of the Hall, governing it according to the laws of the Order, as HE whose Image I am is the Master of all who work for the Hidden Knowledge. My (cloak/tabard/stole) is red because of Uncreated Fire and Created Fire, and I hold the Banner of the Morning Light which is the Banner of the East. I am called Power and Mercy and Light and Abundance, and I am the Expounder of the Mysteries.** (Sits down.)

HIEROPHANT: **(Frater/Soror) Stolistes and (Frater/Soror) Dadouchos, I command you to purify and consecrate the Hall with Water and with Fire.**

ALL except STOLISTES and DADOUCHOS are seated.

For the Purification and Consecration, STOLISTES and DADOUCHOS give the Projection Sign in unison toward the East.

19. Insert whichever form of mantle the temple uses.

a. Then both turn clockwise and walk to the next quarter. (STOLISTES stops in the East, DADOUCHOS stops in the West facing North.) STOLISTES begins purifying by tracing a cross followed by sprinkling water to mark the three points of the Invoking Water Triangle[20] toward the East, while DADOUCHOS waits in the West facing North.

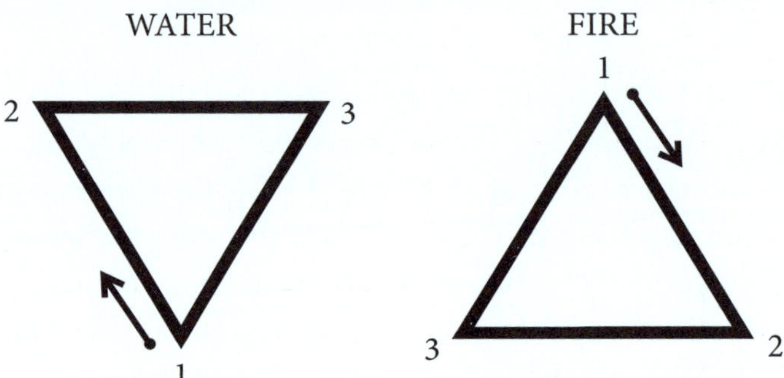

Figure 2: Invoking Water and Fire Triangles

b. Both officers move in unison to the next quarter. STOLISTES traces the same symbols toward the South, while DADOUCHOS waits in the North facing East.

c. Both officers move to the next quarter. STOLISTES traces the same symbols toward the West, while DADOUCHOS begins consecrating by tracing the cross and the Invoking Fire Triangle in the East with the incense.

d. Both move again to the next quarter. STOLISTES traces the purifying symbols in the North while DADOUCHOS traces the consecrating symbols in the South.

e. They move in unison to the next quarter. STOLISTES turns toward the East, raises the Cup, and says, **I purify with Water**, while DADOUCHOS traces the consecrating symbols toward the West.

f. Both officers move to the next quarter: STOLISTES waits in the South facing West while DADOUCHOS traces the consecrating symbols toward the North.

20. Trace the Cross with the Cup. Then dip one or two fingers into the Cup of Water and flick water toward the East while marking the three points of the Water Triangle.

g. They move in unison to the next quarter. STOLISTES waits in the West facing North while DADOUCHOS turns toward the East, raises the Censer, and says, **I consecrate with Fire.**

h. STOLISTES and DADOUCHOS return to their places and in unison give the Sign of Silence but remain standing.

HIEROPHANT: (Rises) **Let the Mystic Circumambulation take place in the Pathway of Light.**

HIEROPHANT stands in the position of the Tau Cross, holding the Scepter in the right hand and the Banner of the East in the left. KERYX goes to the Northeast with Lamp and Wand. Then follow HEGEMON, HIEREUS with Banner and Sword, STOLISTES with Cup, and last, DADOUCHOS with Censer. (The PHYLAX remains at his station.) They all line up in this order behind the KERYX, who leads the procession past Hierophant, making the Signs of Horus (Enterer) and Harpocrates (Silence) as they pass. Each Officer in turn does the same.

HIEREUS falls out as soon as the procession reaches his throne, but remains standing in the Tau Cross position, holding out the Sword and the Banner. HEGEMON returns to place after passing Hierophant twice. The other Officers pass Hierophant three times and then take their seats as they come to them.

HIEROPHANT and HIEREUS replace their Banners on the banner stands.

HIEROPHANT: **The Mystical Circumambulation symbolical of the Rise of Light is accomplished. Let us adore the Lord of the Universe and Space.**

ALL MEMBERS, including DAIS OFFICERS, rise. ALL face East for the Adoration: They salute with the Projection Sign three times following the lead of Hierophant. The Sign of Silence is given at the end of the Prayer:

ALL: **Holy art Thou, Lord of the Universe!** (Salute)
Holy art Thou, Whom Nature hath not Formed! (Salute)
Holy art Thou, the Vast and the Mighty One! (Salute)
Lord of the Light and of the Darkness! (Sign of Silence)

Hierophant, Hiereus, and Hegemon raise implements then slowly sink them. All remain standing.

Hierophant: **Frater/Soror Keryx, in the Name of the Lord of the Universe, I command you to declare that I have opened the Hall of the Neophytes.**

Keryx rises and projects to East, then goes clockwise to the Northeast, faces West, and raises the Wand.

Keryx: **In the Name of the Lord of the Universe, Who works in Silence and Whom naught but Silence can express, I declare that the Sun has arisen and the Shadows flee away.** (Returns clockwise to station, gives the Sign of Silence, then sits.)

Hierophant: (Knocks ٦)
Hiereus: (Knocks ٦)
Hegemon: (Knocks ٦)

Hierophant: (Knocks ٦) **Khabs.**
Hiereus: (Knocks ٦) **Am.**
Hegemon: (Knocks ٦) **Pekht.**

Hiereus: (Knocks ٦) **Konx.**
Hegemon: (Knocks ٦) **Om.**
Hierophant: (Knocks ٦) **Pax.**

Hegemon: (Knocks ٦) **Light.**
Hierophant: (Knocks ٦) **In.**
Hiereus: (Knocks ٦) **Extension.**

When the Battery of Knocks is done, All make the Signs toward the Altar in unison and then sit down.

✠✠✠

The Work

The Middle point of the ritual will be the main magical Working. This could be any of the rituals that follow in chapters 2 and 3 or any similar group ceremonies created for the Outer Order. When the Work is completed, proceed with the Closing of the Neophyte Hall.[21]

....

Closing of the Hall of the Neophytes

Hierophant: (Gives knock ו)

Keryx rises and projects toward the East, then goes to the Northeast, faces West, and raises Lamp and Wand.

Keryx: **Hekas! Hekas! Este Bebeloi!**
Keryx returns to his place, gives the Sign of Silence, and is seated.

Hierophant: (Knocks ו) **Fratres and Sorores of the (______) Temple of the (______) Order of the Golden Dawn, assist me to close the Hall of the Neophytes.** All rise.

Hiereus: (3 knocks ווו)
Hegemon: (3 knocks ווו)
Hierophant: (3 knocks ווו)

Hierophant: **(Frater/Soror) Keryx, see that the Hall is properly guarded.**

Keryx goes to the door and gives one knock ו.
On the outside of the door, Phylax replies with one knock ו.

Keryx: **The Hall is properly guarded, Very Honoured Hierophant.**

---

21. The Phylax is traditionally stationed just outside the closed western door. If the ritual takes place in a Masonic Hall or other space where interruption is a real possibility, then the Phylax should remain outside, just as a Masonic Sentinel would. If the ritual space is totally private, with no risk of intrusion, the Phylax may sit just inside the western entrance (sitting outside part-time as necessary for the admission of candidates, etc.). The Outer Order rituals in this book were written with the second, totally private scenario in mind, allowing all installed Officers to have an active role in the main Working.

HIEROPHANT: **Honoured Hiereus, assure yourself that all present have beheld the Golden Dawn.**

HIEREUS: **Fratres and Sorores, give the signs.**

ALL except Officers on Dais and Hiereus give the Signs in unison toward the Altar. This done, HIEREUS gives the Signs toward the Hierophant, and says:

HIEREUS: **Very Honoured Hierophant, all present have been so honoured.**

HIEROPHANT: **Let the Hall be purified by Water and by Fire.**

ALL except STOLISTES and DADOUCHOS are seated. They purify and consecrate exactly as they did in the Opening of the Hall. [...] STOLISTES: **I purify with Water.** [...] DADOUCHOS: **I consecrate with Fire.** (When finished, STOLISTES and DADOUCHOS return to their places and in unison give the Sign of Silence but remain standing.)

HIEROPHANT: **Let the Mystical Reverse Circumambulation take place in the Pathway of Light.**

HIEROPHANT stands in the position of the Tau Cross, holding the Scepter in the right hand and the Banner of the East in the left. KERYX goes South to the Southeast with Lamp and Wand. After KERYX, then follow HEGEMON, HIEREUS with Banner and Sword, STOLISTES with Cup, and last, DADOUCHOS with Censer. (The PHYLAX remains at station.) They all line up in this order behind the KERYX, who leads the procession counterclockwise past Hierophant, making the Signs of Horus (Enterer) and Harpocrates (Silence) when passing the east. EACH OFFICER in turn does the same.

HIEREUS falls out as soon as he reaches his Throne, but remains standing in the Tau Cross position, holding out the implements. HEGEMON passes Hierophant twice and then takes her place between the Pillars. The other Officers pass Hierophant three times and then take their seats as they come to them.

HIEROPHANT and HIEREUS replace their Banners on the Banner Stands.

HIEROPHANT: **The Mystical Circumambulation is accomplished. It is the symbol of Fading Light. Let us adore the Lord of the Universe.**

ALL members including DAIS OFFICERS rise and turn East.

ALL: **Holy art Thou, Lord of the Universe!** (Salute)
Holy art Thou, Whom nature hath not formed! (Salute)
Holy art Thou, the Vast and the Mighty One! (Salute)
Lord of the Light and of the Darkness! (Sign of Silence)

HIEROPHANT, HIEREUS, and HEGEMON raise implements in salute then slowly lower them. ALL face as usual but remain standing.

HIEROPHANT: **Nothing now remains but to partake together in silence, of the Mystic Repast, composed of the symbols of the Four Elements, and to remember our pledge of secrecy.**

ALL are seated. HIEROPHANT puts down the Scepter. HIEROPHANT goes to the East of the Altar, faces west, and recites the following prayer:[22]

HIEROPHANT: **For Osiris Onnophris who is found perfect before the Gods, hath said: These are the Elements of my Body, Perfected through Suffering, Glorified through Trial.**

For the scent of the Dying Rose is as the repressed Sigh of my suffering: And the flame red Fire as the Energy of mine Undaunted Will: And the Cup of Wine is the pouring out of the Blood of my Heart: Sacrificed unto Regeneration, unto the Newer Life: And the Bread and Salt are as the Foundations of my Body, Which I destroy in order that they may be renewed.

For I am Osiris Triumphant, even Osiris Onnophris, the Justified: I am He who is clothed with the Body of Flesh, Yet in whom is the Spirit of the Great Gods: I

22. From *Z.1: The Enterer of the Threshold*, in book five of Regardie's *The Golden Dawn*, 419.

am the Lord of Life, triumphant over Death. Those who partaketh with me shall arise with me.

I am the Manifestor in matter of Those Whose Abode is in the Invisible. I am purified. I stand upon the Universe. I am its Reconciler with the Eternal Gods. I am the Perfector of Matter, and without me, the Universe is not.

HIEROPHANT goes to the West of the Altar, facing East. HIEROPHANT gives the Saluting Sign but not the Sign of Silence, and taking up the Rose says:

HIEROPHANT: **I invite you to inhale with me the perfume of this Rose, as a symbol of Air.** (Smells Rose.) **To feel with me the warmth of this sacred Fire.** (Spreads hands over it.) **To eat with me this Bread and Salt as types of Earth.** (Dips bread in Salt and eats.) **And finally to drink with me this Wine, the consecrated emblem of Elemental Water.** (Makes a Cross with the Cup [up, down, left, right] and drinks.)

HIEROPHANT puts down the Cup between the Cross and Triangle, then goes East of the Altar and faces West. The PRAEMONSTRATOR then comes to the West of the Altar and makes the Saluting Sign. HIEROPHANT replies with the Sign of Silence and then hands the Elements to Praemonstrator beginning with the Rose, which PRAEMONSTRATOR smells and returns; feels the warmth of the Lamp, eats the Bread and Salt, and receives from the HIEROPHANT the Cup and makes a Cross with it, and having drunk, returns it. HIEROPHANT then passes by West and South and returns to station. PRAEMONSTRATOR comes to the East of the Altar. IMPERATOR comes to the West, exchanges Signs, and partakes. IMPERATOR returns to station after serving CANCELLARIUS, who in turn serves PAST HIEROPHANT.

After the Chiefs, the Officers partake in this order: HIEREUS, HEGEMON, STOLISTES, DADOUCHOS, PHYLAX. (The KERYX assumes the station of PHYLAX long enough for PHYLAX to partake of the Elements.) When all the Officers except Keryx have partaken, the INNER ORDER MEMBERS, in order of seniority of admission, partake but do not wait for instruction in this. If there is a pause, one comes forward. Next come the MEMBERS OF THE OUTER ORDER in the same manner—the Neophytes coming last, piloted by

Hegemon or any Officer appointed. The Order of procedure for Outer members is PHILOSOPHI, PRACTICI, THEORICI, ZELATORES, NEOPHYTES. When the last Neophyte stands East of the Altar, KERYX comes to the West, exchanges the Signs, and partakes. (HEGEMON directs Neophyte to return to place as soon as KERYX takes the Cup.) KERYX, on receiving the Cup, drains it, inverts it over their left open palm, and says:

KERYX: **It is finished!** (Keryx replaces the Cup and returns to station.)

ALL RISE.

HIEROPHANT: (Knocks ٦) **Tetelestai!**
HIEREUS: (Knocks ٦)
HEGEMON: (Knocks ٦)

HIEROPHANT: (Knocks ٦) **Khabs.**
HIEREUS: (Knocks ٦) **Am.**
HEGEMON: (Knocks ٦) **Pekht.**

HIEREUS: (Knocks ٦) **Konx.**
HEGEMON: Knocks ٦) **Om.**
HIEROPHANT: (Knocks ٦) **Pax.**

HEGEMON: (Knocks ٦) **Light.**
HIEROPHANT: (Knocks ٦) **In.**
HIEREUS: (Knocks ٦) **Extension.**

ALL except Dais Officers make the Signs in unison toward the Altar.

HIEROPHANT: **May what we have partaken maintain us in our search for the Quintessence, the Stone of the Philosophers. True Wisdom, Perfect Happiness, the Summum Bonum.** Knocks ٦, then raises the wand and says: **And by the Power invested within this Scepter, I now declare this Temple duly closed. So mote it be.**

✠ ✠ ✠

The Ceremony of the Sephiroth

Qabalah means "tradition" in Hebrew. Its principles and roots are based in Jewish mysticism and are the cornerstone of the Western Esoteric Tradition. Qabalah is ideally suited to esoteric work because it permits us a view of the organization and construction of the universal energies that influence all areas of our lives. It is a very practical system that contains several different layers of working.

For Golden Dawn students, Qabalah is the root and foundation of our magical practice. The various grades, officers, and even the layout of the Neophyte Hall are all based on the Sephirotic structuring of the Qabalistic Tree of Life. In the Outer Order of the Golden Dawn, students learn a great deal of Qabalistic knowledge, including the attributes of the Sephiroth, gematria, names of Hebrew angels and archangels, the planets and elements, and the principal parts of the human soul as defined by Qabalists. They must also memorize the Hebrew alphabet along with all its correspondences and be able to draw the Hebrew letters to form angelic and divine names. Understanding the various arrangements that are formed by the Sephiroth on the Tree of Life is also essential. Golden Dawn students are taught the various patterns that help elucidate the Tree's function and essence. In short, there is no Golden Dawn without the spiritual philosophy known as the Qabalah.

The Ceremony of the Sephiroth given here is a ritual exploration of the ten emanations on the Qabalistic Tree of Life, from their formation out of the Three Negative Veils of Existence to explanations of their specific qualities and symbolism.

NOTE: An additional officer will be needed for this ritual—the *Psaltis* (Greek: "chanter, singer"), who will be required to sound a bell, gong, or chimes at regular intervals.[23]

Synopsis: (Immediately after the Opening, Phylax moves their chair just inside the door of the temple, until the closing.) After the Hierophant announces the ritual's objective, he leads the group through an abbreviated Middle Pillar exercise that emphasizes the importance of the triad.

Hierophant traces a Fire Triangle, Hiereus traces a Water Triangle, and Hegemon links the two by tracing both, forming a hexagram. In the next section of the ritual entitled *Genesis,* the Dais Officers narrate the beginning of the Universe as described in the

23. This officer is nontraditional but often helpful.

Book of Genesis and the creation of the Sephiroth from the Three Negative Veils of Existence.

Three Dais Officers light small votive candles to represent the first emanations that were unstable. They snuff out their candles to represent the Qabalistic Breaking of the Vessels that were imbalanced. The Hierophant reveals a large white Pillar candle to represent the Divine Light.

This is followed by a narration of the Garden of Eden and the formation of the river Naher, which flowed out into four streams representing the Four Elements. Four elemental triangles are traced, one for each river.

Hiereus goes before the Dais and traces the figure of the Flaming Sword to represent the Flaming Sword placed in the east of the Garden of Eden to keep the Supernals from falling with the rest of the Tree.

In the next section, ten officers represent the ten Sephiroth. Starting with Kether and ending with Malkuth, each officer follows the path of the Flaming Sword to their position on the Tree of Life. Each invokes their Sephirah, describes their symbol, and vibrates the Divine name associated with it. As they do this, everyone visualizes the officer surrounded by an aura in the Sephirah's color. Psaltis announces each Sephirah's entrance by ringing the bell the appropriate number of times.

After each Sephirotic Triad is completed, the Past Hierophant, acting as the Shekinah, or Presence of God, announces the event and the triad officers vibrate a Divine Hebrew name that has a certain number of Hebrew letters equal to the sum of the Sephiroth at that point: 3—יהו (Yod Heh Vav), 6—עמנואל (Emmanuel), and 9—קדשים קדוש (Qadesh Qadeshim).

After the tenth Sephirah of Malkuth is finished, the Past Hierophant, acting as the Shekinah, announces the completion of the Tree of Life and leads everyone in the Qabalistic Prayer.

Ritual Personae. All officers have additional roles and duties in this ceremony, as listed in table 2:

Officer	*Role*	*Optional Lamens/ Symbols*
Praemonstrator	Kether	Circle and Point Lamen
Imperator	Chokmah	Line Lamen
Cancellarius	Binah	Triangle Lamen
Hierophant	Chesed	Square Lamen

Table 2: Additional Officer Roles in the Ceremony of the Sephiroth (*continued*)

Officer	*Role*	*Optional Lamens/ Symbols*
Hiereus	Geburah	Pentagram Lamen
Hegemon	Tiphareth	Hexagram Lamen
Dadouchos	Netzach	Heptagram Lamen
Stolistes	Hod	Octagram Lamen
Keryx	Yesod	Nonagram Lamen
Phylax	Malkuth	Quartered Cross Lamen
Past Hierophant	The Shekinah	Dove Lamen
Psaltis		Bell or Chimes

Table 2: Additional Officer Roles in the Ceremony of the Sephiroth (*continued*)

Additional Items needed:

- Three small votive candles in glass, along with lighters, for the Praemonstrator, Imperator, and Cancellarius
- Large white pillar candle in glass, along with lighter, for the Hierophant
- Optional Lamens for the Sephirotic Officers

Perform the Opening of the Hall of the Neophytes. Then continue with the Work.

HIEROPHANT: (Knocks ו) **Fratres and Sorores of the (______) Temple of the (________) Order of the Golden Dawn in the Outer, we are here assembled in our commitment to the work of the divine theurgy, that we may awaken the balanced powers of the Sephiroth and rebuild the Temple of Solomon within our souls. The Qabalistic Tree of Life is the blueprint of the Heavens, the mind of God, and the unfoldment of creation. It is the path of involution from Deity into countless forms of manifestation. And it is the path of evolution back to our Sacred Source, our Way of Return.**

Solomon's Temple is the archetypal dwelling place of God, a restored Eden, a cosmic center, and a bulwark against chaos. It is an image of the God-indwelled Soul. The Temple of Solomon the Wise was built upon a sturdy Stone, made without hands.

As a house built upon the Sand cannot endure, so without the cornerstone of the Lapis Philosophorus the heights of the Hekheloth cannot be scaled. Except Adonai build the house, their labor is but lost that build it. Except Adonai keep the City, the watchman waketh in vain. Through this ceremony, we may be enabled to understand the true nature of the magical art and be better equipped to carry out the Great Work. Within the Souls of all here present, may the Temple of Solomon be rebuilt, may the Gates of Understanding be opened, may the Tree of Life be restored, and may the Gates of the Garden of Eden be unbarred. YHVH! To the glory of the Ineffable name, Amen.

Let us first establish a link with the Higher and Divine Self—that inexhaustible Treasure of Light to which we aspire unceasingly—that the Powers of the Divine may be reawakened in the spheres of those present and in the Sphere of this Order. For by names and Images are all Powers Awakened and Reawakened.

Awakening the Triad of Manifestation

All are seated and close their eyes as the Hierophant leads them through an abbreviated Middle Pillar exercise, using only the Sephiroth of *Kether* (Power Source), *Tiphareth* (Power Outlet), and *Malkuth* (Power Ground). The Hierophant vibrates the Divine Name one time first to establish the vibrational note for the other officers. Then All Officers including the Hierophant vibrate the name three times:

Hierophant: **EHEIEH.**
All: **EHEIEH. EHEIEH. EHEIEH.**

Hierophant: **YHVH ELOAH VE-DAATH.**
All: **YHVH ELOAH VE-DAATH.**
YHVH ELOAH VE-DAATH.
YHVH ELOAH VE-DAATH.

Hierophant: **ADONAI HA-ARETZ.**
All: **ADONAI HA-ARETZ. ADONAI HA-ARETZ. ADONAI HA-ARETZ.**

HIEROPHANT (stands): **Three Spheres vibrated on the Tree of Life—Kether, Tiphareth, and Malkuth. Source, Center, and Completion. Three is the number of the Supernal Sephiroth—Kether, Chokmah, and Binah. Three is the number of the eternal Triad of Life—that Triune Light that moved in Darkness—the triangle of the measureless Heavens reflected in the triangle of the measureless Waters.**

HIEROPHANT traces an Invoking Fire Triangle.

HIEREUS (stands): **Three is the number of the Alchemical Principles, the eternal building blocks of all things within the manifest universe—Salt, Sulphur, and Mercury—which signify the principles of Body, Soul, and Spirit. Three is the number of the alchemical Kingdoms of Nature—animal, vegetable, and mineral. The triangle of the measureless Heavens reflected in the triangle of the Kingdoms of Nature.**

HIEREUS traces an Invoking Water Triangle.

HEGEMON (stands): **Three is the number of the Mother Letters of the Hebrew alphabet—Shin, Aleph, and Mem. Three is the number of the most ancient elements of Fire, Air, and Water, symbolized by the three Primary colors of red, yellow, and blue. Three is the number of two opposing forces and one that balances between them. And these three have their image in the Threefold Flame of our Being and in the threefold wave of the sensual world.**

HEGEMON traces an Invoking Fire Triangle followed by an Invoking Water Triangle (forming a complete hexagram).

HIEREUS: **Three is the number of the Paths shown on my Lamen of Office and on the Banner of the West, and three is the number of the points of the Triangle of Manifestation.**

HIEROPHANT: **Three Times Great was Hermes Trismegistus called. Three is the number of Understanding. Three is the number of our Hermetic Work—Purification, Consecration, and Initiation. And three times did the Seraphim of Isaiah**

intone the Trisagion around the throne of God: "Qadesh, Qadesh, Qadesh!—Holy, Holy, Holy!"

All stand. Hierophant leads All in performance of the Qabalistic Cross: **ATAH, MALKUTH, VE-GEBURAH, VE GEDULAH, LE-OLAHM, AMEN.**

Hierophant: **Thus shall we begin the work of embodying and revitalizing the ten Sephiroth on the Qabalistic Tree of Life. May the shining brilliance of the Divine illuminate our Path in the Magic of Light and lay a foundational stone for the rebuilding of Solomon's Temple within each of us.**

Genesis: The Macrocosmic Temple

All are seated. The lights are dimmed. There is a brief pause.

Cancellarius: **In the beginning was the Logos—the Word—and the Word was with God, and the Word was God.**

Imperator: **In the beginning, the Elohim created the heaven and earth. And the earth was without form and void, and darkness was upon the face of the deep.**

Praemonstrator: **And the Ruach Elohim moved upon the face of the waters.**

Hierophant: **I arise in the place of the Gathering of the Waters, through the rolled-back Cloud of Night. From the Father of the Waters went forth the Spirit, rending asunder the Veils of Darkness.**

Cancellarius: **And there was but a Vastness of Silence and of Depth in the Place of the Gathering Waters.**

Imperator: **Terrible was the Silence of that Uncreated World, Immeasurable the depth of that Abyss. And the Countenances of Darkness half-formed arose, they abode not, they hastened away.**

HIEROPHANT: **And in the Darkness of Vacancy, the Spirit moved and the Light-bearers existed for a space.**

PRAEMONSTRATOR, IMPERATOR, AND CANCELLARIUS light small votive candles in glass. There is a brief pause as ALL contemplate the three lights.

PRAEMONSTRATOR: **Before all things are the Waters and the Darkness and the Gates of the Land of Night.**

CANCELLARIUS: **And the Chaos cried aloud for the Unity of Form!**

IMPERATOR: **Long have we dwelt in Darkness!**

PRAEMONSTRATOR: **Quit the night and Seek the Day!**

CANCELLARIUS: **Glory be unto the Ruach Elohim, for the Rending of Darkness is near!**

PRAEMONSTRATOR: **The first Creation was made void. The Holy Place was made waste and the Sons of the House of Wisdom were taken away into the captivity of the Senses.**

IMPERATOR: **The Face of the Eternal arose. Before the Glory of that Countenance, the Night rolled back and the Darkness hastened away.**

PRAEMONSTRATOR: **The day of the Lord is near. What was once high has been brought low. The first Light-bearers were unbalanced. Half-formed they arose, they abode not, they hastened away, as though they had not been.**

PRAEMONSTRATOR, IMPERATOR, AND CANCELLARIUS snuff out their candles. Lights are dimmed. There is a brief pause as ALL contemplate the Breaking of the Vessels.

CANCELLARIUS: **The voice of him that crieth in the wilderness, prepare ye the way of the Lord, make straight the paths of the Elohim. Every valley shall be exalted**

and every mountain and hill shall be brought low: and the crooked ways shall be made straight and the rough places plain: And the glory of the Lord shall be revealed and all flesh shall behold: for Adonai hath spoken it.

HIEROPHANT: **And the Elohim said, YEHI AUR! Let there be light!**

HIEROPHANT lights a large white pillar candle in the east and holds it aloft.

PSALTIS strikes bell once.

HIEREUS: **Elohim said, Let there be light: and there was light. And Elohim saw the light, that it was good: and Elohim divided the light from the darkness.**

Lights are turned back up. (ALL stand.)

HIEROPHANT: (Knocks ו)
HIEREUS: (Knocks ו)
HEGEMON: (Knocks ו)

HIEROPHANT: (Knocks ו) **Khabs.**
HIEREUS: (Knocks ו) **Am.**
HEGEMON: (Knocks ו) **Pekht.**

HIEREUS: (Knocks ו) **Konx.**
HEGEMON: (Knocks ו) **Om.**
HIEROPHANT: (Knocks ו) **Pax.**

HEGEMON: (Knocks ו) **Light.**
HIEROPHANT: (Knocks ו) **In.**
HIEREUS: (Knocks ו) **Extension.**

ALL give the Neophyte Signs toward the central Altar, then remain standing.

HIEROPHANT: **Sh'ma Israel Adonai Eloheinu Adonai Achad. Hear, Israel, the Lord is our God, the Lord is One.**

PSALTIS strikes bell once.

HEGEMON: **Barukh Shem k'vod Malkhuth le-Olam va'ed. Blessed be the Name of His glorious kingdom forever and ever.**

PSALTIS strikes bell once.

HIEREUS: **Achad Rosh Achdotho Rosh Ichudo Temurahzo Achad. One is His Beginning; One is His Individuality; His Permutation is One.**

PSALTIS strikes bell once.

KERYX: **And Tetragrammaton Elohim planted a Garden eastward in Eden and out of the Ground made Tetragrammaton Elohim to grow every tree that is pleasant to the sight and good for food; the Tree of Life also, in the midst of the Garden, and the Tree of the Knowledge of Good and Evil.**

HIEROPHANT: **And this is the tenth Sephirah, Malkuth, and it has about it Seven Columns, and the Four Splendours whirl around it as in the Vision of the Mercabah of Ezekiel.**

PRAEMONSTRATOR: **And a River Naher went forth out of the Garden, from the Supernal Triad, to water the Garden, and from thence it was divided into four heads in Daath.**

DADOUCHOS: **The First head is Pison, which flows into Geburah, whence there is gold.** With the Censer, traces a Cross toward the altar, followed by an Invoking Fire Triangle (figure 3).

HIEREUS: **The Second head is Gihon, the River of Waters, flowing into Chesed.** With the Sword, traces a Cross toward the altar, followed by an Invoking Water Triangle.

HIEROPHANT: **The Third is Hiddekel, the River of Air, flowing into Tiphareth.** With the Scepter, traces a Cross, followed by an Invoking Air Triangle.

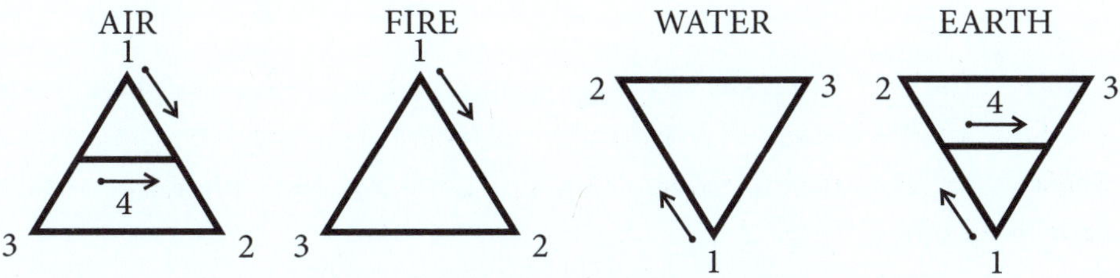

Figure 3: Invoking Elemental Triangles

STOLISTES: **The Fourth is Phrath, Euphrates, which floweth down upon the Earth.** With the Cup, traces a Cross, followed by an Invoking Earth Triangle.

HIEROPHANT: **And the Elohim said, Let us make Adam in Our Image, after our likeness, and let them have dominion over the fish of the sea and over the fowl of the air and over the cattle and over all the Earth, and over every creeping thing that creepeth over the Earth.**

HEGEMON: **And the Elohim created Eth ha-Adam in their own Image, in the Image of the Elohim created they them.**

HIEROPHANT: **And Tetragrammaton placed Kerubim at the east of the Garden of Eden and the Flaming Sword which turned every way to keep the Path of the Tree of Life.**

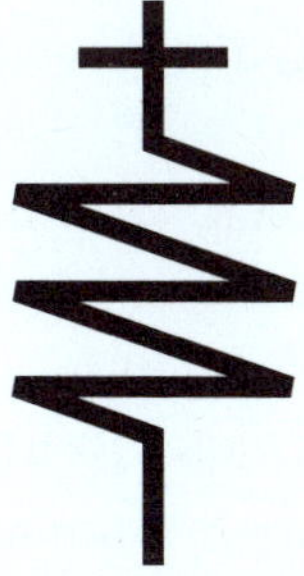

Figure 4: The Sigil of the Flaming Sword

Hiereus, with sword and Banner, goes to the east before the Dais and turns to face West. With the Sword he traces the Sigil of the Flaming Sword (figure 4). Hiereus remains in the east.

Hierophant: **The first Creation was made void. The Holy Place was made waste and the Sons of the House of Wisdom were taken away into the captivity of the Senses. We have worshipped since then in a house made with hands, receiving a reflected Light.**

Hegemon: **But He has created Nature that Man, being cast out of Eden, may not fall into the Void.**

Keryx: **He has bound Man with the Stars as with a chain.**

Stolistes: **He allures him with Scattered Fragments of the Divine Body in bird and beast and flower.**

Dadouchos: **He laments over him in the Wind and in the Sea and in the birds.**

Hegemon: **By the Waters of Babylon we have sat down and wept, but we have ever remembered Zion.**

Hierophant: **Our Memorial of Tears is a Witness in the Temple of the Heart, testifying that we shall yet return with the exultation into the House of our Father.**

Hiereus: **When the times are ended, He will call the Kerubim from the East of the Garden and all shall be consumed and become Infinite and Holy.**

Hegemon: **You are my lamp, O Adonai, keep my lamp burning; turn my darkness into light. By day Adonai went ahead of the Israelites in a Pillar of Cloud to guide them on their way and by night in a Pillar of Fire to give them light, so that they could travel by day or night. Neither the pillar of cloud by day nor the pillar of fire by night left its place in front of the people.**

HIEREUS: **Except Adonai build the house, their labor is but lost that build it. Except Adonai keep the City, the watchman waketh in vain.**

HIEREUS returns to his station. ALL are seated.

INVOCATION OF THE SEPHIROTH

HEGEMON moves her chair from between the pillars and is seated in the southeast.

PAST HIEROPHANT: **Before the Universe was made manifest, there was the Ain Soph, the Limitless. No Form, No Force, No Thing. Before the Universe could be manifested, the contraction occurred, a space in which All that is, was, and is to come could be. Thus the Tzim Tzum, the great contraction, made way for the concretion of Kether.**

PSALTIS strikes bell once.

PRAEMONSTRATOR goes to stand at the first Station of the Flaming Sword, facing west. (See figure 5.) PRAEMONSTRATOR raises hands. ALL vibrate: **EHEIEH.** ALL visualize Praemonstrator surrounded by an aura of white light.

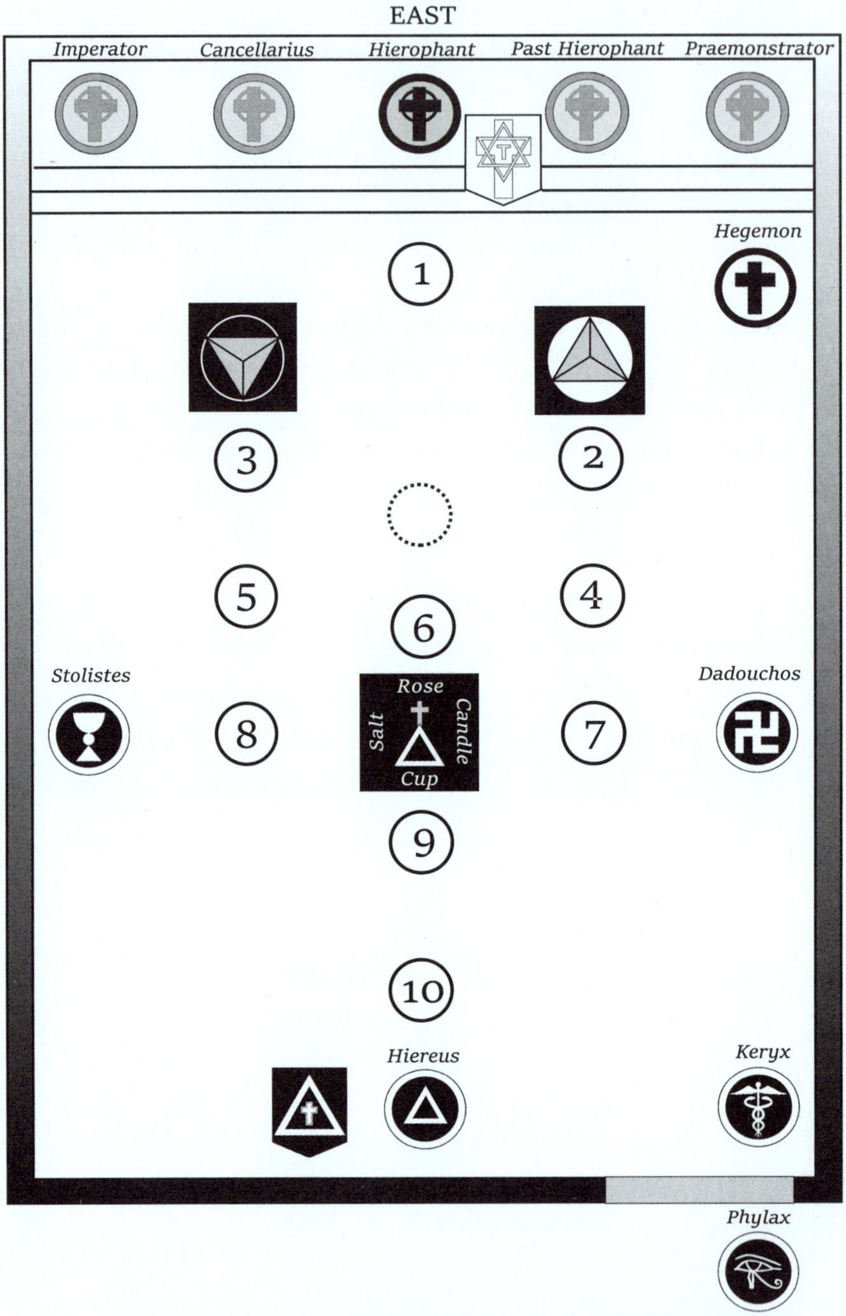

EAST

Imperator Cancellarius Hierophant Past Hierophant Praemonstrator

Hegemon

1

3 2

5 4

6

Stolistes Dadouchos

8 Rose Salt Candle Cup 7

9

10

Hiereus Keryx

Phylax

Figure 5: The Sephirotic Stations of the Flaming Sword

PRAEMONSTRATOR: **Kether the Crown! Concreted out of the Unmanifest, I am the First and I stand at the Head of the Pillar of Mildness. I am the Light giving power of comprehension, for as it is written, I am the Hidden Intelligence, the Primal Glory.**

The first is incorruptible, eternal, unbegotten, and indivisible. The Mind of the First whirled forth in reechoing roar, comprehending by invincible Will ideas omniform, which, flying forth from that one fountain issued. For from the First was alike the Will and the End.

The Point with the Circle is my symbol, containing all that is and will be, the symbol of first emanation and ultimate return. The Potentiality of All contained within the Circle of the Manifested Universe.

PSALTIS strikes bell twice.

IMPERATOR follows the path of the Flaming Sword and stands at the second station, facing north. IMPERATOR raises hands. ALL vibrate: **YAH.** ALL visualize IMPERATOR surrounded by an aura of gray light.

IMPERATOR: **Chokmah, the emanation of Wisdom! Brought forth by the outpouring of Kether, I am the Second and I stand at the Head of the Pillar of Mercy. I am the Splendor of the Unity, equaling it and exalted above every head, for as it is written, I am the Illuminating Intelligence, the Second Glory.**

Where the Paternal Monad is, the Monad is enlarged and generateth two, and beside Him is seated the Duad. All things are sprung from that One Fire, for all things did the Father of all things perfect, and delivered them over to the Second Mind Whom all races of men call First. The Dyad glittereth with intellectual sections, governing all things and ordering everything not ordered.

The Line within the Circle is my symbol, the extension of Kether, the overflowing of the Divine into a Second which is a reflection of the First. Power made manifest and set in motion, the Spirit of God which hovered over the face of the Waters.

Psaltis strikes bell three times.

Cancellarius follows the path of the Flaming Sword and stands at the third station, facing south. Cancellarius raises hands. All vibrate: **YHVH ELOHIM.** All visualize Cancellarius surrounded by an aura of black light.

Cancellarius: **Binah, the emanation of Understanding! Brought forth by the outpouring of Chokmah, I am the Third and I stand at the Head of the Pillar of Severity. I am the foundation of Primordial Wisdom, which is called the Creator of Faith. For as it is written, I am the Sanctifying Intelligence, receiving the dynamic current of Force from Chokmah and providing it Form.**

The Mind of the First said that all things should be cut into Three, whose Will assented, and then all things were divided. For the Mind of the Eternal said, Into Three, governing all things by Mind. And there appeared in it the Triad, Virtue, Wisdom and Multicient Truth. Thus floweth forth the form of the Triad, being Pre-existent, not the first Essence, but that whereby all things are measured.

My symbol is the Triangle, the figure into which all surfaces can be reduced. It is the Triad operating in all things. Even as I am the Neshamah within the Greater Neshamah. All form operates through me.

Praemonstrator, Imperator, and Cancellarius, together: **We are the Supernals, formed in Trinity.**

Praemonstrator: **The Crown Above All Heads.**
Imperator: **Wisdom.**
Cancellarius: **And Understanding.**

Past Hierophant: **And thus the Supernal Eden was Formed. For thou must know that all things bow before the Three Supernals.**

Praemonstrator, Imperator, and Cancellarius, together: **YOD HEH VAV.**

PSALTIS strikes bell four times.

HIEROPHANT follows the path of the Flaming Sword and stands at the fourth station, facing north. HIEROPHANT raises hands. ALL vibrate: **EL.** ALL visualize HIEROPHANT surrounded by an aura of blue light.

HIEROPHANT: **Chesed, the emanation of Mercy! Brought forth by the outpouring of Binah, I am the Fourth and I stand within the Pillar of Mercy. I am that which contains all the Holy Powers and from me all the spiritual virtues emanate. For as it is written, I am the Receptive Intelligence, for I gather all the holy powers from the Supernals.**

All Quaternity lies here. In Wisdom the Eternal hath founded all of Creation upon the Tetrad, for the Triad is completed by the Tetrad. And within the Tetractys is found the Decad, the number of the Kingdom.

My symbol is the Square, the figure of stability and equation. It is the Holy Name of Four Letters operating through the four elements.

PSALTIS strikes bell five times.

HIEREUS follows the path of the Flaming Sword and stands at the fifth station, facing south. HIEREUS raises hands. ALL vibrate: **ELOHIM GIBOR.** ALL visualize HIEREUS surrounded by an aura of red light.

HIEREUS: **Geburah, the emanation of Power! Brought forth by the outpouring of Chesed, I am the Fifth and I stand within the Pillar of Severity. To know me is to know Fear, the Awe of God. For as it is written, I am the Radical Intelligence, the absolute and unmitigated Truth.**

The Voice of the Lord is upon the Waters. The God of Glory thundereth. The Lord is upon many Waters. The Voice of the Lord is powerful. The Voice of the Lord is full of Majesty. The Voice of the Lord breaketh the Cedars of Lebanon.

The Voice of the Lord divideth the Flames of Fire. The Voice of the Lord shaketh the wilderness of Kadesh.

My symbol is the Pentangle, the power of the Pentad operating in Nature by the dispersal of the Spirit and the Four Elements. It is the sign of the Microcosm of Man.

PSALTIS strikes bell six times.

HEGEMON follows the path of the Flaming Sword and stands at the sixth station, facing west. HEGEMON raises hands. ALL vibrate: **YHVH ELOAH Ve-DAATH.** ALL visualize HEGEMON surrounded by an aura of yellow light.

HEGEMON: **Tiphareth, the emanation of Beauty! Brought forth by the outpouring of Geburah, I am the Sixth and I stand within the Pillar of Equilibrium. In the center of the Tree I receive and harmonize the powers of all the other Spheres. For as it is written, I am the Mediating Intelligence, for in me is multiplied the influxes of the emanations.**

The Eternal made them six in number, and cast into their midst thereof the Fire of the Sun. Into that Center from which all lines are equal—that the Swift Sun may come around that Center eagerly urging itself toward that Center of Resounding Light. The Sun more true measureth all things by time, for He is the Time of Time, and his disc is in the Starless above the inerratic Sphere, and he is the center of the Triple World. The Sun is Fire and the Dispenser of Fire. He is also the channel for the Higher Fire.

My symbol is the Hexangle, the power of the hexad operating in Nature by the dispersal of the rays of the planets and of the Zodiac emanating from the Sun in the center, even as I stand in the center of the Tree.

HIEROPHANT, HIEREUS, and HEGEMON, together: **We are the ethical spheres, formed in Trinity.**

HIEROPHANT: **Through Mercy.**
HIEREUS: **And Severity.**
HEGEMON: **And Balanced in Beauty.**

PAST HIEROPHANT: **And thus the Powers of the Supernals were reflected down through Da'ath, and the first reflected triad was formed.**

HIEROPHANT, HIEREUS, and HEGEMON, together: **EMMANUEL.**

PSALTIS strikes bell seven times.

DADOUCHOS follows the path of the Flaming Sword and stands at the seventh station, facing north. DADOUCHOS raises hands. ALL vibrate: **YHVH TZABAOTH.** ALL visualize DADOUCHOS surrounded by an aura of green light.

DADOUCHOS: **Netzach, the emanation of Victory! Brought forth by the outpouring of Tiphareth, I am the Seventh and I stand at the base of the Pillar of Mercy. I am the dwelling place of instincts, emotions, and desires, where creativity is born. For as it is written, I am the Occult Intelligence, for through me the Brilliant Splendour of the Divine Light is reflected into Manifestation.**

The Eternal congregated the Seven Firmaments of the Kosmos, circumscribing the Heavens with convex form. He constituted a Septenary of wandering Existences. Suspending their disorder in Well-disposed Zones.

My symbol is the Heptangle, the power of the heptad dispersing the powers of the Seven Planets. It is the Star of Venus and of Isis.

PSALTIS strikes bell eight times.

STOLISTES follows the path of the Flaming Sword and stands at the eighth station, facing south. STOLISTES raises hands. ALL vibrate: **ELOHIM TZABAOTH.** ALL visualize STOLISTES surrounded by an aura of orange light.

STOLISTES: **Hod, the emanation of Splendor! Brought forth by the outpouring of Netzach, I am the Eighth and I stand at the base of the Pillar of Severity. I am the rational mind which organizes and categorizes. The Origin of all Words and Names of Power is from me. For as it is written, I am the Perfect Intelligence, the Mean of the Primordial, the balance between extremes.**

The Mind of the Father whirled forth in reechoing roar, comprehending by invincible Will Ideas omniform. Hence the inscrutable God is called silent by the divine ones, and is said to consent with Mind, and to be known to human souls through the power of the Mind alone. Measuring and bounding all things.

My symbol is the Octangle, the power of the Ogdoad operating in Nature by the dispersal of the Elements in their dual aspect. It is the Star of Mercury.

PSALTIS rings the Bell nine times.

KERYX follows the path of the Flaming Sword and stands at the ninth station, facing west. KERYX raises hands. ALL vibrate: **SHADDAI EL CHAI.** ALL visualize KERYX surrounded by an aura of violet light.

KERYX: **Yesod, the Foundation! Brought forth by the outpouring of Hod, I am the Ninth and I stand within the Pillar of Equilibrium. I am the Astral Light, that which underlies All, the foundation of Matter. For as it is written, I am the Pure Intelligence, purifying the Numerations, proving and correcting the designs before manifestation.**

The number nine is Sacred, receives its completion from three triads, and attains the summits of Divine Wisdom. O Æther, Sun, and Spirit of the Moon, ye are the chiefs of the Air. And the wide Air, and the Lunar Course, and the Pole of the Sun. Unwearied doth Nature rule over the Worlds and Works, so that the Period of all things may be accomplished.

My symbol is the Enneangle, the power of the Ennead operating in Nature by the dispersal of the rays of the Seven Planets and of the Head and Tail of the Dragon of the Moon. It is the Star of Luna.

Dadouchos, Stolistes, and Keryx, together: **We are the astral spheres, formed in Trinity.**

Dadouchos: **Through Victory.**
Stolistes: **And Glory.**
Keryx: **And Balanced in Foundation.**

Past Hierophant: **And thus the Powers of the Supernals were reflected down through the Veil of Paroketh, and the second reflected triad was formed.**

Dadouchos, Stolistes, and Keryx, together: **QADESH QADESHIM.**

Psaltis: Strikes bell ten times.

Phylax follows the path of the Flaming Sword and stands at the tenth station, facing east. Phylax raises hands. All vibrate: **ADONAI HA-ARETZ.** All visualize Phylax surrounded by an aura of citrine, olive, russet, and black light.

Phylax: **Malkuth, the Kingdom! Brought forth by the outpouring of Yesod, I am the Tenth and final Sphere, and I stand at the base of the Pillar of Equilibrium. I am the Kingdom and the place of final manifestation. The Crucible of all that came before. For as it is written, I am the Resplendent Intelligence, exalted above every head, illuminating the splendor of all the Lights.**

The Maker of all things, self-operating, framed the World. And there was a certain Mass of Fire: all these things Self-Operating He produced, that the Body of the Universe might be conformed, that the World might be manifest, and not appear membranous. Matter—the Matrix containing All. And above the shoulders of the Great Goddess is Nature in her vastness exalted.

My symbol is the Dekangle, the power of the Dekad dispersing the powers of the rays of the ten Sephiroth.

PAST HIEROPHANT: **And thus the Tree of Life was Formed, the Unmanifest made Manifest through the operation of the powers of the Sephiroth in equilibration and harmony. Flowing through the Tree and dwelling in its many palaces was the Shekinah. And through the Presence of the Shekinah we will all be blessed by the Power of the Sephiroth.** (Pause.) **Let us rehearse the Qabalistic Prayer:**[24]

ALL: **Be favorable to me, oh ye Powers of the Kingdom Divine.**
May Glory and Eternity be in my left and right hands,
so that I may attain to Victory.
May Mercy and Justice restore my soul to its original purity.
May Understanding and Wisdom Divine conduct me to the imperishable Crown.
Spirit of Malkuth, Thou who hast laboured and hast overcome;
set me in the Path of Good.
Lead me to the two pillars of the Temple, to Jachin and Boaz,
that I may rest upon them.
Angels of Netzach and of Hod, make my feet stand firmly on Yesod.
Angel of Gedulah, console me.
Angel of Geburah, strike, if it must be so, but make me stronger,
so that I may become worthy of the influence of Tiphereth.
Oh Angel of Binah, give me Light.
Oh Angel of Chokmah, give me Love.
Oh Angel of Kether, confer upon me Faith and Hope.
Spirits of the Yetziratic World,
withdraw me from the darkness of Assiah.
Oh luminous triangle of the world of Briah,
cause me to see and understand the mysteries of Yetzirah and of Atziluth.
Oh Holy Letter Shin.
Oh ye Ishim, assist me by the name Shaddai.
Oh ye Kerubim, give me strength through Adonai.

24. From Levi, *The Magical Ritual of the Sanctum Regnum*, 87–88.

O Beni Elohim, be my companions in the name of Tzabaoth.
O Elohim, fight for me by the Holy Tetragrammaton.
O Melakim, protect me through YHVH.
O Seraphim, give me holy love in the name Eloah.
O Chashmalim, enlighten me by the torches of Eloi and the Shekinah.
O Aralim, angels of power, sustain me by Adonai.
O Ophanim, Ophanim, Ophanim,
forget me not, and cast me not out of the Sanctuary.
O Chaioth ha-Qadesh, cry aloud as an eagle,
speak as a man, roar and bellow.
Qadesh! Qadesh! Qadesh! Shaddai! Adonai! YHVH!
Eheieh Asher Eheieh!
Amen! Selah! Amen!

All Sephiroth Officers go back to their seats, following the path of the Flaming Sword from Kether to Malkuth.

Any announcements, comments, or temple business can be conducted at this time.

Proceed to the Closing of the Neophyte Hall.

✠✠✠

Consecration of a Tiphareth Talisman

A talisman is an object that has been charged or consecrated with magical energies toward the achievement of a specific goal. An unconsecrated talisman is considered a lifeless object, but through the rite of consecration, the once inert object is infused with specific energies that are often astrological or Qabalistic in nature. Charged with a powerful current of divine force, a talisman emanates magical energy that has been tailored to create the precise change the magician desires to achieve.

The Qabalistic Sephiroth of the Tree of Life are particularly suited for talismanic work in the Outer Order, as they form an important component of the Golden Dawn teachings. The following ritual, Consecration of a Tiphareth Talisman, is specifically designed for infusing a talismanic object with the energies of Tiphareth, the sixth Qabalistic Sephirah of beauty and harmony.

Tiphareth is the center of balance on the Tree of Life, the place of equilibrium that connects the higher levels of the Tree with the lower levels. The sixth Sephirah is therefore an essential conduit for passing energy and information to all levels and back again, marking Tiphareth as the sphere of mediation and reconciliation. It is also the Sephirah of healing, illumination, true peace, inner tranquility, and mystical experience. Additionally, Tiphareth is the heart of what is sometimes called Christ consciousness, the mystical center of devotion and the Higher Self. The luminary of the Sun, the source of life and light, is assigned to Tiphareth.

Synopsis: After the Hierophant announces the ritual's objective, he leads the group through an abbreviated Middle Pillar exercise that emphasizes the importance of the triad. The divine names of Tiphareth are vibrated to orient the Working toward the sixth Sephirah.

Keryx places the wrapped talisman on the central altar and the process of purifying and consecrating begins. Following a potent invocation of the forces of Tiphareth over the talisman by the Hierophant, pairs of Officers step up to the altar to further purify and consecrate the talisman by tracing symbols associated with their office over it. The Hierophant performs another powerful invocation ending with all present propelling energy at the talisman with the Projection Sign of the Neophyte, ending with the Sign of Silence. When the Hierophant is satisfied with the outcome of the Work, he thanks the Divine Powers and wraps the newly consecrated talisman in white cloth.[25]

Also needed:

- A talisman (or talismans) of Tiphareth
- A black cloth (or bag) and cord for wrapping the unconsecrated talisman
- A white or yellow cloth or bag for wrapping the consecrated talisman
- An additional officer will be needed—the *Psaltis*, who will be required to sound a bell, gong, or chimes at regular intervals.

25. The design of the talisman does not have to follow the drawing shown here. It could be either more complex or simplified. It could be a gemstone or other object that corresponds to Tiphareth. Or it could be a number of drawn talismans, stones, or other objects that are consecrated together so that each participant may receive a consecrated talisman at the end of the ritual.

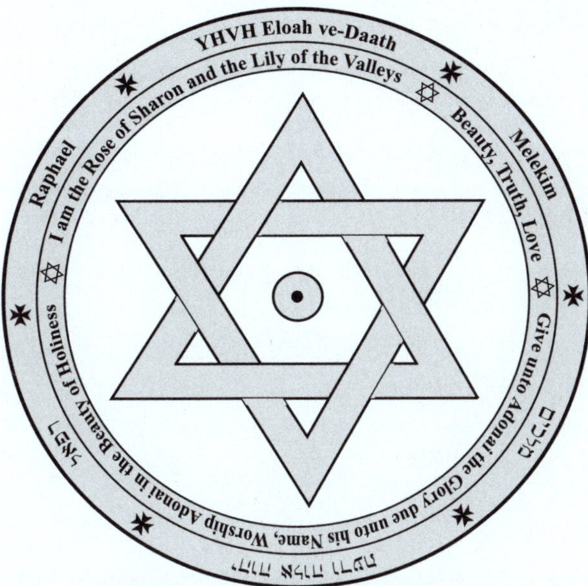

Figure 6: Tiphareth Talisman

Perform the Opening of the Hall of the Neophytes. Then continue with the Work.

HIEROPHANT: (Knocks ו) **Fratres and Sorores of the (______) Temple of the (________) Order of the Golden Dawn in the Outer, we are here assembled in our commitment to the work of the divine theurgy, to charge and consecrate a Talisman of Tiphareth, so that through this ceremony we may be better able to understand the true nature of the magical art and be better equipped to carry out the Great Work, to the glory of the Ineffable name.**

Let us first establish a link with the Higher and Divine Self—that inexhaustible Treasure of Light, to which we aspire unceasingly—that the Powers of the Divine may be reawakened in the spheres of those present and in the Sphere of this Order. For by names and Images are all Powers Awakened and Reawakened.

ALL OFFICERS close their eyes as the HIEROPHANT leads them through an abbreviated Middle Pillar exercise, using only the Sephiroth of Kether (Power Source), Tiphareth

(Power Outlet), and Malkuth (Power Ground). The HIEROPHANT vibrates the Divine Name one time to establish the vibrational note for the other officers. Then ALL OFFICERS including the HIEROPHANT vibrate the name for a total of three times:

HIEROPHANT: **EHEIEH.**
ALL: **EHEIEH. EHEIEH. EHEIEH.**

HIEROPHANT: **YHVH ELOAH VE-DAATH.**

ALL: **YHVH ELOAH VE-DAATH.**
YHVH ELOAH VE-DAATH.
YHVH ELOAH VE-DAATH.

HIEROPHANT: **ADONAI HA-ARETZ.**
ALL: **ADONAI HA-ARETZ. ADONAI HA-ARETZ. ADONAI HA-ARETZ.**

HIEROPHANT: **Three Spheres vibrated on the Tree of Life—Kether, Tiphareth, and Malkuth. Source, Center, and Completion. Three is the number of the Supernal Sephiroth—Kether, Chokmah, and Binah. Three is the number of the eternal Triad of Life—that Triune Light that moved upon the face of the Waters—the triangle of the measureless Heavens, reflected in the triangle of the measureless Waters.**

HIEREUS: **Three embodied twice is six, the number of the days in which God was said to have created the world in the Book of Genesis. According to medieval Christian thought, there were six ages of the world. And six is the number of directions in space: East, West, North, South, Above, and Below.**

HEGEMON: **Three embodied twice is attributed to the figure of the Six-pointed Star, which is the hexagram or seal of Solomon. It represents the Sun at the center of the other planets and is a symbol of the Ruach Elohim, or Spirit of God.**

HIEREUS: **The Hexagram is composed of the two triangles of Water and Fire, which, when combined, form the symbols of the triangles of Air and Earth. Placed**

upon the Tree of Life, the six points of the Hexagram align with Daath, Chesed, Geburah, Netzach, Hod, and Yesod, with the balancing Sephirah of Tiphareth at the center. It represents the union of the Divine and human natures—between active and passive, spirit and matter.

Hegemon: **The Hexagram is an even greater figure than the pentagram, because unlike the five-pointed star, the six-pointed star cannot be inverted for evil. The pentagram is the symbol of man, but the hexagram is the symbol of perfected man or enlightened humanity. It is the Star of the Macrocosm.**

Hiereus: **The Hexagram is also affiliated with the Double Triquetra, or doubling of the Celtic Knot, a symbol of the Triple Goddess in Pagan belief and a symbol used by Christians to represent the Holy Trinity.**

Hierophant: **Three Times Great was Hermes Trismegistos called. Three is the number of Understanding. Three is the number of our Hermetic Work—Purification, Consecration, and Initiation. And three times did the Seraphim of Isaiah intone the Trisagion around the throne of God: "Qadesh, Qadesh, Qadesh!—Holy, Holy, Holy!"**

All stand. Hierophant leads All in performance of the Qabalistic Cross: **ATAH, MALKUTH, VE-GEBURAH, VE GEDULAH, LE-OLAHM, AMEN.**

Hierophant: **Thus shall we begin the work of purifying and consecrating this object as a telesma of this temple, initiating it as a talisman for Theurgic work and re-creating it to be a fitting vessel for the Light Divine.**

Hierophant leads All in vibration of divine names associated with Tiphareth (three times for each):

YHVH ELOAH VE-DAATH.
YHVH ELOAH VE-DAATH.
YHVH ELOAH VE-DAATH.
RAPHAEL. RAPHAEL. RAPHAEL.
MELEKIM. MELEKIM. MELEKIM.

ALL are seated.

PHYLAX hands the talisman, which is wrapped in black cloth, to the KERYX, who brings it to the altar and places it on the white triangle, then returns to place. STOLISTES and DADOUCHOS advance to either side of the altar.

STOLISTES traces a cross and sprinkles water thrice over talisman.
PSALTIS rings bell once.

HIEROPHANT: **The Voice of my Undying and Secret Soul said unto me, "Let me shroud myself in Darkness, peradventure thus shall I manifest myself in Light. I am the only Being an abyss of Darkness. From the Darkness came I forth ere my birth, from the silence of a primal sleep."**

DADOUCHOS traces a cross and censes thrice over talisman.
PSALTIS rings bell once.

HIEROPHANT: **And the Voice of Ages answered unto my Soul and said, "Creature of Telesmata, I am he who formulates in Darkness—the Light that shineth in Darkness, yet the Darkness comprehendeth it not."**

STOLISTES traces a cross and sprinkles water thrice over talisman.
PSALTIS rings bell once.
DADOUCHOS traces a cross and censes thrice over talisman.
PSALTIS rings bell once.

HIEREUS, bearing Banner and sword, steps up to the west of the altar and lays the sword blade on the talisman.

HIEREUS: **Thou canst not pass from concealment unto manifestation save by the virtue of the name ELOHIM. Before all things are the Chaos and the Darkness and the Gates of the Land of Night. I am he whose name is Darkness. I am the Great One of the Paths of the Shades. I am the Purifier in the midst of the Purification. Take on therefore manifestation before me. For I am he in whom fear is not.**

STOLISTES pulls back the black covering, exposing the talisman.
STOLISTES traces a cross and sprinkles water thrice over talisman.
PSALTIS rings bell once.
DADOUCHOS traces a cross and censes thrice over talisman.
PSALTIS rings bell once.
HIEREUS returns to his station.

HEGEMON steps up to the east side of the altar and lays the head of their Wand on the Talisman.

HEGEMON: **Thou canst not pass from concealment unto manifestation save by the virtue of the name YHVH. After the formless and the Void and the Darkness, then cometh the knowledge of the Light. I am that Light which ariseth in Darkness. I am the Consecrator in the midst of the Consecration. Take on therefore manifestation before me, for I am the wielder of the forces of Balance.**

DADOUCHOS removes the black cord from the talisman.
STOLISTES traces a cross and sprinkles water thrice over talisman.
PSALTIS rings bell once.
DADOUCHOS traces a cross and censes thrice over talisman.
PSALTIS rings bell once.

STOLISTES and DADOUCHOS return to their places. HEGEMON removes their chair from between the Pillars and is seated in the Southeast.

HIEROPHANT goes to the east of the altar and traces a clockwise circle over the Talisman. In this circle he traces the symbol of Sol. HIEROPHANT leads ALL in vibrating the divine name of Tiphareth three times:

YHVH ELOAH VE-DAATH.
YHVH ELOAH VE-DAATH.
YHVH ELOAH VE-DAATH.

HIEROPHANT traces a cross over the figure.

HIEROPHANT goes to the east of the Altar, puts the Wand aside for a moment, and forms a triangle with his hands over the talisman as he says: **Behold the Initiator in the midst of the Initiation. And the power of the Divine said unto the Creature of Talismans, "Let us enter the presence of the Ancient of Days. I am the Secret of Secrets, hidden in the heart of all things. I am the grace of the majesty divine. I am the Lord of Perfection and Splendor. Long hast thou dwelt in Darkness. Quit the night and seek the Day!"**

HIEROPHANT traces a cross over the talisman with the right hand.

HIEROPHANT takes up the wand and traces a clockwise circle over the Talisman. In this circle he traces the symbol of Sol. HIEROPHANT leads ALL in vibrating the divine name of Tiphareth three times:

YHVH ELOAH VE-DAATH.
YHVH ELOAH VE-DAATH.
YHVH ELOAH VE-DAATH.

HIEROPHANT: **O thou divine Forces of the sphere of Tiphareth, we invoke thee in the divine name of YHVH Eloah ve-Daath, the mighty archangel Raphael, and the Choir of Angels known as the Melekim, the Kings. Thou art the Heart and Soul of all things, and seat of the Higher Self. The Lord God Made Manifest in the Sphere of the Mind. Holy Child and King! Thou who art the Reconciler with the Ineffable. Augoeides and Divine Genius! Holy Angel of Adonai! Descend from your celestial abode to dwell with the children of the gods on Earth. Thou whose descent from on high connects the heart of humanity with the heart of the Eternal One, whose true name is unknown and unpronounceable. I beseech Thee, manifest though this ceremony thy power and splendor. Consecrate this talisman that lies before us. Give us of Thy substance so that this talisman may have power to assist us in the Great Work. O Secret of Secrets that art hidden in the being of all that lives, Secret and Most Holy! Source of Light, Source of Life, Source of Love, Source of Liberty. We invoke Thee to make a divine link with all those powers of Healing, balance, and Rebirth summed up in the Holy name of Tiphareth, the sixth sphere of Beauty!**

HIEROPHANT again traces a circle around the talisman. In this circle he traces the symbol of Sol. HIEROPHANT leads ALL in vibrating the divine name of Tiphareth three times:

YHVH ELOAH VE-DAATH.
YHVH ELOAH VE-DAATH.
YHVH ELOAH VE-DAATH.

PSALTIS rings bell three times.

HIEROPHANT steps back to a position between the Pillars facing West and visualizes the Banner of the East as the other Officers proceed:

PHYLAX and KERYX go to the altar (PHYLAX on the north side of Altar, KERYX on the South side). PHYLAX traces the Flaming Sword over the talisman with the sword.

PHYLAX: **YHVH ELOAH VE-DAATH, blessed be Thy name. Defeated are the warriors of ignorance and empty are their thrones. Broken are the Lords of Chaos and fallen are the powers in which they trusted! In the name of the Highest, and by the power of YHVH Eloah ve-Daath, and the mighty archangel Raphael, I purify thee with the symbol of the Lightning Flash!**

PHYLAX takes up the talisman, holding it by the black cloth underneath it, and touches it to his Lamen.

PHYLAX: **And through the virtue of the Lamen and the Sword of the Phylax, who guards the Pronoas of the Temple, keeping strict watch without, lest the evil and the unbalanced enter our sacred Hall, I invoke thee to make a divine link with all those powers of connection, reconciliation, and mediation summed up in the Holy name of Tiphareth, the sixth sphere of Beauty!**

PHYLAX replaces the talisman on the altar.
KERYX traces the letter Yod over the talisman with the Lamp.

KERYX: **YHVH ELOAH VE-DAATH, blessed be thy name. Thou art the sun in its rising, passing through the hour of cloud and of night. Under the shadow of thy Wings do I find refuge. In the name of the Highest, and by the power of YHVH Eloah ve-Daath, and the mighty archangel Raphael, I consecrate thee with the symbol of the tongue of Flame!**

KERYX takes up the talisman, holding it by the black cloth underneath it, and touches it to his Lamen.

KERYX: **And through the virtue of the Lamen and the Caduceus Wand of the Keryx, who guards the inner side of the Temple, keeping strict watch within, and leading all Mystic Circumambulations bearing the Lamp of the hidden Gnosis, I invoke Thee to make a divine link with all those powers of illumination, inner vision, and harmony summed up in the Holy name of Tiphareth, the sixth sphere of beauty!**

KERYX replaces the talisman on the altar.

HIEROPHANT steps up to the altar and traces a circle around the talisman. In this circle he traces the symbol of Sol. HIEROPHANT leads ALL in vibrating the divine name of Tiphareth three times:

YHVH ELOAH VE-DAATH.
YHVH ELOAH VE-DAATH.
YHVH ELOAH VE-DAATH.

PSALTIS rings bell three times.
KERYX and PHYLAX return to places.

HIEROPHANT steps back to a position between the Pillars facing West and visualizes the Banner of the East as the other Officers proceed:

STOLISTES and DADOUCHOS go to the altar (STOLISTES on the north side of Altar, DADOUCHOS on the South side). STOLISTES traces a cross and sprinkles water thrice in the form of the Water Triangle over the talisman.

STOLISTES: **YHVH ELOAH VE-DAATH, blessed be thy name. The Voice of the Lord is upon the Waters. Thy way is in the Sea and thy Path in the Great Waters. To that abyss of Waters do I raise my soul to receive thy truth. In the name of the Highest, and by the power of YHVH Eloah ve-Daath, and the mighty archangel Raphael, I purify thee with Water!**

STOLISTES takes up the talisman, holding it by the black cloth underneath it, and touches it to her Lamen.

STOLISTES: **And through the virtue of the Lamen and the Cup of the Stolistes, who guards the Well of Living Water and purifies the Hall, the Fratres, and the Sorores, and the Candidates with the lustral Waters of the loud resounding Sea, I invoke Thee to make a Divine Link with all those powers of devotion, regeneration, and resurrection summed up in the Holy name of Tiphareth, the sixth sphere of Beauty!**

STOLISTES replaces the talisman on the altar. DADOUCHOS traces a cross and censes thrice over talisman in the form of the Fire Triangle.

DADOUCHOS: **YHVH ELOAH VE-DAATH, blessed be thy name. The God of Glory thundereth. The Voice of the Lord divideth the Flames of Fire. The Voice of the Lord shaketh the Wilderness of Kadesh. In the name of the Highest, and by the power of YHVH Eloah ve-Daath, and the mighty archangel Raphael, I consecrate thee with Fire!**

DADOUCHOS takes up the talisman, holding it by the black cloth underneath it, and touches it to his Lamen.

DADOUCHOS: **And through the virtue of the Lamen and the Censer of the Dadouchos, who guards the Lake of Living Fire and consecrates the Hall, the Fratres, and**

the Sorores, and the Candidates with that Holy and Formless Fire which darts and flashes through the hidden depths of the Universe, I invoke Thee to make a Divine Link with all those powers of connection, reconciliation, and illumination summed up in the Holy name of Tiphareth, the sixth sphere of Beauty!

Dadouchos replaces the talisman on the altar. Hierophant steps up to the altar and traces a circle around the talisman. In this circle he traces the symbol of Sol. Hierophant leads All in vibrating the divine name of Tiphareth three times:

YHVH ELOAH VE-DAATH.
YHVH ELOAH VE-DAATH.
YHVH ELOAH VE-DAATH.

Psaltis rings bell three times.
Stolistes and Dadouchos return to places.

Hierophant steps back to a position between the Pillars facing West and visualizes the Banner of the East as the other Officers proceed:

Hiereus and Hegemon go to the altar (Hiereus on the north side of Altar, Hegemon on the South side). Hiereus traces a Circle and a Triangle over the talisman with the Sword.

Hiereus: **YHVH ELOAH VE-DAATH, blessed be thy name. This is the Lord of the Gods! This is the Lord of the Universe. This is he whom the Winds fear! Broken is the strength of hell. Fallen are its walls of deception! In the name of the Highest, and by the power of YHVH Eloah ve-Daath, and the mighty archangel Raphael, I purify thee with symbols of circle and triangle!**

Hiereus takes up the talisman, holding it by the black cloth underneath it, and touches it to his Lamen.

Hiereus: **And through the virtue of the Banner of the West, and the Lamen and Sword of the Hiereus, who guards the Sacred Hall from the Chaos and shadow**

of the Qliphotic Powers, the one who is called Fortitude and known by the titles Lord of Twilight and Master of Darkness, I invoke Thee to make a Divine Link with all those powers of the Higher Genius, the Higher Mind, and the Holy Guardian Angel summed up in the Holy name of Tiphareth, the sixth sphere of Beauty!

HIEREUS replaces the talisman on the altar.
HEGEMON traces a cross over the talisman with the wand.

HEGEMON: **YHVH ELOAH VE-DAATH, blessed be thy name. O Thou Circle of Stars whereof my Genius is but the younger sibling, marvel beyond imagination, Soul of Eternity before whom time is ashamed, not unto thy majesty may I attain unless thy image be that of love. In the name of the Highest, and by the power of YHVH Eloah ve-Daath, and the mighty archangel Raphael, I consecrate thee with the symbols of the equated cross!**

HEGEMON takes up the talisman, holding it by the black cloth underneath it, and touches it to her Lamen.

HEGEMON: **And through the virtue of the Scepter of Wisdom and the Lamen of the Hegemon, who keeps the Threshold of the Gate of the Mysteries, serving as Preparer of the Pathway and Reconciler between Light and Darkness I invoke Thee to make a Divine Link with all those powers of grace, equilibrium, and spiritual harmony summed up in the Holy name of Tiphareth, the sixth sphere of Beauty!**

HEGEMON replaces the talisman on the altar. HIEROPHANT steps up to the altar and traces a circle around the talisman. In this circle he traces the symbol of Sol. HIEROPHANT leads ALL in vibrating the divine name of Tiphareth three times:

YHVH ELOAH VE-DAATH.
YHVH ELOAH VE-DAATH.
YHVH ELOAH VE-DAATH.

Psaltis rings bell three times.
Hiereus and Hegemon return to their places.

Hierophant traces a circle and cross over the talisman. Invokes with raised arms.

Hierophant: **YHVH Eloah ve-Daath, blessed be thy name. O Lord of the Universe, Thou art above all things and thy name is in all things. Before thee the shadows of Night roll back and the Darkness hastens away. After the formless and the void and the Darkness, then cometh knowledge of the Light. So in the place of the Threshold of the Gate of the East, I draw thee into my heart, O vision of the Rising Sun. Lead us in our aspirations after that divine and only selfhood which is in thee, enabling us to live in purity of mind, body, and soul, so that we may have no other desire than to become fit vessels for the Higher and Divine Genius.**

Thou dwellest in the place of balanced forces, where alone is perfect justice. I beseech thee, O YHVH Eloah ve-Daath, Lord God of Knowledge Made Manifest in the Sphere of the Mind, to look with favor upon our rite of consecration. Cause the Divine Influx to descend from your mighty Archangel Raphael and charge this talisman with all the powers of Tiphareth, the sixth sphere of Beauty and Harmony, that through its use we may be aided in our quest for the Light Divine—through intelligence and through love. In the name of the Highest, and by the power of YHVH Eloah ve-Daath, and the mighty Archangel Raphael, I initiate and charge thee with the symbols of the circle and cross!

Hierophant takes up the talisman, holding it by the black cloth underneath it, and touches it to his Lamen.

Hierophant: **And through the virtue of the Banner of the East, the Scepter of Power and the Lamen of the Hierophant who is the Expounder of the Mysteries and the steward of the temple, governing it according to the laws of the Order, I invoke Thee to make a Divine Link with all those powers of balance, mystical vision, and holy union summed up in the Holy name of Tiphareth, the sixth sphere of Beauty!**

HIEROPHANT replaces the talisman and visualizes the Divine White Light, drawn down through Kether, grounding itself in Malkuth, and rising up again to the Tiphareth center. When ready, he projects at the Talisman at least three times, with the Sign of the Enterer, imagining the Divine Light radiating from his Tiphareth center to charge the talisman. When satisfied with the amount of energy projected at the talisman, HIEROPHANT puts the Wand aside for a moment and forms a triangle with his hands over the talisman and concentrates on it, trying to see an aura of light around it. Once the aura is seen, HIEROPHANT gives a nod to the HIEREUS, who leads ALL in three projections (in unison) at the talisman. When satisfied, HIEROPHANT gives the Sign of Silence, after which ALL give the Sign of Silence.

HIEROPHANT: **Through the aid of the Highest, and the Work of the Temple, I declare that the talisman has been duly consecrated with the powers of Tiphareth.**

PSALTIS rings bell six times.

HIEROPHANT goes to the west of the altar and faces east, arms upraised.

HIEROPHANT: **Unto Thee, Sole Wise, Sole Merciful, and Sole Eternal One, we give thanks for overseeing our efforts and empowering our rites. Not unto our names, but to thine, be the praise and Glory forever. Glory be to Thee, Lord of the Land of Life, for thy Glory flows out rejoicing to the ends of the earth!**

PSALTIS rings bell six times.

HIEROPHANT wraps the talisman in a white cloth and carries it back to his station in the East. KERYX replaces the Elements on the altar. HEGEMON moves her throne to between the pillars.

Any announcements, comments, or temple business can be conducted at this time.

Proceed to the Closing of the Neophyte Hall.

✠ ✠ ✠

Invocations

The word *invoke* means "to call." There are actually two forms of invocation. The first form is a prayer of entreaty that calls upon a deity for help, support, or simply to "be present." The second form is an invocation that the magician uses in order to act as a living representative of the deity. For the sake of convenience, we can refer to these two types as *invocation prayer* and *godform invocation*. Ritual magic usually employs both forms.

Godform invocation often forms a part of the Golden Dawn ritual practice known as the *assumption of godforms*.[26] This practice is taught at the Adept level as part of the curriculum of the Second Order. A godform is an archetypal image of a god or goddess built up in the imagination and constructed by visualization on the astral plane. Assumption of a godform is a magical technique wherein the Adept works with the energies of a particular deity by "assuming its form." The image of the deity is created on the astral by focused visualization, vibration of the deity's name, the tracing of its sigil, etc. The magician then steps into this astral image and wears it like a garment or mask, continuing to strengthen the image with intense concentration. This is performed in order to create a vehicle for that particular aspect of the Divine that the magician is working with. The magician imitates and is inspired by the deity and can receive communication from the deity, but does not totally identify or immerse themselves completely with the deity.[27] Nevertheless, the act of assuming a god's form in the astral light brings a form of intimacy with the deity that can result in an increase in spiritual communication and insight. In the Outer Order, Adept Officers, particularly those seated on the Dais, inhabit specific Egyptian godforms during the initiation ceremonies. For example, in the Neophyte Ceremony, the Hierophant assumes the godform of Osiris. Certain godforms are built up at specific places in the Hall but remain unassumed by any Officer. These "invisible stations" are viewed as astral batteries that store magical energies used in ritual.

The two invocation rituals that follow focus on a single Officer who performs a godform assumption. This technique requires preparation and psychological balance and should only be performed by a qualified Adept.

---

26. See Assumption of Godforms in chapter 5, page 331.

27. A channeler allows a deity to inhabit their own body as if it were a garment. For the magician, it is the exact opposite. We inhabit the astral form of a deity that we have constructed. Allowing a deity to have complete control over the magician is antithetical to our work.

Figure 7: The God Thoth

Invocation of Thoth

The goal of this ritual is to invoke Thoth, the Egyptian god of wisdom, in order to provide opportunities for spiritual conversation and the furtherance of knowledge.

Thoth, also called Djehuti and Tahuti, is known as the "lord of books and learning." According to legend he is the patron god of wisdom and inventions, science and literature, and his name is derived from the Egyptian word for *ibis*, a bird that is sacred to him. Thoth is the spokesman of the gods, as well as the record-keeper and moon god. He is self-begotten and self-created. Thoth is credited with inventing all the arts and sciences: geometry, arithmetic, astronomy, astrology, surveying, medicine, music, drawing, writing, and all knowledge in general. He is also the god of magic and the world's first magician and priest. Ancient disciples of Thoth claimed to have access to the god's magical books. When deciphered, these formulas could command all the forces of nature and subdue the gods themselves. This infinite power is the reason his followers referred to him as "Thoth, three times very, very Great," which became the basis for the Greek version, Hermes Trismegistus. Thoth is the one who divided time into months, years, seasons, and aeons. He is the divine calculator, adviser, arbiter, chief historian, and keeper of the divine archives. Herald of the gods, Thoth also serves as their clerk and scribe. In the Judgment of the Soul in the Hall of Truth, he records the final verdict. Thoth is pictured as a human figure with the head of an ibis, wearing the kilt, collar, and headdress, sometimes with the disc and crescent of the Old Kingdom. He often holds the tablet and writing stylus of a scribe.

All participants are encouraged to prepare a personalized prayer to Thoth as well as a small offering for the deity at the appropriate point in the ritual. The offering could be anything that relates to Thoth, such as an instrument of writing, a drawing, a poem, a bit of grain, a votive candle, incense, etc.

Synopsis: After the Hierophant announces the ritual's objective, he leads everyone in the Invoking Star of the Gods, a rite that is based upon the Lesser Invoking Ritual of the Pentagram but utilizes Egyptian words and phrases and the symbol of the Egyptian star. This rite creates a magic circle and lays the groundwork for the Khemetic nature of the Invocation.

Next, four Officers invoke the Four Pillars of the Earth (the four Elements), bringing them to life in the temple by tracing the figure of the Ankh, the Egyptian symbol of life, toward the four cardinal directions.

The Hierophant leaves his throne, which is assumed by the Cancellarius, the Officer who has a direct affiliation with the Godform of Thoth. The Hierophant lights charcoal and incense in the cauldron, draws down a veil in front of the Cancellarius, and goes to the west of the Altar to begin a powerful invocation prayer to Thoth, accompanied by the rest of the participants chanting the name of Thoth.

The Cancellarius begins to assume the Godform of Thoth and chants the deity's name to commence the godform invocation of the Deity.

The Hierophant continues with prayers and invocations to Thoth until at length he advances to the east and quietly gives a personalized prayer to Thoth. Cancellarius, speaking as Thoth's envoy, communicates with the Hierophant for a brief time while the rest of the participants continue to chant. When their communication is finished, the Hierophant offers a gift at Thoth's Altar. One by one, all participants do the same, advancing to the east, communicating with Thoth, and offering their gifts.

When everyone has had a chance to commune with Thoth, the chanting stops. Any final communications from Thoth to the temple are given before the Hierophant thanks the deity. The Cancellarius releases the godform of Thoth and returns to his throne. The veil is withdrawn.

(NOTE: Because this ritual involves a godform assumption of Thoth, it is important that the person taking on the role of Cancellarius be a skilled Adept.)

Preparation: In addition to the setup of the Neophyte Hall, there should be a low, portable Altar that can be moved into position at the beginning of the Work. The Altar should be white or covered with a white cloth. Once the Altar is in place near the throne of the Cancellarius, set the following items on it: a statue or image of Thoth; a white, yellow, or orange candle; a cauldron with charcoal; powdered incense; and any appropriate symbolism attributed to Thoth. (If possible, a thin white veil should be set up so it can be lowered at the appropriate time just in front of the Hierophant's throne. If this is not possible, the veil can be draped over the Cancellarius's head at the appropriate time, or simply do without the veil altogether.)

Words of Power for the Invocation of Thoth	
Djehuti (Jeh-HO-tee)	**Entek Pau** (En-TEK Pow)
Ta Sutenit (Tah SOO-ten-eet)	**Ta Sakhem** (Tah SAA-Kem)
Hena Khut (Hen-ah KOOT)	**En Heh, En Heh** (En-Hey, En-Hey)
Amma (Ah-mah)	**Djehuti Nef** (Jeh-HO-tee Nef)[28]
Djehuti Ash (Jeh-HO-tee Ash)[29]	**Djehuti Mu** (Jeh-HO-tee Moo)[30]
Djehuti Ta (Jeh-HO-tee Tah)[31]	**Tahuti** (Teh-HO-Tee)

Table 3: Words of Power for the Invocation of Thoth

Perform the Opening of the Hall of the Neophytes. Then continue with the Work.

When ready for the main Work to commence, move the Thoth Altar into place in front of the Cancellarius's throne.

HIEROPHANT: (Knocks ٦) **Fratres and Sorores of the (______) Temple of the (_______) Order of the Golden Dawn in the Outer, we are here assembled in our commitment to the work of the divine theurgy, to invoke the great God of Wisdom, the Thrice Great Thoth, Lord and Priest of All Knowledge, so that through this ceremony we may be better able to understand the true nature of the magical art and be better equipped to carry out the Great Work, to the glory of the Ineffable name.**

Let us first establish within this temple a link to the names and images of ancient Khem, the kingdom of the Two Lands! Eternal Egypt, steeped in Majesty and Magic. Let the Powers of the Divine be reawakened in the spheres of those present and in the Sphere of this Order. For by names and Images are all Powers Awakened and Reawakened.

HIEROPHANT leads ALL in the *Invoking Star of the Gods,* beginning with the Egyptian Cross:

28. Meaning "Air of Thoth."

29. Meaning "Fire of Thoth."

30. Meaning "Water of Thoth."

31. Meaning "Earth of Thoth."

The Egyptian Cross

ALL: Stand and face east. Touch the forehead and vibrate: **ENTEK PAU.**

Touch the breast and vibrate: **TA SUTENIT.**

Right shoulder: **TA SAKHEM.**

Left shoulder: **HENA KHUT.**

Clasp the fingers over the breast: **EN HEH, EN HEH.**

Bow and vibrate: **AMMA.**[32]

The Invoking Star of the Gods

Face east.[33] Trace the invoking form of the Egyptian Star. Charge the center by vibrating **NEF** (meaning "Air"). Keep the right arm extended throughout; never let it drop. The star should be visualized in a flaming white light.

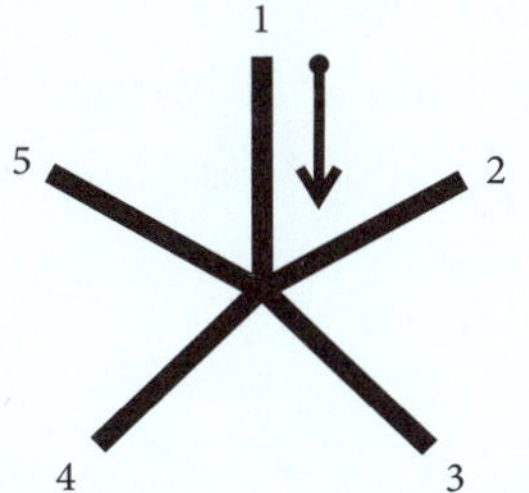

Figure 8: The Egyptian Star

Face the south and draw the star. Charge it in the center by vibrating: **ASH** ("Fire").
Face the west and draw the star. Charge it in the center by vibrating: **MU** ("Water").
Face the north and draw the star. Charge it in the center by vibrating: **TA** ("Earth").

32. Meaning "Thou who art the Self-Existent, the Kingdom, the Divine Power, and the Glory, for eternity, for eternity. Grant that it be so."

33. Participants can simply turn in place.

The Invocation of the Four Deities

All face east and stand in the form of the Tau Cross. Say:

Before me, HATHOOR, the Mother of Light.
Behind me, TOUM of the setting sun.
On my right hand, SAKHMET, mighty lady of Flame.
On my left hand, HAPI-WER, the Bull of the Earth.
For about me flames a heaven of stars.
And above me shines the star of God!

All repeat the *Egyptian Cross* as in the beginning:

Stand and face east. Touch the forehead and vibrate: **ENTEK PAU.**

Touch the breast and vibrate: **TA SUTENIT.**

Right shoulder: **TA SAKHEM.**

Left shoulder: **HENA KHUT.**

Clasp the fingers over the breast: **EN HEH, EN HEH.**

Bow and vibrate: **AMMA.**

All are seated.

Invoking the Four Pillars of the Earth

Hierophant stands, faces west, and says: **The ancient Gods are all things, and all things are the ancient Gods. Their breath is the Air and the wind. Their Will is the Fire. Their blood is the Water. Their bodies are the celestial stars and the terrestrial Earth. The ancient Gods are all things, and all things are the ancient Gods. All Goddesses are but one Goddess. The God and the Goddess are One. All Gods are but One God. All are One. Yet the One has many names and countenances. In this time and in this place, we call upon the One under the name of Thoth.**

All vibrate: **THO-OTH. THO-OTH. THO-OTH.**

Hierophant faces east, raises arms, and says: **Hail to you, O Living Breath which fills all things at their birth. You wind from the Wings of the Ibis, it is you who causes the hawk to fly and all creatures to live.**

Hierophant: **O Air, O Invisible Living One. O Breath of Knowing, I invoke you with this Sign of Life!**

Hierophant traces the Ankh while visualizing it in glowing yellow light.

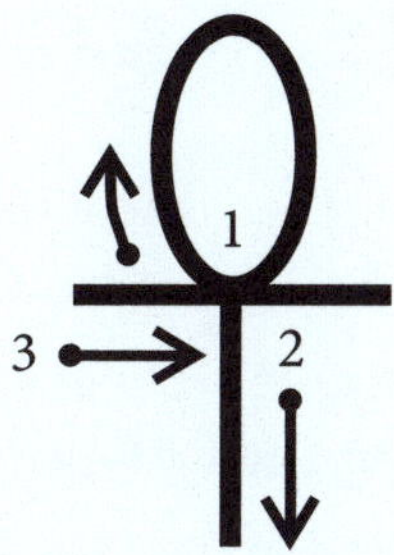

Figure 9: The Ankh

Hierophant: **DJEHUTI NEF. Air of Thoth! Inspire and protect us by the Holy Power of the Sacred and Living Breath! Live, O Breath of Djehuti, live for us!** (Turns to face west.)

Dadouchos stands, faces south, raises arms, and says: **Hail to you, O Burning Flame, O Fiery Disk, you igniter of the life of all things. You are the heat of work and of passion. You are the Light that destroys evil. O Fire, O Creator, O Destroyer, O Purifier, O energy of the Will of Thoth, I invoke you with this sign of Life!**

Dadouchos traces the Ankh while visualizing it in glowing red light.

Dadouchos: **DJEHUTI ASH. Fire of Thoth! Empassion and enflame us by the Holy Power of the Sacred Fire! Live, O Will of Djehuti, live for us!** (Turns to face north.)

HIEREUS stands, faces west, raises arms, and says: **Hail to you, O Inundation, O River of Heaven and Earth. You who makes fertile all things. You are the balm from the hands of the Ibis-headed One. You are the purifying waters of the Nile. O Blood of Thoth, O Power of Magic, O Living Soul, I invoke you with this sign of Life!**

HIEREUS traces the Ankh while visualizing it in glowing blue light.

HIEREUS: **DJEHUTI MU. Waters of Thoth! Deepen and renew us by the Holy Power of the Divine Flow. Live, O Blood of Djehuti, live for us!** (Turns to east.)

STOLISTES stands, faces north, raises arms, and says: **Hail to you, O Mass of Creation! You who did rise from out of the watery Nu wherein was Nothing before your Becoming. By you are all things manifested and sustained. O Earth, O World, O Body of the Universe, I invoke you with this Sign of Life.**

STOLISTES traces the Ankh while visualizing it in glowing black light.

STOLISTES: **DJEHUTI TA. Earth of Thoth! Strengthen and uphold us by the Holy Power of the Earth. Live, O manifestation of Djehuti, live for us!** (Turns to face south.)

ALL vibrate: **DJEHUTI. DJEHUTI. DJEHUTI.**

ALL keep vibrating this name until Hierophant is ready. HIEREUS, STOLISTES, and DADOUCHOS are seated.

At this point, the HIEROPHANT leaves his throne, lights charcoal in the cauldron, and adds a small bit of incense. The CANCELLARIUS assumes the Hierophant's Throne. The HIEROPHANT draws down the veil in front of (or over) the Cancellarius. The CANCELLARIUS begins the assumption of the Godform of Thoth. ALL but HIEROPHANT are seated. HIEROPHANT goes to the West of the Altar, facing East. ALL chanting stops for a while.

HIEROPHANT stands with raised arms and says: **All hail Thoth, Tehuti, Djehuti, the Ibis-Headed author of the world. Poet of the first poem! Writer of the first scroll! Singer of the first hymn, and speaker of the first speech! Hail to the wordsmith and the narrator of all forms. Lord of Holy Words! Be here now!**

God of the Highest Magic! Prince of the Divine Speech! Lord of the whispered incantation that thunders across the firmament like a reechoing roar! We beseech Thee in thy Holy name of Djehuti-Thoth to grant thine aid unto the highest aspiration of our souls, and clothe us with thy Wisdom and knowledge. Live and dwell among us!

Teacher of Secrets and legends. Sacred Storyteller! You are the Master builder of the Door to the Mysteries, and you light the flame that can raze that door to the ground. Lift us up and grant unto us an unshakable link to all those Powers of Wisdom and Magic which rise rank upon rank to the feet of the Holy One. Grant that the Knowledge and Light of the Divine Ones may descend and manifest unto us True holiness and unsullied vision of the Light.

You who wear the head of an Ibis! Lord Djehuti! We invoke thee! You who are also called Tahuti and Hermes Thrice Great! Master of Balance and counter of the Stars! Knower of all that is hidden under the heavenly vault! Bring us into the circle of thy deepest mystery. O Lord Thoth, you are the crafter of the True, you hold the key to an unbreakable code, you are the encrypter of the inscrutable cipher. You alone can decode it.

All hail Thee, Thoth-Hermes thrice greatest. All hail Thee, Prince of Men. All hail Thee, who standeth upon the head of Typhon.[34] Guide our hands that we may know. Scribe of Gods—Lord of Divine Books. We wish to know that we may serve. All hail Thee, Thoth-Hermes. O Djehuti, hear and bestow.

CANCELLARIUS begins to chant **Tho-oth** softly.

34. From Hall, *The Secret Teachings of All Ages*, xxxvii.

HIEROPHANT traces the figure of the Ankh toward the East and continues: **Procul O Procul Ete Profani. Balasti! Ompehda! In the name of the Mighty and Terrible One, I proclaim that I have banished the shells unto their habitations.**

I invoke Tahuti, the Lord of Wisdom and of Utterance; the god that cometh forth from the veil. O thou, majesty of the godhead, wisdom-crowned Tahuti, Lord of the gates of the universe. Thee, thee I invoke.

O thou of the ibis head. Thee, thee I invoke. Thou who wieldest the wand of double power. Thee, thee I invoke. Thou who bearest in thy left hand the rose and cross of light and life. Thee, thee I invoke. Thou whose head is as an emerald, and thy nemyss as the night sky blue. Thee, thee I invoke. Thou whose skin is a flaming orange as though it burned in a furnace. Thee, thee I invoke.

Behold, I am yesterday, today, and the brother of tomorrow. I am born again and again. Mine is the unseen force whereof the gods are sprung, which is as life unto the dwellers in the Watchtowers of the Universe. I am the charioteer of the east; Lord of the past and the future. I see by my own inward light; Lord of resurrection who cometh forth from the dust, and my birth is from the house of death. O ye two Divine hawks upon your pinnacles who keep watch over the universe.

Ye who company the Bier to the house of rest, who pilot the ship of Ra, ever advancing onward the heights of heaven. Lord of the shrine which standeth in the center of the earth. Behold! He is me and I in him. Mine is the radiance wherein Ptah floateth over the firmament. I travel upon high. I tread upon the firmament of Nu. I raise a flashing flame with the lightning of mine eye.

Ever rushing on in the splendor of the daily glorified Ra, giving my life to the dwellers of earth. If I say come up upon the mountain, the celestial waters shall flow at my command. For I am Ra incarnate, Kephra created in the flesh. I am the Eidolon of my father Tmu, Lord of the city of the sun. The god who commands is in my mouth. The god of wisdom is in my heart. My tongue is the sanctuary of truth and a god sitteth upon my lips. My word is accomplished

> **every day, and the desire of my heart realizes itself as that of Ptah when he created his works. I am eternal, therefore all things are as my designs. Therefore do thou come forth unto me from thine abode in the silence, unutterable wisdom, all light, all power.**
>
> **THOTH. HERMES. MERCURY. ODIN. By whatever name I call thee, thou art still nameless to eternity. Come thou forth, I say, and aid and guard me in this work of art. Thou star of the east that didst conduct the magi. Thou art the same all present in heaven and in hell. Thou that vibratest between the light and the darkness, rising, descending, changing ever, yet ever the same. The sun is thy father; thy mother the moon. The wind hath borne thee in its bosom and earth hath ever nourished the changeless godhead of thy youth. Come thou forth, I say, come thou forth and make every spirit of the firmament and of the ether, upon the earth and under the earth, on dry land and in the water, of whirling air and of rushing fire, and every spell and scourge of God the Vast One may be obedient unto me.**[35]

ALL except HIEROPHANT begin to chant **Tho-oth** softly and continuously. HIEROPHANT again traces the figure of the Ankh toward the East. After a pause, the HIEROPHANT continues:

> **Let all the Nature of the world entertain the hearing of this Hymn.**
> **Be opened, O Earth, and let all the Treasure of the Rain be opened.**
> **You Trees tremble not, for I will sing,**
> **and praise the Lord of the Creation,**
> **and the All, and the One.**
> **Be opened you Heavens, ye Winds stand still,**
> **and let the immortal Circle of God, receive these words.**
> **For I will sing, and praise him that created all things,**
> **that fixed the Earth, and hung up the Heavens, and commanded the sweet Water to come out of the Ocean,**
> **into all the World inhabited, and not inhabited,**
> **to the use, and nourishment of all things, or men.**

35. Adapted from *Liber Israfel.* Printed in Regardie, *The Tree of Life,* 396–97.

That commanded the fire to shine for every action, both to Gods, and Men.
Let us altogether give him blessing, which rideth upon the Heavens,
the Creator of all Nature.
This is he, that is the Eye of the Mind, and will accept the praise of my Powers.
O all ye Powers that are in me, praise the One, and the All.
Sing together with my Will, all you Powers that are in me.
O Holy Knowledge, being enlightened by thee, I magnify the intelligible Light,
and rejoice in the Joy of the Mind.
All my Powers sing praise with me, and thou my Continence,
sing praise my Righteousness by me; praise that which is righteous.
O Communion which is in me, praise the All.
By me the Truth sings praise to the Truth, the Good praiseth the Good.
O Life, O Light from us, unto you comes this praise and thanksgiving.
I give thanks unto thee, O Father, the operation or act of my Powers.
I give thanks unto thee, O God, the Power of my operations.
By me thy Word sings praise unto thee,
receive by me this reasonable Sacrifice in words.
The powers that are in me, cry these things, they praise the All,
they fulfill thy Will; thy Will and Counsel is from thee unto thee.
O All, receive a reasonable Sacrifice from all things.
O Life, save all that is in us; O Light enlighten, O God the Spirit;
for the Mind guideth the Word: O Spirit bearing Workman.
Thou art God, thy servant crieth these things unto thee through,
by the Fire, by the Air, by the Earth, by the Water, by the Spirit,
by thy Creatures.
From eternity I have found the means to bless and praise thee,
and I have what I seek; for I rest in thy Will.[36]

(Pause.)

All continue to softly chant **Tho-oth** as Hierophant advances to the east before the Cancellarius. The Hierophant (kneeling or standing) gives a personalized invocation to Thoth. Cancellarius (in godform) may communicate to Hierophant at this

36. Adapted from "The Secret Song, The Holy Speech," in Everard, *The Divine Pymander*, 63–66.

time. When finished, Hierophant goes to the Thoth Altar and offers a gift, placing it on the Altar. (If HIEROPHANT has no gift, he may offer a small bit of incense to the Cauldron.) When finished, Hierophant returns to stand west of the cubical altar and chants **Tho-oth** with the other members.

The rest of the Members each take their turn in the usual order: HIEREUS, HEGEMON, STOLISTES, DADOUCHOS, PHYLAX, and sideliners, ending with KERYX. Each member stands or kneels before the Cancellarius and delivers their Thoth invocation, possibly receives communication, and then goes to the Thoth Altar to offer their gifts, or a small bit of incense to the cauldron.

When the KERYX is finished, the Thoth chant stops. (Let CANCELLARIUS in godform speak to the group if they desire to do so.) The HIEROPHANT, west of the Cubical Altar, gives thanks to Thoth:

HIEROPHANT: **At the Ending at the Night: At the Limits of the Light:**
Tho-oth stood before the Unborn Ones of Time!
Then was formulated the Universe: Then came forth the Gods thereof:
The Aeons of the Bornless Beyond:
Then was the Voice vibrated: Then was the Name declared.
At the Threshold of the Entrance, Between the Universe and the Infinite,
In the Sign of the Enterer, stood Tho-oth,
As before him were the Aeons proclaimed.
In Breath did he vibrate them: In Symbols did he record them:
For betwixt the Light and Darkness did he stand.

The Speech in the Silence: The Words against the Son of Night:
The Voice of Thoth before the Universe in the presence of the eternal Gods:
The Formulas of Knowledge: The Wisdom of Breath:
The Radix of Vibration: The Shaking of the Invisible:
The Rolling Asunder of the Darkness:
The Becoming Visible of Matter:
The Piercing of the Coils of the Stooping Dragon:

The Breaking forth of the Light:
All these are in the Knowledge of Tho-oth.[37]

HIEROPHANT traces the Ankh and continues:

> **Magic courses through us like ink flowing from the pen of Thoth, magic of magic, spirit of spirit. We awake as from a dream. Our hearts open, filled with Light.**[38] **We give thanks to Djehuti, the God of Magic, Thoth, Thrice Very Great.**
>
> **Lord of the Divine Words! For your wisdom, we give thanks. For your blessings, Mighty Prince of Incantation, we thank thee. Our hearts open, the door, the way. Our senses are radiant. Words of Truth flow over us. We know the golden song of day. We hear the name of Light. We shine as the points of stars in the ubiquitous heart of God.**[39]

CANCELLARIUS releases the godform of Thoth, traces the Qabalistic Cross in silence, and returns to the throne of the CANCELLARIUS. The HIEROPHANT returns to station.

At this point, any comments, announcements, or temple business may be discussed. (After the closing, be sure that the gifts to Thoth are dispersed according to their nature. Seeds, fruit, and other natural items or perishables can be placed in the garden. Incense may be burned.)

Proceed to the Closing of the Neophyte Hall.

✠ ✠ ✠

INVOCATION OF IOPHIEL

This ritual, like the previous one, involves invocation prayer as well as godform invocation. The goal of this rite is to invoke Iophiel, the angelic intelligence of Jupiter, into the Hall in order to commune with those present.

The name Iophiel (pronounced "Yoh-fee-el") means "the Beauty of God." This angel is one of the Shinanim, a high class of fiery angels associated with Jupiter. Iophiel is often invoked as an amulet or talisman angel.

37. Adapted from *Liber Israfel*. Printed in Regardie, *The Tree of Life*, 396–97.

38. Adapted From Ellis, *Awakening Osiris*, 140, 164–65.

39. Adapted From Ellis, *Awakening Osiris*, 164–65.

The planet Jupiter, named after the primary Roman god, was called the Greater Benefic by the ancients. Jupiter is the lawmaker, the judge, and the benefactor of humankind. This planet rules leisure time, wealth, growth, prosperity, opportunity, assimilation, indulgence, optimism, big business, morality, the higher (abstract) mind, higher education, ambitions, philosophy, and luck. Jupiter's action is orderly and efficient and fosters growth and increase.

Figure 10: Iophiel

Synopsis: After the Hierophant announces the ritual's objective, he leads everyone in the Lesser Invoking Ritual of the Pentagram to create a magic circle conducive to the nature of the working. This is followed by an invocation to the Highest. In the east, the Hierophant traces a number of sigils connected to the divine and angelic forces of Jupiter.

Next, four Officers invoke the Four Pillars of the Earth (the Elements), bringing them to life in the temple by tracing Aleph, the first letter of the Hebrew alphabet, toward the four cardinal directions. Aleph is the letter attributed to air and affiliated with the breath of life. It is also the first letter of the word *emeth*, which means truth.

The Hierophant leaves his throne, which is assumed by the Praemonstrator, the Officer most aligned with the planet Jupiter through the Sephirah of Chesed. The Hierophant lights charcoal and incense in the cauldron, draws down a veil in front of the Praemonstrator, and goes to the west of the Altar to begin a powerful invocation prayer to Iophiel accompanied by the rest of the participants chanting the name of the angel.

The Praemonstrator begins to assume the godform of the angel and chants Iophiel's name.

The Hierophant continues with prayers and invocations to the forces of Jupiter and to Iophiel until at length he advances to the east and quietly gives a personalized invocation to Iophiel. The Praemonstrator, speaking as the envoy to the angel, communicates with the Hierophant for a brief time while the rest of the participants continue to chant. When their communication is finished, the Hierophant offers a gift at Iophiel's Altar. One by one, all participants do the same, advancing to the east, communicating with Iophiel, and offering their gifts.

When everyone has had a chance to commune with the angel, the chanting stops. Any final communications from Iophiel to the temple are given before the Hierophant thanks the Angel. The Imperator releases the godform of Iophiel and returns to their throne. The veil is withdrawn.

(NOTE: Because this ritual involves a godform invocation of Iophiel, it is important that the Adept taking on the role of the Praemonstrator have the proper preparation and psychological balance and be skilled in assuming godforms.)

Preparation: In addition to the setup of the Neophyte Hall, there should be a low, portable Altar that can be moved into position at the beginning of the Work. The Altar should be white or covered with a white cloth. Once the Altar is in place (near the throne of the Praemonstrator), set the following items on it: a statute or image of Iophiel; a white, blue, or violet candle; a cauldron with charcoal; powdered incense; and any appropriate symbolism attributed to Jupiter. (If possible, a thin, white veil should be set up so it can be lowered at the appropriate time just in front of the Hierophant's throne. If this is not possible, then the veil can be draped over the Praemonstrator's head at the appropriate time, or simply do without the veil altogether.)

Perform the Opening of the Hall of the Neophytes.

When ready for the main Work to commence, move the Iophiel Altar into place in front of the throne of the Praemonstrator.

HIEROPHANT: (Knocks ו) **Fratres and Sorores of the (______) Temple of the (________) Order of the Golden Dawn in the Outer, we are here assembled in our commitment to the work of the divine theurgy, to invoke Iophiel, the angelic intelligence of Jupiter, so that through this ceremony we may receive the bounties of positive growth and increase, understand the true nature of magical philosophy and the Higher Mind, and be better equipped to carry out the Great Work, to the glory of the Ineffable name.**

Let us first establish within this temple a link to the names and images of the Invoking Pentagram and the Conjuration of the Four.[40] **Let the Powers of the Divine be reawakened in the spheres of those present and in the Sphere of this Order. For by names and Images are all Powers Awakened and Reawakened.**

HIEROPHANT leads ALL in the *Lesser Invoking Ritual of the Pentagram*, starting and ending with the Qabalistic Cross. After the LIRP, ALL are seated.

INVOCATION OF THE HIGHEST

HIEROPHANT stands, faces East, and says:

Unto Thee, sole wise, sole eternal, and sole merciful One,
Be the praise and the glory forever.
Who hath permitted us, who now standeth humbly before Thee,
To enter thus far into the sanctuary of Thy mysteries.
Not unto us, but unto Thy name be the glory.
Let the influence of Thy Divine Ones descend upon our heads,
And teach us the value of self-sacrifice,
So that we shrink not in the hour of trial,
But that thus our names may be written on high,
And our Genius may stand in the presence of the Holy Ones—
In that hour when the Son of Man is invoked before the Lord of Spirits
And His name in the presence of the Ancient of Days.

---

40. The four Archangels of the Elements as given in the LRP.

(Pause.)

Thou that standest above the Waters where from all things were created,
Thee, Thee I invoke, by the name of EHEIEH and the power of AGLA.
O Thou Divine Silence, Thou that bearest the Rose and Cross of Life and Light!
Thee, Thee I invoke, for my exaltation to that Light.
Thou art the Alpha and the Omega, the First and the Last.
And Thy Life is as a circle of Infinite Heaven.
Thy throne is set on high, Thou art the center and the shrine,
The Silence and the Eternal Light.
Behold! I am in Thee Lord, and Thou also in me.
Thou art my Father, the Might and Strength of the Almighty God.
Thou art my Mother, Immortal Wisdom veiled in Eternal Beauty and Love.
Therefore I ask Thee to bring me unto Thine abode of All-Wisdom,
All-Light, All-Love.
Father, Celestial Fire; Mother, Heavenly Sea; Thou who art the Air of Life,
The Harmony of all.
Bring me, I say, to thine abode of Loving Majesty that I may awaken to the glory of my Godhead, which is in Thee. Amen.

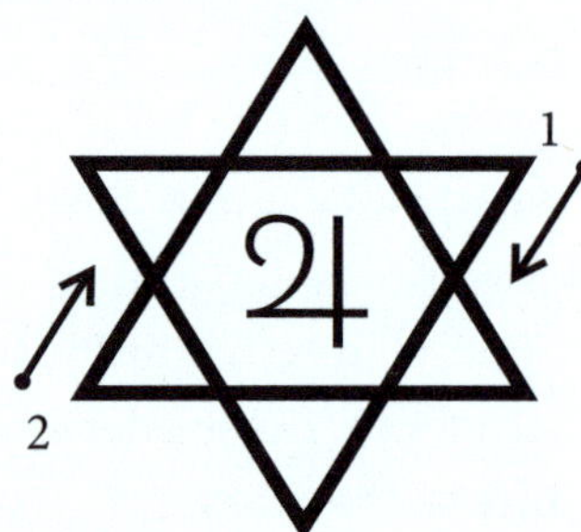

Figure 11: Greater Invoking Hexagram of Jupiter

HIEROPHANT traces the *Greater Invoking Hexagram of Jupiter* over the throne of the Hierophant, then continues to trace the appropriate sigils over the throne during the following invocation:

In the Divine Name EL (draws sigil), **Most Treasured Father, Thou Great Founder of Benevolent Priesthood and the Loving Wisdom which underlies all Authority. Thee, Thee I invoke! Grant that Thy Divine Light flow through my being to**

manifest unto me the Beneficent Powers of TZEDEK (draws sigil)**, so that in the enhancement of our true spiritual natures, we may continually aspire unto Thy Wisdom and Love.**

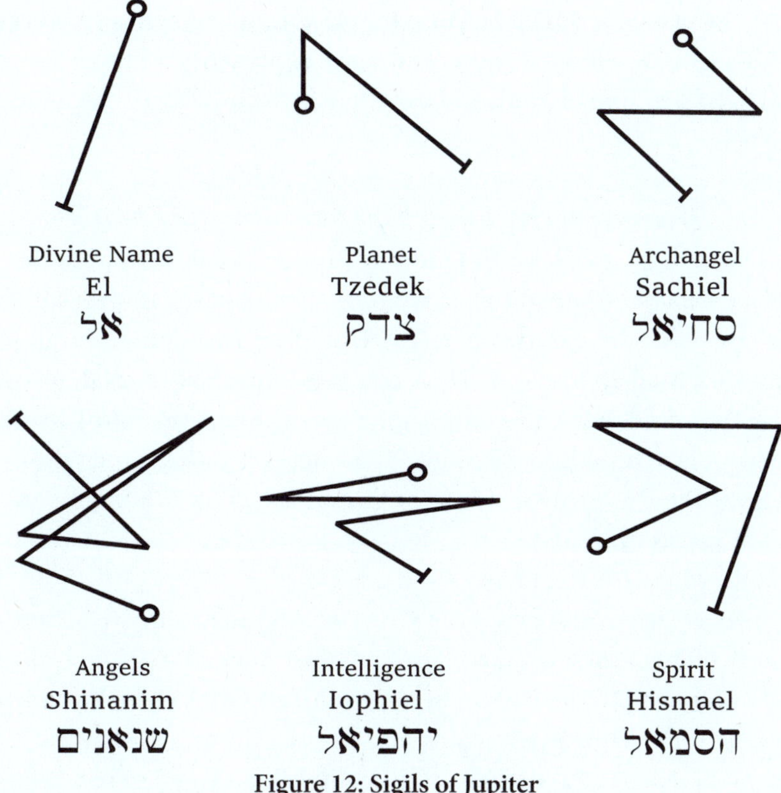

Figure 12: Sigils of Jupiter

Grant unto us the strength and aid of Thy Mighty and Great Archangel SACHIEL (draws sigil)**, who is an Essence of Thy Holy Power.**

SACHIEL, I ask you to command to our assistance your Angelic Host, the SHINANIM (draws sigil)**, that they may impart to us the Expansive, Sagacious, and Uplifting Authority of Jupiter.**

IOPHIEL (draws sigil)**, Great Archangelic Intelligence of the Sphere of Tzedek, ruling therein by the virtue of EL, whose Name you must obey, and in the Name**

of Sachiel, your most potent Archangel, I call you hither that you may concentrate and bring forth the Holy Powers of Tzedek.

IOPHIEL, Thou who art the Messenger of Jupiter-Tzedek. Call forward and command the presence of HISMAEL (draws sigil), **that a true and vibrant link may be formed between the Fratres and Sorores present and those powers of Love and Wisdom, Expansion and Growth, which show forth the majesty of thy Realm.**

Invoking the Four Pillars of the Earth

Hierophant faces west and says: **EL! God of Jupiter-Tzedek! Thou Father of all the Great Gods above, whose name is strength, whose being is love, whose nature is benign, thee do I invoke through Thy Holy Servant Iophiel. Mighty, merciful, magnificent, thee do I invoke. Thou whose Sephirah is Chesed, whose lordship is the realm of whirling fire and raging storm, thee, thee do I invoke. O thou whose head is of amethystine blue, whose heart is pitiful, and whose judgment just, where the Rose Dawn shines out amid the gold. We invoke thee through Thy Holy Servant Iophiel!**

Holy Tzedek! Royal and generous Giver of Abundance from a Cup Unfailing! Shepherd of the Golden Stars! Lord of the Tides of Fortune! Glorious Dispenser of Mercy! Divine Patron of Paternal and Filial Love! Thou whose blessings are without end. Bless peace and amity between all beings. Thou Great Father of Benevolent Rule and of Priesthood, and of Loving Wisdom.[41] **Thy Majesty, Golden, Vast, and Eternal, shineth above the Heaven of Stars. We invoke thee through Thy Holy Intelligence Iophiel!**

All vibrate four times: **IOPHIEL. IOPHIEL. IOPHIEL. IOPHIEL.**

Hierophant faces east, raises arms, and says: **Hail unto Thee, O Living Breath of the Ruach Elohim who breathed upon the Face of the Waters when the Earth was formless and void! Thou art the Spirit of Life whose breath giveth forth and withdraweth the form of all things. Thou before Whom the life of beings is but**

41. Adapted from Denning and Phillips, *Planetary Magic*, 179.

a shadow which changeth, and a vapor which passeth. We invoke thee through Thy Holy Servant—the Angelic Intelligence of Iophiel!

Hierophant: **O Invisible Living One. O Breath of Knowing, I invoke you with the Symbol of Life.**

Figure 13: Hebrew Letter Aleph

Hierophant traces the Hebrew letter Aleph in the air while visualizing it in glowing yellow light.

Hierophant: **IOPHIEL. Breath of the Ruach Elohim! Inspire and protect us by the Holy Power of the Sacred and Living Breath! Live, O Breath of Jupiter-Tzedek, live for us!** (Turns to face west.)

Dadouchos stands, faces south, raises arms, and says: **Hail unto Thee, O Burning Flame, O Flashing Fire. Igniter of the life of all beings. You are the heat of passion and of love. You are the Light that destroys evil. O Fire, O Creator, O Destroyer, O Purifier, O energy of the Will of Jupiter-Tzedek, I invoke you with the Symbol of Life.**

Dadouchos traces the Hebrew letter Aleph in the air while visualizing it in glowing red light.

Dadouchos: **IOPHIEL. Fire of the Holy Mercabah! Empassion and enflame us by the Holy Power of the Sacred Fire! Live, O Will of Jupiter-Tzedek, live for us!** (Turns to face north.)

HIEREUS stands, faces west, raises arms, and says: **Hail unto Thee, O Thou Ocean of Infinite Perfection! King of the Deluge and the Rains of Spring. Thou who openest the sources of the rivers and of the fountains. Speak to us also in the murmur of the limpid Waters, and we shall desire Thy love. O Living Soul, I invoke you with this Symbol of Life!**

HIEREUS traces the Hebrew letter Aleph in the air while visualizing it in glowing blue light.

HIEREUS: **IOPHIEL. Water of Chesed! Deepen and renew us by the Holy Power of the Waters of Creation. Live, O Life-blood of Jupiter-Tzedek, live for us!** (Turns to east.)

STOLISTES stands, faces north, raises arms, and says: **Hail unto Thee, O King of Manifestation! Thou who took the Earth for Foundation, and didst hollow its depths to fill them with Thy Almighty Power. Thou who causest the Seven Metals to flow in the veins of the rocks. By you are all things manifested and sustained. O Earth, O World, O Body of the Universe, I invoke you with this Symbol of Life!**

STOLISTES traces the Hebrew letter Aleph in the air while visualizing it in glowing black light.

STOLISTES: **IOPHIEL! Earth of Creation! Strengthen and uphold us by the Holy Power of the Kingdom. Live, O manifestation of Jupiter-Tzedek, live for us!** (Turns to face south.)

ALL vibrate at least four times: **IOPHIEL. IOPHIEL. IOPHIEL. IOPHIEL.**

ALL keep vibrating this name until HIEROPHANT is ready. HIEREUS, STOLISTES, and DADOUCHOS are seated.

At this point, the HIEROPHANT leaves his throne, lights charcoal in the cauldron, and adds a small bit of incense. The PRAEMONSTRATOR assumes the Hierophant's Throne. The Hierophant draws down the veil. The PRAEMONSTRATOR begins the assumption of the godform of Iophiel. ALL but HIEROPHANT are seated. HIEROPHANT goes to the West of the Altar, facing East. ALL chanting stops for a while.

HIEROPHANT stands with raised arms and says: **EL! God of Jupiter-Tzedek! Thou Father of all the Great Gods above, whose name is strength, whose being is love, whose nature is benign, thee do I invoke through Thy Holy Servant Iophiel. Mighty, merciful, magnificent, thee do I invoke. Thou whose Sephirah is Chesed, whose lordship is the realm of whirling fire and raging storm, thee, thee do I invoke. O thou whose head is of amethystine blue, whose heart is pitiful, and whose judgment just, where the Rose Dawn shines out amid the gold. We invoke thee through Thy Holy Servant Iophiel!**

I invoke the Angelic Intelligence Iophiel, the messenger of Jupiter-Tzedek! O Thou Circle of Stars whereof my Genius is but the younger brother, marvel beyond imagination, soul of Eternity before whom time is ashamed, the Ruach bewildered, and the Neschamah dark! Not unto thy majesty may I attain unless thine image be that of love.

Therefore, by seed and root, and by bud and leaf, and by flower and fruit of my entire being, do I invoke thee, whose name and power is love. O Secret of Secrets that art hidden in the being of all that lives, lord secret and most holy—source of light, source of life, source of love, source of liberty, be thou ever constant and mighty within me that I may forever remain in thine abundant joy.

Sublime and Shadowed One! Awakener of high aspiration and mystical hope! Thou art the Giver of the Silent Will to Endure! Thou art the Spirit's creativity and the Force of preservation and renewal. Open within us the impenetrable gates of Thy Sphere that Thy Power may arise within our Souls. We invoke thee through Thy Holy Servant Iophiel!

May we be blessed with the generous Spirit which both gives and attracts the bounties of all levels of existence! Ours be that Cup Unfailing, overflowing and ever replenished by the Powers of Celestial Abundance! Ours be the far vision which transcends the images and emotions of the moment! Ours be the regardful

Love which seeks the highest good in all and for all. Ours be it to dispose with True Wisdom all matters which fall within our judgment.

May our hearts be filled with Royal Freedom and the Divine Expansion of infinite blue skies; and may that bright amplitude exalt our minds to share in its magnificence, so that our whole being may be imbued, and may give forth again its high peace and noble rhapsody. So mote it be, in the Holy Name of EL through his servant Iophiel.[42]

THE PRAEMONSTRATOR begins to chant **Iophiel** softly.
HIEROPHANT traces an Aleph toward the East and continues:

Let all the Nature of the world entertain the hearing of this Hymn.
Be opened, O Earth, and let all the Treasure of the Rain be opened.
You Trees tremble not, for I will sing, and praise the Lord of the Creation,
and the All, and the One.
Be opened you Heavens, ye Winds stand still,
and let the immortal Circle of God, receive these words.
For I will sing, and praise him that created all things, that fixed the Earth,
and hung up the Heavens, and commanded the sweet Water to come out of the
Ocean, into all the World inhabited, and not inhabited,
to the use, and nourishment of all things, or men.
That commanded the fire to shine for every action, both to Gods, and Men.
Let us altogether give him blessing, which rideth upon the Heavens,
the Creator of all Nature.
This is he, that is the Eye of the Mind, and will accept the praise of my Powers.
O all ye Powers that are in me, praise the One, and the All.
Sing together with my Will, all you Powers that are in me.
O Holy Knowledge, being enlightened by thee, I magnify the intelligible Light,
and rejoice in the Joy of the Mind.
All my Powers sing praise with me, and thou my Continence,
sing praise my Righteousness by me; praise that which is righteous.
O Communion which is in me, praise the All.

42. Adapted from Denning and Phillips, *Planetary Magic*, 180.

By me the Truth sings praise to the Truth, the Good praiseth the Good.
O Life, O Light from us, unto you comes this praise and thanksgiving.
I give thanks unto thee, O Father, the operation or act of my Powers.
I give thanks unto thee, O God, the Power of my operations.
By me thy Word sings praise unto thee,
receive by me this reasonable Sacrifice in words.
The powers that are in me, cry these things, they praise the All,
they fulfill thy Will; thy Will and Counsel is from thee unto thee.
O All, receive a reasonable Sacrifice from all things.
O Life, save all that is in us; O Light enlighten, O God the Spirit;
for the Mind guideth the Word:
O Spirit bearing Workman.
Thou art God, thy servant crieth these things unto thee through,
by the Fire, by the Air, by the Earth, by the Water, by the Spirit, by thy Creatures.
From eternity I have found the means to bless and praise thee,
and I have what I seek; for I rest in thy Will.[43]

(Pause.)

Lord El, god of the High Heavens and the fertile Earth,
and all that dwells therein.
I am one who has come forth from Thee.
Thou art my Mind, my Wealth, My Completion, and my Rest.
I invoke Thee, the Divine One Who Was, Is, and Is to Be,
Who existed previously in the Sacred Name,
Which is extolled above every other.
Grant me authority through Thy Holy Spirit.
Bestow healing for my body and mind.
And restore my Eternal Soul,
formed after the image of the Elohim
When it was created before Time existed.
I have trust and I have hope.
Place upon me Thy blessed Mercy.

43. Adapted from "The Secret Song, The Holy Speech," in Everard, *The Divine Pymander*, 63–66.

That the Love and Illumination of the Divine Ones
May descend into my Heart
And I will dwell in the Light of the Spirit forever.

ALL except HIEROPHANT begin to chant **IOPHIEL** softly and continuously. HIEROPHANT again traces the letter Aleph toward the East. After a pause, the HIEROPHANT continues:

Father of my Soul, before thee have I covered my face.
Arise, great King, arise and shine in me, for I have hidden myself
and stand humbly before the glory of thy face.
In the chariot of life eternal is thy seat,
and thy steeds course the firmament of Nu. Behold!
Thou didst lift up thy voice, and the hills were shaken!
Thou didst cry aloud, and the everlasting hills did bow.
O my Father, my Father; the chariots of Israel and the horsemen thereof.
The sound of thy voice was freedom.
Thy lightnings were kindled and lighted.
Thy thunder was heard on the deep.
The stars with thy fear shook and whitened, while the voice of the Lord was
uplifted. The wilderness also obeys. For the flames of thy fire are rifted,
and the waves of the Sea know thy ways.
They did hear thee, the cedars of Lebanon;
and the desert of Kadesh hath known. O Holy Tzedek.
Thou Spirit of Limitless Light and Life and Love.
Thou with the plume and the Wand, is thy path in the Waters?
The marvelous deeps of the Sea?
To that abyss of waters do I raise my soul to receive thy truth.
God EL of the Waters! I invoke thee; exalt my soul to the feet of thy glory.
Hear me and manifest in splendor to the one who worships at thy throne.

(Pause.)

I have passed through the Gates of Wisdom and come unto the palace of Peace. Give me your hands, O ye Lords of Truth, for I am made as ye. Ye are the teachers of the soul.

ALL continue to softly chant **IOPHIEL** as HIEROPHANT advances to the east before the PRAEMONSTRATOR. The HIEROPHANT (kneeling or standing) gives a personalized invocation to Iophiel. PRAEMONSTRATOR in godform may communicate to Hierophant at this time. When finished, HIEROPHANT goes to the Iophiel Altar and offers a gift, placing it on the Altar. (If HIEROPHANT has no gift, he may offer a small bit of incense to the cauldron.) When finished, HIEROPHANT returns to stand west of the cubical altar and chants **IOPHIEL** with the other members.

The rest of the members each take their turn in the usual order: HIEREUS, HEGEMON, STOLISTES, DADOUCHOS, PHYLAX, and sideliners, ending with KERYX. Each member stands or kneels before the Praemonstrator and delivers their Iophiel invocation, possibly receives communication, then goes to the Iophiel Altar to offer their gifts, or a small bit of incense to the cauldron.

When the KERYX is finished, the Iophiel chant stops. (Let PRAEMONSTRATOR in godform speak to the group if desired.) The HIEROPHANT, west of the Cubical Altar, gives thanks to Iophiel:

HIEROPHANT: **Holy servant of Jupiter-Tzedek! Divine Lord of Heaven! Compassionate Father of Earthly Life! Thou Who art ever with us to sustain us in being, be with us now in the working of this Rite! And in the partaking of this Mystery, may we be blessed with a generous Spirit, which both gives and attracts bounties on all levels of existence.**

May ours be that Cup unfailing, overflowing, and ever replenished by the Powers of Celestial Abundance. May ours be that far vision which transcends the images and emotions of the moment. May ours be that regardful Love which seeks the highest good in all, for all; and may ours be it to dispose with True Wisdom all matters which fall within our judgment. May we attain a greater

Enlightenment and Love, whereby we may be better enable to assist those to whom we are called. This we ask in the Divine Name EL. (Traces the Aleph.)

The Grace of Gedulah courses through us like the rivers of Eden. We awake as from a dream. Our hearts open, filled with Light. We give thanks to Iophiel, the Holy Servant of Jupiter-Tzedek.[44]

Messenger of EL, we give Thee thanks. For your blessings, Mighty Angel of Abundance, we thank thee. Our hearts open, the door, the way. Our senses are radiant. The Pure Love of the Divine flows over us. We know the golden song of day. We hear the name of Light. We shine as the points of stars in the ubiquitous heart of God.[45]

THE PRAEMONSTRATOR releases the godform of Iophiel. She traces the Qabalistic Cross in silence and returns to her seat. The HIEROPHANT returns to station.

At this point, any comments, announcements, or temple business may be discussed. (After the closing, be sure that the gifts to Iophiel are dispersed according to their nature. Seeds, fruit, and other natural items or perishables can be placed in the garden. Incense may be burned.)

Proceed to the Closing of the Neophyte Hall.

✠ ✠ ✠

INVOCATION OF THE MAZZOLOTH

The word Mazzoloth (מזלות) is a Hebrew term for the Zodiac, or the Zodiacal constellations as a group. The Golden Dawn assigns the realm of the Zodiac and all its associated astrological signs to the Second Sephirah of Chokmah, "wisdom."

Astrology is the study of the stars and one of the oldest known sciences. It is a subjective and intuitive science that not only deals with the astronomical delineation of horoscopes but also embraces philosophical ideas that help to explain the spiritual

44. Adapted from Ellis, *Awakening Osiris*, 140, 164–65.

45. Adapted from Ellis, *Awakening Osiris*, 140, 164–65.

essence of life. As an esoteric science, astrology reveals the universal pattern of living and the means by which human beings can align themselves with the divine matrix of the universe. It is a system for understanding celestial energies and a method for viewing the universe as a symmetrical whole.

In the Outer Order of the Golden Dawn the student learns basic astrological information concerning the Zodiacal wheel, the twelve Signs, the twelve Houses, the thirty-six Decanates, the four Triplicities, the three Quadruplicities, and the various aspects. All this knowledge is later used for elemental, planetary, and Zodiacal magic in the higher grades of the Inner Order. Next to the teachings of the Qabalah, astrological correspondences are the most prevalent form of esoteric knowledge used in both the Outer and Inner Orders.

The twelve Signs of the Zodiac are distributed among the four Triplicities, or sets of three Signs. Each of these Triplicities is attributed to one of the Four Elements, and they represent the operation of the Elements in the Zodiac. The Triplicities emphasize the various attributes of the Elements: The Fire Signs (Aries, Leo, and Sagittarius) are impassioned, spontaneous, independent, and enthusiastic. Water Signs (Cancer, Scorpio, and Pisces) are intuitive, receptive, emotional, sensitive, compassionate, and complex. Air Signs (Libra, Aquarius, and Gemini) are expressive, communicative, intellectual, logical, open-minded, idealistic, and objective. Earth Signs (Capricorn, Taurus, and Virgo) are stable, practical, dependable, conservative, and sensual.

The Outer Order Invocation of the Mazzoloth is designed to invoke the positive energies of the twelve Zodiacal Signs. It is also constructed to be performed in a typical Neophyte Hall of the Golden Dawn, wherein the rank of participants may vary from Neophyte through the Adept levels. Only one skilled Adept, holding the office of Hierophant, is actually needed for the performance of a few Second Order techniques of invocation. Everyone else will be invoking at a level that is appropriate for Outer Order members. And because the ceremony is intended to accommodate a large number of people, its structure is simple—there are few complicated movements.

Synopsis: After the Hierophant announces the ritual's objective, he leads everyone in the Qabalistic Cross. All are seated and the Hierophant begins a back-and-forth discussion about the attributes of the Mazzoloth. Following this, the Hierophant traces the Greater Invoking Hexagram of Chokmah toward the East and gives a powerful invocation of the Mazzoloth through the Second Sephirah.

The Hierophant goes to the central Altar, traces the figure of Lesser Invoking Pentagram, lights the central white candle, and gives a short invocation.

Next, the invocation of the individual Zodiacal Signs begins. In turn, each of the twelve Zodiacal officers who serve as the Priests and Priestesses of the various Signs goes to the central altar, traces their Zodiacal symbols, and invokes the positive energies of their Sign. Then they light the candle attributed to their Sign. All vibrate the Divine Hebrew name attributed to the Sign's triplicity. The Psaltis rings a bell to mark each sign's invocation and the invoking officer takes their seat. (This process continues until all twelve signs have been invoked.)

The Hierophant gives thanks to all the powers invoked. When the Work is concluded, all the Zodiacal symbolism is removed from the central Altar, to setup for the Closing of the Neophyte Hall.

Preparation: An additional officer will be needed—the *Psaltis*. The rite also requires twelve members previously chosen to be the Priests and Priestesses of the Zodiacal Signs. If there are not enough sideliners to fill these roles, they may be filled by any regular Officer.

Additional Items needed:

- Protective Altar cloth[46]
- In the center of the Altar, the diagram of the Table of Shewbread, or a simplified form of the diagram that shows only a pentagram within a dodecahedron (See figures 14 and 15.)
- Around the diagram should be four three-branched candelabras painted in the elemental colors of red, blue, yellow, and black. The four elemental triplicity candelabras are to be placed around the diagram in accordance with the directions of the cardinal signs (Fire–Aries–East, Water–Cancer–North, Air–Libra–West, Earth–Capricorn–South). (See figure 16). The branches of the four candelabras are attributed to the signs as follows:
    - » *Red Fire candelabra*: Aries, Leo, Sagittarius
    - » *Blue Water candelabra:* Cancer, Scorpio, Pisces
    - » *Yellow Air candelabra:* Libra, Aquarius, Gemini
    - » *Black Earth candelabra:* Capricorn, Taurus, Virgo

46. To protect both the Altar and the Altar cloth, have a piece of clear plexiglass cut to the dimensions of the Altar top. You can cover the Altar with the Altar cloth and lay the plexiglass on top.

- Twelve Zodiacal-colored candles[47] for the candelabras
- White pillar candle or votive candle in the center of the diagram
- Barbecue lighter or simple lighter (This should be removed once the central candle is lit.)
- A separate white taper candle for lighting the main candles (placed on an incense stick holder to protect the altar top)
- A bell, chimes, or gong for Psaltis Officer
- Twelve Zodiacal Lamens for the Priests and Priestesses

Figure 14: Altar Setup of the Elemental Candelabras with Table of Shewbread

47. The twelve colors of the Zodiac are found in Table 5: Correspondences of the Lotus Wand on page 250.

Figure 15: The Table of Shewbread

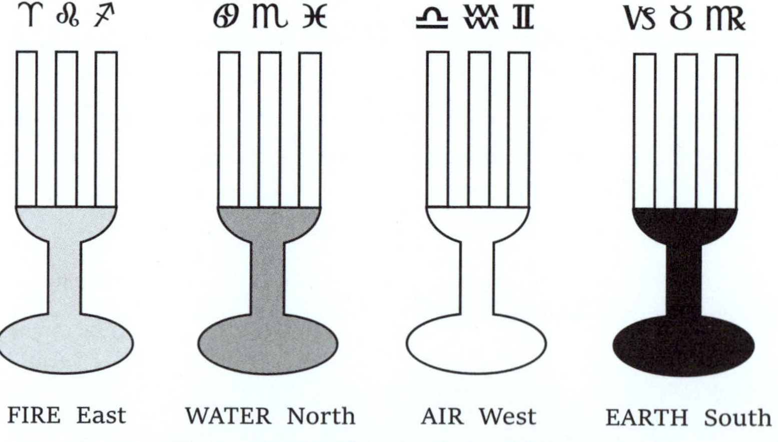

Figure 16: The Elemental Candelabras

Perform the Opening of the Hall of the Neophytes, then continue with the Work.

After the Hall is opened, the usual implements on the Altar are temporally removed. The Altar is set up for the work at hand.

HIEROPHANT: (Knock ן) **Fratres and Sorores of the (______) Temple of the (________) Order of the Golden Dawn in the Outer, we are here assembled in our commitment to the work of the divine theurgy, that we may rebuild the Temple of Solomon within our souls. To this end we shall light and awaken the twelve-fold archetypal Luminaries of the Zodiac, the Mazzoloth within. The Temple of Solomon the Wise was built upon a sturdy Stone, made without hands. As a house built upon the Sand cannot endure, so without the cornerstone of the Lapis Philosophorum the heights of the Heavens cannot be scaled. Except Adonai build the house, their labor is but lost that build it. Except Adonai keep the City, the Watchman waketh in vain.**

Through this ceremony, may we be enabled to understand the true nature of the magical art and be better equipped to carry out the Great Work. Within the Souls of all here present, may the Temple of Solomon be rebuilt, may the Gates of Understanding be opened, may the Tree of Life be restored, and may the Gates of the Garden of Eden be unbarred. YHVH. To the glory of the Ineffable name, Amen.

Let us first establish a link with the Higher and Divine Self—that inexhaustible Treasure of Light, to which we aspire unceasingly—that the Powers of the Divine may be reawakened in the spheres of those present and in the Sphere of this Order. For by names and Images are all Powers Awakened and Reawakened.

ALL stand.

HIEROPHANT leads ALL in performance of the Qabalistic Cross:

ATAH, MALKUTH, VE-GEBURAH, VE GEDULAH, LE-OLAHM, AMEN.

ALL remain standing.

HIEROPHANT: **The Heavens are above, and the Earth is beneath, and between the Light and the Darkness the starry animals of the Rota Zodiacus vibrate. We supplicate the Powers and Forces governing the realm and place and authority of the Twelve Signs, through the power of the Angel Raziel, by the Twelve Simple Letters of the Hebrew Aleph-Bet, to bestow this present day and hour and confirm their mystic and potent influence upon this rite, which we dedicate to the occult work of the Mazzoloth, the circle of the Zodiac!**

Hierophant: (Knocks ꞁ) All are seated.

HIEROPHANT: **(Frater/Soror) Dadouchos, what know you of the Mazzoloth?**

DADOUCHOS: **It is an ancient Hebrew word for the constellations of the Zodiac, taken as a whole. In later times it came to be used as a term for astrology in general, and it is the origin of the expression *mazel tov*, meaning "good luck."**

HIEROPHANT: **(Frater/Soror) Stolistes, what know you of the Mazzoloth?**

STOLISTES: **It is attributed to twelve Hebrew letters. The twenty-two sounds and letters of the Hebrew alphabet are the foundation of all things. Three Mothers, Seven Doubles, and Twelve Simples. The Twelve Simple letters are allotted to the 12 directions in space, and those diverge to Infinity, and are in the arms of the Eternal.**

HIEROPHANT: **(Frater/Soror) Keryx, what know you of the Mazzoloth?**

KERYX: **It is attributed to the Table of Shewbread in the northern side of the Holy Place in the Temple of Solomon. On it twelve loaves were laid as emblems of the Bread of Life. It is an image of the Mystery of the Rose of Creation. The 12 circles are the 12 Signs of the Zodiac, while the Lamp in the Center is symbolic of the Sun, which is the source of heat and life.**

HIEROPHANT: **(Frater/Soror) Hegemon, what know you of the Mazzoloth?**

HEGEMON: **The 12 Signs of the Zodiac are divided into four triplicities, or sets of three signs that correspond to Fire, Earth, Air, and Water. Every sign contains 3 decanates or phases of ten degrees of each sign. And each is referred to a specific permutation of the Divine Name, Yod Heh Vav Heh, as well as one of the names of the 12 tribes of Israel which is also attributed to it.**

HIEROPHANT: **Honored Hiereus, what know you of the Mazzoloth?**

HIEREUS: **The Lord of the Universe crafted all of Creation out of twelve. These Twelve letters he designed and combined, and formed with them the Twelve Celestial Constellations of the Zodiac. They are over the Universe as a King traversing his dominions, and they are in the heart of man as a King in warfare.**

HIEROPHANT: **The Twelve candles upon our Sacred Altar are the Outer Petals of the Rose; while the candelabras that hold them are the Four Archangels ruling over the Four Quarters, and the Kerubic emblems of the Lion, Man, Bull, and Eagle.**

HEGEMON: **Around the great central lamp, which is an image of the Sun, is the Great Mother of Heaven, symbolized by the letter Heh, the first of the Simple Letters, and by its number 5, the Pentagram, Malkah the Bride, ruling in her kingdom Malkuth, crowned with a crown of Twelve stars.**

HIEREUS: **The twelve candles further represent the 12 Foundations of the Holy City of the Apocalypse, while in Christian Symbolism the Sun and the twelve signs are referred to Christ and his Twelve Apostles.**

HIEROPHANT: **The Sun in the center of the universe is the mediator of all powers, earthly and celestial, and in the Sun of the mortal body are the divine and the human united in one soul. The force of the Sun is outpouring, but its essence draws us inward, for the Sun draws all bodies to itself, causing them to seek the center. In this seeking, the person must sacrifice the base and imbalanced parts**

of the self, stripping away the outworn and the useless, revealing within themselves the Divine Light, ever shining—a body of pure Quintessence surrounded by Starlight.

To this end we invoke the powers of the Twelve to bestow their potent influence and benefits upon this temple and its members.

All: **So mote it be!**

Hierophant (knocks ו): **Let us invoke the forces of the Mazzoloth through the sphere of Chokmah!**

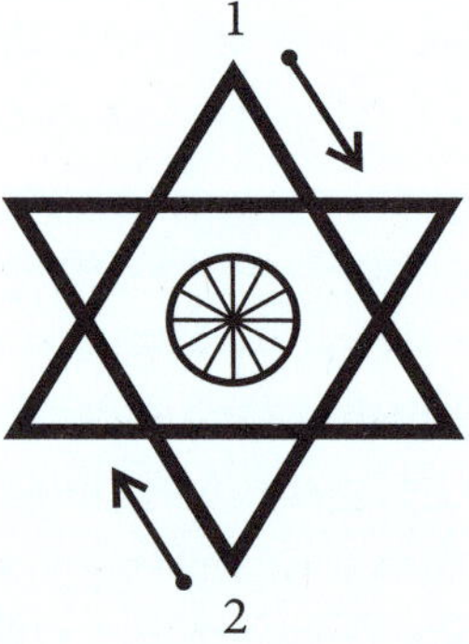

Figure 17: Greater Invoking Hexagram of Mazzoloth

Hierophant faces east and traces the Greater Invoking Hexagram of Mazzoloth, vibrating **ARARITA, YAH,** and **ALEPH.**

Psaltis rings the bell twice וו.

Hierophant (still facing east): **O Thou Celestial One, Ring of the Ecliptic! O Thou circle of stars whereof my Genius is but the younger (brother/sister)! Marvel beyond imagination! Soul of Eternity before whom time is ashamed, the Ruach bewildered, and the Neshamah dark. Not unto thy majesty may we attain unless thine image be that of Wisdom.**

Therefore, by atom and molecule, by muscle and bone, by body and spirit of our entire being do we invoke thee, whose name and power is Wisdom. O secret of secrets that art hidden in the blueprint of all that has come into manifestation!

Secret and most holy! Source of Light, Source of Life, Source of Liberty, be thou ever constant within us, that we may forever remain in thy abundant Wisdom.

Thou Father of all the Great Gods above, whose name is Movement, whose being is Wisdom, and whose nature is benevolent. We invoke Thee. Thou who manifests through the Wisdom of the god Thoth and the starry heavens of the goddess Nuet, we invoke Thee. Thou whose Sephirah is Chokmah and whose lordship is the realm of the highest Heavens, Thee do we invoke.

O thou whose head is of pure star ruby, whose heart is paternal, and whose judgment is just, where the Rose Dawn shines out amid the gold, thee do I invoke. Arise, great King! Arise and shine within us who have humbled ourselves before the glory of thy face. Thy seat is in the chariot of Life Eternal, and thy steeds traverse the firmament of Nu. We invoke thee! Exalt our souls to the feet of Thy glory. Hear us and manifest in splendor to those who worship at Thy Throne.

Hierophant turns to face west and descends from the Dais to move west of the Altar, facing east.

Hierophant: **Through the forces of the Mazzoloth, we invoke the elemental triplicities of the Zodiac, by the power of the fourfold name, the Tetragrammaton crowned by the guidance and majesty of the fifth element of Spirit.**

Hierophant traces the *Lesser Invoking Pentagram* over the Altar.

Figure 18: Lesser Invoking Pentagram

As Hierophant traces the figure, Psaltis rings the bell five times ווווו.

Hierophant lights the central white candle on the Altar.

Hierophant raises wand and says: **Spirit of Life, Spirit of Wisdom! Cause of all Creation! Origin and everlasting fount of every living soul! From Deity we are born, through the Light of Mediation we die, and through the Divine Presence we live in the embrace of Eternity. Thou art the Supreme Source of Wisdom and Truth. Permit us to rise, rank upon rank, from the feet of Malkuth even unto the throne of Aima Elohim.**[48] **Guide us over the deserts and seas, and lift us out of the pits and chasms. Become for us the catalyst of change and the root of liberation. May a ray of Thine infinite Glory illuminate the path before us, and allow us to ascend to the Heavens as if upon a ship of Starlight. May we come to know the celestial realms and the limitless grace of the Divine. So mote it be.**

All (speaking, not vibrating): **Amen. Selah. Amen.**

Hierophant returns to the Dais.

48. Adapted from Regardie, *The Golden Dawn,* 521.

The Invocation of the Zodiacal Signs

ARIES

Priest (or Priestess) of Aries rises and gives the Projection Sign to the Banner of the East, walks to the west of the Altar facing east, and then traces the symbol of Aries ♈ over the Altar and vibrates: **ELOHIM.**

To the forces of Aries that we now invoke, we have awakened the powers of cardinal Fire. Come forth under the aegis of Mars who is your Lord. Come forth and be present in this sacred rite. You who are the power of fiery impulse and the spark necessary for a new life, we call you forth. New beginnings, the direct release of energy, and enthusiasm shall reign in this temple. Open your realm to us, that we may know you and awaken your powers within our souls.

In the Tarot card of the Emperor, you are the Warrior King who laid down his sword and took up the scepter. You are power, authority, and symbol of experience. Be present in the working of this rite, and bestow upon us your gifts of courage and the ability to embrace our true purpose in Life. In the Divine Name YHVH (Yod Heh Vav Heh) and in the name of the great archangel Malkhidael, we invoke the powers of Aries. In the letter Heh and in the Sign of the Ram, we invoke thee! Come thou forth.

Priest (or Priestess) of Aries lights the Red Candle on the Red Fire Candelabra on the East side of the Altar. (NOTE: Take the flame from the central candle and transfer it with the taper candle.)

All vibrate: **ELOHIM.**

Psaltis rings the bell once ٦.

Priest (or Priestess) of Aries then returns to place, gives the Sign of Silence, and is seated.

TAURUS

Priest (or Priestess) of Taurus rises and gives the Projection Sign to the Banner of the East, walks to the west of the Altar facing east, and then traces the symbol of Taurus ♉ over the Altar and vibrates: **ADONAI.**

> **To the forces of Taurus that we now invoke, we have awakened the powers of Kerubic Earth. Come forth under the aegis of Venus who is your Ruler. Come forth and be present in this sacred rite. You who are the power of diligence and focus, I call you forth. Productiveness, material pleasure, and heightened perception shall reign in this temple. Open your realm to us, that we may know you and awaken your powers within our souls.**
>
> **In the Tarot card of the Hierophant, you are the Magus of the Eternal Gods, Expounder of the Mysteries. You are the ruler over the Earthly realm and the teacher in the quest for wisdom. Be present in the working of this rite, and bestow upon us your gifts of beauty, fulfillment, and comfort. In the Divine Name YHHV (Yod Heh Heh Vav) and in the name of the great archangel Asmodel, we invoke the powers of Taurus. In the letter Vav and in the Sign of the Bull, we invoke thee! Come thou forth.**

Priest (or Priestess) of Taurus lights the Red-orange Candle on the Black Earth Candelabra on the South side of the Altar. (NOTE: Take the flame from the central candle and transfer it with the taper candle.)

All vibrate: **ADONAI.**

Psaltis rings the bell twice ꜙ.

Priest (or Priestess) of Taurus then returns to place, gives the Sign of Silence, and is seated.

GEMINI

Priest (or Priestess) of Gemini rises and gives the Projection Sign to the Banner of the East, walks to the west of the Altar facing east, and then traces the symbol of Gemini ♊ over the Altar and vibrates: **YHVH.**

> **To the forces of Gemini that we now invoke, we have awakened the powers of mutable Air. Come forth under the aegis of Mercury who is your Lord. Come forth and be present in this sacred rite. You who are the power of communication and expressive speech, I call you forth. Adaptability and inspiration shall reign in this temple. Open your realm to us, that we may know you and awaken your powers within our souls.**
>
> **In the Tarot card of the Lovers, you are the Children of the Voice Divine, the Oracle of the Mighty Gods. You are the synergy, the spiritual and the physical, the container and the contained, the one and the many, the observer and the observed, the human and the Divine. Be present in the working of this rite, and bestow upon us your gifts of knowledge in the magical arts, and a true understanding of the signs, symbols, and words of Power. In the Divine Name YVHH (Yod Vav Heh Heh) and in the name of the great archangel Ambriel, we invoke the powers of Gemini. In the letter Zayin and in the Sign of the Twins, we invoke thee! Come thou forth.**

Priest (or Priestess) of Gemini lights the Orange Candle on the Yellow Air Candelabra on the West side of the Altar. (NOTE: Take the flame from the central candle and transfer it with the taper candle.)

All vibrate: **YHVH.**

Psaltis rings the bell three times ꟾꟾꟾ.

Priest (or Priestess) of Gemini then returns to place, gives the Sign of Silence, and is seated.

CANCER

Priest (or Priestess) of Cancer rises and gives the Projection Sign to the Banner of the East, walks to the west of the Altar facing east, and then traces the symbol of Cancer ♋ over the Altar and vibrates: **EL.**

> **To the forces of Cancer that we now invoke, we have awakened the powers of cardinal Water. Come forth under the aegis of Luna who is your Ruler. Come forth and be present in this sacred rite. You who are the power of growth and security, we call you forth. Emotional support, sensitivity, fellowship, and a sense of belonging shall reign in this temple. Open your realm to us, that we may know you and awaken your powers within our souls.**
>
> **In the Tarot card of the Chariot, you are the Lord of the Triumph of Light. You are loyalty, faith, and Victory. Be present in the working of this rite, and bestow upon us your gifts of nurturing and empathy, and the ability to value ourselves and others. In the Divine Name HVHY (Heh Vav Heh Yod) and in the name of the great archangel Muriel, we invoke the powers of Cancer. In the letter Cheth and in the Sign of the Crab, we invoke thee! Come thou forth.**

Priest (or Priestess) of Cancer lights the Yellow-orange Candle on the Blue Water Candelabra on the North side of the Altar. (NOTE: Take the flame from the central candle and transfer it with the taper candle.)

All vibrate: **EL.**

Psaltis rings the bell four times ווו - ו.

Priest (or Priestess) of Cancer then returns to place, gives the Sign of Silence, and is seated.

LEO

Priest (or Priestess) of Leo rises and gives the Projection Sign to the Banner of the East, walks to the west of the Altar facing east, and then traces the symbol of Leo ♌ over the Altar and vibrates: **ELOHIM.**

> **To the forces of Leo that we now invoke, we have awakened the powers of Kerubic Fire. Come forth under the aegis of Sol who is your Lord. Come forth and be present in this sacred rite. You who are the power of self-awareness and self-confidence, we call you forth. Generosity, creativity, and radiance shall reign in this temple. Open your realm to us, that we may know you and awaken your powers within our souls.**
>
> **In the Tarot card of Strength, you are the Daughter of the Flaming Sword, Leader of the Lion. You are discipline and compassion. Be present in the working of this rite, and bestow upon us your gifts of honest pride for our accomplishments and the proper recognition for those accomplishments. In the Divine Name HVYH (Heh Vav Yod Heh) and in the name of the great archangel Verkhiel, we invoke the powers of Leo. In the letter Teth and in the Sign of the Lion, we invoke thee! Come thou forth.**

Priest (or Priestess) of Leo lights the Yellow Candle on the Red Fire Candelabra on the East side of the Altar. (NOTE: Take the flame from the central candle and transfer it with the taper candle.)

All vibrate: **ELOHIM.**

Psaltis rings the bell five times ווו - וו.

Priest (or Priestess) of Leo then returns to place, gives the Sign of Silence, and is seated.

VIRGO

Priest (or Priestess) of Virgo rises and gives the Projection Sign to the Banner of the East, walks to the west of the Altar facing east, and then traces the symbol of Virgo ♍ over the Altar and vibrates: **ADONAI.**

> **To the forces of Virgo that we now invoke, we have awakened the powers of mutable Earth. Come forth under the aegis of Mercury who is your Lord. Come forth and be present in this sacred rite. You who are the power of analysis and practical skills, we call you forth. Precision and adaptation shall reign in this temple. Open your realm to us, that we may know you and awaken your powers within our souls.**
>
> **In the Tarot card of the Hermit, you are the Magus of the Voice of Light and the Prophet of the Gods. You are the Light-bearer who shows the way to Hidden Knowledge. Be present in the working of this rite, and bestow upon us your gifts of clarity of mind, and the development of our true talents. In the Divine Name HHYV (Heh Heh Yod Vav) and in the name of the great archangel Hamaliel, we invoke the powers of Virgo. In the letter Yod and in the Sign of the Virgin, we invoke thee! Come thou forth.**

Priest (or Priestess) of Virgo lights the Yellow-green Candle on the Black Earth Candelabra on the South side of the Altar. (NOTE: Take the flame from the central candle and transfer it with the taper candle.)

All vibrate: **ADONAI.**

Psaltis rings the bell six times 111 - 111.

Priest (or Priestess) of Virgo then returns to place, gives the Sign of Silence, and is seated.

LIBRA

Priest (or Priestess) of Libra rises and gives the Projection Sign to the Banner of the East, walks to the west of the Altar facing east, and then traces the symbol of Libra ♎ over the Altar and vibrates: **YHVH.**

> **To the forces of Libra that we now invoke, we have awakened the powers of cardinal Air. Come forth under the aegis of Venus who is your Ruler. Come forth and be present in this sacred rite. You who are the power of harmony and equilibrium, we call you forth. Balance and symmetry shall reign in this temple. Open your realm to us, that we may know you and awaken your powers within our souls.**
>
> **In the Tarot card of Justice, you are the Daughter of the Lord of Truth and the Holder of the Balances. You are Truth in Action and the arbiter of equality. Be present in the working of this rite, and bestow upon us your gifts of tranquility, fairness, and friendship. In the Divine Name VHYH (Vav Heh Yod Heh) and in the name of the great archangel Zuriel, we invoke the powers of Libra. In the letter Lamed and in the Sign of the Scales, we invoke thee! Come thou forth.**

Priest (or Priestess) of Libra lights the Green Candle on the Yellow Air Candelabra on the West side of the Altar. (NOTE: Take the flame from the central candle and transfer it with the taper candle.)

All vibrate: **YHVH.**

Psaltis rings the bell seven times ווו – ווו - ו.

Priest (or Priestess) of Libra then returns to place, gives the Sign of Silence, and is seated.

SCORPIO

Priest (or Priestess) of Scorpio rises and gives the Projection Sign to the Banner of the East, walks to the west of the Altar facing east, and then traces the symbol of Scorpio ♏ over the Altar and vibrates: **EL.**

> **To the forces of Scorpio that we now invoke, we have awakened the powers of Kerubic Water. Come forth under the aegis of Mars who is your Lord. Come forth and be present in this sacred rite. You who are the power of change and transformation, we call you forth. Determination, power, and depth of passion shall reign in this temple. Open your realm to us, that we may know you and awaken your powers within our souls.**
>
> **In the Tarot card of Death, you are the Child of the Great Transformers, Lord of the Gates of Death. You are renewal and rebirth. Be present in the working of this rite, and bestow upon us your gift of understanding the importance of silence and secrecy, and an appreciation of change and release. In the Divine Name VHHY (Vav Heh Heh Yod) and in the name of the great archangel Barkhiel, we invoke the powers of Scorpio. In the letter Nun and in the Sign of the Scarabeus, we invoke thee! Come thou forth.**

Priest (or Priestess) of Scorpio lights the Blue-green Candle on the Blue Water Candelabra on the North side of the Altar. (NOTE: Take the flame from the central candle and transfer it with the taper candle.)

All vibrate: **EL.**

Psaltis rings the bell eight times 111 – 111 - 11.

Priest (or Priestess) of Scorpio then returns to place, gives the Sign of Silence, and is seated.

SAGITTARIUS

Priest (or Priestess) of Sagittarius rises and gives the Projection Sign to the Banner of the East, walks to the west of the Altar facing east, and then traces the symbol of Sagittarius ♐ over the Altar and vibrates: **ELOHIM.**

> **To the forces of Sagittarius that we now invoke, we have awakened the powers of mutable Fire. Come forth under the aegis of Jupiter who is your Ruler. Come forth and be present in this sacred rite. You who are the power of persistence and aspiration, I call you forth. Idealism, steadfastness, and the pursuit of wisdom shall reign in this temple. Open your realm to us, that we may know you and awaken your powers within our souls.**
>
> **In the Tarot card of Temperance, you are the Daughter of the Reconcilers, the Bringer Forth of Life. Be present in the working of this rite, and bestow upon us your gifts of the desire and ability to seek what lies beyond the horizon, and to discover the possibilities which answer our greatest questions. In the Divine Name VYHH (Vav Yod Heh Heh) and in the name of the great archangel Adnakhiel, we invoke the powers of Sagittarius. In the letter Samekh and in the Sign of the Archer, we invoke thee! Come thou forth.**

Priest (or Priestess) of Sagittarius lights the Blue Candle on the Red Fire Candelabra on the East side of the Altar. (NOTE: Take the flame from the central candle and transfer it with the taper candle.)

All vibrate: **ELOHIM.**

Psaltis rings the bell nine times ווו – ווו - ווו.

Priest (or Priestess) of Sagittarius then returns to place, gives the Sign of Silence, and is seated.

CAPRICORN

Priest (or Priestess) of Capricorn rises and gives the Projection Sign to the Banner of the East, walks to the west of the Altar facing east, and then traces the symbol of Capricorn ♑ over the Altar and vibrates: **ADONAI.**

> **To the forces of Capricorn that we now invoke, we have awakened the powers of cardinal Earth. Come forth under the aegis of Saturn who is your Lord. Come forth and be present in this sacred rite. You who are the power of responsibility and practicality, we call you forth. Fortitude, organization, and accomplishment shall reign in this temple. Open your realm to us, that we may know you and awaken your powers within our souls.**
>
> **In the Tarot card of the Devil, you are Lord of the Gates of Matter and the Child of the Forces of Time. You are materialization and physicality. Be present in the working of this rite, and bestow upon us your gifts of steadfast determination and resolve, and an ability to establish pragmatic leadership. In the Divine Name HYHV (Heh Yod Heh Vav) and in the name of the great archangel Hanael, we invoke the powers of Capricorn. In the letter Ayin and in the Sign of the Sea-Goat, we invoke thee! Come thou forth.**

Priest (or Priestess) of Capricorn lights the Blue-violet Candle on the Black Earth Candelabra on the South side of the Altar. (NOTE: Take the flame from the central candle and transfer it with the taper candle.)

All vibrate: **ADONAI.**

Psaltis rings the bell ten times ווו – ווו – ווו - ו.

Priest (or Priestess) of Capricorn then returns to place, gives the Sign of Silence, and is seated.

AQUARIUS

Priest (or Priestess) of Aquarius rises and gives the Projection Sign to the Banner of the East, walks to the west of the Altar facing east, and then traces the symbol of Aquarius ♒ over the Altar and vibrates: **YHVH.**

> **To the forces of Aquarius that we now invoke, we have awakened the powers of Kerubic Air. Come forth under the aegis of Saturn who is your Lord. Come forth and be present in this sacred rite. You who are the power of reason, complex thought, and meditation, we call you forth. Philosophy, intuition, and education shall reign in this temple. Open your realm to us, that we may know you and awaken your powers within our souls.**
>
> **In the Tarot card of the Star, you are the Daughter of the Firmament, Dweller between the Waters. You are spiritual insight and clarity of vision. Be present in the working of this rite, and bestow upon us your gifts of philosophical wisdom, simplicity, and a detachment from material desire. In the Divine Name HYVH (Heh Yod Vav Heh) and in the name of the great archangel Kambriel, we invoke the powers of Aquarius. In the letter Tzaddi and in the Sign of the Water-bearer, we invoke thee! Come thou forth.**

Priest (or Priestess) of Aquarius lights the Violet Candle on the Yellow Air Candelabra on the West side of the Altar. (NOTE: Take the flame from the central candle and transfer it with the taper candle.)

All vibrate: **YHVH.**

Psaltis rings the bell eleven times ווו – ווו – ווו - וו.

Priest (or Priestess) of Aquarius then returns to place, gives the Sign of Silence, and is seated.

PISCES

Priest (or Priestess) of Pisces rises and gives the Projection Sign to the Banner of the East, walks to the west of the Altar facing east, and then traces the symbol of Pisces ♓ over the Altar and vibrates: **EL.**

> **To the forces of Pisces that we now invoke, we have awakened the powers of mutable Water. Come forth under the aegis of Jupiter who is your Lord. Come forth and be present in this sacred rite. You who are the power of the visionary and the mystic, we call you forth. Creativity, imagination, and unity shall reign in this temple. Open your realm to us, that we may know you and awaken your powers within our souls.**
>
> **In the Tarot card of the Moon, you are the Ruler of Flux and Reflux, Child of the Sons of the Mighty. You are dreams and the power of the subconscious mind. Be present in the working of this rite, and bestow upon us your gifts of religious and mystical experience, and the ability to see and experience realms beyond the physical. In the Divine Name HHVY (Heh Heh Vav Yod) and in the name of the great archangel Amnitziel, we invoke the powers of Pisces. In the letter Qoph and in the Sign of the Fishes, we invoke thee! Come thou forth.**

Priest (or Priestess) of Pisces lights the Red-violet Candle on the Blue Water Candelabra on the North side of the Altar. (NOTE: Take the flame from the central candle and transfer it with the taper candle.)

All vibrate: **EL.**

Psaltis rings the bell twelve times ווו – ווו – ווו - ווו.

Priest (or Priestess) of Pisces then returns to place, gives the Sign of Silence, and is seated.

HIEROPHANT (knocks ו): **It is written: "And the Elohim said, 'Let there be lights in the vault of the sky to separate the day from the night, and let them serve as signs to mark sacred times, and days and years, and let them be lights in the vault of the sky to give light on the earth.'" And it was so.**

HIEROPHANT stands, raises both hands (with scepter), and says: **Glory be unto Thee, Father of the Undying, for thy Glory goes out rejoicing to the ends of the earth!**

ALL (speaking, not vibrating): **Amen.**

HIEROPHANT (with hands still raised): **Hail to Thee, Thou glorious and divine Spirit, extending from the heights of heaven to the depths of the earth! Hail to Thee, invisible Spirit, who fills the depth of our souls and clings to us in goodness! We give you thanks and praise, and may we continue to walk in your Light now and forevermore.**

ALL (speaking, not vibrating): **Amen.**

HIEROPHANT: **We give thanks and praise to all heavenly and Zodiacal powers. May your gifts be ours to hold and share and may they ever abide in this sacred hall of the Mysteries.**

ALL (speaking, not vibrating): **Amen. Selah. Amen.**

PSALTIS rings the bell three times ווו.

This signifies the end of the Work. Candelabras may be moved to a side altar. Any announcements may be made at this time.

Proceed to the Closing of the Neophyte Hall.

✠ ✠ ✠

Tarot Divination Ritual

The word *divination* is based upon the Latin word *divinatio*, which means "the faculty of foreseeing." The root word is itself based upon the Latin term for "divine power" or "of the Gods," and thus exposes the true meaning of the word *divination*, which is "to make divine." This is a spiritual science that deals with discovering the divine significance of "chance" events. And like other methods included in the magical arts, divination has existed as a tool for psychic well-being and spiritual health long before the development of modern psychology.

Forms of divination are as varied as the inventive minds from which they sprang. The earliest type of divination was probably as simple as gazing into a fire or listening to the wind. A multitude of methods developed from that point forward. It often doesn't seem to matter what form a divination takes; it is more important that the diviner be able to quiet the mind enough to attune with the Higher Forces and perceive certain signs or symbols by means of an inner perception that can interpret their sacred implications.

Divinatory methods such as Tarot have become fundamental to the understanding of the Divine Universe by today's hermetic students. These techniques are now used by magicians of many different traditions to communicate with the Deity by seeking out knowledge from within. This, too, is a fulfillment of the Hermetic axiom "As above, so below," for by learning how to interpret the subtle cosmic influences within us, we can learn to understand those unseen influences that exist outside of ourselves through a universal law of correspondences.

The ceremony that follows is a ritualized group Tarot reading that is based on the energies of the Neophyte Hall itself. Each of the Officers invokes the energies and duties of their stations as they choose a card to add to the Tarot Tableau, a diagram showing the placement of fourteen cards that make up the Temple Card Spread, which is then interpreted by and for the group (see figure 19).

Synopsis: After the Hierophant announces the ritual's objective, he leads the group through an abbreviated Middle Pillar exercise. The Hierophant extols the importance of divination and then invokes the Spirit of Life under the auspices of the divine names of Tiphareth, the sixth Sephirah. The angels of the celestial spheres are called upon to guard the ceremony, and the query is stated.

Hierophant leads everyone in the Qabalistic Cross, then unwraps and shuffles the Tarot Cards. Hierophant invokes the angel HRU over the cards to anoint them with truth, then fans the cards out face down in a semicircle and traces the figure of the Lesser Invoking Pentagram over them.

Next, the Praemonstrator goes to the Altar, speaks an invocation, selects a card, and returns to their seat. One by one, each of the Officers does the same. After the Phylax has selected a card, the Imperator returns to the Altar and picks another card—the card of the Black Pillar. Praemonstrator returns to the Altar and picks another card—the card of the White Pillar. Hegemon returns to the Altar and picks another card—the card of the Altar.

In total, fourteen cards are chosen for the Temple Spread:

1. The Praemonstrator Card
2. The Imperator Card
3. The Cancellarius Card
4. The Past Hierophant Card
5. The Hierophant Card
6. The Hiereus Card
7. The Hegemon Card
8. The Keryx Card
9. The Stolistes Card
10. The Dadouchos Card
11. The Phylax Card
12. The Boaz (Black Pillar) Card
13. The Jachin (White Pillar) Card
14. The Altar Card

After the fourteen cards are chosen, the Keryx places the diagram of the Tarot Tableau in the East before the throne of the Hierophant. Starting with the Praemonstrator, the officers call out the name of their card and place it on the Tableau, from card 1 through card 14. The Tableau is studied for any insights it brings. The explanation of the Temple Spread and how it can be interpreted is given at the end of the Ritual.

Also needed:

- A Tarot deck wrapped in linen or a Tarot bag
- White pillar candle in glass

- Altar cloth
- Small cauldron with charcoal and incense
- A Tarot Tableau showing the Temple Card Spread

Perform the Opening of the Neophyte Hall. Then continue with the Work.

Keryx removes the elements from the Altar and drapes an Altar cloth on top of it. On the top right Keryx places a cauldron with lighted charcoals, plus a container of powered incense. On the top left Keryx places a white pillar candle and lights it. At the center he places the wrapped Tarot deck. Keryx is seated.

Hierophant: (Knocks ו) **Fratres and Sorores of the (______) Temple of the (________) Order of the Golden Dawn in the Outer, we are here assembled in our commitment to the work of the divine theurgy, for the purpose of performing a ritual divination using the Sacred Tarot Images of Art. To this end we shall invoke the Divine forces represented by the Officers of this Hall of the Neophytes, to aid and guide us in our search for Truth, so that through this ceremony, we may be better able to understand the true nature of the magical art, and be better equipped to carry out the Great Work, to the glory of the Ineffable name.**

Let us first establish a link with the Higher and Divine Self—that inexhaustible Treasure of Light, to which we aspire unceasingly—that the Powers of the Divine may be reawakened in the spheres of those present and in the Sphere of this Order. For by names and Images are all Powers Awakened and Reawakened.

All Officers close their eyes as the Hierophant leads them through an abbreviated Middle Pillar exercise, using only the Sephiroth of *Kether* (Power Source), *Tiphareth* (Power Outlet), and *Malkuth* (Power Ground). The Hierophant vibrates the Divine Name one time by himself, to establish the vibrational note for the other officers. Then All Officers including the Hierophant vibrate the name for a total of three times:

HIEROPHANT: **EHEIEH.**
ALL: **EHEIEH. EHEIEH. EHEIEH.**

HIEROPHANT: **YHVH ELOAH VE-DAATH.**
ALL: **YHVH ELOAH VE-DAATH.
YHVH ELOAH VE-DAATH.
YHVH ELOAH VE-DAATH.**

HIEROPHANT: **ADONAI HA-ARETZ.**
ALL: **ADONAI HA-ARETZ. ADONAI HA-ARETZ. ADONAI HA-ARETZ.**

HIEROPHANT: (Knocks ׀) **Divination is the daughter of inspiration. The whole of the world is indeed divinatory and teems with divinatory symbols. And it is truly divine law that the Divine is not separate from the human. For to divine is nothing else than to see in advance, in the proper way to Deity. Divination is a participation in the Divine which comes from the gods to humans, and a unification of human souls with the divine natures. The Soul's act of divination takes place in a state most alike to the Divine, to the One.**

We call upon Divine Forces of the Ruach Elohim and the Spirit of Life, under the Majesty of the Divine Name YHVH Eloah Ve-Daath, the Archangel Raphael, and the Angelic host of the Melekim, to bestow this present day and hour, and confirm their mystic and potent influence upon this ceremonial divination!

HIEROPHANT stands and faces East.

Sacred Breath of Life! Spirit of Life! Spirit of Wisdom! We adore Thee and we invoke Thee! Bless the Work we undertake this day! Grant us a true Message from the abode of the Divine! Grace us with your Wisdom in all things relating to our spiritual query. Look with favor upon this Ceremony and grant thine aid unto the Higher aspirations of our Souls. To the Glory of the Ineffable Name! AMEN!

I invoke ye, ye Angels of the celestial spheres, whose dwelling is in the invisible. Ye are the Guardians of the Gates of the Universe, be ye also the Guardians of this Sacred Hall. Keep far removed the evil and the unbalanced. Strengthen and inspire us, so that we may preserve unsullied this abode of the mysteries of the eternal Gods. Let our Temple be pure and holy, so that we make partake of the secrets of the Light Divine.

Through these Cards of Art, we seek an answer to our query (state the question).

Hierophant goes to the west of the Altar, facing east.
Hierophant leads All in performance of the Qabalistic Cross:
ATAH, MALKUTH, VE-GEBURAH, VE GEDULAH, Le-OLAHM, AMEN.

Hierophant places a small amount of incense in the cauldron.

Hierophant leads all in vibrating **IAO. IAO. IAO.** All keep vibrating as Hierophant unwraps and shuffles cards thoroughly. (When he is finished, All stop vibrating.)

Hierophant traces a cross ✚ over the deck, followed by the letters HEH, RESH, VAV (הרו), and says: **In the Divine Name IAO I invoke the great angel HRU,**[49] **who art set over the operations of this Secret Wisdom. Strengthen and establish us in our search for the Mysteries of the Divine Light! Increase the Spiritual perception of all present within this Temple! Lay thine hand invisibly on these Cards of Art and give them life. Anoint them with the Divine Science, so that through their use we may obtain True Knowledge of hidden things, and rise above that lower self-hood which is nothing, unto that Highest Self-hood which is in God the Vast One. To the glory of the ineffable Name. Amen.**

All visualize the hand of a Mighty Angel held over the Deck of Cards, which glows with a bright white light. The Tarot deck should be seen in a brilliant halo of light.

All vibrate four times: **IAO. HRU. IAO. HRU. IAO. HRU. IAO. HRU.**

---

49. The Angel of the Tarot.

HIEROPHANT: **Arise before us, clear as a mirror, O Magical Vision required for the accomplishment of this Divination! With the Power of Heka and the Balance of Maat, let these Symbols be true of Voice! Maa Kheru!**

HIEROPHANT fans the cards out in a semicircle on the altar, face down. Hierophant traces a cross ✚ in the air above cards and says: **By Names and Images are all Powers awakened and reawakened.**

HIEROPHANT traces the figure of a *Lesser Invoking Pentagram* over the cards and vibrates: **ROTA. TARO. ORAT. TORA. ATOR.** HIEROPHANT thrusts the wand through the center of the figure then says: **The wheel of Tarot speaks the law of Hathor!**

HIEROPHANT returns to station.

PRAEMONSTRATOR rises, gives the Projection Sign toward the Banner of the East, walks to the west of the Altar and sprinkles a small amount of incense into the censer, then performs the Qabalistic Cross.

PRAEMONSTRATOR: **I am the Praemonstrator of the Mysteries and the messenger of Osiris Onnophris. My station in the Southeast is the Gate which leadeth to the Realm of Mercy. I represent the Great Goddess Isis, Mother of the Gods. Queen of Heaven. Great Lady of Magic. Mistress of the House of Life. High Priestess of the Silver Star! Accept our offerings, She Who Knows How to Make Right Use of the Heart! Lead us to the Truth and guide all our wanderings in darkness as we travel the Path of Light to the Eternal Crown. Come forth, O gracious Mother. Come unto us and dwell within our hearts. O Goddess crowned with starlight, who shineth amid the Lords of Truth, whose place is in the abode of Heaven! Speak the Names of Magic, as we call upon Thy Wisdom.**

PRAEMONSTRATOR traces a cross ✚ over the Tarot cards, then says: **By the authority of my office and the command of the Great Goddess Isis! With the Power of Heka and the Balance of Maat! Let these Symbols be True of Voice! Maa Kheru!**

ALL vibrate one time: **ROTA. TARO. ORAT. TORA. ATOR.**

Praemonstrator: **The wheel of Tarot speaks the law of Hathor!**

Praemonstrator selects a card from the Altar, takes it back to her station, gives the Sign of Silence, and is seated.

Imperator rises, gives the Projection Sign toward the Banner of the East, walks to the west of the Altar and sprinkles a small amount of incense into the censer, then performs the Qabalistic Cross.

Imperator: **I am the Imperator of the Mysteries and the messenger of Osiris Onnophris. My station in the North-East is the Gate that leadeth to the Realm of Power. I represent the Mighty Goddess Nephthys, Lady of the Duat, Mistress of the Gods, Lady of the Temple. Excellent Goddess who purifies all things. Guardian and Protector! Weeper of Tears and Singer of Songs. Mother of Darkness, who dwellest in the Night to which no man can approach, Wherein is Mystery and Depth Unthinkable, and Awful silence. Thou Voice of Hidden Things! Sing the Charm of Living as we call upon Thy Wisdom.**

Imperator traces a cross ✚ over the Tarot cards, then says: **By the authority of my office and the command of the Mighty Goddess Nephthys! With the Power of Heka and the Balance of Maat! Let these Symbols be True of Voice! Maa Kheru!**

All vibrate one time: **ROTA. TARO. ORAT. TORA. ATOR.**

Imperator: **The wheel of Tarot speaks the law of Hathor!**

Imperator selects a card from the Altar, takes it back to his station, gives the Sign of Silence, and is seated.

Cancellarius rises, gives the Projection Sign to the Banner of the East, walks to the west of the Altar and sprinkles a small amount of incense into the censer, then performs the Qabalistic Cross.

CANCELLARIUS: **I am the Cancellarius of the Mysteries and the messenger of Osiris Onnophris. My station in the East is the Gate that leadeth to the Realm of Beauty. I represent the Great God Thoth, Scribe of the Gods, Lord of Holy Words, Thrice Great God of Divination and Magic! May the Ibis-headed One look with favor upon our rites! O Holy Knowledge, being enlightened by Thee, magnify the intelligible Light, and rejoice in the Joy of the Mind! O Light, enlighten!**

O God the Spirit! For the Mind guideth the Word.
The Speech in the Silence. The Voice of Thoth!
The Formulas of Knowledge! The Wisdom of Breath!
The Source of Vibration! The Shaking of the Invisible!
The Rolling Asunder of the Darkness!
The Becoming Visible of Matter!
The Piercing of the Coils of the Stooping Dragon!
The Breaking forth of the Light!
All these are in the Knowledge of Thoth!
Speak the Words of Magic as we call upon Thy Wisdom.

CANCELLARIUS traces a cross ✚ over the Tarot cards, then says: **By the authority of my office and the command of the Great God Thoth! With the Power of Heka and the Balance of Maat! Let these Symbols be True of Voice! Maa Kheru!**

ALL vibrate one time: **ROTA. TARO. ORAT. TORA. ATOR.**

CANCELLARIUS: **The wheel of Tarot speaks the law of Hathor!**

CANCELLARIUS selects a card from the Altar, takes it back to his station, gives the Sign of Silence, and is seated.

PAST HIEROPHANT rises, gives the Projection Sign to the Banner of the East, walks to the west of the Altar and sprinkles a small amount of incense into the censer, then performs the Qabalistic Cross.

PAST HIEROPHANT: **I am the Past Hierophant of the Mysteries and the messenger of Osiris Onnophris. My station in the East is the Place of the Ever-present Past. I represent Mighty God Haroueris, Horus the Elder. The Overcomer of obstacles. Radiant in Battle. The Bright One of Heaven and Heart of the Sun. God of two Eyes and a Thousand Names. Lord of the vast Horizon! Peace be upon You, Lord of the Two Lands who illuminateth the darkness! May your lifetime be that of the Sky, enduring for Eternity before the Souls of the living forever! Open the Gates of Magic as we call upon Thy Wisdom.**

PAST HIEROPHANT traces a cross ✚ over the Tarot cards, then says: **By the authority of my office and the command of the Mighty god Haroueris! With the Power of Heka and the Balance of Maat! Let these Symbols be true of Voice! Maa Kheru!**

ALL vibrate one time: **ROTA. TARO. ORAT. TORA. ATOR.**

PAST HIEROPHANT: **The wheel of Tarot speaks the law of Hathor!**

PAST HIEROPHANT selects a card from the Altar, takes it back to his station, gives the Sign of Silence, and is seated.

HIEROPHANT rises, gives the Projection Sign toward the West and walks to the west of the Altar and sprinkles a small amount of incense into the censer, then performs the Qabalistic Cross.

HIEROPHANT: **I am the Hierophant of the Mysteries and the messenger of Osiris Onnophris. My station in the East is the Place of the Guardian of the Dawning Sun. I represent the Great God Osiris, who is found perfect before the Gods. Beautiful Being, Osiris Triumphant, even Osir Meekheru, the Justified One. God of Eternity! Lord of both the Outer and the Inner. The Leaders of the Five-fold Star give glory unto Thee. When Thou resideth in the firmament, when Isis folds Thee in her arms in peace, when she turns back the storm from the Gate of Thy paths. When Thou showest Thy face to the West, Lighting up the Two Lands with Thy silver-gold. Our hearts know peace when we see Thee! Thou who art the eternal Aeon. Hail, thou living soul of Osiris, diademmed with the**

moon. There is no part of Thee that is not of the Gods! Whisper the Prayers of Magic as we call upon Thy Wisdom.

HIEROPHANT traces a cross ✚ over the Tarot cards, then says: **By the authority of my office and the command of the Great God Osiris! With the Power of Heka and the Balance of Maat! Let these Symbols be True of Voice! Maa Kheru!**

ALL vibrate one time: **ROTA. TARO. ORAT. TORA. ATOR.**

HIEROPHANT: **The wheel of Tarot speaks the law of Hathor!**

HIEROPHANT selects a card from the Altar, takes it back to his station, gives the Sign of Silence, and is seated.

HIEREUS rises, gives the Projection Sign and walks to the west of the Altar and sprinkles a small amount of incense into the censer, then performs the Qabalistic Cross.

HIEREUS: **I am the Hiereus of the Mysteries and the messenger of Osiris Onnophris. I represent the god Horus, Golden Hawk-headed God of the Sun! Lord of the diadems, and beloved Son of Isis! Fill us with courage and Right Action, that we may learn when to know, to dare, to will, and to be silent! That we may know when to draw the Sword and when to sheath it.**

My station in the West is the Place of the Setting Sun. I am the Keeper of the Gateway of the West, defending against the Multitudes that sleep through the Light and awaken at Twilight. I guard our Sacred Hall from the chaos and the shadow of the Qlipothic Powers. I protect the Temple and its members from the evil and the unbalanced. I am called Fortitude, Lord of Twilight, and the Master of Darkness.

HIEREUS traces a cross ✚ over the Tarot cards, then says: **By the authority of my office, and the command of the Mighty God Horus! With the Power of Heka and the Balance of Maat! Let these Symbols be True of Voice! Maa Kheru!**

ALL vibrate one time: **ROTA. TARO. ORAT. TORA. ATOR.**

HIEREUS: **The wheel of Tarot speaks the law of Hathor!**

HIEREUS selects a card from the Altar, takes it back to his station, gives the Sign of Silence, and is seated.

HEGEMON rises, gives the Projection Sign and walks to the west of the Altar and sprinkles a small amount of incense into the censer, then performs the Qabalistic Cross.

HEGEMON: **I am the Hegemon of the Mysteries and the messenger of Osiris Onnophris. I represent the Great Goddess Maat, Lady of the Eternal Feather and the Scales of Balance! Thou whose name is Justice and whose Word is Truth. Thy feather is weighed against the heart of the Initiate in the Hall of Judgement. Thou art the eye of the storm and center of the wheel, and the heavens revolve around Thee.**

My station between the two Pillars is the Place of Perfect Equilibrium, between the Ultimate Light and the Ultimate Darkness. I keep watch over the Threshold of the Gate of the Mysteries. I serve as Guide and Mystagogue for the Candidate, the Preparer of the Pathway. And within the Hall of Two Truths I serve as the Reconciler between Light and Darkness.

Hegemon traces a cross over the Tarot cards, then says: **By the authority of my office and the command of the Righteous Goddess Maat! With the Power of Heka and the Balance of Maat! Let these Symbols be True of Voice! Maa Kheru!**

ALL vibrate one time: **ROTA. TARO. ORAT. TORA. ATOR.**

HEGEMON: **The wheel of Tarot speaks the law of Hathor!**

HEGEMON selects a card from the Altar, takes it back to her station, gives the Sign of Silence, and is seated.

KERYX rises, gives the Projection Sign and walks to the west of the Altar and sprinkles a small amount of incense into the censer, then performs the Qabalistic Cross.

KERYX: **I am the Keryx of the Mysteries and the messenger of Osiris Onnophris. I represent the Great God Anubis, Guardian of the tomb and Lord of the Duat. He Who is Upon his Sacred Mountain. Master of Secrets. Minder of the Scales of Balance in the Hall of Two Truths. Lord of the Sacred Land and Gatekeeper of the Cavern. Thou who standeth between the worlds in the midst of Time. Grant us safe passage through our hour of trial.**

My station is within the Portal of the Temple to guard against the profane. I lead the Mystic Circumambulations bearing the Lamp of the Hidden Gnosis. I am the true Herald and Harbinger of the Gods. I proclaim the Word of Truth and the Dawn of Light. I am the Watcher Within, just as the Phylax is the Watcher Without.

KERYX traces a cross ✚ over the Tarot cards, then says: **By the authority of my office and the command of the Great God Anubis! With the Power of Heka and the Balance of Maat! Let these Symbols be True of Voice! Maa Kheru!**

ALL vibrate one time: **ROTA. TARO. ORAT. TORA. ATOR.**

KERYX: **The wheel of Tarot speaks the law of Hathor!**

KERYX selects a card from the Altar, takes it back to his station, gives the Sign of Silence, and is seated.

STOLISTES rises, gives the Projection Sign, and walks to the west of the Altar and sprinkles a small amount of incense into the censer, then performs the Qabalistic Cross.

STOLISTES: **I am the Stolistes of the Mysteries and the messenger of Osiris Onnophris. I represent the Goddess Mut, Great Mother, Lady of Thebes, Eye of Ra, Mistress of Heaven! Gracious World Mother and Queen of the Gods! Thou art the Vulture's Wings! Lady of the primordial waters, wash us, thy children! Cleanse us with Thy tears! We thank thee for the many Blessings thou hast bestowed on us.**

My station at the Gate of the North is the Place of the Guardian of the Cauldron and the Well of Water; of Cold and Moisture. I keep the Sacred Cup and cleanse

all within the Temple with the Living, Lustral Waters of the loud-resounding Sea. Hear thou the voice of Water!

STOLISTES traces a cross ✚ over the Tarot cards, then says: **By the authority of my office and the command of the Mother Goddess Mut! With the Power of Heka and the Balance of Maat! Let these Symbols be True of Voice! Maa Kheru!**

ALL vibrate one time: **ROTA. TARO. ORAT. TORA. ATOR.**

STOLISTES: **The wheel of Tarot speaks the law of Hathor!**

STOLISTES selects a card from the Altar, takes it back to her station, gives the Sign of Silence, and is seated.

DADOUCHOS rises, gives the Projection Sign, and walks to the west of the Altar and sprinkles a small amount of incense into the censer, then performs the Qabalistic Cross.

DADOUCHOS: **I am the Dadouchos of the Mysteries and the messenger of Osiris Onnophris. I represent the Mighty Goddess Neith, Lady of the West. Self-created Goddess of the two Arrows. Red of Crown and fierce of heart! Mighty Huntress! We take refuge in your strength, Holy Flame!**

My station at the Gate of the South is the Place of the Guardian of the Lake of Fire and the Burning Bush. I keep the Censer of Living Fire, and consecrate all within the Temple with that Holy and Formless Fire, that Fire which darts and flashes through the hidden depths of the Universe. Hear thou the Voice of Fire!

DADOUCHOS traces a cross ✚ over the Tarot cards, then says: **By the authority of my office, and the command of the Mighty Goddess Neith! With the Power of Heka and the Balance of Maat! Let these Symbols be True of Voice! Maa Kheru!**

ALL vibrate one time: **ROTA. TARO. ORAT. TORA. ATOR.**

DADOUCHOS: **The wheel of Tarot speaks the law of Hathor!**

DADOUCHOS selects a card from the Altar, takes it back to his station, gives the Sign of Silence, and is seated.

PHYLAX rises, gives the Projection Sign, and walks to the west of the Altar and sprinkles a small amount of incense into the censer, then performs the Qabalistic Cross.

PHYLAX: **I am the Phylax of the Mysteries and the messenger of Osiris Onnophris. I represent the god Opowet, the Opener of the Ways. Master of Gates and Lord of Roads. Thou who openeth the path for the Virtuous, and barreth the path for the Wicked. Wolf-headed God, clear the path before us and unlock the hidden door to the Mysteries. Open the Way for us.**

My station is in the Pronaos of the Temple. I keep strict watch over the Portal, lest the profane enter our sacred Hall. I am the Watcher Without, just as the Keryx is the Watcher Within.

PHYLAX traces a cross ✚ over the Tarot cards, then says: **By the authority of my office and the command of the Great God Opowet! With the Power of Heka and the Balance of Maat! Let these Symbols be True of Voice! Maa Kheru!**

ALL vibrate one time: **ROTA. TARO. ORAT. TORA. ATOR.**

PHYLAX: **The wheel of Tarot speaks the law of Hathor!**

PHYLAX selects a card from the Altar, takes it back to his station, gives the Sign of Silence, and is seated.

IMPERATOR rises, gives the Projection Sign toward the Banner of the East, walks to the west of the Altar and sprinkles a small amount of incense into the censer, then performs the Qabalistic Cross.

IMPERATOR: **The station of the Great Goddess Nephthys is at the Black Pillar of Severity known as Boaz. The Feet of the Goddess rest upon the Sephirah of Hod and her Mighty image extends upwards into the Heavens beyond.**

IMPERATOR traces a cross ✚ over the Tarot cards, then says: **By the authority of my office and the command of the Mighty Goddess Nephthys! With the Power of Heka and the Balance of Maat! Let these Symbols be true of Voice! Maa Kheru!**

ALL vibrate one time: **ROTA. TARO. ORAT. TORA. ATOR.**

IMPERATOR: **The wheel of Tarot speaks the law of Hathor!**

IMPERATOR selects a card from the Altar, takes it back to <u>his</u> station, gives the Sign of Silence, and is seated.

PRAEMONSTRATOR rises, gives the Projection Sign toward the Banner of the East, walks to the west of the Altar and sprinkles a small amount of incense into the censer, then performs the Qabalistic Cross.

PRAEMONSTRATOR: **The station of the Great Goddess Isis is at the White Pillar of Mercy known as Jachin. The Feet of the Goddess rest upon the Sephirah of Netzach and her Mighty image extends upwards into the Heavens beyond.**

PRAEMONSTRATOR traces a cross ✚ over the Tarot cards, then says: **By the authority of my office and the command of the Great Goddess Isis, Mighty Mother! With the Power of Heka and the Balance of Maat! Let these Symbols be True of Voice! Maa Kheru!**

ALL vibrate one time: **ROTA. TARO. ORAT. TORA. ATOR.**

PRAEMONSTRATOR: **The wheel of Tarot speaks the law of Hathor!**

PRAEMONSTRATOR selects a card from the Altar, takes it back to <u>her</u> station, gives the Sign of Silence, and is seated.

HEGEMON rises, gives the Projection Sign, and walks to the west of the Altar and sprinkles a small amount of incense into the censer, then performs the Qabalistic Cross.

HEGEMON: **The Double Cubical Altar in the center of the Hall is an emblem of visible Nature or the Material Universe, concealing within Herself the mysteries of all dimensions while revealing Her surface to the exterior senses. It is a double cube because, as the Emerald Tablet has said, "The things that are below are a reflection of the things that are above." Qadesh! Emeth! Qadesh!**

HEGEMON traces a cross ✚ over the Tarot cards, then says: **By the authority of my office and the command of the Righteous Goddess Maat! With the Power of Heka and the Balance of Maat! Let these Symbols be True of Voice! Maa Kheru!**

ALL vibrate one time: **ROTA. TARO. ORAT. TORA. ATOR.**

HEGEMON: **The wheel of Tarot speaks the law of Hathor!**

HEGEMON selects a card from the Altar, takes it back to her station, gives the Sign of Silence, and is seated.

KERYX places the Tarot Tableau of the Temple Card Spread in the East before the throne of the Hierophant, and is seated.

At this point the OFFICERS may call out the names of the cards that they have chosen in order from 1 to 14. After each card is called out, it is placed on the Tarot Tableau in accordance with the diagram so it may be recorded. The Tableau can be studied at length after the ritual is closed.

When finished, the Hierophant thanks any entities that may have aided the ceremony.

HIEROPHANT: **Unto Thee Sole Wise, Sole Merciful, and Sole Eternal One, we give thanks for overseeing our efforts and empowering our rites. Not unto our names, but to thine be the praise and Glory forever. Glory be to Thee, Lord of the Land of Life, for thy Glory flows out rejoicing to the ends of the earth!**

Any comments, announcements, or temple business may be discussed. Then proceed to the closing.

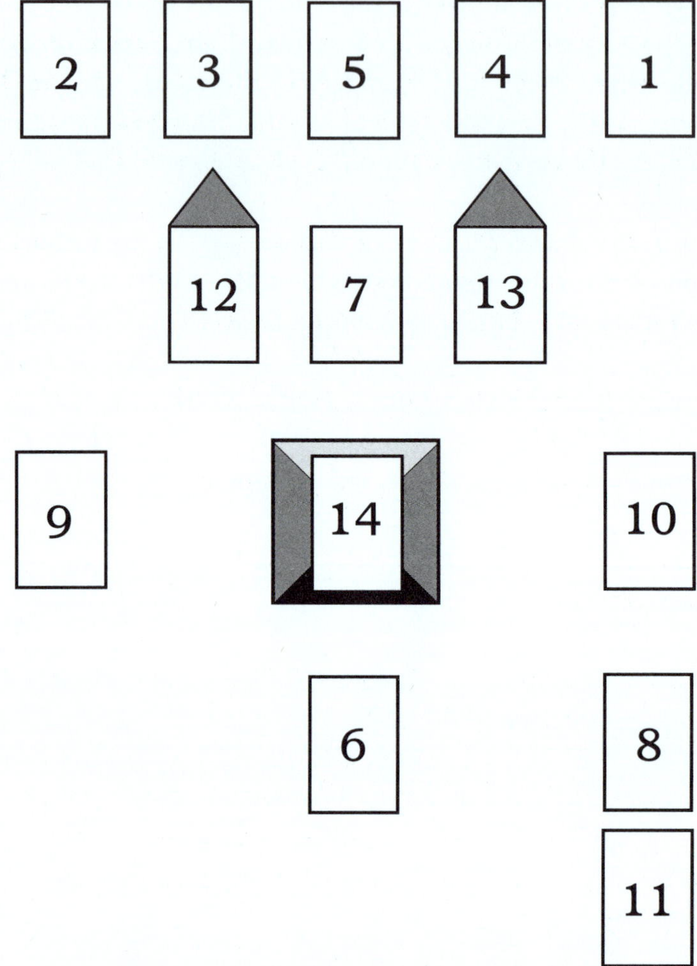

Figure 19: Tarot Tableau of the Temple Spread

1. Praemonstrator Card: The Teacher. The Spiritual essence of Water. The Sphere of Mercy (Chesed). *Interpretation:* That which provides spiritual nourishment. A lesson that the teacher is offering. A lesson or force that might seem harsh but is actually a mercy. A helpful influence. A force that seeks to expand and manifest.
2. Imperator Card: The Commander. Law Giver. The Spirit of the Law. Enforcer of Divine Law. The Spiritual essence of Fire. The Sphere of Power

and Severity (Geburah). *Interpretation:* That which provides spiritual justice. A judgment from the Divine. A force that might seem merciful but is actually and by necessity harsh. A force that seeks to limit and contain. An oppressive influence.

3. CANCELLARIUS CARD: The Mystic. The Divine Voice. The Oracle. The Spiritual essence of Air. The Sphere of Beauty (Tiphareth). *Interpretation:* Divine Aid and advice. A hidden influence that connects everything. A mystery to be solved. Something that can clarify the issue. The heart of the matter. A center point to which all roads lead.
4. PAST HIEROPHANT CARD: The Sage. *Interpretation:* That which is passing from the physical plane back to the Divine (evolution). The Past. A force that is leaving. That which has completed its task. Something that needs to be remembered. A force that can step back into the matter, if needed.
5. HIEROPHANT CARD: Presiding Official. Initiator. The Revealer of the Mysteries. Channeler of the Higher. Master of Ceremonies. The Power of Spirit. The Higher and Divine Genius. Higher Self. *Interpretation:* A Spiritual Force that is descending into view. That which was hidden but is now being revealed. That which connects the Higher with the Lower or the Inner with the Outer. The energy that is the connecting link in the issue. A force that initiates and orchestrates all action in the matter. That which has initiated the matter.
6. HIEREUS CARD: The Guardian. The Protector. The Power of Earth. The Active Will. *Interpretation:* Divine Protection. That which defends and stands guard. That which acts without hesitation. A harsh force that is needed. Conversely, something harmful that must be barred or banished. Something that must be sacrificed.
7. HEGEMON CARD: The Guide. The Reconciler. The Power of Air. The Neshamah, or intuitive consciousness. *Interpretation:* A mediating force. A guiding force that prepares the pathway. The middle path. The road that is clear. That which adds balance. Something that harmonizes opposing forces. Conversely, something that needs to be balanced. (That which mediates between cards 12 and 13.)
8. KERYX CARD: The Herald. The Ruach, or conscious mind. *Interpretation:* A message from the Divine. That which must be invoked. That which leads to the solution. A force that will come full circle.

9. STOLISTES CARD: The Power of Water. Thoughts. Creativity. Intuition. *Interpretation:* A calming force. A rational force. Creative energy that can be used in the matter. Something that is known intuitively. That which will calm the situation. Something that will purify the matter. Conversely, that which needs to be calmed or purified.
10. DADOUCHOS CARD: The Power of Fire. Emotions. Feelings. Passions. *Interpretation:* A stimulating force. Something that will bring fresh energy to the situation. That which shakes things up. An agitating force. Conversely, an irrational force, a destructive force. An obsession.
11. PHYLAX CARD: The Sentinel. *Interpretation:* Mundane influences. Outer distractions. That which must be kept outside the matter.
12. THE BOAZ CARD: The Black Pillar. Severity. Darkness. Night. Feminine Force. *Interpretation:* That which either balances or opposes card 13.
13. THE JACHIN CARD: The White Pillar. Mercy. Light. Day. Masculine Force. *Interpretation:* That which either balances or opposes card 12.
14. THE ALTAR CARD: The Manifest Universe. The Sphere of Malkuth. The Spiritual essence of Earth. Completion. *Interpretation:* The Divine reflected into the Physical. As Above, so Below. That which will manifest. That which must be dealt with or confronted. The Resolution. The final solution of the matter.

✠ ✠ ✠

chapter 3

HEALING, SEASONAL RITUALS, AND RITES OF PASSAGE

Healing and magic have been linked together since the beginning of history. In ancient times, magicians were the doctors of their day. They were called upon to expel evil spirits, lift curses, and placate gods—whatever was believed necessary to heal a sick child, an ailing relative, or an injured member of the community.

In the modern era, we are blessed with many advances in the science of modern medicine. Rather than look for perpetrators of family curses, today we look to physicians trained to find microscopic pathogens in order to cure the sick. Nevertheless, contemporary magicians are still healers. Healing magic is without a doubt an important focus of much of our work, just as healing rituals remain a cornerstone of our tradition.

Physical well-being is only one of the many benefits that rites of healing have to offer. The real power of these rituals is in their capacity to repair spiritual wounds, emotional injuries, and psychic imbalances. Healing rituals function as a salve for the soul, reconciling the conflicting impulses within the psyche and removing obstacles that impede a person's health and wellness. Ritualists performing the rite become conduits for the therapeutic energies of the Divine, allowing for the restoration of both recipients and healers alike.

Healing rituals are more than just a method for restoring health; they are a powerful manifestation of our integration with the sacred.

Archangelic Rite of Healing

The following ritual invokes the powers of the Archangels of the five elements to bestow healing upon a member of the temple.

Ritual Personae. Some officers have additional roles and duties. Five officers, known collectively as "the Five," act as the emissaries of the Archangels:

1. Hiereus: Emissary of Uriel and Earth
2. Stolistes: Emissary of Gabriel and Water
3. Keryx: Emissary of Raphael and Air
4. Dadouchos: Emissary of Michael and Fire
5. Hierophant: Emissary of Nuriel and Spirit

The ritual also calls for a Psaltis.

Synopsis: After the Hierophant announces the ritual's objective and invokes the highest aspects of Deity, the Hiereus performs the Lesser Invoking Ritual of the Pentagram to establish a magic circle that is conducive to elemental forces. Then the Hierophant goes to the west of the Altar to invoke the Archangels[50] and charge the five elemental symbols.

The beneficiary of the rite, hereafter called the Aspirant, is led to the west of the Altar by the Hegemon. The Aspirant asks the Archangels of the Elements for healing. Hegemon leads Aspirant to the seat of the invisible station of Harpokratês.[51]

In turn, each of the Five,[52] acting as an emissary to their respective archangel, goes to the west of the altar and speaks to the Aspirant. Then, taking up one of the elemental symbols from the Altar, each emissary blesses the Aspirant, traces an elemental figure, and lights a candle on the Pentagrammaton candelabra.

Aspirant sits in a meditative state as Hegemon leads all members (except for the Five) in a chant of healing. As the chant continues, the Five gather around the Aspirant in a pentagram formation for a final invocation of healing Light and breath. When ready, Hierophant motions for the chant to stop. Aspirant takes their original seat

---

50. The order of the Archangels here is in alignment with the Conjuration of the Four as given in the Lesser Ritual of the Pentagram (East, West, South, North).

51. At the center of the temple between the Hegemon and the Altar.

52. The order and numbering of the Archangels here (1. Hiereus, 2. Stolistes, etc.) is in alignment with the tracing of a Lesser Invoking Pentagram (Earth, Water, Air, Fire, and back to Spirit, as the element of connection and final unity).

amongst the members. The Hierophant thanks the Archangels invoked. The Altar is reset for the Closing of the Neophyte Hall.

Additional Items needed:

- Protective Altar cloth
- The Pentagrammaton candelabra with five candles in the elemental colors of black, blue, yellow, red, and white
- Small white votive candle
- A separate white taper candle for lighting the candelabra[53]
- A quartz crystal
- A small vial of anointing oil
- A hand fan
- A red scented candle
- A bright LED light
- A bell, chimes, or gong for the Psaltis Officer
- An extra chair for the Aspirant

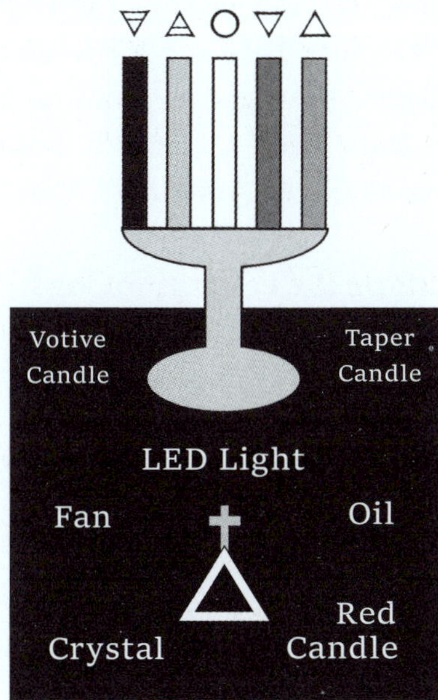

Figure 20: Altar Setup for Archangelic Rite of Healing

53. This taper is used to transfer the flame from the small white votive to the candelabra. Place the taper on a stick incense holder to protect the altar top.

Perform the Opening of the Hall of the Neophytes. Then continue with the Work.

After the Hall is opened, the usual items on the Altar, except for Cross and Triangle, are temporally removed. The Altar is set up for the work at hand. A seat for the Aspirant is placed upon the invisible station of Harpokratês.

HIEROPHANT: (Knocks— ו) **Fratres and Sorores of the (______) Temple of the (________) Order of the Golden Dawn, we are here assembled in our commitment to the work of the divine theurgy, to perform a ritual of healing for (Frater/Soror ________). To that end we call upon the mighty Archangels of the Elements to administer their curative powers on our (Brother/Sister) and bring them peace and convalescence. Working as emissaries to these great Angelic Companions, we invoke the therapeutic Light of the Divine to restore the health of our beloved (Frater/Soror).**

ALL stand and face east.

HIEROPHANT: **Lord of the Universe—the Vast and the Mighty One! Ruler of the Light and of the Darkness! We adore Thee and We invoke Thee! Look with favor on us, and grant Thine aid unto the higher aspirations of our souls. To the glory of Thine Ineffable Name. Unto Thee, O Tetragrammaton be ascribed, Malkuth, Geburah, Gedulah, Unto the Ages, Amen.**

Honoured Hiereus, perform the Lesser Invoking Ritual of the Pentagram, and establish a circle for the influx of the five elemental forces in Malkuth.

HIEREUS performs the LIRP. At the end, ALL present perform the Qabalistic Cross with the HIEREUS: **ATAH, MALKUTH, VE-GEBURAH, VE GEDULAH, LE-OLAHM, AMEN.**

ALL are seated.

HIEROPHANT goes to west of the Altar, lights the small white votive candle, and gives the Angelic Invocations: **In the most holy and ineffable name of the Tetragramma-**

ton, YOD HEH VAV HEH, and in the quintessential name of the Pentagrammaton, YOD HEH SHIN VAV HEH, I call upon the mighty Archangels of the elements to be in attendance and bestow their health-giving powers to our ceremony. Bless us with your presence! Honor us with your wisdom! Fill us with the Healing Love of the Divine!

O Raphael, Angel of the purest Air. You ride the four winds and create the clouds that wrap the earth, as it were, in a garment. Holy Breath of Life! We call upon you to descend from your abode in the Eastern heavens and breathe into us with your powers of restoration. (Traces the figure of a cross over the fan.)

O Gabriel, Angel of the purest Water. You emerge from the heavens in the purifying rains that fill the Oceans and the Rivers of being. Holy Waters of Life! Sprinkle us with the lustral waters of the loud resounding sea. We call upon you to descend from your abode in the Western heavens and cleanse us with your powers of purification. (Traces the figure of a cross over the oil.)

O Michael, Angel of the purest Fire. You blaze forth from the heavens in that holy and formless fire, that Fire which darts and flashes through the hidden depths of the universe. Holy Fires of Life! We call upon you to descend from your abode in the Southern heavens and purify us with your powers of rejuvenation. (Traces the figure of a cross over the red candle.)

O Uriel, Angel of the purest Earth. You materialize from the heavens to fill the earth with the multifarious forms, urging forth the growth of vegetable matter, crowning the earth with golden harvest and the purple vintage of the vine. Holy Earth of Life! We call upon you to descend from your abode in the Northern heavens and stabilize us with your powers of renewal. (Traces the figure of a cross over the crystal.)

ALL: **Before me, RAPHAEL! Behind me, GABRIEL! On my right hand, MICHAEL! On my left hand, URIEL! For about me flames the Pentagram, and in the column shines the Six-rayed Star!**

HIEROPHANT: **It is written: In the center there is another. The Light. The Mind. The God. But first conceive well the Light in thy mind and know it.**

O Nuriel, Angel of the purest Spirit. You ascend from the Mind of God to connect all things with the illuminating power of the Divine, giving forth Light, Logos, and Love. Holy Spirit of Life! We call upon you to descend from your abode in the celestial heavens and infuse us with your powers of reintegration. (Traces the figure of the Lesser Invoking Pentagram over the fan, oil, candle, crystal, and LED light.)

ALL are seated.

HIEROPHANT: **Let the Aspirant come forward and make their request.**

HEGEMON leads ASPIRANT to the west of the Altar, facing east. ASPIRANT assumes a position of supplication: arms bent at the elbow forward, with palms facing upward. HEGEMON holds the script for ASPIRANT during the following prayer.

ASPIRANT: **Mighty Archangels of the Elements, hear my prayer! I come before Thee in all humility. I am in need of healing. Hear my prayer! My heart is reverent. I am in need of rest and convalesce. Hear my Prayer! I request your presence. I beseech your guidance. Hear my Prayer! Grant me the soothing balm of your healing energy. Free me from illness. Hear my Prayer! Mend my wounds. Soothe my thoughts and dreams. Hear my Prayer! Grant me solace and serenity. Cure what ails me. Hear my Prayer! Cure all ills that trouble me, both seen and unseen.** (Here Aspirant can specify what exact form of healing is needed, if desired.) **Hear my Prayer! O Mighty Archangels of Life and Light, I ask for your restorative powers to permeate the whole of my being and infuse me with good health, peace, and comfort. May your heavenly grace and wisdom beam down upon me and bring me the renewal I seek. This I humbly ask. Amen. Selah. Amen.**

HIEROPHANT knocks ו: **Ask and it will be given to you; seek and you will find; knock and the door will be opened. So mote it be.**

ALL: **So mote it be.**

ALL: **Before me, RAPHAEL! Behind me, GABRIEL! On my right hand, MICHAEL! On my left hand, URIEL! For about me flames the Pentagram, and in the column shines the Six-rayed Star!**

PSALTIS chimes once ℸ.

HEGEMON leads ASPIRANT to the invisible station of Harpokratês, facing west. ASPIRANT is seated. HEGEMON is seated.

HIEREUS goes to stand west of the Altar and says: **Uriel, the First of the Five, spake to the Aspirant and said: I am the Light of God and Archangel of Elemental Earth. I rule over that quarter we name Tzaphon, the North. I am clothed in the colors of Malkuth and I carry sheaves of grain. My symbol is an open hand carrying a flame. I grant protection from natural disasters and I act as a channel between the earth and the Divine. In the body, elemental Earth governs the bones, teeth, joints, musculature, throat, and lower limbs. I support the entire physical body as a unified whole. By what Signs doest thou seek my aid?**

HEGEMON speaking for ASPIRANT: **By the Signs of Prayer and Supplication.**

ASPIRANT brings hands together as if praying and then opens them as if to receive water from a stream.

HIEREUS: **Hear thou the voice of Uriel, the First of the Five: It is written: Visita Interiora Terrae Rectificando Invenies Occultum Lapidem—Visit the interior of the Earth; by rectification thou shalt find the hidden stone.**

There is a Secret Song and a Holy Speech. Let all of Nature entertain the hearing of this Hymn. Be opened, O Earth, and let all the Treasure of the Rain be opened. You Trees tremble not, for I will sing and praise the Lord of the Creation, and the All and the One. Be opened you Heavens, ye Winds stand still, and let the Immortal Circle of God receive these words. For I will sing, and

praise the One that created all things, that fixed the Earth, and hung up the Heavens, and commanded the sweet Water to come out of the Ocean; into all the World inhabited, and not inhabited, to the use and nourishment of all things.[54]

HIEREUS takes up the quartz crystal, walks to the east of the Altar facing the Aspirant, holds the crystal on the crown of the Aspirant's head, and says: **In the name of Uriel, the Light of God, may Adonai nourish thy bones and teeth. May Adonai nourish thy muscles and lower limbs. May Adonai strengthen thy body.**

HIEREUS traces the invoking Triangle of Earth over the ASPIRANT with the crystal and says: **In names of Adonai Ha-Aretz, the Lord of Earth, and Malkah, the Queen of the Kingdom, and in the Sign of the inverted and bifurcated Triangle, Child of Earth, thou art purified. Be thou healed! Hereunto is the Speech of Uriel.**

ALL: **Before me, RAPHAEL! Behind me, GABRIEL! On my right hand, MICHAEL! On my left hand, URIEL! For about me flames the Pentagram, and in the column shines the Six-rayed Star!**

HIEREUS returns to the west of the Altar, replaces the crystal, lights the black candle of Earth on the candelabra, and returns to station.

PSALTIS chimes once ו.

STOLISTES goes to stand west of the Altar and says: **Gabriel, the Second of the Five, spake to the Aspirant and said: I am the Strong One of God and Archangel of Elemental Water. I rule over that quarter we name Mearab, the West. I am clothed in the colors of blue and orange and I carry the Cup of Living Water. I am the Archangel of hope and glad tidings. I am the spirit of Truth and Mercy as well as the angel of revelation. In the human body, elemental Water governs internal fluids, veins and arteries, the stomach, the spleen, the loins, the fluids of reproduction, the hormones, digestion, and elimination. By what Signs doest thou seek my aid?**

---

54. Adapted from "The Secret Song, The Holy Speech," in Everard, *The Divine Pymander*, 63–66.

HEGEMON SPEAKING FOR ASPIRANT: **By the Signs of Devotion and Supplication.** (ASPIRANT makes signs as before.)

STOLISTES: **Hear thou the voice of Gabriel, the Second of the Five: It is written: Why, O Off-spring of the Earth, why have you delivered Yourselves over unto Death, having Power to Partake of Immortality; Repent and Change your Minds, you that have together Walked in Error, and have been Darkened in Ignorance. Depart from that dark Light, be Partakers of Immortality, and Leave or Forsake Corruption. And some of Them That Heard Me, mocking and scorning, went away and delivered themselves up to the way of death. But others, casting themselves down before my feet, besought me that they might be taught; but I, causing them to rise up, became a guide of mankind, teaching them the reasons how and by what means they may be saved. And I sowed in them the words of Wisdom, and nourished them with Ambrosian Water of Immortality.**[55]

STOLISTES takes up the vial of oil and walks to the east of the Altar and anoints ASPIRANT with the oil, tracing a cross on their forehead, then says: **In the name of Gabriel, the Strong One of God, may the Great God El strengthen thy heart, and cleanse and purify thy blood and fluids. May El restore balance to thy hormones and gastric organs.**

STOLISTES traces the invoking Triangle of Water over the ASPIRANT with the vial of oil, then says: **In names of the Mighty El and Elohim Tzabaoth, God of Armies, and in the Sign of the inverted Triangle, Child of Water, thou art purified. Be thou healed! Hereunto is the Speech of Gabriel.**

ALL: **Before me, RAPHAEL! Behind me, GABRIEL! On my right hand, MICHAEL! On my left hand, URIEL! For about me flames the Pentagram, and in the column shines the Six-rayed Star!**

STOLISTES returns to the west of the Altar, replaces the oil, lights the blue candle of Water on the candelabra, and returns to station.

55. Adapted from "The Secret Song, The Holy Speech," in Everard, *The Divine Pymander*, 63–66.

PSALTIS chimes once ˥.

KERYX goes to stand west of the Altar and says: **Raphael, the Third of the Five, spake to the Aspirant and said: I am the Healer of God and Archangel of Elemental Air. I rule over and that quarter we name Mizrach, the East. I am clothed in the colors of yellow and violet and I carry the Caduceus Staff of Hermes. I have the power to heal all wounds and diseases, whether physical, emotional, or spiritual. In the body, elemental Air governs the lungs, the shoulders, respiration, absorption, the nervous system, and mental balance. By what Signs doest thou seek my aid?**

HEGEMON SPEAKING FOR ASPIRANT: **By the Signs of Prayer and Supplication.** (Done.)

KERYX: **Hear thou the voice of Raphael, the Third of the Five: It is written: The Letter *H* is the Letter of Life; because the Letter *H* is our mode of representing the ancient Greek aspirate or breathing, and Breath is the evidence of Life.**

Were it possible for thee to have wings, and to fly into the Air, and being taken up in the midst, between Heaven and Earth, to see the stability of the Earth, the fluidness of the Sea, the courses of the Rivers, the largeness of the Air, the sharpness or swiftness of the Fire, the motion of the Stars; and the speediness of the Heaven, by which it travels about all these.[56] Of the Matter, the most subtle and slender part is Air, of the Air the Soul, of the Soul the Mind, of the Mind God.[57]

KERYX takes up the fan and walks to the east of the Altar and fans the air around the Aspirant, then says: **In the name of Raphael, the Healing One of God, may YHVH breathe healing into thy lungs, calm thy nerves, and mend thy mental wounds and injuries of the mind.**

KERYX traces the invoking Triangle of Air over the Aspirant with the fan, then says: **In the names of YHVH, the Ineffable One, and of Shaddai El Chai, the Almighty**

56. Adapted from "The Secret Song, The Holy Speech," in Everard, *The Divine Pymander*, 63–66.

57. Adapted from "The Secret Song, The Holy Speech," in Everard, *The Divine Pymander*, 63–66.

and Living God, and in the Sign of the upright and bifurcated Triangle, Child of Air, thou art purified. Be thou healed! Hereunto is the Speech of Raphael.

ALL: **Before me, RAPHAEL! Behind me, GABRIEL! On my right hand, MICHAEL! On my left hand, URIEL! For about me flames the Pentagram, and in the column shines the Six-rayed Star!**

KERYX returns to the west of the Altar, replaces the fan, lights the yellow candle of Air on the candelabra, and returns to station.

PSALTIS chimes once ו.

DADOUCHOS goes to stand west of the Altar and says: **Michael, the Fourth of the Five, spake to the Aspirant and said: I am He Who is as God and Archangel of Elemental Fire. I rule over that quarter we name Darom, the South. I am clothed in the colors of red and green and I wield the Sword of Justice. I am the Prince of Light who defends the Just and the Innocent. In the body, elemental Fire governs the head and face, the brain, the heart and the blood, the liver, the hips, the thighs, energy, and vitality. By what Signs doest thou seek my aid?**

HEGEMON speaking for ASPIRANT: **By the Signs of Prayer and Supplication.** (Done.)

DADOUCHOS: **Hear thou the voice of Michael, the Fourth of the Five: It is written: The first mover of nature is External Fire, the Moderator of Internal Fire, and of the whole Work.**

Nature uses Fire, so also does Art after its example, as an Instrument and Mallet in cutting out its works. In both operations therefore Fire is Master and Perfector of Matter. Wherefore the knowledge of Fire is most necessary for a Philosopher, without which he shall turn about the Whorl of Nature to no purpose. Nature acknowledgeth a Threefold Fire: Celestial, Terrestrial, and Innate. The First flows from Sol into the Bosom of the Earth, and is a spur to vegetation. The Second lurketh in the depths of the Earth, wherein it creates metals and changes the composition of the seeds of vegetation, softening and preparing

them for generation. The third Fire, Innate, is also solar yet internal, springing from within matter itself in accordance with the Laws of Nature.[58]

DADOUCHOS takes up the red scented candle and walks to the east of the Altar, moves the candle in circles close to the ASPIRANT, then says: **In the name of Michael, Who is as God, may Elohim protect thy head and heart. May Adonai grant thee abundant energy and vitality.**

DADOUCHOS traces the invoking Triangle of Fire over the ASPIRANT and says: **In the names of Elohim and YHVH Tzabaoth and in the Sign of the upright Triangle, Child of Fire, thou art purified. Be thou healed! Hereunto is the Speech of Michael.**

ALL: **Before me, RAPHAEL! Behind me, GABRIEL! On my right hand, MICHAEL! On my left hand, URIEL! For about me flames the Pentagram, and in the column shines the Six-rayed Star!**

DADOUCHOS returns to the west of the Altar, replaces the scented red candle, lights the red candle of Fire on the candelabra, and returns to station.

PSALTIS chimes once ו.

HIEROPHANT goes to stand west of the Altar and says: **Nuriel, the Fifth of the Five, spake to the Aspirant and said: I am the Light and Fire of the Divine and the Archangel of Elemental Spirit. I rule over that area in space known as Merkaz,**[59] **the Center. I am clothed in the colors of white and royal purple or Argaman.**[60] **I am the Angel of Spell-binding Power and a protector against evil. When descending from the side of Geburah, I manifest as a hailstone, but when issu-**

---

58. From the *Hermetic Arcanum* published in Westcott's *Collectanea Hermetica*.

59. Spelled Mem Resh Kaph Zayin.

60. The name of Nuriel can be found in the acronym of the Hebrew word *argaman*, which means "purple," a color that has long been associated with royalty and with the holy day of Pentecost, commemorating the descent of the Holy Spirit. The word *argaman* is spelled from the Hebrew letters aleph, resh, gimel, mem, and nun, which stand for Uriel (or Auriel–earth), Raphael (air), Gabriel (water), Michael (fire), and Nuriel (spirit)—ARGMN.

ing from the side of Chesed, I take on the form of an Eagle. In the body, Elemental Spirit governs the wholeness of the human organism in body and soul, and rules over the faculty of balance in all things, physical, psychic, and spiritual. By what Signs doest thou seek my aid?

Hegemon speaking for Aspirant: **By the Signs of Prayer and Supplication.** (Done.)

Hiereus: **Hear thou the voice of Nuriel, the Fifth of the Five: It is written: For it is the greatest evil not to know God. But to be able to know and to will, and to hope, is the straight way, and Divine way, proper to the Good; and it will everywhere meet thee, and everywhere be seen of thee, plain and easy, when thou dost not expect or look for it; it will meet thee, waking, sleeping, sailing, travelling, by night, by day, when thou speakest, and when thou keepest silence.**

Whether thou speak of Matter, or Body, or Essence, know that all these are acts of God. And yet thou sayest, God is invisible, but be advised, for who is more manifest than He? For therefore hath he made all things, that thou by all things mayest see him. This is the Good of God, this is his Virtue, to appear, and to be seen in all things. The Mind is seen in Understanding, and God is seen in doing or making.[61]

We live in Power, in Act and in Eternity. Life is the union of the Mind and the Soul. And Man was made of Life and Light into Soul and Mind, of Life the Soul, of Light the Mind. O Communion which is in me, praise the All. By me the Truth sings praise to the Truth, the Good praiseth the Good. O Life, O Light from us, unto you comes this praise and thanksgiving. O Life, save all that is in us: O Light enlighten, O God the Spirit; for the Mind guideth or feedeth the Word; O Spirit bearing Workman.[62]

Thou art God, thy Man crieth these things unto thee through by the Fire, by the Air, by the Earth, by the Water, by the Spirit, by thy Creatures. For there is nothing which is not the Image of God.

---

61. Adapted from "The Secret Song, The Holy Speech," in Everard, *The Divine Pymander*, 91.

62. Adapted from "The Secret Song, The Holy Speech," in Everard, *The Divine Pymander*, 64–65.

HIEROPHANT takes up the LED light and walks to the east of the Altar, holding the light above ASPIRANT's head, then says: **In the name of Nuriel, the Light and Fire of the Divine, may Eheieh nourish, strengthen, purify, protect, and balance thy entire being. May Adonai heal every aspect of thy body, soul, and spirit.**

HIEROPHANT traces a circle clockwise over the ASPIRANT with the light and says: **In the names of Eheieh and Adonai and in the Sign of the Circle, Child of Spirit, thou art purified. Be thou healed! Hereunto is the Speech of Nuriel.**

ALL: **Before me, RAPHAEL! Behind me, GABRIEL! On my right hand, MICHAEL! On my left hand, URIEL! For about me flames the Pentagram, and in the column shines the Six-rayed Star!**

HIEROPHANT replaces the LED light, then lights the white candle of Spirit on the candelabra.

PSALTIS chimes once 1.

HEGEMON says to ASPIRANT: **Accept the gift of healing.** ASPIRANT closes their eyes and remains in a meditative state. HEGEMON quietly moves her chair to the Southeast of the temple.

HEGEMON leads ALL (except for the FIVE) in a soft chant of **Therápefse** (Ther-ah-pef-say), Greek for "(he/she/it) will heal."[63] Keep chanting for the duration of the next section.

The FIVE gather around the seated ASPIRANT in a pentagram formation, arms bent at the elbow, with palms facing forward toward the ASPIRANT.

---

63. Can also be pronounced "ther-ah-pew-say." An alternative Greek chant would be "Oule!" (pronounced "oo-leh," meaning "Be whole!," "Be healthy!," "Be well!," or loosely "Be healed!").

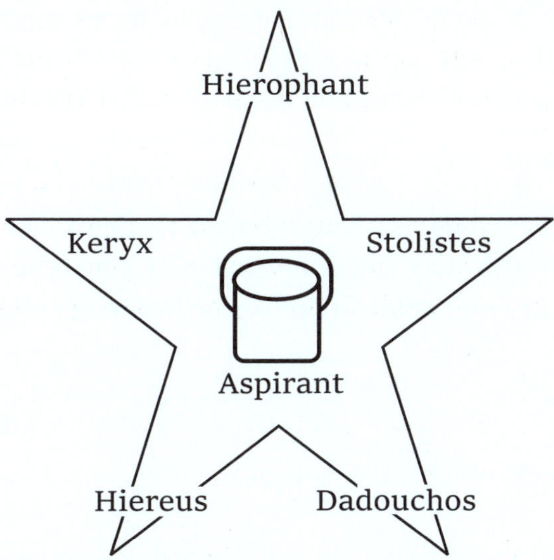

Figure 21: Pentagram Formation of the Five

HIEREUS: **I come in the power of the Light.**
STOLISTES: **I come in the Light of Wisdom.**
KERYX: **I come in the Mercy of the Light.**
DADOUCHOS: **The Light has Healing in its wings.**

HIEROPHANT slowly raises his arms like giant wings and brings his hands down to rest on the Aspirant's shoulders.

PSALTIS chimes five times ᒣᒣᒣᒣᒣ.

The FIVE perform five deep inhalations and exhalations of breath, inhaling through the nose and exhaling through the mouth, with each officer concentrating on their element as they do so.

HIEREUS, STOLISTES, KERYX, and DADOUCHOS return to place and join in the chant. HIEROPHANT remains with hands on Aspirant's shoulders while the chanting continues for a short time.

When HIEROPHANT feels the meditation is at an end, he motions for the chant to stop. HIEROPHANT indicates to Aspirant to remain seated for a while in meditative silence, but when ready, Aspirant should return to her original seat. (Done.)

HIEROPHANT returns to the east and says: **We give thanks and praise to the heavenly powers, and to the mighty archangels of the elements who have graced us with their presence in this holy rite of healing. May your gifts be ours to hold and share and may they ever abide in this sacred hall of the Mysteries. Amen!**

ALL: **AMEN!**

HEGEMON returns her chair to between the pillars.

KERYX removes Aspirant's chair from the station of Harpokratês and resets the Altar for the Closing of the Neophyte Hall.

Any comments, announcements, or temple business may be discussed. Then proceed to closing.

✠ ✠ ✠

MAGICIANS ARE HEALERS, NOT DOCTORS!

Physical illness is a part of the human condition. At some point, many magicians perform healing rituals for themselves or others as an aid to overcome disease. But as we like to say, "The angels help those who help themselves." No responsible magician would think that ritual alone could overcome a serious illness. Healing rites are meant to complement medical science, not replace it. Our work is to overcome the inner causes of illness within the soul and psyche, while letting medical professionals do what they are good at—combating physical illness with physical tools and medicines.

The Flame of the Sacred Heart: A Rite of Planetary Healing

Human beings have had a massive effect on our planet, and often not for the better. Our problems are enormous and the answers are illusive. Today we find ourselves in a world of exploding populations, shrinking resources, conflict, pollution, and climate change. In short, we must change our ways or risk leaving an uninhabitable world for future generations. One small step toward righting these wrongs is to perform a ritual of healing for the Earth itself. How, you might ask, can our little temple hope to put a dent in the Earth's problems with a simple ceremony? The answer: one prayer, one heart, one mind, one invocation, one act of kindness, one positive action, one ritual at a time. It is certainly not an easy task, but it is one we must undertake.

The Flame of the Sacred Heart is a ceremonial healing. It calls upon the Great Mother Goddess Isis, Lady of Magic, to bless and heal the denizens of the Earth and the planet itself.

Isis is the most important and beloved of all Egyptian goddesses. Over time she absorbed the functions and attributes of all the other goddesses combined. Isis is the sister and wife of Osiris, to whom she bore the child Horus. Mother goddess extraordinaire, Isis is often said to be the most powerful magician in the universe, even rivaling the great Thoth. Her many deeds include learning Ra's secret name of power, protecting the infant Horus from the evil Set, and resurrecting Osiris from the dead. Isis is credited with teaching the arts of healing, cloth-weaving, and the magical arts. She rules over marriage, fertility, medicine, weaving, magic, maternity, divination, and protection. The goddess is usually depicted as a woman who wears a throne, the symbol of her name, upon her head. She sometimes appears with wings or wearing the solar disk and lunar crescent.

Synopsis: After the Hierophant announces the ritual's objective, he leads the group through an abbreviated Middle Pillar exercise that emphasizes the importance of the triad. The divine names of Binah are vibrated to orient the working toward the third Sephirah, to which Isis corresponds.

Four Officers invoke the Four Pillars of the Earth, bringing them to life in the temple by tracing the figure of the Ankh, the Egyptian symbol of life, toward the four cardinal directions.

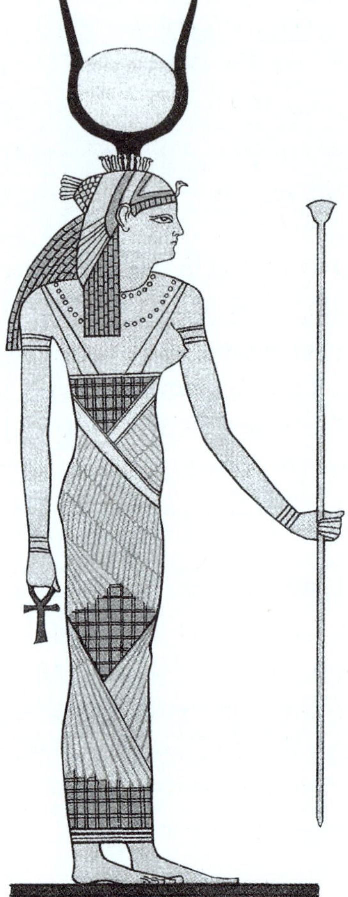

Figure 22: The Goddess Isis

The Hierophant leaves <u>his</u> throne and the Praemonstrator, the Officer most closely affiliated with the Goddess Isis, goes to stand between the Pillars. The main officers begin potent invocations of the goddess as the Praemonstrator takes on the godform of Isis. Praemonstrator makes a cross over the candle and continues with a godform invocation.

The next section involves the cleansing of the elements of the Earth, wherein the Stolistes and Dadouchos purify and consecrate the symbols on the Altar: the elemental symbols, the vessel of transmutation, and the Work of Transmutation. (NOTE: The Work of Transmutation is comprised of a crystal-growing kit that can be purchased online. During the course of the ritual, the crystal-growing solution is mixed, charged, and consecrated with the energies called upon to heal the planet.)

The Praemonstrator continues a potent invocation to heal the Earth. Then the Praemonstrator, aided by the Keryx, mixes the chemicals of the transmutation and sets the vessel of transmutation upon the Seal of Universal Unity. Praemonstrator traces a cross over the Work of Transmutation and continues with a healing invocation before taking off the godform of Isis.

Gifts may be offered to the Divine for the healing of the planet. Finally, the Hierophant leads a brief guided visualization of the planet as it receives healing.

Items needed for the central Altar:

- The Seal of Universal Unity (a laminated diagram—See figure 23)
- A crystal or crystal sphere to represent the Earth
- A white pillar candle in glass to represent the Sacred Heart
- The elements of the Mystic Repast
- A crystal-growing kit and the vessel of transmutation (a small container appropriate for growing crystals)[64]
- A separate side Altar ready in the Southeast
- Prior to the Ritual, each member should bring a small, simple offering (incense, oil, gemstone, grain, written prayer, etc.) to offer up to the Divine for the healing of the Planet and the collective Human soul.

Words of Power for the Flame of the Sacred Heart	
Isis (Eye-sis)	**Iset** (EE-set)
Iset Nef (EE-set Nef)	**Iset Ash** (EE-set Ash)
Iset Mu (EE-set Moo)	**Iset Tah** (EE-set Tah)
Isis Khabhuet (I-sis Ka-boo-ET)	**Isis Thiouis** (I-sis The-oh-OO-is)

Table 4: Words of Power for the Flame of the Sacred Heart

64. Read all instructions that come with the kit thoroughly and become familiar with them prior to the ritual.

Figure 23: The Seal of Universal Unity

Perform the Opening of the Hall of the Neophytes.

KERYX should arrange items on the central Altar as follows: The Seal of Universal Unity should be placed underneath the Cross and Triangle, surrounded by the four Elements of the Mystic Repast. In the center of the Seal should be placed a crystal (or crystal sphere), to represent the planet Earth. A white candle in glass is placed just west of the rose. Also in the center should be a small container (the Vessel of Transmutation) and any items needed for the crystal growing.

HIEROPHANT: (Knocks ו) **Fratres and Sorores of the (______) Temple of the (________) Order of the Golden Dawn in the Outer, we live in a time of critical change. In many nations our fellow human beings are oppressed and abused. War rages while people starve. Animals face extinction through loss of habitat. Our lands, rivers, oceans, and atmosphere are choked with pollution. The world over people are reverting to extreme tribalism and are choosing lies over**

truth, hate over love, violence over charity, and darkness over light. Greed, selfishness, and lust for power threaten future generations. The Earth itself is in danger of climate change.

Fratres and Sorores, we are here assembled in our commitment to the Work of the Divine Theurgy, that we may bring healing to the planet and restore balance to world. Through this ceremony, we seek to take back our roles as caretakers of the Earth. We petition the Divine for strength and courage—for the wisdom to heal, to love one another, and to finally realize peace. We invoke the Power and the Vision to make a more loving, compassionate, thriving, and vibrant world. We invoke the Power and the Vision to restore the integrity of the planet and to build a sustainable future for our children.[65]

May all the work we do here today be for the highest good of all concerned and in strict accordance with Divine Will. For Good alone is Mighty and Truth alone shall prevail. Let us first establish a link with the Higher and Divine Self—that inexhaustible Treasure of Light, to which we aspire unceasingly—that the Powers of the Divine may be reawakened in the spheres of those present and in the Sphere of this Order. For by names and Images are all Powers Awakened and Reawakened.

All close their eyes as the Hierophant leads them through an abbreviated Middle Pillar exercise, using only the Sephiroth of *Kether* (Power Source), *Tiphareth* (Power Outlet), and *Malkuth* (Power Ground). The Hierophant vibrates the Divine Name one time first to establish the vibrational note for the other officers. Then All vibrate the name three times:

Hierophant: **EHEIEH.**
All: **EHEIEH. EHEIEH. EHEIEH.**

Hierophant: **YHVH ELOAH VE-DAATH.**

65. Adapted from Vaspra, "Prayer for the Healing and Care of Our Mother Earth."

ALL: **YHVH ELOAH VE-DAATH.**
YHVH ELOAH VE-DAATH.
YHVH ELOAH VE-DAATH.

HIEROPHANT: **ADONAI HA-ARETZ.**
ALL: **ADONAI HA-ARETZ. ADONAI HA-ARETZ. ADONAI HA-ARETZ.**

HIEROPHANT: **Three Spheres vibrated on the Tree of Life—Kether, Tiphareth, and Malkuth. Source, Center, and Completion. Three is the number of the Supernal Sephiroth—Kether, Chokmah, and Binah. Three is the number of the eternal Triad of Life—that Triune Light that moved upon the face of the Waters—the triangle of the measureless Heavens, reflected in the triangle of the measureless Waters.**

HIEREUS: **Three is the number of the Alchemical Principles, the eternal building blocks of all things within the manifest universe—Salt, Sulphur, and Mercury—which signify the principles of Body, Soul, and Spirit. Three is the number of the alchemical Kingdoms of Nature—animal, vegetable, and mineral. The triangle of the measureless Heavens reflected in the triangle of the Kingdoms of Nature.**

HEGEMON: **Three is the number of the Mother Letters of the Hebrew alphabet—Shin, Aleph, and Mem. Three is the number of the primary colors, and of the most ancient elements of Fire, Air, and Water, symbolized by the three Primary colors of red, yellow, and blue. Three is the number of two opposing forces and one that balances between them. And these three have their image in the Threefold Flame of our Being and in the threefold wave of the sensual world.**

HIEREUS: **Three is the number of the Paths shown on my Lamen of Office, and on the Banner of the West, and three is the number of the points of the Triangle of Manifestation.**

HIEROPHANT: **Three Times Great was Hermes Trismegistos called. Three is the number of Understanding. Three is the number of our Hermetic Work—Purifica-**

tion, Consecration, and Initiation. And three times did the Seraphim of Issiah intone the Trisagion around the throne of God: "Qadesh, Qadesh, Qadesh!—Holy, Holy, Holy!"

ALL stand. HIEROPHANT leads ALL in performance of the Qabalistic Cross:

ATAH, MALKUTH, VE-GEBURAH, VE GEDULAH, LE-OLAHM, AMEN.

HIEROPHANT: **Thus shall we begin the work of healing, purifying, and restoring balance to our Planet and all life which abides thereon. To this end we call upon the Divine forces of the Third Sephirah, Binah, under the personage of the Great Lady Isis, Goddess of Nature, to be present at our ceremony and bless our Work of healing and purification!**

HIEROPHANT leads ALL in vibration of the divine names associated with Binah:

YHVH ELOHIM. YHVH ELOHIM. YHVH ELOHIM.
TZAPHQIEL. TZAPHQIEL. TZAPHQIEL.
ERELIM. ERELIM. ERELIM.

ALL except HIEROPHANT, HIEREUS, STOLISTES, and DADOUCHOS may be seated.

Invoking the Four Pillars of the Earth

HIEROPHANT: **The ancient Gods are all things, and all things are the ancient Gods. Their breath is the Air and the wind. Their Will is the Fire. Their blood is the Water. Their bodies are the celestial stars and the terrestrial Earth. The ancient Gods are all things, and all things are the ancient Gods. All Goddesses are but one Goddess. The God and the Goddess are One. All Gods are but One God. All are One. Yet the One has many names and countenances. In this time and in this place, we call upon the One under the name of ISIS!**

ALL vibrate three times: **ISIS. ISIS. ISIS.**

HIEROPHANT faces east, raises arms, and says: **Hail to you, O Living Breath which fills all things at their birth. You wind from the Wings of Isis, it is you who causes**

the hawk to fly and all creatures to live. O Air, O Invisible Living One. O Breath of the Goddess, I invoke you with this Sign of Life.

HIEROPHANT traces the Ankh while visualizing it in glowing yellow light and then continues: **ISET NEF! Air of Isis! Inspire and protect us by the Holy Power of the Sacred and Living Breath! Live, O Breath of Isis, live for us!**

HIEROPHANT turns to face west.

DADOUCHOS faces south, raises arms, and says: **Hail to you, O Burning Flame, O Fiery Disk, you igniter of the life of all things. You are the heat of work and of passion. You are the Light that destroys evil. O Fire, O Creator, O Destroyer, O Purifier, O energy of the Will of Isis, I invoke you with this sign of Life!**

DADOUCHOS traces Ankh while visualizing it in glowing red light and then continues: **ISET ASH! Fire of Isis! Empassion and enflame us by the Holy Power of the Sacred Fire! Live, O Will of Isis, live for us!**

DADOUCHOS turns to face north.

HIEREUS faces west, raises arms, and says: **Hail to you, O Inundation, O River of Heaven and Earth. You who makes fertile all things. You are the balm from the hands of Isis. You are the purifying waters of the Nile. O Blood of Isis, O Power of Magic, O Living Soul, I invoke you with this sign of Life!**

HIEREUS traces Ankh while visualizing it in glowing blue light and then continues: **ISET MU! Water of Isis! Deepen and renew us by the Holy Power of the Divine Flow. Live, O Blood of Isis, live for us!**

HIEREUS turns to face east.

STOLISTES faces north, raises arms, and says: **Hail to you, O Mass of Creation! You who did rise from out of the watery Nu wherein was Nothing before your Becoming.**

By you are all things manifested and sustained. O Earth, O Mother, O Body of the Universe, I invoke you with this Sign of Life.

STOLISTES traces Ankh while visualizing it in glowing green light and then continues: **ISET TA! Earth of Isis! Strengthen and uphold us by the Holy Power of the Earth. Live, O Body of Isis, live for us!**

STOLISTES turns to face south.

ALL vibrate: **ISET. ISET. ISET.**

Invocation of Isis

HIEROPHANT goes to the West of the Altar, facing East, and lights the white candle.
HEGEMON moves their chair from between the pillars and stands off to the Southeast.
PRAEMONSTRATOR descends to stand between the Pillars.
STOLISTES and DADOUCHOS are seated.
KERYX goes to his heraldic station in the Northeast (balancing the Hegemon).

HIEROPHANT traces the figure of the Ankh toward the East and says: **Lady of the Stars who dwellest in the Night to which no man can approach, wherein is Mystery and Depth unthinkable. We beseech Thee in thy Holy name of Isis to grant thine aid unto the highest aspiration of our souls, and clothe us with thy Wisdom and Understanding. O Celestial Goddess of the Heavens and the Earth! High Priestess of the Silver Star! Live!**

Divine Light that shineth in the Darkness! Thou springest from the Sun of splendor, shrouded from all. Come and dwell within our hearts! Crowned with Star-light and clothed with the Sun. Thou who art the Spirit of the Waters of Life, for thy righteousness and love are the foundation of the universe. Be here now!

We invoke Thee, O thou Great Goddess of Nature who clothest thyself with the forces of Life as with a garment. O thou who art Isis, the High Priestess of the Silver Star—the perfect purity of the Supernal Light. Lift us up and grant unto us an unshakable link to all those Powers of Love and Understanding which

rise rank upon rank to the feet of the Holy One. Grant that the Wisdom and Light of the Divine Ones may descend and manifest unto us True holiness and unsullied vision of the Light.

KERYX: **And I beheld a great wonder in Heaven. A woman clothed with the Sun, with the Moon at her feet, and on her head was the diadem of the Twelve Stars. O thou Queen of Love and Mercy, thou crowned with the Throne, horned as the Moon, whose countenance is mild and glowing, hear us, O Isis, hear and bestow.**

HEGEMON: **Thou who art in matter manifest, Mother, Queen, and Daughter of the Justified One, we invoke thee. O Virgin Glory of the Godhead unspeakable, immortal Queen of the Gods, we invoke Thee, O Isis. By the Lotus, by the sacred flower of thy Life, we invoke thee! We who dwell in the vast Hall of living death, crying as thy child Horus toward the Golden Dawn. O Isis!**

KERYX: **Bid us awake, O Mother, from the darkness of this man-made tomb, that each of us may, as the living Osiris, be blessed! O Isis, thou Khemetic form of the Holy Spirit and the Divine Shekinah, from the marble halls of life, the immeasurable deep, the sea of sacred love, we invoke thee! O Isis, descend from thy Palace of the Stars.**

HEGEMON: **O Mother. O Archetype Eternal of Maternity and Love. O Mother, the flower of all Mothers, whose voice all Amenti heareth. Speak unto us of Truth and Vision. Lift us up from the chaos and the evil, from the world of illusory goals and useless pursuits. O Isis, great queen of Heaven, supernal splendor which dwellest in that Light to which no man may approach! Lift us up and make open the Gates of Bliss.**

HIEROPHANT: **Hail unto Thee, O Mighty Mother. Isis! Unveil thy Mystery, O Soul of Nature, giving life and energy to the Universe. From thee all things do proceed and unto thee all things must return. Accept our prayers, Bright Maiden. Lead us to the Truth and guide all our wanderings in darkness as we travel upwards to the Light of the Eternal Crown. Come forth, O gracious Mother. Come unto**

us and dwell within our hearts. O Goddess crowned with starlight, who shineth amongst the Lords of Truth, whose place is in the abode of the Light of Heaven! Lady, live for us!

We ask Thee, Isis, to come. Bless us and bless this temple, this Order, this race of humanity, this planet. The inheritors of a dying world beseech thine aid. We pray for Planet Earth, and the holy terrestrial essence of Gaia and all creatures living above, on, or below her surface. We pray for healing on all levels and a return to balance, beauty, happiness, and peace. We pray for the purity of the Celestial Fire to cleanse the air, the land, and the waters—the hardened arteries of the ravished Earth. Grant us, O Isis, the Celestial Flame of the Sacred Heart, to provide warmth and comfort to all creatures in need, and to melt the cold and hardened hearts of those have forgotten the paradise from whence they came.

All vibrate: **ISET. ISET. ISET.**

Praemonstrator invokes the Godform of Isis and says: **With the Sign of Life, we call upon Isis the Giver of Life, Isis the Ever-Living, Isis Great of Love. We ask Thee, Isis, to come. Bless us and bless this temple, this Order, this race of humanity, this planet. The inheritors of a dying world beseech thine aid. O Isis, come now to Thy Prophetess. O Lady of All, come and dwell with me. Thou Who art the Living Spirit, Mind, Soul, and Body of All Things, come to this, Thy temple, and to this, Thy Prophetess. Let me take on Thy form, Thou Goddess. Isis the Great, I ask Thee: Let me know Thee and speak for Thee!** (Pause.)

Praemonstrator in the godform of Isis says: **Be still thy mind. Make thee One with the Source of Life. Be thy heart a center of the Light.**

Keryx and Hegemon return to their stations.
Hierophant returns to his Throne.
Praemonstrator goes clockwise to the West of the Altar, facing East.

Praemonstrator: **At the ends of the Universe is a cord that ties death to life, man to woman, will to destiny. We awake as from a dream. Is the hand that soothes us**

that of a mother or priestess? We rise and we walk. The sky arcs ever around, the world spreads itself beneath our feet. We are bound mind to Mind, heart to Heart—no difference arises between the shadow of our footsteps and the will of the Divine. We walk in harmony, heaven in one hand and earth in the other. We are the knot tied where the two worlds meet. Magic courses through us like the blood of Isis, magic of magic, spirit of spirit. We awake as from a dream. Our hearts open, filled with Light—the brilliant Flame of the Sacred Heart.[66]

PRAEMONSTRATOR places left hand over her heart and traces a Cross ✚ over the central white candle, then says: **And Isis said, I am She Who is the Only One, Isis Thiouis, the Great One Who Initiated Existence. I am Isis Khabhuet, the Great Watery Abyss. I am the Libationess Who pours forth Her Blessings from Beyond, the Spirit Who—from the Beginning—is, was, and ever shall be.**

With what shall I offer to heal the World, but that which is only mine to give? I am Isis. This is my heart. This is the fire of the Sacred Heart, the purifying flame and the Celestial spark of Life and Light. In my heart, I am. In my heart, I exist. In my heart, I live.

My heart is that place where, entering within, one journeys to Most Self—and then transcends Self, becoming No Self and All Self. I am the Gateway of becoming. I am the pure drop of dew. I am the ultimate root of all things and the foundation of the Universe. My heart is a heart of Love. My womb is the boundless sea. My bones are the mountains at the top of the world. My feet are the roots of the Tree of Life. My blood is the sap of the fruitful plants. My tears are a healing balm that soothes the soul. My children are all creatures living above, on, or below the surface of the Earth. My heart is a heart of Love. Blessed is the Flame of my Sacred Heart, which restores the health and harmony of every living Being on all planes of existence. I am the incoming Celestial Fire of Love.

PRAEMONSTRATOR remains west of the Altar, holding the white candle.

---

66. Portions of this have been adapted from Ellis, *Awakening Osiris*, 180, 207–8.

The Cleansing of the Elements of the Earth

Hierophant speaking from the East: **(Frater/Soror) Stolistes, bring forth the Lustral Waters of Creation, to purify the elements of the Earth.**

Stolistes walks straight up to the North side of the Altar and with the Stolistes Cup traces a Cross ✚ over each of the elements in turn: the rose, the red Candle, the Cup of Wine, Bread and Salt, the crystal of Earth, the vessel of transmutation, and the Work of Transmutation. Stolistes then raises the Cup and says:

> **In the name of Isis and of the Flame of the Sacred Heart, who works in Love and Light, I purify these Elements of Earth with the Life-giving Waters, purifying and cleansing all that is polluted, diseased, imbalanced, and unhealthy; making clear the way for the incoming purity of the Divine!**

Stolistes returns to place.

Hierophant speaks from the East: **(Frater/Soror) Dadouchos, bring forth the Terrestrial Fire, to consecrate the elements of the Earth.**

Dadouchos walks straight up to the South side of the Altar and with the Censer traces a Cross ✚ over each of the elements in turn: the rose, the red Candle, the Cup of Wine, Bread and Salt, the crystal of Earth, the vessel of transmutation, and the Work of Transmutation. Dadouchos then raises the censer and says:

> **In the name of Isis and of the Flame of the Sacred Heart, who works in Love and Light, I consecrate these Elements of Earth with the Terrestrial Fire, purifying and cleansing all that is polluted, diseased, imbalanced, and unhealthy; making clear the way for the incoming purity of the Divine!**

Dadouchos returns to place.

Praemonstrator places left hand over her heart and with the White Candle traces a Cross ✚ over the rose, the red Candle, the Cup of Wine, Bread and Salt, the crystal of Earth, the vessel of transmutation, and the Work of Transmutation.

PRAEMONSTRATOR: **And Isis said, I am She Who is the Throne itself—the One upon Whom you rest and Whose Presence rests always with you. I am the Breath, the Life, the Blood, and the Flesh. I am the manifestor in matter, the seat and Mother of all blessings.**

Spirit joined to spirit; Mind joined to mind; Soul joined to soul; Body joined to body. Thus is Magic joined to magic. Isis is with me—and with us all. My heart is a heart of Love. The Flame of the Sacred Heart is a Celestial Fire—that Holy and Formless Fire which darts and flashes through the Hidden Depths of the Universe!

O Elements and Inhabitants of Earth, hear thou the Voice of Isis! Be without evil! Be without hate! Be without pollution! Be without war! Be without hunger! Be without imbalance!

O Elements and Inhabitants of Earth, receive now the blessings of Isis! Be healed! Be cleansed! Be purified! Be consecrated! Be liberated! Be vitalized! Be restored! Be balanced! Be joyous! Be enlightened! Be at peace! Be at One!

By the magic of Isis, it is so. By the love of Isis, so mote it be!

The Work of Transmutation

ALL vibrate: **ISET. ISET. ISET.**

ALL keep vibrating several times while the transmutation (the crystal-growing kit) is set up.

PRAEMONSTRATOR, aided by the KERYX or another member who has had experience with creating the crystals, mixes the necessary chemicals and places the contained mixture on the center of the Seal of Universal Unity.

After the transmutation is set up, the KERYX returns to place.

ALL stop vibrating.

Praemonstrator places left hand over heart. With the White Candle she traces a Cross ✚ over the Work of Transmutation and says:

> **Spirit joined to spirit; Mind joined to mind; Soul joined to soul; Body joined to body. Thus is Magic joined to magic. Isis is with me—and with us all. My heart is a heart of Love. The Flame of the Sacred Heart is a Celestial Fire—that Holy and Formless Fire which darts and flashes through the Hidden Depths of the Universe!**
>
> **O Work of Transmutation, hear thou the Voice of Isis! Encapsulate the blessings of the Celestial Fire! Transform into a true talisman and vessel of Love! Manifest our invocation into crystalline forms! Embody the blessings of Isis, so that through meditation upon these consecrated talismans, we may manifest those blessings to Planet Earth, to the holy terrestrial essence of Gaia and all creatures living above, on, or below her surface. We pray for healing on all levels and a return to balance, beauty, happiness, and peace.**
>
> **O Work of Transmutation, receive now the blessings of Isis! Be healed! Be cleansed! Be purified! Be consecrated! Be liberated! Be vitalized! Be restored! Be balanced! Be joyous! Be enlightened! Be at peace! Be at One! By the magic of Isis, it is so. By the love of Isis, so mote it be!**

HIEROPHANT: **The Blessings of Isis are upon us, and upon our Work this day. We give thanks to Thee, O Isis, thou Great Goddess, Mighty Mother, Priestess of the Silver Star. For your wisdom, O Isis, we give thanks. For your blessings, Bright Maiden, we thank thee. Our hearts open, the door, the way. Our senses are radiant. Words of Truth flow over us. We know the silver song of day. We hear the name of Light. We shine as the points of stars in the ubiquitous heart of the Divine.**[67]

PRAEMONSTRATOR takes off the Godform of Isis and is seated.

HEGEMON moves their throne back between the Pillars.

---

67. Adapted from Ellis, *Awakening Osiris*, 140, 164–65.

ALL are seated.

HIEROPHANT directs any member who has brought a simple gift to offer up to the Divine for the healing of the Planet and the collective Human soul to approach the central Altar, place their gift on the Seal of Universal Unity, and offer a short, silent prayer. (This should be done in the usual order, starting with the officers.)

Guided Visualization

HIEROPHANT leads a brief guided visualization. The exact form of the visualization is left up to the HIEROPHANT, but it should focus on imagery wherein each member connects himself or herself to the Earth crystal on the Altar. EACH MEMBER should visualize our planet being completely purified and raised to an entirely new level in its spiritual evolution.

At the end of the visualization, HIEROPHANT directs KERYX to move the Seal of Universal Unity, the Flame of the Sacred Heart, the Earth Crystal, and the Work of Transmutation to a separate side Altar in the Southeast. (STOLISTES and DADOUCHOS may help if KERYX requests it.)

KERYX makes sure that the Mystic Repast is properly arranged on the central Altar, then returns to place.

At this point, the HIEROPHANT thanks the members and makes any necessary announcements before proceeding with the regular Closing of the Neophyte Hall and the Mystic Repast.

Proceed to the Closing of the Neophyte Hall.

✠ ✠ ✠

Rites of Passage

Rites of passage are important rituals that underscore significant transitions in a person's life within the framework of their community or religion. The Golden Dawn is not a religion, and while religious symbolism and concepts play an important role in the Order's teachings, rites of passage are not traditionally a part of the system. Ceremonies of initiation, particularly the Neophyte Ritual, correspond to a spiritual rebirth and are the closest equivalent to a rite of baptism in the Golden Dawn system. Advancement ceremonies from one grade to the next can be likened to "coming of age" rituals within a magical context. Nevertheless, these cannot be considered true rites of passage because their primary purpose is not to celebrate an important life stage of a child or a youth, but rather to advance an Initiate to a higher level of learning and spiritual education. Many Golden Dawn practitioners do perform one true rite of passage, however—a ritual requiem. The word *requiem* comes from the Latin *requies*, meaning "rest," and indicates a service for the deceased. It comes from the Catholic Mass for the Dead, which is spoken or sung in Latin.

A requiem ritual is the final rite of passage for a member of a temple or Order. Designed to celebrate the life and accomplishments of a Frater or Soror who has passed beyond the veil, requiem ceremonies also serve to help the group cope with the loss of a magical companion. For the participants, it offers emotional and psychological support. In addition, it supplies a framework that recognizes death as part of the inherent life cycle of the universe; the wheel of life, death, and rebirth, wherein we acknowledge this transitional step in our evolutionary journey back to the Source of All.

One of the earliest Golden Dawn requiems was written by Israel Regardie and included in his book *The Golden Dawn*. That ritual was written for use by a single Adept and was based upon many Inner Order techniques.

A Requiem Rite

The Requiem Rite given here is for use by the members of the Outer Order temple to mark the passing of a fellow Initiate on the Path of Light. It employs the energies and forces of Binah to bless the deceased's journey.

Binah is the third Sephirah and the sphere of divine understanding. Although wisdom is the quality of Chokmah, understanding is assigned to Binah. Wisdom alludes to complete and infinite knowledge, while understanding imparts the notion of an ability to grasp the ideas that are intrinsic to wisdom. The understanding of Binah is the divine understanding of what difficulties and hardships have to teach us in life. The Qabalistic text known as the *Sefer Yetzirah* tells us that Binah is still in a sanctified or blessed state because it remains above the abyss in an unmanifest condition. Sanctification expresses the idea of that which is holy and set apart. This Sephirah is given the title "Primordial Wisdom" because it is the primary source of organization at this stage of divine emanation where a distinct polarity has been defined on the Tree of Life. Binah is also referred to as the "Creator of Faith." Faith rests upon understanding, whose parent is Binah. Faith is also defined as belief and veneration, but in the light of mystical consciousness, faith can be defined as the conscious result of superconscious experience.

Binah is the great organizer and form-builder of the universe. It takes the raw energy from the second Sephirah, Chokmah, and begins to organize it into form. This is the sphere of patience, limitation, time, and creation. Binah is said to be the great archetypal feminine or maternal force of the universe. Saturn, the planet of time, limitation, restriction, age, significant life events, and life lessons, is attributed to this Sephirah. Binah completes the triad of the Supernals, and is the first of the Supernals that any Initiate scaling the Tree of Life would see when passing through the Abyss.

The ritual provided is for a group working in a temple of the Outer Order. The rite calls for the Dais Adepts to perform the Adept-level workings. However, their duties can be performed by the Hierophant alone if need be.

Components of this ritual were adapted from the Equinox Ceremony as well as Regardie's Requiem.

Synopsis: After the Opening of the Neophyte Hall, the Hierophant makes a statement of intention. The Hegemon places a photo of the deceased on the central altar. The Lord of the Universe is invoked to lend aid to the Ritual.

The Praemonstrator traces the Greater Invoking Hexagram of the Supernals. The powers of the Sephirah Binah and the planet Saturn are called upon to assist the ceremony and bring peace and rest to the deceased.

The Imperator traces the Greater Invoking Hexagram of Saturn and appeals to the powers of Saturn to further aid the deceased, who is visualized as standing in the East of the Temple between the two pillars.

The three Dais Adepts form a triangle around the Altar. The Cancellarius traces Spirit Pentagrams over the elements and the photo. The Divine Light of Kether is strongly invoked and everyone visualizes this light descending upon the image of the deceased.

The Three Adepts push the Light with one circumambulation around the Hall. The image of the deceased is visualized as having passed the Eastern Veil. All project three times to seal the image. The Spirit Pentagrams are retraced over the elements and photo.

The Hierophant leads everyone in reciting the Prayer of the Sylphs, or Air Spirits, from the Theoricus Ceremony. Then Hierophant seals the image in the east with the figure of the Circled Cross, and a final invocation prayer is given.

Officers needed:

- The Regular Officers of the Outer Order
- The Psaltis who rings a bell or chime at regular intervals

Additional Items needed:

- A photo of the deceased (preferably in ritual regalia) or some magical item or symbol used by or belonging to the deceased

✠ ✠ ✠

Group Requiem Rite

By Jayne Gibson, OZ, and Chic and Tabatha Cicero

Perform the Opening of the Hall of the Neophytes.

The Work may commence.

HIEROPHANT: (Knocks— ו) **Fratres and Sorores of the (______) Temple of the (________) Order of the Golden Dawn in the Outer, we are here assembled in our commitment to the work of the divine theurgy, and to mark the passing of beloved (Frater/Soror** *name and magical motto***). We honor our magical companion and cherish the memory of their life. We ask the blessings of Deity to look with favor on our ceremony, and grant eternal life and peace upon our (Frater/Soror). Make clear the celestial pathway before them, and ease their transition into the higher realms of Being. And grant that we who celebrate our (brother/sister) today are healed within our hearts; that our sorrows will subside over time as we remember our companion with fondness and affection. Until such time as we are joined together within the Light Divine. Grant that through this ceremony, we may be better able to understand the true nature of the magical art and be better equipped to carry out the Great Work, to the glory of the Ineffable name.** (Pause.)

PSALTIS rings the bell once ו.

HIEROPHANT: **Cleansed and purified through suffering, like the Great Ones hast thou known tribulation. These have been but the purification of the gold. In the alembic of Thine heart, through the Athanor of Aspiration, seek thou the true Stone of the Wise.**

HEGEMON goes to stand at West of Altar, facing East. HEGEMON brings a photograph or symbol of the deceased, places it within the triangle on the altar, then returns to place.

HIEROPHANT: **As above**

HIEREUS: **So below**

HEGEMON: **As in life**

KERYX: **So in death**

STOLISTES: **As in joy**

DADOUCHOS: **So in sadness**

HIEROPHANT: **One creator**

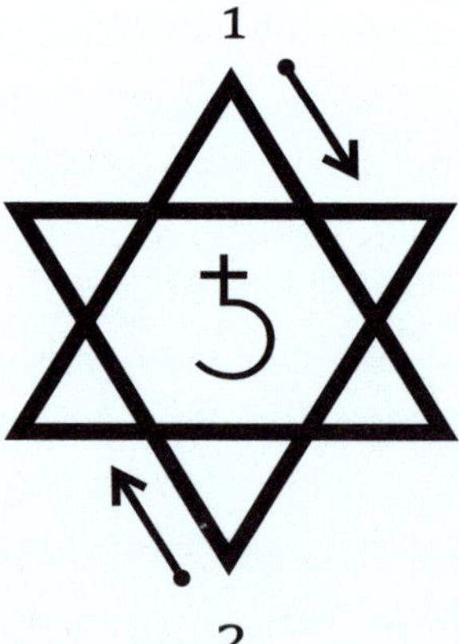

Figure 24: Greater Invoking Hexagram of the Supernals

HIEREUS: **One preserver**

HEGEMON: **One destroyer**

KERYX: **One redeemer**

STOLISTES: **One incarnation**

DADOUCHOS: **One dis-incarnation**

HEGEMON: (Knocks ן) **One reconciler between them**

PSALTIS rings the bell slowly, three times ןןן.

HIEROPHANT: **O Lord of the Universe, Thou Vast and Mighty One, Ruler of the Light and of the Darkness, We adore Thee and We invoke Thee. Look with favor upon us who are now before thee, and grant thine aid unto the highest aspirations of our souls, to the glory of Thy Ineffable Name.**

ALL: (Vibrate) **Amen.**
PRAEMONSTRATOR stands before the Dais facing East and traces the Greater Invoking Hexagram of the Supernals, then returns to place.

HIEROPHANT: **EHEIEH—Spiral of Sanctity, Bond of all Natures.**
HIEREUS: **YHVH—Life of the Lives of All Beings, Father of All.**
HEGEMON: **YHVH ELOHIM—House of the Spirit, Mother of the Soul.**

HIEROPHANT: **Supernal Splendor, which dwellest in the Light to which no human can approach, wherein is Mystery and depth Unthinkable, and awful Silence. I beseech Thee who art Shekinah and Aima Elohim, to look down upon us in this Ceremony which we perform to Thine Honour, and for the assistance of those who have passed through the Veil. Grant Thine aid unto the Highest aspirations of our Souls, in Thy Divine Name YHVH ELOHIM by which Thou dost reveal Thyself as the Perfection of Creation and the Light of the World to Come.**

HIEREUS: **We implore Thee to grant unto us the Presence of Thine Archangel TZAPHQIEL. O Tzaphqiel, Thou Prince of Spirit Initiation through suffering and of strife against evil, aid us to transcend the evil that is in us, so that we may be enabled to perform a higher and divine work.**

HEGEMON: **O ye strong and Mighty Ones of the Sphere of Shabbathai. O ye Erelim, we call Thee by the Mighty Name YHVH ELOHIM, the Divine Ruler of Thy Realm, and by the Name of Tzaphqiel, Thine Archangel.**

Grant unto us the Power of the Spirit to bring the brilliance of the eternal splendor to those who have now entered the invisible. Lift us so that we may be made divine messengers bearing the peace and harmony of higher spheres to (Frater/Soror *magical motto*), whose death to this earthly plane we do now commemorate. Wherever they may now be, and on whatever plane they may now pursue their ideal, let them be blessed with a divine rest and utter cessation from strife.

ALL: **So Mote it Be!**

PSALTIS rings the bell slowly, three times ווו.

IMPERATOR stands before the Dais facing East and traces the *Greater Invoking Hexagram of Saturn*[68] toward the East, with Saturn sigil in center.

IMPERATOR: **Term of all that liveth, whose Name is Death and Whose Being is incomprehensible, be Thou favorable unto us in Thine Hour. And unto them, from whose mortal eyes the Veil of physical life hath fallen, grant that there may be the accomplishment of their True Will and Divine Purpose. Should they will absorption into the Infinite, or to be united with their chosen and preferred, or to be in contemplation, or to be at peace, or to achieve the labor and heroism of incarnation on this planet or another, or in any star, or ought else, unto them may there be granted the accomplishment of their True Will and Divine Purpose.**

---

68. This is identical in form to the Supernal Hexagram in figure 24 on page 180.

PRAEMONSTRATOR goes to the South of the Altar. IMPERATOR goes to the North of the Altar. CANCELLARIUS goes to the West of the Altar.

ALL visualize the deceased at the East, facing West.

CANCELLARIUS makes all the Spirit Pentagrams over the Elements.[69]

CANCELLARIUS: **I invoke Thee by the Divine Name IAO, Thou Great Angel HRU, who art set over the operations of the Secret Wisdom. Strengthen and establish (Frater/Soror *magical motto*) in their search for the Divine Light. Increase their spiritual perception so that they may accomplish their True Will and Divine Purpose, and that thus they may be enabled to rise beyond that lower self-hood which became as nothing unto that highest self-hood which is the Clear Light of the Spirit.**

ALL perform the Qabalistic Cross.

PRAEMONSTRATOR: **For Osiris Onnophris, who has been found perfect before the Gods, hath said: These are the elements of my body, perfected through suffering, glorified through trial. The scent of the dying Rose is as the repressed sigh of my suffering. And the flame red Fire as the energy of mine undaunted Will. And the Cup of Wine is the pouring out of the blood of my heart, sacrificed unto regeneration, unto the new life. And the bread and salt are as the foundations of my body, which I destroy in order that they may be renewed.**

IMPERATOR: **For I am Osiris Triumphant, even Osiris Onnophris the Justified. I am He who is clothed in the body of flesh yet in whom flames the spirit of the eternal Gods. I am the Lord of Life. I am triumphant over Death, and whosoever partaketh with me shall arise with me. I am the manifester in Matter of those Whose above is in the Invisible. I am purified. I stand upon the Universe. I am its Reconciler with the eternal Gods. I am the Perfector of Matter, and without me the Universe is not.**

---

69. Two Invoking Spirit Active Pentagrams (EXARP and BITOM) and two Invoking Spirit Passive Pentagrams (HCOMA, and NANTA). See Ciceros, *Golden Dawn Magic*, 228–30.

ALL visualize Kether brightly in the crown center.

CANCELLARIUS: **Buried with that Light in a mystical death, rising again in a mystical resurrection, cleansed and purified through Him our Master, O thou dweller of the invisible. Like Him, thou pilgrims of the ages, hast thou toiled. Like Him hast thou suffered tribulation. Poverty, torture, and death hast thou passed through. They have been but the purification of the gold. In the alembic of thine heart, through the Athanor of Affliction, seek thou the True Stone of the Wise.**

HIEROPHANT: **Come in peace, O beautiful and Divine One, to a body glorified and perfected. Herald of the Gods, knowing his speech among the living! Pass thou through every region of the invisible unto the place wherein Thy Genius dwelleth, because thou comest in peace, provided with Thy Wealth. Dwell thou in that sacred land that far-off travelers call naught. O land beyond honey and spice and all perfection! Dwell therein with Thy Lord Adonai forever.**

ALL turn and face the West and raise their eyes to the heavens.

PRAEMONSTRATOR: **O Lord of the Universe, the vast and the mighty One, Ruler of the Light and the Darkness, we adore Thee and we invoke Thee. Look Thou with favor upon this pilgrim, who is now before Thee, and grant Thine aid unto the highest aspiration of their soul, to the glory of the ineffable Name.**

HEGEMON moves her chair from between the pillars.

ALL turn and face as usual. Visualize the deceased between the Pillars and see the brilliance descend upon this image.

HIEROPHANT: **I come in the Power of the Light, I come in the Light of Wisdom, I come in the Mercy of the Light, the Light hath healing in its Wings. (Frater/ Soror *magical motto*), I tell thee that as the Light can manifest from the darkness so by these rites shall the Light descend unto thee. Long hast thou dwelt in the Darkness. Quit the Night and Darkness and seek the Light.**

ALL visualize the deceased now completely engulfed in the Light of the Divine.

KERYX: (Gives the 0=0 Signs) **The Light Shines upon you.**
HIEREUS: (Gives the 0=0 Signs) **The Light Embraces you.**
HEGEMON: (Gives the 0=0 Signs) **The Light Welcomes you.**
HIEROPHANT: (Gives the 0=0 Signs) **The Light Hath Healing in its wings.**
STOLISTES: (Gives the 0=0 Signs) **The Light Shines upon you.**
DADOUCHOS: (Gives the 0=0 Signs) **The Light Embraces you.**
PHYLAX: (Gives the 0=0 Signs) **The Light Welcomes you.**
HIEROPHANT: (Gives the 0=0 Signs) **The Light Hath Healing in its wings.**
PRAEMONSTRATOR: (Gives the 0=0 Signs) **The Light Shines upon you.**
IMPERATOR: (Gives the 0=0 Signs) **The Light Embraces you.**
CANCELLARIUS: (Gives the 0=0 Signs) **The Light Welcomes you.**
HIEROPHANT: (Gives the 0=0 Signs) **The Light Hath Healing in its wings.**

HIEROPHANT: **With One Voice!**

ALL: **The Light Shines upon you.** (All give the Projection Sign.)
The Light Embraces you. (All give the Projection Sign.)
The Light Welcomes you. (All give the Projection Sign.)
The Light Hath Healing in its wings. (All make Sign of Silence.)

PSALTIS rings the bell slowly three times ווו.

PRAEMONSTRATOR: **I am the Resurrection and the Life. Whosoever believeth in me though they were dead, yet shall they live, and whosoever liveth and believeth in me shall never die. I am the First and the Last. I am He that liveth and was dead, and behold I am alive forever more and hold the keys of death and of hell. For I know that my Redeemer liveth, and that He shall stand at the latter day upon the earth. I am the Way, the truth, and the Life. No one cometh unto the Father but by me. I am the Purified. I have passed through the Gates of Darkness unto Light. I have fought upon the earth for good, and I have finished my work. I have entered the invisible.**

ALL VIBRATE: **YEHESHUAH. YEHESHUAH. YEHESHUAH.**

The DAIS OFFICERS circumambulate the Hall once and then return to the Altar: PRAEMONSTRATOR to South, IMPERATOR to North, CANCELLARIUS to West.

IMPERATOR: **I am the Sun in his rising, passed through the hour of cloud and of night. I am Amoun the concealed one, the Opener of the day. I am Osiris Onnophris the Justified, Lord of Life, Triumphant over Death. There is no part of me that is not of the Gods. I am the preparer of the pathway, the rescuer unto the Light. Out of the darkness, let that Light arise.**

CANCELLARIUS: **I am the Reconciler with the Ineffable, the dweller of the invisible.**

ALL turn and face East. Visualize the deceased now standing beyond the Veil in the East.

HIEROPHANT: **Whoever thou art in reality, and wheresoever thou now mayest be, by the power of the Spirit devolving upon us by this ceremony, we do project unto thee this ray of the Divine White Brilliance that it may bring thee peace and happiness and rest.**

ALL make the Sign of the Enterer to the East three times. Then give one Sign of Silence at the end.

CANCELLARIUS: **May thy mind be opened unto the Higher.** (Projection Sign)
IMPERATOR: **May thy heart be a center of the Light.** (Projection Sign)

PRAEMONSTRATOR: **May thy body, whatsoever its nature, be a Temple of the Holy Spirit.** (Projection Sign)

ALL give the Sign of Silence.
ALL pause and then make Qabalistic Cross.

IMPERATOR: **Unto Thee sole wise, sole Eternal, and Sole Merciful One be the praise and the glory forever, who has permitted (Frater/Soror** *magical motto***) who now**

standeth invisibly and humbly before Thee to enter into the sanctuary of Thy Mystery. Not unto us but unto Thy Name be the glory.

Praemonstrator: **Let the influence of Thy Divine Ones descend upon their head, and teach them the value of self-sacrifice so that they shrink not in their hour of trial. But that thus their name may be written upon high and their Genius stand in the presence of the Holy Ones, in that hour when the Son of Man is invoked before the Lord of Spirits and His name in the presence of the Ancient of Days.**

Cancellarius again draws all Spirit Invoking Pentagrams over the elements.

Psaltis rings the bell slowly three times 111.

Hierophant: **Let us Rehearse the Prayer of the Sylphs.**

All (facing East): **Spirit of Life! Spirit of Wisdom! Whose breath giveth forth and withdraweth the form of all things. Thou before Whom the life of beings is but a shadow which changeth, and a vapor which passeth. Thou who mountest upon the clouds, and who walkest upon the Wings of the Wind. Thou who breathest forth Thy Breath, and endless space is peopled.**

Thou drawest in Thy Breath and all that cometh from Thee returneth unto Thee! Ceaseless Motion, in Eternal stability, be Thou eternally blessed! We praise Thee and we bless Thee in the Changeless Empire of Created Light, of Shades, of Reflections, and of Images.

And we aspire without cessation unto Thy Immutable and Imperishable Brilliance. Let the Ray of Thy Intelligence and the warmth of Thy Love penetrate even unto us! Then that which is volatile shall be fixed; the Shadow shall be a Body; the Spirit of Air shall be a soul; the Dream shall be a Thought. And no more shall we be swept away by the Tempest, but we shall hold the bridles of the Winged Steeds of Dawn. And we shall direct the course of the Evening Breeze to fly before Thee!

O Spirit of Spirits! O Eternal Soul of Souls! O Imperishable Breath of Life! O Creative Sigh! O Mouth which breathest forth and withdrawest the life of all beings, in the flux and reflux of Thine Eternal Word, which is the Divine Ocean of Movement and of Truth!

HIEROPHANT motions with Scepter to seal the deceased's aura with the circled cross and says: **And now, in the name and power of the Divine Spirit, I invoke ye, ye Angels of the Watchtowers of the Universe, and charge ye by the divine names YEHESHUAH, YEHOVASHAH, to guard the sphere of (Frater/Soror** *magical motto***). Keep far from them all evil and the unbalanced, that they penetrate not into the spiritual abode of our (Frater/Soror). Inspire and sanctify our departed companion so that they may enter into the center of their being and there receive the vision of the Clear Light into which they have recently passed.** (Knocks 1.)

ALL visualize the image of the deceased entering into the Light beyond the Veil and becoming One with It.

ALL vibrate together as HIEROPHANT continues sealing motion with circled cross:

IAO. IAO. IAO.

PSALTIS rings the bell once 1.

HIEROPHANT: (Knocks 1)

ALL return to place. HEGEMON replaces her seat between Pillars.

HIEROPHANT asks if anyone wishes to say some personal words about the deceased. The photograph or symbol of the deceased remains on the Altar through the Eucharist.

Proceed to the Closing of the Neophyte Hall.

✠ ✠ ✠

TO HOLD THE BRIDLES OF THE WINGED STEEDS OF DAWN

Israel Regardie often told us that his favorite prayer was the Prayer of the Sylphs, or Air Spirits, an invocation prayer penned by Eliphas Levi in his book *Dogma and Ritual of High Magic* (1854–56). All four of Levi's elemental prayers were added to the Elemental grade ceremonies of the Golden Dawn: The Prayer of the Sylphs was adopted into the Theoricus Ritual. After Regardie's death in 1985, our temples performed the Requiem that Regardie himself had written and included in his book *The Golden Dawn*, with the addition of the Prayer of the Sylphs to honor him. Since then it has become a tradition in our Order to include this prayer in Requiem Rites.

Seasonal Rituals

Seasonal rituals are ceremonies that mark the changing of the seasons and other significant events that involve the passage of time. Unlike rites of passage, which mark important transitions for the individual, seasonal rituals mark important transitions for entire communities. Seasonal rites and festivals originated in agrarian societies where people observed the four key seasonal times of the year that governed the raising of crops: planting, growing, harvesting, and storing.

Modern pagans observe eight temporal festivals based on the Wheel of the Year: Imbolc (February 1), Spring Equinox or Ostara (March 20 or 21), Beltane (May 1), Summer Solstice or Litha (June 20 or 21), Lughnasadh (August 1), Autumnal Equinox or Mabon (September 22 or 23), Samhain (November 1), and Winter Solstice or Yule (December 21 or 22).[70]

Of these, the Golden Dawn tradition only observes the Vernal and Autumnal Equinoxes, and one ritual is used for both. The Ceremony of the Equinox can be found in Regardie's *The Golden Dawn*.[71]

A Summer Solstice Ritual

The word *solstice* comes from the Latin *sol*, or "sun," and *sistere*, meaning "to stand still." The solstices are points in the Ecliptic at which the Sun is at its greatest distance north or

70. These dates are for the Northern Hemisphere. In the Southern Hemisphere, the Spring (or Vernal) Equinox falls on September 22 or 23, Summer Solstice on December 21 or 22, Autumnal Equinox on March 20 or 21, and Winter Solstice on June 20 or 21.

71. See Regardie, *The Golden Dawn*, 321–33.

south of the Equator, times at which the Sun appears to stand still before reversing direction. In the Northern Hemisphere the Summer Solstice occurs when the Sun is at 0 degrees Cancer, around June 20th or 21st, and the Winter Solstice occurs at 0 degrees Capricorn, about December 20th or 21st. In the Southern Hemisphere the seasons are reversed, and so are the solstices.

The Summer Solstice occurs once a year when the North Pole of the Earth is tilted closest to the Sun. It is the longest day of the year in the Northern Hemisphere; sunrise comes early and sunset is late. Following the Summer Solstice, the days begin to shorten and the nights get longer as the season of autumn approaches. Observed by various cultures for centuries, the event signifies the peak of summer and has long been celebrated with festivals, bonfires, feasts, and rituals such as the Roman festival of Vestalia, dedicated to the Goddess Vesta, and the Celtic festival of Litha. For many, the Summer Solstice signifies the triumph of Light over darkness. It is a time of spiritual renewal, fertility, personal growth, connection with the natural world, and abundance. It is also a time of reflection and taking stock of one's goals.

Traditionally the Golden Dawn only observed the equinoxes, not the solstices. But many magicians enjoy celebrating the solstices as well, and there are certainly plenty of reasons to want to celebrate the four mid-seasonal points of the year, not the least of which is the significance of the number four to our Hermetic Work. Therefore, although they are not official rituals in the same sense or importance as the Equinox Ceremony, Solstice rituals are another welcome addition to the growing body of Golden Dawn–based rites.

The following ritual is just such a ceremony. It is based on the idea of spiritual renewal that is emblematic of the Summer Solstice. It also has echoes of the Second Order's Consecration of the Vault of the Adepti, a ceremonial recharging of the Inner Order's ritual chamber that occurs in the summer, anywhere from the end of May to the end of June. In both rituals, portions of the temple are symbolically deconstructed, reconsecrated, and reconstructed, reaffirming the sanctity of temple with a renewed dedication and a replenishment of purpose. This reconsecration of ritual symbolism such as regalia marks a difference between this ritual and that of the traditional Equinox ceremony. Eric V. Sisco's Ceremony of the Rising of the Light is marginally based on a short Alpha et Omega ritual (dated 1921) for Consecrating a Temple, found in the private archives of our Order.

Synopsis: Hierophant instructs Keryx to announce the arrival of the Summer Solstice, then explains the significance of the Solstice and the intention to reconsecrate the temple and the Lamp of the Hidden Knowledge. Hierophant initiates a dialogue with the other officers concerning their roles and responsibilities at the time of the Summer Solstice.

Stolistes and Dadouchos perform an expanded version of the purification and consecration, establishing the cardinal points at the edges of the temple.

The Hierophant announces the next section of the Work: to establish Paths of the Forces by performing the Rising of the Light. The Hegemon goes to the Keryx station and veils the lamp of the Keryx. The following officers stand guard in the four quarters (Hierophant with rose and white wine, Dadouchos with candle flame and incense, Hiereus with Chalice of wine and cross, and Stolistes with salt and water).

Keryx leads Hegemon in a procession around the Hall as the two begin a series of three circumambulations. During each circuit the pair is stopped in each of the four quarters.

The first circumambulation is the Path of the Human Body. In this circuit the pair is barred at every turn and asked by what symbols they expect to gain entrance. When the correct answer is given, they are allowed to move on.

The second circumambulation is the Path of the Light and Soul. In this circuit the procession is asked to give the proper homage to the Sun God who is set over that particular quarter. After giving the proper homage, the pair is allowed to move on. At the midpoint of the circumambulation, the Hegemon unveils the Keryx Lamp.

The third and final circumambulation is the Path of the Word and of Spirit. During this circumambulation the Keryx invokes and blesses each quarter and traces a cross with the lamp as Hegemon vibrates the tetragrammic name of each element in its respective quarter. Keryx lights the elemental candles in each quarter.

After the Triple Circumambulation is accomplished, all present perform the Hermetic Adoration. Hierophant declares the temple and the Lamp of the Mysteries reconsecrated. Hierophant instructs Keryx to read the temple Warrant.

The officers in turn place their mantles, collars, lamens, and insignia on the Dais. Hierophant purifies, consecrates, and sanctifies all regalia. Hierophant reinvests Keryx, who returns the elements of the Mystic Repast to the central Altar and places the Keryx Lamp on the white triangle. The rest of the officers are reinvested with their regalia.

Stolistes and Dadouchos purify and consecrate the temple to balance out the energies of the Work. Hierophant asks the Lord of the Universe to bless the temple and its members. Hierophant places the image of the temple patron on the red cross on the altar and gives thanks. All members spend time in contemplation of the Light symbolized by the Lamp of the Keryx before proceeding with the closing of the Neophyte Hall.

The Ceremony of the Rising of the Light: A Summer Solstice Ritual

By Eric V. Sisco

Ritual Personae:
Hierophant—Priest of Khepera, Guardian of the Rising Sun
Dadouchos—Priest of Ra, Guardian of the Noonday Sun
Hiereus—Priest of Temu, Guardian of the Setting Sun
Stolistes—Priest of Amun, Guardian of the Midnight Sun
Hegemon—Priest of Ma'at, Guardian of the Incarnation of Light
Keryx—Priest of Anubis, Steward of the Incarnation of Light

Preparation: Black Central Altar. Upon Altar are a Rose in the East, a red Lamp in the South, a Cup of Red Wine in the West, and a Paten of Bread and Salt in the North. Red Cross above White Triangle at the center of the Altar. White Veil for the Lamp at Station of Hegemon. Temple Warrant at Heraldic Station of Keryx in the Northeast. Statue or Image of Temple Patron on Dais behind Station of Hierophant.

In each quarter there is a small altar on which are placed the following articles:

- On the Eastern Altar is a Cup of White Wine and a yellow candle.
- On the Southern Altar is the Censer of the Dadouchos and a red candle.
- On the Western Altar is a silver Latin Cross and a blue candle.
- On the Northern Altar is the Cup of the Stolistes and a black candle.

Perform the Opening of the Hall of the Neophytes. After the Opening, the Keryx distributes the elements of the Mystic Repast to the four quarter Altars.

HIEROPHANT: **Fratres et Sorores of the Temple of ________ of the ________ Order of the Golden Dawn, let us celebrate the Arrival of the Aestival Solstice. Frater Keryx, I direct you to announce this fact and declare the Solstice has come.**

KERYX *(moves to NE and holds Lamp on high)*: **In the Name of the Lord of the Universe, who works in Silence and Whom naught but Silence can express, I proclaim the Aestival Solstice has arrived in the semester of [Password].** *(Returns to Station.)*

HIEROPHANT: Sisters and Brothers, it is at the time of the solstices where the Sun finds itself at its extremities, the zenith and nadir of its circumgyration. Upon the Aestival Solstice, the Sun of Life and Light stands at its pinnacle, marking its point of greatest influence. As such, it indicates an auspicious time for consecration, more especially of those things which symbolize the Light and Life bestowed upon the world by the Sun.

In all of our wanderings along the Pathway to Occult Knowledge, the Lamp of the Keryx has gone before us. It is the symbol of the Hidden Light of the Mysteries. It is ever-burning and all-illuminating, and it is critical for our guidance on the path, lest our souls all wander in the Darkness of Ignorance, groping for the Light.

So therefore, let us consecrate according to ancient custom the Lamp of the Keryx, which is the Light of Hidden Knowledge, and (re)constitute this place designated for the Temple of ________ as an Outer Order Temple of the ________ Order of the Golden Dawn.

(Pause.)

Soror Stolistes, what is your role and responsibility at the Seasonal Crest?

STOLISTES: **As my Station in the North represents the place of greatest symbolic darkness, my charge is to conceal the Sun, even in its greatest strength, by immersing it in the Primordial Waters, and affirming and reaffirming that its very nature is purified.**

HIEROPHANT: **Soror Dadouchos, what is your role and responsibility at Summertide?**

DADOUCHOS: **As my Station in the South represents the place of greatest symbolic eminence, my charge is to glorify the Sun in its most refulgent splendor, by emblazoning it in the highest heavens, and affirming and reaffirming that its very nature is consecrated.**

HIEROPHANT: **Frater Keryx, what is your role and responsibility at the Summer Standstill?**

KERYX: **As my position is responsible for leading all circumambulations and processions while carrying the Lamp of my office, my charge is to accompany the Sun in its revolution, from the underworld, to its ascension above the horizon, then to its pinnacle in the heavens, to its submersion below the horizon, and eternally around again.**

HIEROPHANT: **Honored Hegemon, what is your role and responsibility at Midsummer?**

HEGEMON: **As my office is responsible for leading those through the path of darkness unto light, my charge is to escort the Sun in its orbit, thus securing the cosmic order by ensuring that its journey progresses on its proper pathway and does not wander beyond its extremes.**

HIEROPHANT: **Honored Hiereus, what is your role and responsibility at the Aestival Solstice?**

HIEREUS: **As the Throne of the West represents the increase of darkness and the decrease of light, my charge is to redirect the Sun back toward the balance of the Autumnal Equinox and its continuance through to the Hibernal Solstice, assuring that the Solar revolution finds its fitting completion.**

HIEROPHANT: **As the Throne of the East represents the rise of the Sun of Life and Light, my charge is to elevate the Sun in its emergence from the horizon, exalting it from its most inert state on the Hibernal Solstice, through the balance of**

the Vernal Equinox, and up to and including its most potent day on the Aestival Solstice.

(Pause.)

Soror Stolistes and Soror Dadouchos, establish the Cardinal Points within the Limits designated for the Temple.

(Expanded consecration and purification of the Hall: Stolistes and Dadouchos rise, give Sign of the Enterer, and pick up Cup and Censer, respectively. Stolistes sprinkles a few grains of salt from the Paten into the Cup, and Dadouchos lights Incense from the Fire Lamp. Stolistes moves to E, with Dadouchos balancing her in W as she begins. Dadouchos always balances her as she passes round the Hall. Dadouchos begins consecration upon arriving in E.)

Stolistes: *(Upon sprinkling in E)* **So therefore first, the priest . . .**
(Upon sprinkling in S) **Who governeth the works of Fire . . .**
(Upon sprinkling in W) **Must sprinkle with the lustral Water . . .**
(Upon sprinkling in N) **Of the loud, resounding sea.**
(Upon reaching E, holds Cup on high) **With Salt and Water, I purify.**

(Stolistes will balance Dadouchos as she rounds the Temple.)

Dadouchos: *(Upon censing in E)* **And when after all the Phantoms have vanished . . .**
(Upon censing in S) **Thou shalt see that Holy and Formless Fire . . .**
(Upon censing in W) **That Fire which darts and flashes . . .**
(Upon censing in N) **Through the hidden depths of the Universe.**
(Upon reaching E) **Hear thou the voice of Fire.**
(Holds Censer on high) **With Fire and Incense, I consecrate.**

Both return to place and give Sign of Silence.

Hegemon: **The Cardinal Points have been established.**

Hierophant: **Fratres et Sorores, let us now establish the places of the paths of the Forces therein by performing the Rising of the Light.**

HEGEMON takes Veil, moves sunwise to Keryx station in SW and veils the Lamp. Both KERYX and HEGEMON move sunwise to N of Black Pillar. HIEROPHANT stands in E with Rose and Wine. DADOUCHOS stands in S with Fire Lamp and Incense. HIEREUS stands in W with Wine and Cross. STOLISTES stands in N with Salt and Water. Both KERYX and HEGEMON pause a moment before commencing the First Circumambulation. Then they together move sunwise and are halted in E.

HIEROPHANT: **The Guardian of the East spake and said, "Thou canst not enter the Gateway of the East unless thou canst tell me my Name."**

HEGEMON: **Thou art Khepera, the Guardian of the Rising Sun.**

HIEROPHANT: **By what symbols dost thou expect to gain entrance?**

HEGEMON: **By the symbols of the Rose and Wine, Blossom and Transformation.**

HIEROPHANT *(holds Rose above Wine before Lamp)*: **By the path of the Offering of Sacrifice between them, thou mayst enter the Gateway of the East.**

Both KERYX and HEGEMON move sunwise and are halted in S.

DADOUCHOS: **The Guardian of the South spake and said, "Thou canst not enter the Gateway of the South unless thou canst tell me my Name."**

HEGEMON: **Thou art Ra, the Guardian of the Noonday Sun.**

DADOUCHOS: **By what symbols dost thou expect to gain entrance?**

HEGEMON: **By the symbols of Fire and Incense, Consecration and Prayer.**

DADOUCHOS *(holds Fire Lamp and Incense in Sign of Cross before Lamp)*: **By the path of the Offering of Sacrifice between them, thou mayst enter the Gateway of the South.**

Both KERYX and HEGEMON move sunwise and are halted in W.

HIEREUS: **The Guardian of the West spake and said, "Thou canst not enter the Gateway of the West unless thou canst tell me my Name."**

HEGEMON: **Thou art Temu, the Guardian of the Setting Sun.**

HIEREUS: **By what symbols dost thou expect to gain entrance?**

HEGEMON: **By the symbol of the Cross and Cup, Height and Depth, Aspiration and Humility.**

HIEREUS *(holds Cross above Wine before Lamp)*: **By the path of the Offering of Sacrifice between them, thou mayst enter the Gateway of the West.**

Both KERYX and HEGEMON move sunwise and are halted in N.

STOLISTES: **The Guardian of the North spake and said, "Thou canst not enter the Gateway of the North unless thou canst tell me my Name."**

HEGEMON: **Thou art Amun, the Guardian of the Midnight Sun.**

STOLISTES: **By what symbols dost thou expect to gain entrance?**

HEGEMON: **By the symbols of Water and Salt, Purification and Conservation.**

STOLISTES: *(holds Water and Salt in Sign of Cross before Lamp)*: **By the path of the Offering of Sacrifice between them, thou mayst enter the Gateway of the North.**

Both KERYX and HEGEMON move sunwise to N of Black Pillar.

KERYX: **This is the Path of the Human and of the Body, and the first of the Circumambulations is complete.**

Both KERYX and HEGEMON pause a moment before commencing the Second Circumambulation.

HEGEMON: **In the Beginning, the Elohim created the Heavens and the Earth.**

Both KERYX and HEGEMON begin to move sunwise.

HEGEMON: **And the Earth was formless and void, and Darkness was upon the Face of the Deep.**

Both KERYX and HEGEMON are halted in E.

HIEROPHANT: **The Priest with the Mask of Khepera spake and said, "Thou canst not pass by the Gateway of the East unless thou canst give proper homage."**

KERYX: *(Turns to E and makes Sign of Enterer. All except Hierophant do the same.)*
Praise be to thee, O Khepera in thy rising!
Yet unto thee, O Khepera in thy birth!
Hail, thou Disk, Lord of Rays, Lord of Might!
Hail, thou Reborn One, Lord of Life, Lord of Light!
Isis and Nephthys salute thee, O Risen One of the Sky!
Homage to thee, O Khepera, who art the morning's Eye![72]
(Sign of Silence.)

HEGEMON: **And the Ruach Elohim moved upon the Face of the Waters.**

HIEROPHANT *(sprinkles a few drops of Wine on Lamp under Veil)*: **By the path of the Birth of Creation thencefrom, Incarnation of Light, thou art purified, and thou mayst pass through the Gateway of the East.**

Both KERYX and HEGEMON move sunwise and are halted in S.

---

72. From "Kheperu Nu Ra: The Evolutions of Ra," in Ciceros, *Self-Initiation into the Golden Dawn Tradition*, 87–88.

DADOUCHOS: **The Priest with the Mask of Ra spake and said, "Thou canst not pass by the Gateway of the South unless thou canst give proper homage."**

KERYX: *(Turns to S and makes Sign of Enterer. All except Dadouchos do the same.)*
Praise be to thee, O Ra in thy Zenith!
Yet unto thee, O Ra in thy strength!
Hail, thou Disk, Lord of Rays, Lord of Might!
Hail, thou Shining One, Lord of Life, Lord of Light!
Isis and Nephthys salute thee, O Brilliant One of the Sky!
Homage to thee, O Ra, who art the Midday's Eye! [73]
(Sign of Silence.)

HEGEMON: **And the Elohim said "Let there be Light," and straightway there came the Light.** *(Unveils Lamp.)*

DADOUCHOS *(censes the Lamp)*: **By the path of the Birth of Creation thencefrom, Incarnation of Light, thou art purified, and thou mayst pass through the Gateway of the South.**

Both KERYX and HEGEMON move sunwise and are halted in W.

HIEREUS: **The Priest with the Mask of Temu spake and said, "Thou canst not pass by the Gateway of the West unless thou canst give proper homage."**

KERYX: *(Turns to W and makes Sign of Enterer. All except Hiereus do the same.)*
Praise be to thee, O Temu in thy setting!
Yet unto thee, O Temu in thy peace!
Hail, thou Disk, Lord of Rays, Lord of Might!
Hail, thou Subsiding One, Lord of Life, Lord of Light!
Isis and Nephthys salute thee, O Fading One of the Sky!
Homage to thee, O Temu, who art the Evening's Eye! [74]

---

73. From "Kheperu Nu Ra: The Evolutions of Ra," in Ciceros, *Self-Initiation into the Golden Dawn Tradition*, 87–88.

74. From "Kheperu Nu Ra: The Evolutions of Ra," in Ciceros, *Self-Initiation into the Golden Dawn Tradition*, 87–88.

(Sign of Silence.)

HEGEMON: **Except One be born of Water and of the Spirit, they cannot enter into the Kingdom of God.**

HIEREUS *(swings Cross at Lamp)*: **By the path of the Birth of Creation thencefrom, Incarnation of Light, thou art purified, and thou mayst pass through the Gateway of the West.**

Both KERYX and HEGEMON move sunwise and are halted in N.

STOLISTES: **The Priest with the Mask of Amun spake and said, "Thou canst not pass by the Gateway of the North unless thou canst give proper homage."**

KERYX: *(Turns to N and makes Sign of Enterer. All except Stolistes do the same.)*
Praise be to thee, O Amun in thy hiding!
Yet unto thee, O Amun in thy veil!
Hail, thou Disk, Lord of Rays, Lord of Might!
Hail, thou Eternal One, Lord of Life, Lord of Light!
Isis and Nephthys salute thee, O Concealed One of the Sky!
Homage to thee, O Amun, who art the Midnight's Eye![75]
(Sign of Silence.)

HEGEMON: **And the Elohim saw that the Light was good, and the Elohim separated the Light from the Darkness.** *(Casts Veil aside emphatically.)*

STOLISTES *(sprinkles a few drops of Water on Lamp):* **By the path of the Birth of Creation thencefrom, Incarnation of Light, thou art purified, and thou mayst pass through the Gateway of the North.**

Both KERYX and HEGEMON move sunwise to N of Black Pillar.

---

75. From "Kheperu Nu Ra: The Evolutions of Ra," in Ciceros, *Self-Initiation into the Golden Dawn Tradition*, 87–88.

Keryx: **This is the Path of the Light and of the Soul, and the second of the Circumambulations is complete.**

Both Keryx and Hegemon pause a moment before commencing the Third Circumambulation. Then they together move sunwise and are halted in E.

Hierophant: **Let us adore the Lord of the Universe!** *(All face E.)*

Keryx: **Holy art Thou, who hast created the Firmament! Thine, the Vast and Mighty One, is the Air, in its unresting movement!** *(Makes Cross with Lamp.)*

Hegemon: *(Turns to E and makes Sign of Enterer. All except Hierophant do the same.)* **Yod Heh Vav Heh (י ה ו ה).**

Sign of Silence. Keryx lights candle on Eastern Altar.

Hierophant *(makes Sign of Aquarius with Rose over Lamp)*: **By the Revolving Path of the Name therein, Incarnation of Light, thou art consecrated by Air. Pass thou on.**

Both Keryx and Hegemon move sunwise and are halted in S.

Dadouchos: **Let us adore the Lord of the Universe!** *(All face S.)*

Keryx: **Holy art Thou, wherein Thou hast shown forth the Throne of Thy Glory! Thine, Lord of the Light and of the Darkness, is the Fire, with its Flashing Flame!** *(Makes Cross with Lamp.)*

Hegemon: **(Turns to S and makes Sign of Enterer. All except Dadouchos do the same.) Heh Yod Heh Vav (ה י ה ו).**

Sign of Silence. Keryx lights candle on Southern Altar.

Dadouchos *(makes Sign of Leo with Fire over Lamp)*: **By the Revolving Path of the Name therein, Incarnation of Light, thou art consecrated by Fire. Pass thou on.**

Both Keryx and Hegemon move sunwise and are halted in W.

Hiereus: Let us adore the Lord of the Universe! *(All face W.)*

Keryx: **Holy art Thou, whereon Thy Spirit moved at the Beginning! Thine, whom Nature hath not formed, is the Water, with its Flux and Reflux!** *(Makes Cross with Lamp.)*

Hegemon: *(Turns to W and makes Sign of Enterer. All except Hiereus do the same.)* **Vav Heh Yod Heh (ו ה י ה).**

Sign of Silence. Keryx lights candle on Western Altar.

Hiereus *(makes Sign of Eagle with Wine over Lamp)*: **By the Revolving Path of the Name therein, Incarnation of Light, thou art consecrated by Water. Pass thou on.**

Both Keryx and Hegemon move sunwise and are halted in N.

Stolistes: **Let us adore the Lord of the Universe!** *(All face N.)*

Keryx: **Holy art Thou, who hast made the Earth Thy Footstool! Thine, Lord of the Universe, is the Earth, in its Eternal Stability!** *(Makes Cross with Lamp.)*

Hegemon: (Turns to N and makes Sign of Enterer. All except Stolistes do the same.) **Heh Vav Heh Yod (ה ו ה י).**

Sign of Silence. Keryx lights candle on Northern Altar.

Stolistes *(makes Sign of Ox with Salt over Lamp)*: **By the Revolving Path of the Name therein, Incarnation of Light, thou art consecrated by Earth. Pass thou on.**

Both KERYX and HEGEMON move sunwise to N of Black Pillar.

KERYX: **This is the Path of the Word and of the Spirit, and the third of the Circumambulations is complete.**

Both KERYX and HEGEMON return to places.

HEGEMON: **Thus are the Cardinal Points and the Places of the Paths of the Forces established within the Limits designated for the Temple.**

HIEROPHANT: **The Triple Circumambulation, symbolic of the Rising of the Light, is accomplished! Let us adore the Lord of the Universe!** *(All face E.)*

ALL: *(Sign of Enterer)* **Holy art Thou, Lord of the Universe!**
(Sign of Enterer) **Holy art Thou, Whom Nature hath not formed!**
(Sign of Enterer) **Holy art Thou, the Vast and the Mighty One!**
Lord of the Light and of the Darkness! *(Sign of Silence.)*

HIEROPHANT: **Look thou with favor on this our undertaking, and grant that this Temple and this Lamp of Hidden Knowledge that has been consecrated in thy Name be established unto Thy Glory, both for the Good of the Order and for the benefit of its Members. Grant Thine Aid unto all upon whom the privilege of Initiation herein may be conferred, so that they may prove true and faithful Fraters and Sorors among us, unto the Glory of Thine Ineffable Name. Amen.**

ALL: **So mote it be.**

HIEROPHANT: **Frater Keryx, in the Name of the Lord of the Universe, I command you to declare that this place has been (re)constituted as a Temple of the _______ Order of the Golden Dawn and its Lamp of Occult Knowledge has been consecrated.**

KERYX *(moves to NE):* **In the Name of the Lord of the Universe, and by command of the Very Honored Hierophant, I proclaim that this Temple of _______ has been regularly (re)constituted as an Outer Order Temple of the _______ Order of**

the Golden Dawn, and its Ever-Burning Lamp of the Guardian of the Mysteries has been duly consecrated therein. *(Returns to place.)*

HIEROPHANT: (Knocks ‫ו‬)
HIEREUS: (Knocks ‫ו‬)
HEGEMON: (Knocks ‫ו‬)

HIEROPHANT: (Knocks ‫ו‬) **Khabs.**
HIEREUS: (Knocks ‫ו‬) **Am.**
HEGEMON: Knocks ‫ו‬) **Pekht.**

HIEREUS: (Knocks ‫ו‬) **Konx.**
HEGEMON: (Knocks ‫ו‬) **Om.**
HIEROPHANT: (Knocks ‫ו‬) **Pax.**

HEGEMON: (Knocks ‫ו‬) **Light.**
HIEROPHANT: (Knocks ‫ו‬) **In.**
HIEREUS: (Knocks ‫ו‬) **Extension.**

HIEROPHANT: **I (re)consecrate this Temple under due dispensation and authority from the Greatly Honored Chiefs of the Second Order. Frater Keryx, I delegate upon you to read the Warrant for the Establishment of this Temple of the Order.**

KERYX: *(Moves to NE, reads Warrant, and returns to place.)*

HIEROPHANT: **Let the Robes, Collars, Lamens, and Insignia be placed upon the Dais before me.**

(Done in the following order: PHYLAX, DADOUCHOS, STOLISTES, HEGEMON, HIEREUS, KERYX, HIEROPHANT. ALL return to their stations.)

HIEROPHANT:
(Sprinkling with Water) **I purify with Water.**
(Censing with Incense) **I consecrate with Fire.**
(Swinging Lamp of Keryx) **I sanctify with Light.**

Hierophant reinvests himself with his regalia.

Hierophant: **Let the Elements be replaced upon the Altar.**

Keryx comes round to E. Hierophant reinvests Keryx with his Lamen and Lamp. Keryx then replaces the Elements back on the Central Altar in customary fashion, holding the Lamp above each Element as it is returned. After replacing all Elements, Keryx moves round to E and receives Caduceus Wand from Hierophant. Hegemon moves aside to make way for Keryx. Keryx then proceeds between the Pillars to E of Altar, places Lamp in the middle of the White Triangle, and returns to station.

Hierophant: **Let the Officers be reinvested with their Regalia.**

(Done in the following order: Hiereus, Hegemon, Stolistes, Dadouchos, Sentinel. All return to their stations, facing E.)

Hierophant: **The Robes, Collars, Lamens, and Insignia being thus purified, consecrated, and sanctified, Soror Stolistes and Soror Dadouchos, I call upon you now to purify and consecrate the actual Temple itself with Water and with Fire.**

Stolistes and Dadouchos rise and give Sign of the Enterer. Stolistes picks up Cup and moves to E, Dadouchos picks up Censer and balances her in the W as she begins. Stolistes makes a cross with Cup and sprinkles in the form of a Water Triangle at the Cardinal Points. Stolistes and Dadouchos continue to balance one another, sprinkling and censing as they pass around the Hall. Dadouchos begins censing upon arriving in E. Dadouchos makes a cross with Censer and censes in the form of a Fire Triangle at the Cardinal Points.

Stolistes *(upon reaching E, holds Cup on high)*: **I purify with Water.**

(Stolistes will balance Dadouchos as she rounds the Temple, but does not sprinkle.)

Dadouchos *(upon reaching the E, holds Censer on high)*: **I consecrate with Fire.**

Both return to place, replace their implements, and give Sign of Silence.

HIEROPHANT: **Creator of the World, and Lord of the Universe, we entreat Thee to bless us in the purpose of our present Assembly. Grant unto us Wisdom, Strength, and Knowledge, so that this Temple may be erected to Thy Glory and consecrated to Thy Service.**

Grant Thou unto the Chiefs of this Temple, Wisdom to instruct and guide its members in the Paths of Occult Knowledge. May they ever act together in unbroken accord and harmony, as far as may be possible to imperfect mortals, dealing justly in all things without fear or favor, and ruling this Temple alike to the benefit of the Order, and to the Glory of Thine Ineffable Name.

Bless Thou the Members of this Temple. May fraternal love and harmony ever prevail among us all. May we progress in Occult Knowledge and support and work harmoniously with their Superiors in the Order without discord or jealousy.

May harmony and peace prevail among the various Temples of our Order, wherever they may be found throughout the World. And finally may we all at length attain to that perfect and Divine Wisdom, without which all worldly Wisdom is as nothing. Amen.

ALL: **So mote it be.**

ALL face Cubical Altar. HEGEMON moves aside to make way for HIEROPHANT. HIEROPHANT moves directly to E side of Altar and places image of Temple Patron on Red Cross on Altar. HEGEMON steps back into Station.

HIEROPHANT: **And seeing that this Temple is called after the Name of the God _______, I hereby solemnly dedicate this Temple thereunto, and I invoke by the Ceremonies herein before performed the God ________ to act as the Genius and Watcher hereover, and Patron of this Temple.** *(Steps aside to allow HEGEMON to approach the Altar.)*

HEGEMON *(moves to E side of Altar and lifts Lamp):* **In all our wandering in Darkness, the Lamp of the Keryx went before us all, though it was not seen by our eyes. Thanks be to God for this Admirable Light.**

ALL salute toward the Lamp and vibrate the name of the Patron three times, then conclude with Sign of Silence. HEGEMON replaces Lamp on Altar.

HIEROPHANT: **Let us now spend some time in contemplation of the Lamp of the Keryx, which is the symbol of the Hidden Light of Occult Science, and the symbolic guiding light of our Patron ______.**

ALL approach the Central Altar. Members may stand in a circle holding hands around the Altar for a brief contemplation or sit around the Altar for a more prolonged meditation. For a more elaborate proceeding, an Invocation of the God may be performed by the HIEROPHANT at this time instead of the above monologue. When done, everyone returns to their stations. KERYX takes Lamp and figure of Temple God and returns it to his station.

Proceed with the Closing of the Neophyte Hall.

At the very end, HIEROPHANT may state the following: **Now shall we depart in Peace and retire for a season, for we shall meet again in performance of the Great Work, and in that time we shall once more take up the mantle of this Temple not made with hands when the Light and the Darkness have come back into complete balance at the Autumnal Equinox. And may what we have partaken of sustain us in our search for the Quintessence, the *Lapis Philosophorum,* the Stone of the Wise, True Wisdom, Perfect Happiness, the *Summum Bonum.* And by the Power invested in this scepter, I declare this temple duly closed! So mote it be!**

✠ ✠ ✠

Honor and Remembrance

Throughout the long history of the Western Esoteric Tradition, the threads of wisdom, insight, and transformation have been woven together across generations. As spiritual seekers and practitioners of Golden Dawn magic, we stand not only on the shoulders of our immediate teachers but also on the accumulated wisdom of those who have paved the way before us. The significance of a ritual memorial to honor and celebrate our magical teachers and companions of the past cannot be overstated.

The Ritual of Honor and Remembrance serves as a tangible link to this rich heritage. It is not merely a gesture of remembrance; it is a bridge that connects us to the currents of magical energy and knowledge that have flowed through the veins of our tradition. By recognizing and honoring those who have come before us, we acknowledge the continuity of the tradition and ensure that their teachings continue to influence and inspire us. But more than this, the ceremony becomes a point of convergence, where the energies and intentions of past, present, and future coalesce. It is a place where the boundaries between the physical and the spiritual are blurred, allowing us to tap into the reservoir of knowledge and guidance that transcends time itself.

This ritual presents another opportunity for modern Golden Dawn Initiates to connect with ancient seasonal festivals that were never a part of the original Order but that can nonetheless provide richness to our spiritual experience and well-being.

As a ceremony that celebrates our Order's founders and teachers as well as magical companions who have passed more recently beyond the Veil, this ritual has a natural affiliation with the ancient Celtic festival of Samhain (Gaelic for "summer's end"), which fell around the beginning of November. It signified the end of the harvest season and the beginning of winter, the season most associated with death. At Samhain it was believed that the veil between the living and the dead was particularly thin: The spirits of the dead were believed to walk the Earth at that time and visit the living. In modern times, Samhain is a time for honoring one's departed ancestors.

This ceremony reminds us that we are a part of a living tradition. Through our own dedication, we become contributors to this ongoing narrative. As we honor those who have illuminated our path, we in turn become beacons of light for those who will follow in our footsteps.

Synopsis: After the Opening of the Neophyte Hall, the Hierophant makes a statement of intention. This intention is further elaborated by explanations of the Holy days that coalesce around the end of October and beginning of November: the Celtic Samhain, the Egyptian *Isia*, and the Christian Eve of All Hallows' and All Saints' Day. Hiereus explains that the ritual will open a portal or liminal space between the worlds that will allow the living members and their companions beyond the veil to commune together within the temple.

The portal space is defined by a vesica around the central Altar. The gateway to the vesica is marked by two tall candlesticks just west of the Altar. The Vesica Portal is created by the Keryx and the Phylax, who begin by standing on either side of the Altar, north and south of it.

The Hierophant goes to the west, walks between the candlesticks, and begins to sanctify the portal space by tracing Spirit Pentagrams over the Altar. Hierophant invokes the Angels of the Celestial Spheres to guard the portal space and sanctify all who enter.

All perform the Qabalistic Cross for balance and Divine Light. Stolistes and Dadouchos purify and consecrate the gateway between the two candlesticks.

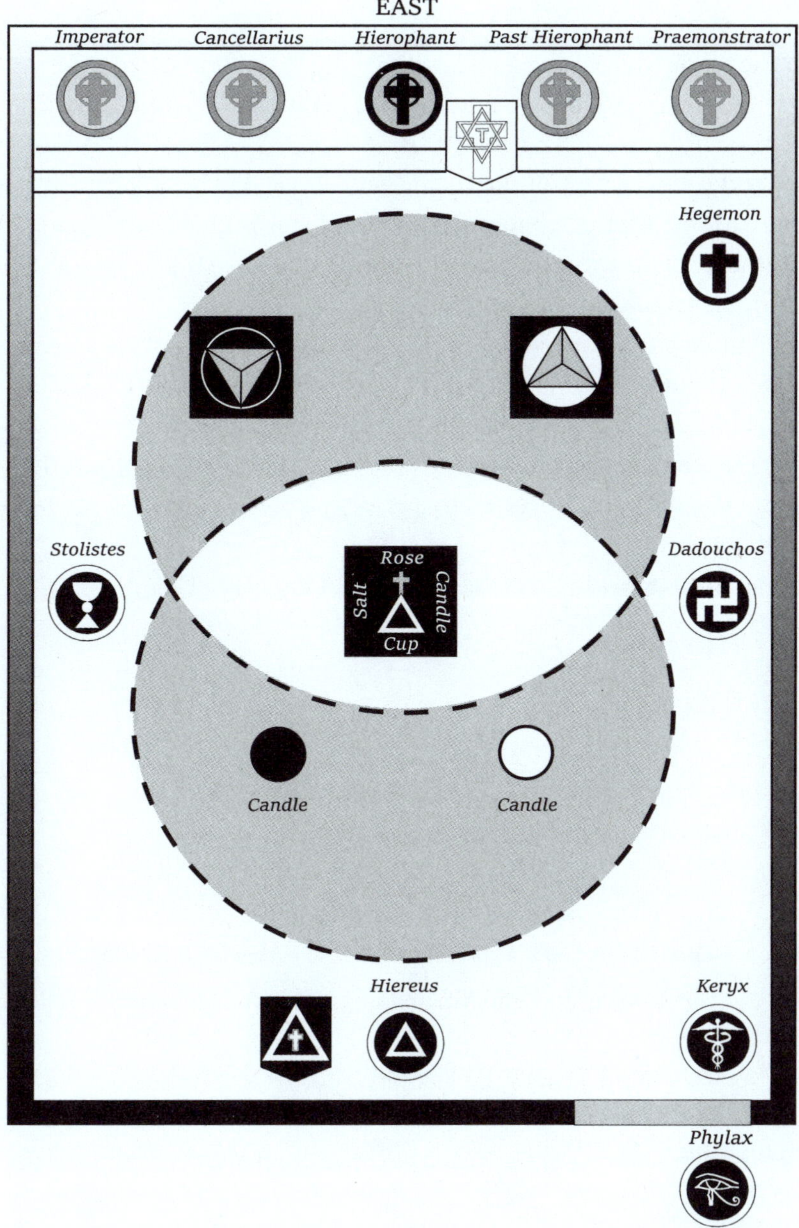

Figure 25: Temple Setup for a Ritual of Honor and Remembrance

Keryx moves to his heraldic station in the Northeast. Phylax moves to a position balancing Keryx in the Southwest. Moving clockwise in unison, they complete three slow circumambulations: Keryx's circle extends east to the foot of the Dais to just west of the Altar. Phylax's circle extends west to the foot of the Hiereus's throne to just east of the Altar. The Vesica formed from the intersection of the two officers' circles forms the Vesica Portal. The Hierophant declares the portal space between the Worlds opened.

In the next section, each officer in turn enters the Vesica Portal to commemorate one of the honored dead of our tradition, including Samuel Mathers, Wynn Westcott, Robert Woodman, Moina Mathers, Florence Farr, William Butler Yeats, Annie Horniman, Maud Gonne, Dion Fortune, and Israel Regardie. Deceased Adepts and Outer Order members from the temple are also remembered.

Blessings and thanks are given to the honored dead, and members are encouraged to enter the Vesica Portal and commune with a deceased companion, friend, or ancestor.

After final blessings, Hierophant enters the gateway and traces Banishing Spirit Pentagrams over the Altar. Keryx goes to the Southeast and Phylax goes to the northwest. Moving counterclockwise in unison, they perform a reverse circumambulation to close down the Vesica Portal.

Preparation: The temple setup is the Opening of the Hall of the Neophytes.

Additional Items needed:

- Two very tall candleholders,[76] one with a white candle and the other a black candle
- A cauldron, charcoal, and powdered incense
- Any personal offerings for one's ancestors

A Ritual of Honor and Remembrance

By Chic and Tabatha Cicero and Jayne Gibson

Perform the Opening of the Hall of the Neophytes. Then continue with the Work.

Hegemon moves her chair from between the Pillars to the foot of the Dais in the SE.

76. These should be between four and six feet in height. They are meant to simulate a doorway, so the taller the better.

HIEROPHANT: (Knocks— ו) **Fratres and Sorores of the (______) Temple of the (________) Order of the Golden Dawn in the Outer, our work today is a celebration of those who have gone before us and passed beyond the veil. The ancient Celts celebrated two hinges or pivotal points of the calendar year: Beltaine, the first of May, and Samhain, the first of November, which was also the traditional Celtic New Year. These two days were the most magical of the entire year. The ancient Celtic people revered times and places that were considered to be "in between," or liminal, and so Beltane and Samhain mark the transitions of summer and winter. Holy times were border times such as twilight and dawn, marking the transitions of night and day.**

HEGEMON: **Samhain marked the end of harvest and the beginning of winter. To the ancient Celts, during the period of Samhain, time lost all meaning. Past, present, and future were merged. Through the thinning of the veil that separates the material world and the Otherworld, the spirits of the dead and the Otherworld denizens walked freely among human beings.**

HIEREUS: **Therefore Samhain, a Fire Festival, is a time to remember those who have passed, to celebrate the harvest and prepare for the dark half of the year. During Samhain, ritual bonfires were lit on hilltops to mimic the Sun, assisting the solar powers of growth and holding back the darkness of winter. These fires, as well as their smoke and ashes, were deemed to have protective and cleansing powers. Sometimes two bonfires would be built side by side, and the participants would walk between them as a cleansing ritual. People often took the flames from the bonfire back to their homes and used them to light their hearth fires. These bonfires were also utilized in divination rituals to foretell what was to happen in the coming year.**

HIEROPHANT: **This time of year was also sacred to the ancient Egyptians. A festival known as the Isia, sacred to the Goddess Isis, was celebrated from October 28 to November 1. Little is known of the Isia Festival. But another festival also took place at this time of the year in the Egyptian month of Khoiak, when the ancients held a festival for Osiris, known as the Osiria. This celebration remembered his conflict with his brother Set, his death, and his resurrection through the holy magic of Isis. The festival reenacted the central Isis-Osiris myth**

wherein Isis searched for the scattered pieces of Osiris, found him, mourned him, reassembled him, and resurrected him. The Egyptians molded images of Osiris from the Nile mud, special spices, talismanic stones, and seeds. The images were watered so that the grain sprouted, a fitting symbol of new life. The festival ended with the raising of the Djed pillar, a symbol of the resurrection of the God himself as Lord of the Otherworld.[77]

HIEREUS: **In Christian times, November 1st was designated as a day to honor the saints. Soon after, All Saints' Day, also called All Hallows' Day (as "hallows" meant "holy," indicating saints), was established. It was also called Hallowmas, or Feast of All Saints, and came to incorporate some of the traditions of Samhain. The evening before All Saints' Day was known as All Hallows' Eve, and later it came to be called Halloween.**

All Hallows' Eve marked the beginning of Allhallowtide, and in the Christian calendar it covers a three-day span—All Hallows' Eve (October 31st), All Saints' Day (November 1st), and All Souls' Day (November 2nd). During the course of these three holy days, the worshipers honor and remember the dead, the saints and martyrs, and all of the faithful departed.

HEGEMON: **At this liminal time, we are gathered here to open the gate of the Otherworld in order that we may enter the Assembly Hall of the Ancestors. We will honor the Adepts of our tradition as well as Loved Ones who now reside there, the fruits of whose wisdom and efforts have been handed down to us.**

HIEREUS: **To that end we will open a doorway between the worlds and allow our departed Loved Ones and the Masters of the Past to come to be honored and commune with us in peace and fellowship.**

HIEROPHANT: **(Frater/Soror) Keryx and (Frater/Soror) Phylax, as guardians of our temple, stationed within and without our Sacred Hall, I call upon you to trace the circles of this World and the Next, creating a portal in between, a Vesical**

77. Forrest, M. Isidora. "What Is the Isia? 'Samhain' for Isis Devotees?"

Portal, where companions Past and Present may meet each other and give thanks.

Keryx and Phylax rise and give the Projection Sign. Both walk to the Altar and stand on either side facing east, with Keryx on the north side and Phylax on the South.

Keryx: **I am the Keryx of the Mysteries and the messenger of Osiris Onnophris. I represent the god Anubis, Guardian of the tomb and Lord of the Duat. I am the Minder of the Scales of Balance in the Hall of Two Truths. Gatekeeper and Lord of the Cavern in the Sacred Land, the Foremost of the Two Lands! I grant safe passage through the realm of the Underworld. I protect those who pass into the realm of Shadows. I guide the steps of the Initiated just as I would guide the souls to the Chamber of Judgment. I keep all who pass the gateway safe from harm from above or from below. I am the Watcher Within, as my brother Opowet is the Watcher Without.**

Phylax: **I am the Phylax of the Mysteries and the messenger of Osiris Onnophris. I represent the god Opowet, the Opener of the Ways. Master of Gates and Lord of Roads. I open the path for the Virtuous and close the path for the Wicked. I unbar the road to victory for the Living and the Dead, blessing their coming and going. I open the way for every prayer and guard against every harm. I am the Watcher Without, as my brother Anubis is the Watcher Within.**

Keryx and Phylax together: **Open our eyes so we may see. Open our ears so we may hear. Open our mouths so we may speak. Open our hearts that we may love. Open our souls that the Gods may aid us. Open our Spirits that we may soar like eagles. Under the blessings of Deity, make open the Veil between Past and Present. Make open the Hall of the Ancestors.**

Hierophant descends and walks clockwise to west of the candlesticks. He walks between the Candles and traces the Pentagrams of Invoking Spirit Active and Invoking Spirit Passive over the altar.

HIEROPHANT: **I invoke ye, ye Angels of the celestial spheres, whose dwelling is in the invisible. Ye are the guardians of the gates of the Universe, be ye also the guardians of this mystic gateway. Keep far removed the evil and the unbalanced. Strengthen and inspire all those who enter herein, so that we may preserve unsullied this abode of the mysteries of the eternal gods. Let our spheres be pure and holy so that we may enter the space between the Worlds and meet in the Great Assembly of the Ancestors. Selah!**

ALL TOGETHER: **Open our eyes so we may see. Open our ears so we may hear. Open our mouths so we may speak. Open our hearts that we may love. Open our souls that the Gods may aid us. Open our Spirits that we may soar like eagles. Under the blessings of Deity, make open the Veil between Past and Present. Make open the Hall of the Ancestors. Selah!**

HIEROPHANT leads everyone in vibrating the Qabalistic Cross.

HIEROPHANT returns to Dais.

STOLISTES and DADOUCHOS rise and give the Projection Sign. They walk clockwise to the west of the temple, to the west of the candlesticks facing east, with STOLISTES on the north side and DADOUCHOS on the south.

KERYX moves to his heraldic station in the NE.
At the same time, PHYLAX moves to the KERYX station in the SW.

STOLISTES purifies (with cross and Invoking Water triangle) the area between the two candlesticks, then returns to station.

DADOUCHOS consecrates (with cross and Invoking Fire triangle) the area between the two candlesticks, then lights the candles and returns to station.

KERYX and PHYLAX then begin their clockwise circles of the Two Worlds. They make three circuits of the Hall slowly as the HIEREUS reads Psalm 23.

HIEREUS: **The Lord is my shepherd; I shall not want. He maketh me to lie down in green pastures: he leadeth me beside the still waters. He restoreth my soul: he leadeth me in the paths of righteousness for his name's sake. Yea, though I walk through the valley of the shadow of death, I will fear no evil: for thou art with me; thy rod and thy staff they comfort me. Thou preparest a table before me in the presence of mine enemies: thou anointest my head with oil; my cup runneth over. Surely goodness and mercy shall follow me all the days of my life: and I will dwell in the house of the Lord forever.**

After completing three circuits, KERYX and PHYLAX return to their stations.

HIEROPHANT leads everyone in vibrating **IAO. IAO. IAO.** ALL should now visualize the space around the altar, the vesical shape wherein the two circles share common space, as a holy place where the veil between the worlds is thinnest.

HIEROPHANT: **Through the shadows of living memory and out across the gulf of years, we call out to our friends, Fratres and Sorores who have crossed into the Beyond; to our ancestors who are the golden threads to the tapestry of our souls; and to the Masters of the Past who have paved the pathways of our Tradition. Our venerated Companions beyond the Veil in the Great Chain of Being!**

We have opened a portal into the Great Assembly of the Ancestors, so that on this (day/night) we may give thanks and honor to the Adepts who have gone before us. In honoring our magical ancestors, we affirm that Spark of the Light within, which they have helped us discover. These Adepts preserved the Western Magical Tradition we share in our Rites to this present day. Through them, the path to wisdom and self-transformation has been increased, defended, safeguarded, and preserved. Come and let us remember their names according to our Tradition.

IMPERATOR goes to the west, then walks between the Candlesticks and up to the Altar: **To William Robert Woodman, our Order's First Imperator. Your mottos include *Magna est Veritas et Praelavebit* (meaning "Great is the Truth and it shall Prevail") and *Vincit Omnia Veritas* (meaning "Truth Conquers All"). We**

here assembled acknowledge your contribution to the Magic of the Light through the Qabalistic Knowledge Lectures. Greatly Honoured Frater, we thank you for your gift of Hebrew scholarship and the passing on of your knowledge of Egyptology, Platonism, Neo-Platonism, Alchemy, and Tarot. We offer this sweet incense in remembrance and honor. (IMPERATOR sprinkles some incense into the censer, then returns to station.)

PRAEMONSTRATOR goes to the west, then walks between the Candlesticks and up to the Altar: **To Samuel Liddell MacGregor Mathers, our Order's First Praemonstrator who later became Imperator. Your mottos include *S Rioghail Mo Dhream* (meaning "Royal is My Tribe") and *Deo Duce Comite Ferro* (meaning "With God as My Leader and the Sword as my Companion"). We here assembled acknowledge your contribution to the Magic of the Light through the fashioning of a true magical fraternity. Greatly Honoured Frater, we thank you for your gift of inspired ceremonial magic, for the brilliance of the Z Documents, and for the five systems of Inner Order Magic known collectively as the Magic of the Light. We offer this sweet incense in remembrance and honor.** (PRAEMONSTRATOR sprinkles some incense into the censer, then returns to station.)

CANCELLARIUS goes to the west, then walks between the Candlesticks and up to the Altar: **To William Wynn Westcott, our Order's First Cancellarius who later became Praemonstrator. Your mottos include *Sapere Aude* (meaning "Dare to Be Wise"), and *Non Omnis Moriar* (meaning "I Shall Not Wholly Die"). We here assembled acknowledge your contribution to the Magic of the Light as a true creator of the Order of the Golden Dawn. Greatly Honoured Frater, we thank you for your gift of the Cipher Manuscripts and for your organizational genius which transformed your vision of an authentic magical fraternity into the reality of the Golden Dawn tradition. We offer this sweet incense in remembrance and honor.** (CANCELLARIUS sprinkles some incense into the censer, then returns to station.)

PAST HIEROPHANT goes to the west, the walks between the Candlesticks and up to the Altar: **To Moina Bergson Mathers, known in our Tradition as Very Honoured Soror Vestigia Nulla Retrorsum, whose motto means "I Leave No Traces." We**

here assembled acknowledge your contribution to the Magic of the Light in your devotion and visionary insight which helped to create the Inner Order rituals. Very Honoured Soror, we thank you for your gift of clairvoyance which, when translated into untiring artistic inspiration, produced the Vault of the Adepti. We offer this sweet incense in remembrance and honor. (PAST HIEROPHANT sprinkles some incense into the censer, then returns to station.)

HIEROPHANT goes to the west, then walks between the Candlesticks and up to the Altar: **To Florence Farr, known in our Tradition as Very Honoured Soror Sapiens Sapienti Dona Data, whose motto means "Wisdom is a gift to the Wise." We here assembled acknowledge your contribution to the Magic of the Light in your teaching to all initiates that rituals are important spiritual and personal experiences. Very Honoured Soror, we thank you for the gift of your melodious voice which still sings today in our sacred rites, and for the passing on of your knowledge of dramatics and staging which are central elements in our rituals. We offer this sweet incense in remembrance and honor.** (HIEROPHANT sprinkles some incense into the censer, then returns to station.)

HIEREUS goes to the west, then walks between the Candlesticks and up to the Altar: **To William Butler Yeats, known in our Tradition as Very Honoured Frater Daemon est Deus Inversus, and whose motto means "The Devil is the Inverse of God." We here assembled acknowledge your contribution to the Magic of the Light through your mystical verse and poetry which tried to show the outer world the inner mysteries. Very Honoured Frater, we thank you for your gift of devotion and determination, even in times of great duress, to maintain the original ideals of the Founders, which insisted that the Order remain magical in its focus and objectives. We offer this sweet incense in remembrance and honor.** (HIEREUS sprinkles some incense into the censer, then returns to station.)

HEGEMON goes to the west, then walks between the Candlesticks and up to the Altar: **To Annie Horniman, known in our Tradition as Very Honoured Soror Fortiter et Recte, and whose motto means "Bravely and With Rectitude." We here assembled acknowledge your contribution to the Magic of the Light as a scholar of Astrology and Tarot. Very Honoured Soror, we thank you for your gift of**

knowledge concerning theater which helped shape our rituals, and we thank you for the time, the patience, and the finances which you contributed to the creation of the Order of the Golden Dawn. We offer this sweet incense in remembrance and honor. (HEGEMON sprinkles some incense into the censer, then returns to station.)

KERYX goes to the west, then walks between the Candlesticks and up to the Altar: **To Maude Gonne, known in our Tradition as Honoured Soror Per Ignem ad Lucem, and whose motto means "Through the Fire to the Light." We here assembled acknowledge your contribution to the Magic of the Light as the prophetess known as the Woman of the Sidhe.[78] Honoured Soror, we thank you for your magical work aimed at awakening the soul of the masses, and for your ritual work with V.H. Frater Yeats and V.H. Sorores Horniman, Mathers, and Farr in the creation of the Castle of the Heroes—a retreat and teaching center grounded in the mystic Forces of the Celtic Tradition wherein you sought to enter the inner worlds and bring back knowledge of the ancient ways. We offer this sweet incense in remembrance and honor.** (KERYX sprinkles some incense into the censer, then returns to station.)

STOLISTES goes to the west, then walks between the Candlesticks and up to the Altar: **To Violet Mary Firth, known to the world as Dion Fortune, and known in our Tradition as Very Honored Soror Deo Non Fortuna, whose motto means "God, not Luck." We here assembled acknowledge your contribution to the Magic of the Light through the establishment of your own magical Order and your many writings, most notably the Mystical Qabalah and the novels entitled *Sea Priestess* and *Moon Magic* that taught many aspiring magicians how to prepare for and perform a powerful magical event. Very Honored Soror, we thank you for your critical emphasis on the masculine and feminine polarity as the basis for magical working, which had a significant influence on both ceremonial magic and Wicca. We offer this sweet incense in remembrance and honor.** (STOLISTES sprinkles some incense into the censer, then returns to station.)

78. Sidhe is pronounced "Shee," Woman of the Fairies.

DADOUCHOS goes to the west, then walks between the Candlesticks and up to the Altar: **To Israel Regardie, known in our Tradition as Very Honoured Frater Ad Majorem Adonai Gloriam, and whose motto means "To the Greater Glory of God." We here assembled acknowledge your invaluable contribution to the Magic of the Light in the preservation of the sacred teachings through the written and published word. You kept the flame of our tradition alive. Very Honoured Frater, we especially thank you for the gift of your devotion to the Western Mystery Tradition and for the passing on of this Tradition to the many generations yet to come. You are the essential link between the original Order and the Golden Dawn of today. We offer this sweet incense in remembrance and honor.** (DADOUCHOS sprinkles some incense into the censer, then returns to station.)

PHYLAX goes to the west, then walks between the Candlesticks and up to the Altar: **To all the other Companions of our Order who have passed beyond the Veil.** (PHYLAX gives the names and Magical Mottos of deceased Adepts of the Order that the temple wishes to acknowledge, followed by the names and Magical Mottos of deceased Outer Order members.) **To these and all other Fratres and Sorores who have departed this world for the Elysian Fields and Summerlands beyond, we give you our thanks and our love. We offer this sweet incense in remembrance and honor.** (PHYLAX sprinkles some incense into the censer, then returns to station.)

IMPERATOR: **It is said that History, with its flickering lamp, stumbles along the trail of the past, trying to reconstruct its scenes, to revive its echoes, and kindle with pale gleams the passion of former days. What is the worth of all this? The only true guide is our conscience; the only true shield is our memory and the integrity and sincerity of our actions in the Great Work. It is very imprudent to walk through a magical life without this shield, because we are so often shackled by the failure of our hopes and the upsetting of our calculations; but with this shield of memory, however the fates may play, we march always in the ranks of honor.**[79]

---

79. Adapted from Churchill, *The Unrelenting Struggle,* 4.

PRAEMONSTRATOR: **Here is to all the brilliant minds who loved deeply, for they wrote the stories that make us dream. Here is to all the visionaries who created paths for us to follow. Here is to all the magicians who created a perspective of the Great Work we can experience in this lifetime. But most of all, here is to the wild souls that the world called abnormal or different because they were the ones who renewed our faith, by what they overcame and created, in a world that desperately needed a sign that the Divine Light rests within us all.**

CANCELLARIUS: **These past Adepts have carved their names on our hearts, not their tombstones; for theirs is a legacy etched into our minds through their stories we now share. There is evidence to suggest that these past Adepts were privy to the secret of the universe, which is simply this: Everything is connected by the Divine Light. Everything. They understood that the focused ray that can uncover and illuminate this connection is the language of the Magical Arts. And just as a sudden revelation often will light our minds more brilliantly than any deep, abiding belief, so an unlikely and unexpected burst of magical inspiration will reveal greater truths than the most exacting scholarship.**

PAST HIEROPHANT: **What matters here is that, after these many years, we are still giving homage to these Adepts, and we have benefited from the offerings they have contributed through their abiding quest for the transformation of their common lead into the precious Gold of Spirit. The greatest tribute we can give them is to carry on the Great Work, making our efforts a tribute equal to the magnitude of the gifts they have left for us.**

HIEROPHANT: **O Hidden Adepts and Companions of our tradition: In this time and in this place you have come forth from Amoun, the Hidden One, Pure of heart. Verily you have come, you are here. You have opened the Ways! Stand with us! Sharing in sacredness and the blessings of Deity.**

Light dwells within the darkness, as beautiful as a god. You have made your way, ascending the Tree of Life back to the Sacred Source. You dwell in that invisible realm where the Seed of Wisdom is sown in silence. You abide within the Sacred Mysteries and stand next to the Throne. Living in the Light of that Perfect Justice before whom our souls now stand.

(Brief pause.)

HIEROPHANT: **In honor of those magicians who have come before us, both named and unnamed, we offer our thanks and blessings. We have claimed our place in the assemblies of our ancestors. While the Portal between the worlds is still open, I now invite anyone present to commune with a departed loved one, be it magical companion, friend, or ancestor. Give thanks or offerings, or commune in whatever manner you wish.**

Any Frater or Soror who wishes to do so may approach the Altar from between the candlesticks and offer thanks, incense, or any other small offering or communication to a deceased companion, friend, or ancestor. When all are finished, the ritual continues.

HIEROPHANT descends and walks clockwise to west of the candlesticks and up to the Altar.

HIEROPHANT: **O Hidden Adepts and Companions of our tradition: You have passed through the Gates of Darkness unto the Light. You have fought upon the Earth for good. You have finished your work. You have entered into the Invisible. You are the Sun in its Rising. You have passed through the hour of cloud and of night. Your labors are at an end: Pass on your Working Tools to us, that we may labor toward the Completion of the Great Work in your name.**

May you fly, may you gather yourself together like a hawk. Beautiful of gold, may your heart come to you from the land of Beginnings! May it come to you among the gods! If ye are in heaven or on Earth, in the east or in the west, in the north or in the south, or at the center of all that is, you are pure of eye and made Maat. You shall not die a second time.

O never-setting stars! Your soul is of the gods! Arise for thyself, O still heart! Shine for thyself and rejoice! Within a Pure Body of Light. You live through your words and deeds. Depart in peace and blessings. Take our love and gratitude as reminders of the connecting links that exist beyond the time and space of momentary life. Go in Peace. Go in Peace.

HIEROPHANT traces the Pentagrams of Banishing Spirit Active and Banishing Spirit Passive over the altar, then returns to station.

KERYX and PHYLAX rise and give the Projection Sign. KERYX and PHYLAX go the Southeast and Northwest, respectively (KERYX to the Southeast, as in the reverse mystical circumambulation, and PHYLAX directly opposite Keryx in the Northwest).

KERYX and PHYLAX then begin their counterclockwise circles of the two Worlds. They make three slow circuits of the Hall. All should visualize the holy place fading as the two Worlds unwind.

HEGEMON replaces her chair between the pillars.

At this point, any comments, announcements, or temple business may be discussed.

Proceed to the Closing of the Neophyte Hall.

✠ ✠ ✠

A Winter Solstice Ritual

The Winter Solstice is an astronomical event that occurs when the Earth tilts on its axis away from the Sun. In the Northern Hemisphere it occurs annually around December 21st or 22nd, while in the Southern Hemisphere it occurs in June. For both hemispheres, the Winter Solstice marks the shortest day and the longest night of the year, when the Sun appears to hang very low in the sky at noon, and as a result, we receive less sunlight and the warmth it brings. It is the turning point of winter, because after the solstice the days gradually start getting longer, and the nights shorter, as the Earth continues its orbit around the Sun. This change in daylight hours is seen as a symbol of hope and the promise of spring's return. It has long been seen as a time for reflection.

The Sun is also the center of our solar system. In magic, the symbol of the Sun is a hexagram, the six-rayed star. The points on the hexagram are attributed to the planets of Saturn, Jupiter, Mars, Venus, Mercury, and Luna. The Sun is placed at the center of the figure as a reflection of the planets in their cosmic dance around the Sun.

The term *planet*, or "wandering star," developed as a word to describe any celestial body visible from the Earth that appeared to move or "wander" in a regular orbit against the backdrop of stars in the night sky. The ancients recognized seven planets, including the luminaries of the Sun and the Moon (Sol and Luna). Planetary energies are used to affect the astral realm, the subtler planes above it, and the physical realm below it. The planets also represent aspects of the human soul.

In magic, the seven ancient planets are widely utilized for their extensive symbolism, more so than the twelve Zodiacal signs. This is because planets are agents of change. As the movers and shakers of astrology, it is their function to act, move, and initiate change. The symbols and powers of the planets are invoked to effect change in their associated sphere of influence and rulership.

Synopsis: After the Opening of the Neophyte Hall, the Hierophant makes a statement of intention concerning the celebration of the Winter Solstice. In turn, the Officers explain the significance of the Winter Solstice, and the desire to witness the Divine Sun emerging from the Darkness.

In *Part 1: The Birth of the Sun: The Creation of a Magical Universe,* Seven Officers move to their planetary stations, which form a macrocosmic hexagram around the Altar with the Sun at the very center. The Hierophant recalls a time before the Divine act of Creation when there was nothing but darkness and silence. The light of the Sun is invoked, and the Solar candle is lit to represent the first spark of creation at the center of the Hall.

The Hierophant brings the Solar Candle to each of the planetary Officers in turn, from Saturn to Jupiter, Mars, Venus, Mercury, and Luna. When the Hierophant stops at their station, each officer invokes their planetary energy and lights their planetary candle, taking the flame from the Solar candle.

In *Part 2: Ascending the Ladder of Lights: Forming the Six-Rayed Star in Sacred Space,* the Keryx places a Menorah on the Altar. Hierophant announces a journey of ascent, awakening the powers of the Sun.

All members visualize their auras in orange solar light as the Hierophant lights the Sun candle on the Menorah, transferring the flame from the orange solar candle. The positive energies of the Sun are invoked, and the negative and unbalanced qualities of Sol are pushed away. This process is repeated by each planetary officer in turn until all the planetary candles on the menorah are lit. The powers of the seven planets are praised and thanked for their gifts.

In *Part 3: A Repast of the Sun*, Sol is invoked and a Mystic Repast of the Sun is partaken by all members present.

Preparation: All is arranged in accordance with the Opening of the Neophyte Hall.

Additional items needed for Planetary stations:

- Pillar Candles in Glass:
    - » Blue-violet Saturn Candle (East)
    - » Violet Jupiter Candle (SE)
    - » Red Mars Candle (NE)
    - » Orange Solar Candle (Altar)
    - » Green Venus Candle (SW)
    - » Yellow Mercury Candle (NW)
    - » Blue Luna Candle (West)
- Easily accessible tapers for lighting candles

Also Needed: A side Altar in the NE with Menorah and seven white candles.

Optional: Seven Lamens ornamented with the colors and symbols of the seven planets.

The Ceremony of the Seven Wanderers: A Winter Solstice Ritual

By Jayne Gibson and Chic and Tabatha Cicero

Perform the Opening of the Hall of the Neophytes. The Work may commence.

Hierophant: (Knocks 1) **Fratres and Sorores of the (______) Temple of the (________) Order of the Golden Dawn in the Outer, our work today is a celebration of the Winter Solstice. The word Solstice means the "sun stands still," for during the time of the Solstice the Sun appears to halt in the sky, hardly moving in its journey through the Heavens for approximately three days before beginning to move to the south or the north, depending on the season. In the Northern Hemisphere, the Winter Solstice is around December 21st, which is the shortest day of the year preceded by the longest night, and when the Sun is at its most southerly point in the sky.**

PRAEMONSTRATOR: **From this point onward, from its nadir in the sky, the Sun ascends toward the north, and the days become longer until both day and night are of equal length at the Vernal Equinox. At the Winter Solstice, the Light is at its lowest ebb, its greatest darkness, and this is the time of the birth of the Sun.**

HIEREUS: **At the Winter Solstice, darkness is at its supreme length, but at its dawning, the Sun gradually begins its increase, giving more and more light as the days progress. And this is why many Deities are said to be born on the Winter Solstice, for this is the time of the birth of the Sun from the darkness, a time of spiritual birth.**

HEGEMON: **The dawning of the Sun on the Winter Solstice, rising out of the darkest night of the year, speaks of the dawning of creation from the darkness of the void. The same process of creation that gave birth to the Universe also gives birth to spiritual development.**

KERYX: **At the Winter Solstice, the birth of the Divine Sun within brings light to the soul which eventually overthrows the powers of darkness. Although the Sun is born at the Winter Solstice, and its light will continually increase, it is still born into darkness and has yet to grow.**

STOLISTES: **As Solar Initiates, we start our journey as a spiritual child, born from the darkness of an unillumined consciousness into the darkness of the Winter Solstice. It is during the process of initiation within the Solar Initiate that the inner Sun gains strength as it moves from Winter to Spring, from the searching in the darkness of the Outer Order into the Light of the Sun in the Inner.**

DADOUCHOS: **As the Inner Sun grows within the self, it works to control the forces of our inner darkness, bringing about a spiritual maturation through the Light of Divine Spirit. On the day of the Winter Solstice the dawning sun emerges from the darkest point of the year, and harkens back to the first day of creation when the dawning light first emerged from the primeval darkness. It signifies a definitive stage in the Work of spiritual enlightenment.**

HIEROPHANT: **Let us then give birth to the Divine Sun within this sacred Hall on this day of the Winter Solstice.**

1. The Birth of the Sun: The Creation of a Magical Universe

The lights are dimmed in the Hall. The Officers move to stand at their Planetary stations.

The members stand for a brief moment in silence and visualize being surrounded by complete darkness, a void wherein nothing exists.

Hierophant: **Nothing exists. There is no light, no sound, only emptiness and silence, a vast stillness in an infinite void. Suddenly, in the depths of the void, there arises a shining light. At first, the smallest of points, single and alone, growing larger and larger, illuminating the darkness of the void.**

Hierophant draws the Sigil of Sol over the Altar.

Hierophant: **And the void was filled with light, scintillating and warm, illuminating the darkness with brilliant inspiration. In the divine name YHVH ELOAH V'DAATH and in the name of the great Archangel MICHAEL, I call forth the light of the Sun.**

Hierophant lights the Solar candle on the altar and says: **The flame of mystical creation is now awakened, and the darkness has been made light.**

Hierophant takes up the Solar candle and goes clockwise to the East of the sacred space, and stands before Praemonstrator at the station of Saturn.

Hierophant: **And the Divine Light of the Sun glowed brightly and illumination reigned supreme but there was no form, neither the cohesion of the Light nor the beginnings of structure. The purpose of the Sun was to create life in the void, but life cannot evolve without form.**

Hierophant gives Praemonstrator the Solar Candle.
Praemonstrator draws the Sigil of Saturn in the air with the Solar Candle.

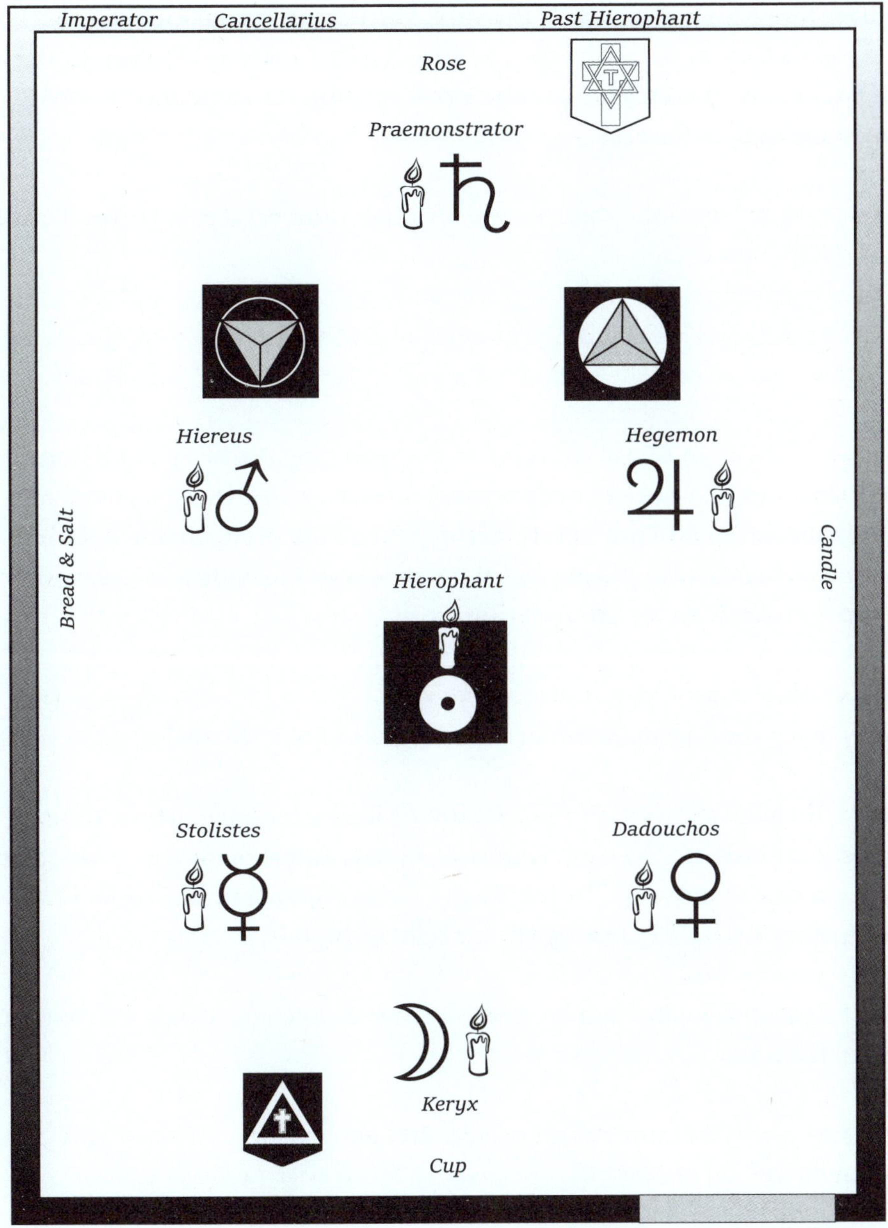

Figure 26: Temple Setup for the Ceremony of the Seven Wanderers

PRAEMONSTRATOR: **Through the power of Saturn the divine imagination was born, whose thoughts gave shape to the void. The patient and laborious process of the crystallization of the universe was begun and time was created. In the divine name YHVH ELOHIM and in the name of the great Archangel KASSIEL, I call forth the light of Saturn.**

PRAEMONSTRATOR lights the Saturn candle from the Sun candle and gives the Sol Candle back to HIEROPHANT.

HIEROPHANT, with the Sun candle, walks diagonally to the Southeast of the Temple and stands before HEGEMON at the station of Jupiter.

HIEROPHANT: **The light of the universe was crystalizing, forming itself, but the laws of formation had not yet been created. Order amidst the chaos was necessary, an organization and preservation, the structuring of the divine light into interacting elements. The purpose of the Sun was to create life in the void, but life cannot evolve without interrelation.**

HIEROPHANT gives the Solar Candle to HEGEMON.
HEGEMON draws the Sigil of Jupiter in the air with the Solar Candle.

HEGEMON: **Through the power of Jupiter divine laws were born, whose thoughts gave beneficent order to the void. Kindness, virtue, and love were embedded into the pattern of the universe. In the divine name EL and in the name of the great Archangel SACHIEL, I call forth the light of Jupiter.**

HEGEMON lights the Jupiter candle from the Sun candle and hands the Solar Candle back to HIEROPHANT.

HIEROPHANT, with the Sun candle, walks straight to the Northeast and faces the HIEREUS at the station of Mars.

HIEROPHANT: **The light of the universe had created interrelationships and laws, but laws must be defended and divine will must prevail. Discipline and dynamism, the energy to project life outward and implement the divine plan was necessary. The purpose of the Sun was to create life in the void, but life cannot evolve without motivation and drive.**

HIEROPHANT gives the Solar Candle to the HIEREUS.
HIEREUS draws the Sigil of Mars in the air with the Solar Candle.

HIEREUS: **Through the power of Mars divine will was born, whose thoughts gave potency and force to the void. Power, determination, and strength were embedded into the pattern of the universe. In the divine name ELOHIM GIBOR and in the name of the great Archangel ZAMAEL, I call forth the light of Mars.**

HIEREUS lights the Mars candle from the Sun candle and returns the Sol Candle to HIEROPHANT.

HIEROPHANT walks diagonally to the East of the altar and faces the West.

HIEROPHANT: **The Sun had created the heavens and the patterns of life. The light of the universe had illuminated the darkness and had placed therein divine imaginings and formation, love and laws, power and will. But yet the work of the Sun was not complete. To be fully realized, life had to be reflected in physical form, to be made manifest, and so humans were born under the light of the Sun. Yet humanity, in whom was embedded the divine pattern of the universe, was to be given a certain purpose and that was to search for and come to know its divine origins.**

HIEROPHANT, with the Sun candle, walks diagonally to the Southwest and faces the DADOUCHOS at the station of Venus.

HIEROPHANT: **The Sun now manifested life on earth through Nature's countless forms, and it was there that humanity was born. Humans were given emotion and desire in order that they may know their divine origins. The purpose of the Sun was to manifest life on earth, but human life cannot evolve without creativity, aspiration, and love.**

HIEROPHANT gives DADOUCHOS the Solar Candle.
DADOUCHOS draws the Sigil of Venus in the air with the Solar Candle.

DADOUCHOS: **Through the power of Venus human love and desire were born, whose imagination gave tangible form to the divine light. Creative inspiration and a yearning for happiness were embedded into the pattern of the human mind. In the divine name YHVH TZABAOTH and in the name of the great Archangel ANAEL, I call forth the light of Venus.**

DADOUCHOS lights the Venus candle from the Sun candle and returns the Solar Candle to HIEROPHANT.

HIEROPHANT, with the Sun candle, walks straight to the Northwest and faces the Stolistes at the station of Mercury.

HIEROPHANT: **Human love and desire had brought about companionship and pleasure to the people of the world, but this was not enough for humans to be complete. Humans possess mind and their minds had to be stimulated and educated in order to know their divine origins. The purpose of the Sun was to manifest life on earth, but human life cannot evolve without intelligence, curiosity, and a thirst for knowledge.**

HIEROPHANT gives the STOLISTES the Solar Candle.
STOLISTES draws the Sigil of Mercury in the air with the Solar Candle.

STOLISTES: **Through the power of Mercury speech, learning and a desire to know the mysteries were born, whose expressions gave tangible form to the divine light. Intelligence and communication were embedded into the pattern of the human mind. In the divine name ELOHIM TZABAOTH and in the name of the great Archangel RAPHAEL, I call forth the light of Mercury.**

STOLISTES lights the Mercury candle from the Sun candle and returns the Solar Candle to HIEROPHANT.

HIEROPHANT, with the Sun candle, walks diagonally to the West and faces KERYX at the station of the Moon.

HIEROPHANT: **Humans now possessed creativity and intellect, but this was not enough to stimulate the desire to know their divine origins. The Sun therefore placed a reflection of itself deep within the human psyche, behind the mind. And there the Sun placed a love of honest science, a delight in novelty, and a steadfast desire for freedom. The purpose of the Sun was to manifest life on earth, but human life cannot evolve without autonomy and liberty.**

HIEROPHANT gives the KERYX the Solar Candle.
KERYX draws the Sigil of the Moon in the air toward the West.

KERYX: **Through the power of the Moon a reflection of the Sun was born in the human mind, whose expression gave a yearning of the intellect to know and manifest the divine light. The love of freedom and a desire to comprehend divine origins were embedded into the pattern of the human mind. In the divine name SHADDAI EL CHAI and in the name of the great Archangel GABRIEL, I call forth the light of the Moon.**

KERYX lights the Moon candle from the Sun and returns the Solar Candle to HIEROPHANT.

HIEROPHANT, with the Sun candle, walks straight to the West of the altar in the center of the Temple. HIEROPHANT places the Sun candle on the center of the altar.

HIEROPHANT: **The higher is reflected in the lower, and the lower reaches to the heights. Through the birth of the Sun we have created a magical universe within this sacred space wherein the human may come to know the Divine and wherein the Divine may manifest in the human.**

(Brief pause.)

2. Ascending the Ladder of Lights: Forming the Six-Rayed Star in Sacred Space

Figure 27: Planetary Candles on the Menorah

Keryx places the menorah on the eastern side of the Altar top, then returns to planet station.

Hierophant is to the East of the altar, facing the West.

Hierophant: **The Sun in the center of the universe is the mediator of all powers, earthly and celestial, and in the Sun of the mortal body are the divine and the human united in one soul. The force of the Sun is outpouring but its essence draws us inward, for the Sun draws all bodies to itself, causing them to seek the center. In this seeking, the person must sacrifice particulars of their mortal selves, stripping away the outworn and the useless, revealing within themselves the Divine Light shining.**

We will now begin the ascending journey by awakening the powers of the Sun within us, for it is the Sun in the self that illuminates the Divine Light within, the Light that shines in the darkness though the darkness comprehends it not.

Hierophant takes up the Sun Candle.

All Members turn their auras to ORANGE and hold this visualization until the image is as strong as possible.

Hierophant: **Powers of the Sun, you who are the Shining Crown of the Day, hear us now. We are ones who are ascending the Ladder of Lights. Swing wide your gates and allow us to enter your realm.**

Hierophant lights the Sun candle on the Menorah, transferring the flame from the orange candle.

All Members visualize the ORANGE symbol of the Sun glowing in the heart.

Hierophant: **In our quest for the Light we sacrifice all arrogance, conceit, self-importance, and sense of superiority over any living creature. As an embodiment of the Sun we shall strive to acquire the qualities of good judgment, honor, faithfulness, and kindness expressed toward all.**

Keryx takes up the Moon candle.

All Members turn the color of the aura to BLUE and hold this visualization until the image is as strong as possible.

Keryx: **Powers of the Moon, you who are the Shining Crown of the Night, hear us now. We are ones who are ascending the Ladder of Lights. Swing wide your gates and allow us to enter your realm.**

Keryx lights the Luna candle on the Menorah, transferring the flame from the blue candle, then returns to planet station.

All Members visualize the BLUE symbol of the Moon glowing in the heart.

Keryx: **In our quest for the Light we sacrifice our energies of increase and decrease. As an embodiment of Luna we shall strive to acquire the qualities of tenderness, peacefulness, and a love of freedom.**

Stolistes takes up the Mercury candle.
All Members turn the color of the aura to YELLOW and hold this visualization until the image is as strong as possible.

Stolistes: **Powers of Mercury, you who are the Swift Ones, hear us now. We are ones who are ascending the Ladder of Lights. Swing wide your gates and allow us to enter your realm.**

Stolistes lights the Mercury candle on the Menorah, transferring the flame from the yellow candle, then returns to planet station.

The members visualize the YELLOW symbol of the Mercury glowing in the heart.

Stolistes: **In our quest for the light we sacrifice all malevolent and spiteful conspiracies or collusions. As an embodiment of Mercury we shall strive, as students of the Mysteries, to acquire the qualities of a true seeker of occult knowledge, desiring to explore all forms of learning.**

Dadouchos takes up the Venus candle.
All Members turn the color of the aura to GREEN and hold this visualization until the image is as strong as possible.

Dadouchos: **Powers of Venus, you who are the Beauteous Ones, hear us now. We are ones who are ascending the Ladder of Lights. Swing wide your gates and allow us to enter your realm.**

Dadouchos lights the Venus candle on the Menorah, transferring the flame from the green candle, then returns to planet station.

All Members visualize the GREEN symbol of the Venus glowing in the heart.

Dadouchos: **In our quest for the light we sacrifice the illusion of longing, for it is the desire for material things that is the root of all unhappiness. As an embodi-**

ment of Venus we shall strive to acquire the qualities of love and mirth, and we shall delight in the arts.

HIEREUS takes up the Mars candle.
ALL MEMBERS turn the color of the aura to RED and hold this visualization until the image is as strong as possible.

HIEREUS: **Powers of Mars, you who are the Valiant Ones, hear us now. We are ones who are ascending the Ladder of Lights. Swing wide your gates and allow us to enter your realm.**

DADOUCHOS lights the Mars candle on the Menorah, transferring the flame from the red candle, then returns to planet station.

ALL MEMBERS visualize the RED symbol of the Mars glowing in the heart.

HIEREUS: **In our quest for the light we sacrifice all unkind and outmoded beliefs and also we sacrifice all careless and rash actions. As an embodiment of Mars we shall strive to acquire the qualities of courage, determination, and discipline.**

HEGEMON takes up the Jupiter candle.

ALL MEMBERS turn the color of the aura to VIOLET and hold this visualization until the image is as strong as possible.

HEGEMON: **Powers of Jupiter, you who are the Beneficent Ones, hear us now. We are ones who are ascending the Ladder of Lights. Swing wide your gates and allow us to enter your realm.**

DADOUCHOS lights the Jupiter candle on the Menorah, transferring the flame from the violet candle, then returns to planet station.

ALL MEMBERS visualize the VIOLET symbol of the Jupiter glowing in the heart.

HEGEMON: **In our quest for the light we sacrifice all selfish impulses for wealth and worldly goods. As an embodiment of Jupiter we shall strive to acquire the qualities of charity and free-thinking spirituality.**

PRAEMONSTRATOR takes up the Saturn candle.

ALL MEMBERS turn the color of the aura to BLUE-VIOLET and hold this visualization until the image is as strong as possible.

PRAEMONSTRATOR: **Powers of Saturn, you who are the Austere Ones, hear us now. We are ones who are ascending the Ladder of Lights. Swing wide your gates and allow us to enter your realm.**

DADOUCHOS lights the Saturn candle on the Menorah, transferring the flame from the blue-violet candle, then returns to planet station.

ALL MEMBERS visualize the BLUE-VIOLET symbol of the Saturn glowing in the heart.

PRAEMONSTRATOR: **In our quest for the light we sacrifice all forms of deceit and dishonesty. As an embodiment of Saturn we shall strive to acquire the qualities of imagination, patience, and diligent labor.**

HIEROPHANT: **A magical universe have we formed from the planetary lights. We have descended through the spheres and risen to the heights. In our journey we have acquired the virtues of the travelers, and through those virtues we have manifested their powers in this sacred space. We shall sing our praises to the Wandering Lights of the universe**

PRAEMONSTRATOR: **We sing praise to the Sower and the Reaper, the one who bears the scepter of elder night. We call to the Ancient One, the one who is veiled, the mother-father of the heavens whose domain is the vast flowing ocean of time. O Silent One who works unseen in the darkness, we praise you. Through your gift of enduring fidelity, we shall bring our labors on earth to their full harvest.**

HEGEMON: **We sing praise to Truth and Fairness, the glorious dispenser of mercy. We call to the Divine Liberality, the source of all brotherhood and sisterhood, the true purveyor of all bounties. Through your power, peace and amity shall exist between us and all beings. O Divine One of Benevolent Rule, the enlightened wisdom which underlies noble authority, we praise you. Through your gift of a generous heart, charitable acts shall we embrace.**

HIEREUS: **We sing praise to the Mighty Guardian who enchains the forces of darkness. We call to the divine defender of justice and truth, the noble inspirer of courage, endurance, and bold resolve. Great power who motivates loyalty and confirms the steadfast heart, we praise you. Through your gift of strong resolve, we will be powerful adversaries of any malevolent force whose path we cross.**

HIEROPHANT: **We sing praise to the Mediator of the Planetary Powers, for through you comes the force of magical ascendance and mystical endeavor. We call to the one who is reborn again and again from the darkest of nights into the gentle light of the dawn. O Divine One of the sky, master of eternity, who fills the heavens with rays of golden fire, we praise you. Through your gift of life and joy renewed, we shall emit your light to the outer world.**

DADOUCHOS: **We sing praise to the Lady of Beauty and Grace, the radiant giver of love and harmony. We call to the one who greens the earth and fills my sanctuary with joy and sweet laughter. O Divine One of loving eyes, who brings peace and elegance into my life, we praise you. Through your gift of the inspiration, creations of great beauty and delight shall be ours to give.**

STOLISTES: **We sing praise to the Traveler between the Worlds, who speaks of secret tidings, who is the far-seeing and sure guide of souls. We call to the one who is the great scribe, the keeper of the signs, the sigils, and the words of power. O Divine One, great in the magical art, who brings skill and knowledge, we praise you. Through your gift of magical learning, we shall know the hidden ways of life and the mysteries shall be ours to behold.**

KERYX: **We sing the praises of the Giver of Dreams and the Maker of Enchantments, whose silver light shines in the nighttime skies. We call to the one who governs**

the tides and all growing things. O Divine One who is the gracious opener of hidden doors, the initial step into the mysteries, we praise you. Through your gift of quietude and freedom, the threshold to the unseen realms has been opened to us.

HIEROPHANT: **We give thanks and praise to all planetary powers. May your gifts be ours to hold and share and may they ever abide in this sacred hall of the mysteries.**

ALL MEMBERS: **So mote it be.**

3. A Repast of the Sun

KERYX moves the Menorah to a side altar. Planetary Officers place their candles on the side Altar as well in this order—KERYX, STOLISTES, DADOUCHOS, HIEROPHANT, HIEREUS, HEGEMON, PRAEMONSTRATOR—then return to their original stations as in the Neophyte Hall *except* for HIEROPHANT, who stays east of the Altar facing West. KERYX replaces the Elements of the Repast upon the Altar in their proper places.

HIEROPHANT: **We invoke the Lord Sun, effulgent gem, destroyer of vice, sadness, poverty, and ailments. Meritorious art Thou, our diamond refuge, the One of a Thousand Rays, Giver of the gifts of prophecy, good fortune, and the Light of Life, we call to you.**

PRAEMONSTRATOR: **Send forth Thy rays unto us, exalted and noble. Thou who gathers all Beauty into Thyself, pure and wise. Thou who holds the reins of the six noble Planets, so that they may be guided by Thee, hear our petition.**

HIEREUS: **Thou who rules over all that is and will be, give ear to our supplications. Let us receive Thy Light and Power; from Thy shining may we also shine. O Source of Power! Foundation of strength, joy of life, Pillar of Exaltation, origin of all good deeds, we take refuge in Thy glorious streams of Light.**

HEGEMON: **Thou who gives us Thy keys to the future, we call to you. By the grace of the Sun, we immediately become like the gods of wealth. By the reins of the Six**

Planets, which are given Thou, may Thou be the cause of our liberation and take away all our pain.

KERYX: **Though Thou hast now to descend into the darkness, Thou will be reborn in Thy Shining Rulership once again. Grant us a part of that which we desire in this world and grant something of Thy Majesty and Thy Beauty unto us.**

STOLISTES: **By Thy quality of firmly establishing those who wish to serve Thy light, listen to our prayer and heed our call! O Cause of Causes, Thou who art sanctified and made Holy with the Unending Rule of Eternity, give us your blessing.**

DADOUCHOS: **Divine One of the Sun, we ask that Thou listen and grant us recognition and kind reception. Victory over difficulties and the fruit of serving the Light be ours to hold. So mote it be.**

HIEROPHANT: **We ask this in the name of YHVH ELOAH V'DAATH, who is set over Thy realm, in the name of the Archangel MICHAEL and the Angelic Choir of the TARSHISHIM, that Thy Light shines through us and supports us in all that we do in the coming season, for you are Master and King of all that is and will be.**

Let us now partake of the Mystic Repast of the Sun.

I invite you to inhale with me the sweet perfume of this Rose as a symbol of Air. Let it be for us a perfume of the Solar Light.
(Makes Blessing Cross and Symbol of the Sun over the Rose.)

To feel with me the warmth of this sacred Flame as a symbol of Fire. Let it be for us a guiding Light on our Solar journey.
(Makes Blessing Cross and Symbol of the Sun over the Candle.)

To eat with me this Bread and Salt as symbols of Earth. May it be for us an embodiment of the powers of the Sun.
(Makes Blessing Cross and Symbol of the Sun over the Bread and Salt.)

> **And finally to drink with me this Wine, a consecrated symbol of Elemental Water. Let it be for us the outflowing of the Light of Sol.**
> (Makes Blessing Cross and Symbol of the Sun over the Wine.)

HIEROPHANT serves the PRAEMONSTRATOR. The rest of the OFFICERS and members partake of the Mystic Repast in the same order that they would in the Closing of the Neophyte Hall.

When the KERYX finishes the Wine, the cup is turned over and the KERYX exclaims: **It is finished!**

The KERYX returns to place.

HIEROPHANT: **In the Divine Names of Sol, we give thanks and praise to the Spirits of the Sun! From falsity lead us to Truth. From darkness lead us to Light. From death lead us to Immortality. May the long-time Sun shine upon us, may all love surround us, and may the Pure Light within guide us on our way.**

ALL MEMBERS: **So mote it be.**

At this point, any comments, announcements, or temple business may be discussed.

Proceed to the Closing of the Neophyte Hall. (NOTE: Skip the Mystic Repast in the Closing.)

✠ ✠ ✠

SECTION TWO

Inner Order Rituals

chapter 4

CONSECRATION OF MAGICAL TOOLS

The First (or Outer) Order of the Golden Dawn is, first and foremost, a school of magic in the Western Esoteric Tradition. The primary goal of the First Order is to teach students the language, theory, and basic principles of magic necessary to aid the magician in their *later* practice. The study of the Knowledge Lectures and assimilation of the energies that students encounter during initiation takes precedence. Other than the Lesser Ritual of the Pentagram and specific meditative work for the elemental grades, very little formalized magic actually happens in the First Order in private, outside of the group ritual setting.

It is not until the Second (or Inner) Order that the Initiate undertakes the practice of magic on a grand scale. Adepts of the Second Order build and consecrate their own magical tools, write and perform their own rituals based on traditional Golden Dawn formulas, practice techniques of skrying and astral traveling, create and assume the images of godforms, and perform advanced magical techniques. Many difficult procedures of magic have to be carefully learned, and certain fundamental rituals must be committed to memory. In a strict sense, the Second Order is not technically a part of the Golden Dawn. It is a separate Order, the *Ordo Roseae Rubeae et Aureae Crucis (R.R. et A.C.)*—the "Order of the Red Rose and Golden Cross."

While Adepts of the *R.R. et A.C.* also meet for initiation ceremonies, lectures, and group rituals, a much larger portion of the work in the higher grades actually takes place in private. By tradition and design, many Inner Order rituals are solo rites performed by the Adept alone on their continuing path toward magical proficiency and spiritual growth.

One of the first orders of business that new Adepts are encouraged to undertake involves the consecration of specific magical tools needed for advanced Workings within our system.

The standard tool kit of magical implements for a Golden Dawn Adept includes seven items that magicians are required to make and consecrate for their personal magical work. We have come to call these the *Working Tools of the Adept.* They include the Lotus Wand, the Rose Cross Lamen, the Magic Sword, and the four Elemental Tools. These seven implements represent specific energies and unique qualities. They are the quintessential magical tools that will serve the Golden Dawn Adept well on the Path of Light, and they will be used for almost all private magical workings outside of and apart from group work.

The Elemental Tools include the Earth Pentacle, the Air Dagger, the Water Cup, and the Fire Wand. These are the Tarot symbols equating to the divine name YHVH. They have a certain bond and sympathy between them so that even if only one is to be used, the others should also be present, just as each of the four Elemental Tablets is divided into four quarters representing all four elements bound together within the same tablet.

Consecration of the Adept's Working Tools

To *consecrate* something means to make it sacred. A consecration ritual is a rite of dedication that empowers a symbol or object, drawing a meaningful, energetic relationship between the symbol and that which it represents.

Consecration is a sacred act of purification, empowerment, and alignment with the Higher. It works to establish a righteous orientation, a true North Star, to guide the magician ever onward toward the Divine. Ritual consecration infuses these essential tools with energetic force, attuning them with the Adept's Higher Self and transforming them from inanimate objects into live conduits for divine power.

The Consecration Rituals of the Adept's Working Tools are among the best-known rituals of the Second Order. Many magicians who have created their own Lotus Wand or Earth Pentacle have charged their implements using the consecrations ritual found in Regardie's *The Golden Dawn*. The rituals provided here are adapted from those traditional rites but have been updated for modern use.[80] We present them here in a format that is more reader-friendly, with clearer instructions, stage directions, and some corrections.

(NOTE: The stage directions in all the solo rites presented in this chapter are numbered. This makes it easier for the solitary practitioner to follow the script and not lose their place in the ritual.)

General Temple Setup for an Adept Working in the Portal Hall

Preparation: The temple setup for the consecration of the Working Tools is virtually the same for all the tools with a few differences as indicated below. In all cases you will need:

- The temple arranged as in the diagram in figure 28
- Chair in the West[81]
- The Enochian Tablets[82] set around the room in their respective quarters, on or above side altars[83] (Glass-enclosed pillar candles in the elemental colors can be placed in front of the Tablets.)
- Black and White Pillars toward the eastern edge of the temple
- Stolistes Cup of Lustral Water in the north
- Dadouchos Censer of Incense in the south[84]

---

80. Adapted from Regardie, *The Golden Dawn*: "Consecration of the Lotus Wand" (385–87), "Consecration of the Rose Cross" (396–98), "Consecration Ritual of the Sword" (401–2), and "Ritual of Consecration of the Four Elemental Weapons" (406–12).

81. Or in the East if preferred.

82. Rituals in this chapter that do not *specifically* call for the Enochian Tablets to be present include the Consecrations of the Lotus Wand, the Rose Cross Lamen, and the Magic Sword. Nevertheless, it is always a good idea to have the Tablets present. The Tablets *must* be present for the Elemental Tools.

83. A side altar can be any convenient small table or nightstand. Industrious magicians can construct four small stands and paint them in the elemental colors.

84. Some rituals in this chapter have traditionally called for the incense to be placed on the Altar next to the rose. But in consecration, the incense represents Fire, not Air. Therefore we place it in the south.

- Central Black Double Cubical Altar upon which are placed:
    - » The Cross and Triangle (center)
    - » Tablet of Union (center)[85]
    - » Elemental Symbols

There are two sets of Elemental Symbols to choose from:

1. *Natural Elemental Symbols:* Rose, Red Candle, Chalice of Water, and platter of Salt[86]
2. *Elemental Tools:* Fire Wand, Water Cup, Air Dagger, and Earth Pentacle

For the consecrations of the Lotus Wand, Rose Cross Lamen, and the Magic Sword, the natural symbols are placed on top of the altar as follows: EAST–Rose, SOUTH–Candle, WEST–Water, NORTH–Salt. When consecrating or using the Elemental Tools, the natural symbols are moved to the side altars and replaced by the four Elemental Tools themselves.

A piece of silk or linen (either white or the color of the implement) will be needed for wrapping the newly consecrated implement or a specially made bag or case created for this purpose.

Adept Regalia: White robe, yellow-and-white-striped nemyss, Adept sash, and yellow socks or slippers. Also, the Rose Cross Lamen hanging from a yellow collar.

Candles and incense are lit just before the start of any ritual. Ambient music may also be helpful.

---

85. When using the Tablet of Union, place a white glass-enclosed pillar candle just to the east of it.

86. If you choose to add a Mystic Repast to the end of any ritual, fill the chalice with wine and add a small piece of bread to the platter of salt. (This is another reason to have a Stolistes Cup of Water in the north for purifying.)

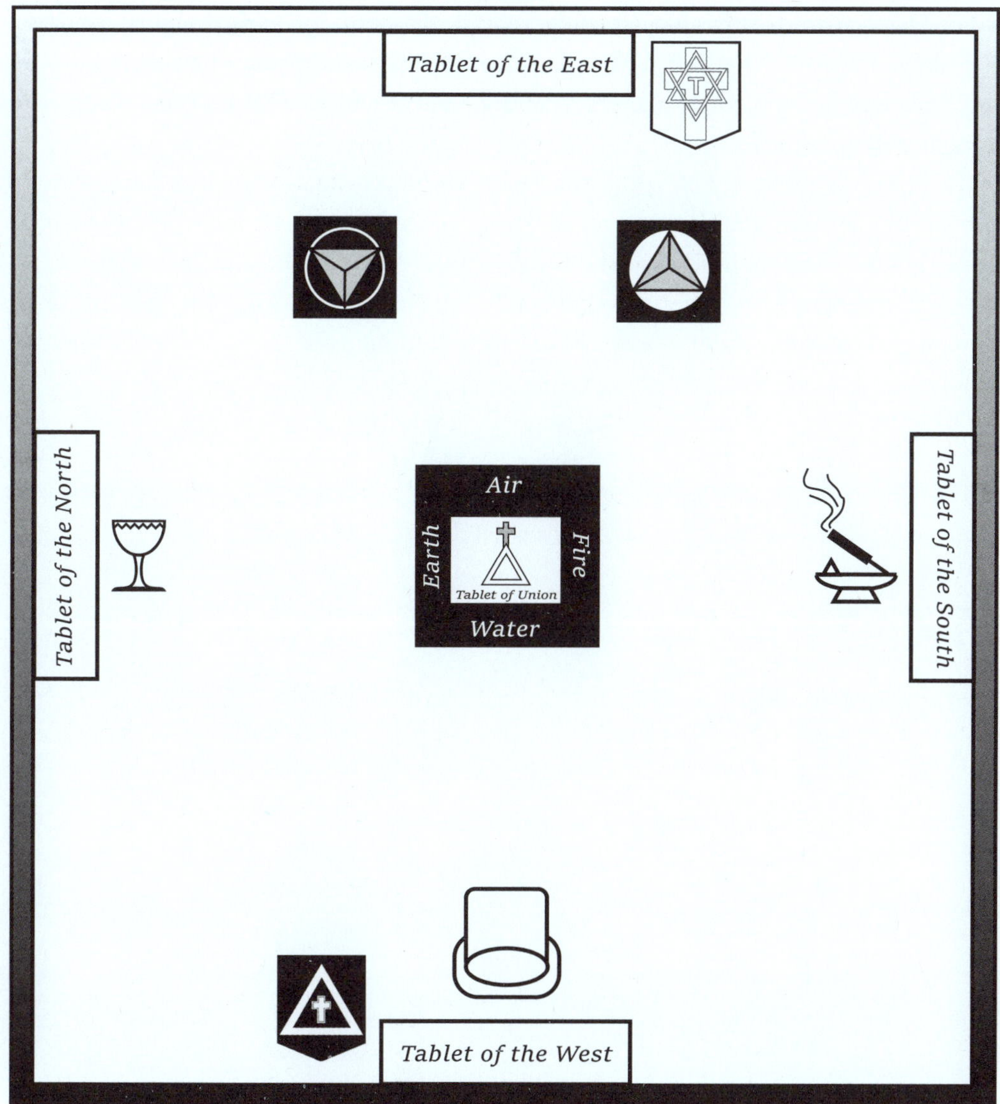

Figure 28: General Temple Setup for the Adept in the Portal Hall

The Lotus Wand

The Lotus Wand is the Swiss army knife of implements—the single most useful tool in Golden Dawn magic. This all-purpose wand can be used for most magical situations and rituals. It is especially useful for fine-tuning the invocation and banishment of any and all elemental, Sephirotic, planetary, and Zodiacal energies. The Lotus Wand is for general use in magical work.

Of all the Adept's Working Tools, the Lotus Wand is arguably the most important. It is carried by the Adeptus Minor at all meetings of the Second Order where the initiate has the right to be present. Ideally, the wand is to be made by the Adept unassisted, and to be consecrated by him or her alone. It is not to be touched by any other person, and is kept wrapped in white silk or linen, free of external influences.

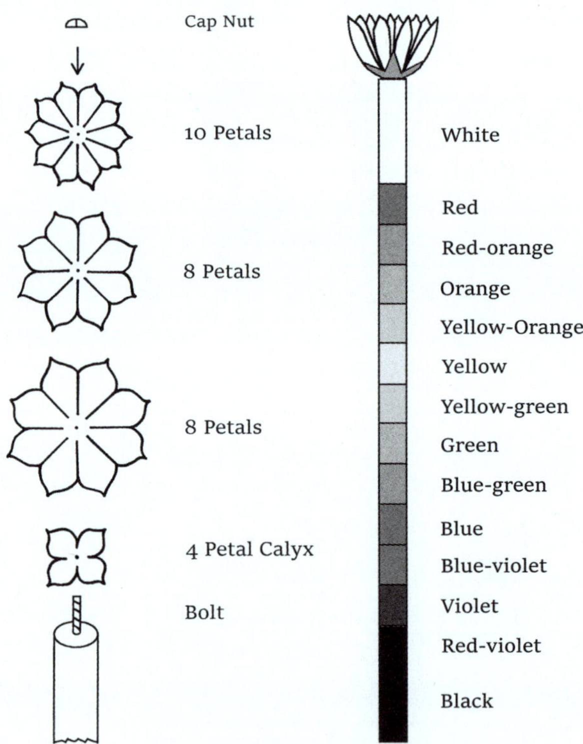

Figure 29: The Lotus Wand

In ancient Egypt, the lotus was a symbol of purity and regeneration. For this reason, the Golden Dawn's Lotus Wand is dedicated to the goddess Isis. The wand head is a 26-petaled lotus flower made from three layers of petals. The outer two layers each have eight petals that are white on the inside and olive with five black veins on the outside. The middle eight petals refer to the counter-charged natural and spiritual forces of air and fire. The lowest and outer eight petals refer to the powers of earth and water. The central interior layer has ten petals that are white on both sides, referring to the purity of the ten Sephiroth. The golden head of the locknut (or screwhead) that attaches the flower to the wand refers to the spiritual Sun, while the outer calyx of four orange sepals shows the action of the Sun upon the variety of life.

The shaft of the wand is divided into the colors of the twelve signs of the Zodiac, between a white band for spirit and a black band for the mundane.

As a general rule, the white end of the Wand is used to invoke and the black end to banish. The white end may be used to banish by tracing a banishing symbol against an evil and opposing force that has resisted other efforts. Hold the wand by the white portion for all divine and spiritual matters as well as for Sephirotic influences and for the process of rising in the planes. Whether you are holding the white portion for spiritual things, or the black portion for the mundane, or the blue band for Sagittarius, etc., invoke by directing the white end to the quarter desired. When banishing, point the black end to that quarter.

The wand is not to be inverted. But if very material forces are concerned, holding the wand by the black end may be the most suitable for invocation, but only with the greatest caution.

For Zodiacal energies, hold the wand by the appropriate band between the thumb and two fingers. If a planetary working is required, hold the wand by the band representing the day or night house of the planet (depending on the time of day for the working—use the day house attributions for the daylight hours or the night house attributions if you are performing the ritual after dark), or else by the sign in which the planet is at the time (table 5).

Planet	*House*	*Sign*	*Band*
SATURN	Day House	Aquarius	Violet
	Night House	Capricorn	Blue-violet
JUPITER	Day House	Sagittarius	Blue
	Night House	Pisces	Red-violet
MARS	Day House	Aries	Red
	Night House	Scorpio	Blue-green
VENUS	Day House	Libra	Green
	Night House	Taurus	Red-orange
MERCURY	Day House	Gemini	Orange
	Night House	Virgo	Yellow-green
SOL	N/A	In Leo only	Yellow
LUNA	N/A	In Cancer only	Yellow-orange

Table 5: Correspondences of the Lotus Wand

For example, if you are working with Venus, hold the Libra band during the day and the Taurus band at night.

If you are performing an elemental working, hold the wand by one of the signs of the elemental triplicity, according to the nature of the element you intend to invoke. (*Fire triplicity:* Aries, Leo, Sagittarius. *Water triplicity:* Cancer, Scorpio, Pisces. *Air triplicity:* Gemini, Libra, Aquarius. *Earth triplicity:* Taurus, Virgo, Capricorn.) Bear in mind that the Kerubic sign represents the most powerful action of the element in the triplicity.

The Lotus Flower should not be touched in working, but in Sephirotic and spiritual things the flower can be inclined toward the forehead, and to rise in the planes the golden-orange-colored center is to be fully directed to the forehead.[87]

Consecration of the Lotus Wand

Preparation: The Temple should be arranged in accordance with the *General Temple Setup for an Adept Working in the Portal Hall.* Ideally the Lotus Wand should be placed on top of the Altar, with the flower toward the east, but this is not always practical. Alter-

87. Regardie, *The Golden Dawn*, 384.

natively, the wand could be placed in a specially made wand stand at the side of the Altar or wherever is most convenient.

You will also need an astrological figure of the heavens for the time of the working—a horoscope for the ritual "birth time" of the wand's consecration.[88] After determining this, you will need a set of astrological drawings—twelve drawings of the Zodiacal signs—to be placed in a circle around the room in accordance with the natal chart.

The Adept should be dressed in the regalia of the Second Order. Also needed:

- The temple arranged as in the diagram (see figure 30)
- Stolistes Cup in the north, Dadouchos Censer in the south
- The Central Black Double Cubical Altar upon which are placed:
    - The Cross and Triangle (center)
    - The Natural Elemental Symbols (rose, red candle, water, salt)[89]
- An astrological figure (chart) of the heavens for the time of the working. Prepare this ahead of time.
- A set of astrological symbolic drawings—twelve drawings of the Zodiacal signs—to be placed in a circle around the room in accordance with the chart of the heavens at the time of the working.
- The new Lotus Wand, and white linen or silk for wrapping
- *Optional:* Twelve small tables or plant stands in a circle around the altar for holding the Zodiacal symbols and candles (This eliminates the need to place the symbols on the floor and makes the consecration easier.)
- Twelve Zodiacal candles in the twelve colors (see table 5)
- A white taper candle near the Aries symbol for transferring the flame (Place on a stick incense holder to protect the floor from dripping wax.)

(NOTE: Light only the red candle on the Altar at the beginning of the ritual.)

---

88. If for some reason you cannot determine this, it is acceptable to place Aries in the east, but this is not the preferred method. See figure 30.

89. The original script calls for incense to be placed next to the rose for consecrations. However, we like to place the Dadouchos Censer in the south and the Stolistes Cup in the north for all purifications and consecrations.

Figure 30: Temple Setup for Lotus Wand Consecration (With Aries in the East Variant)

The Opening

1. Stand west of the Altar, holding the Lotus Wand by the black portion, and say: **HEKAS! HEKAS! ESTE BEBELOI!**

2. Perform the LBRP.

3. Perform the Purification and Consecration as follows:

   a. Take up the Stolistes Cup of Water. Go to the east. Stand at the eastern edge of the Hall facing east. Hold up the Stolistes Cup of Water and trace the figure of a cross (up, down, left, right). Then sprinkle some water thrice in the form of an Invoking Water Triangle.

   b. Purify the temple in the same manner in the south, west, and north while saying the following: **So therefore, first, the Priest who governeth the works of Fire must sprinkle with the lustral water of the loud resounding sea.**[90]

   c. When returning to the east, hold up the cup and say: **I purify with Water!** Replace the cup.

   d. Take up the incense. Go to the east. Stand at the eastern edge of the Hall facing east. Hold up the incense and trace the figure of a cross (up, down, left, right). Then wave the incense thrice in the form of an Invoking Fire Triangle.

   e. Consecrate the temple in the same manner in the south, west, and north while saying the following: **And when after all the Phantoms are banished, thou shalt see that Holy and Formless Fire, that Fire which darts and flashes through the hidden depths of the Universe, hear thou the voice of Fire!**[91]

   f. When returning to the east, hold up the Incense and say: **I consecrate with Fire!** Replace the Incense.

4. Take the wand by the white band. Perform the Mystic Circumambulation.

---

90. This speech can be broken up as the Adept circumambulates the Hall and traces the figures thus: (EAST: ✛ **"So therefore, first"**), (SOUTH: ✛ **"the Priest who governeth the works of Fire"**), (WEST: ✛ **"must sprinkle with the lustral water"**), (NORTH: ✛ **"of the loud resounding sea"**), (RETURNING TO EAST, holds up the cup: **"I purify with Water!"**)

91. This speech can be broken up as the Adept circumambulates the Hall and traces the figures thus: (EAST: ✛ **"And when after all the Phantoms are banished"**), (SOUTH: ✛ **"thou shalt see that Holy and Formless Fire"**), (WEST: ✛ **"that Fire which darts and flashes through the hidden depths of the Universe"**), (NORTH: ✛ **"hear thou the voice of Fire!"**), (RETURNING TO EAST, holds up the incense: **"I consecrate with Fire!"**)

5. Perform the Adoration.

6. Perform the SIRP.

Proclamation of Intention (Optional)[92]

7. Say: **I, (*state your magical motto*), a Frater/Soror of the Rose of Ruby and the Cross of Gold and a member of the Body of the Christos, do this day undertake the Consecration of this Lotus Wand.**

With the Divine permission, I shall consecrate this Lotus Wand as a labor in the Divine Science, in pursuit of the Great Work, which is to purify and exalt my spiritual nature that with the Divine aid I may at length become more than human, and thus gradually raise and unite myself to my Higher and Divine Genius. So mote it be!

Invocation of Harpokratês

8. Stand east of the Altar and face east. Hold the Lotus Wand by the white portion, and give the LVX Signs in silence. Look upward, holding the white band of the wand high, and say: **O Harpokratês, Lord of Silence, who art enthroned upon the Lotus. Twenty-six are the Petals of the Lotus, Flower of thy Wand. O Lord of Creation, they are the Number of Thy Name. In the name of YOD HEH VAV HEH, let the Divine Light descend!**

Invoking the Zodiacal Signs

NOTE: *Stage directions for this section:* Facing consecutively the quarter where each Sign is located according to the Horary Figure for the time of working, repeat in each of the twelve directions the invocation that follows, using the appropriate Divine and Angelic names and Letters for each. Begin with Aries. (Remember that the symbols are to be set out on the floor *counterclockwise* around the room, just as a Zodiacal chart going from Aries to Pisces would be. However, you will have to move *clockwise* around the room to walk from one sign to the next.) Hold the wand by the appropriate colored band (pointing with the flower end), and in your left hand hold the Elemental symbol from the Altar.

---

92. Although this Proclamation of Intention was not a part of the traditional Lotus Wand Consecration, and is therefore optional, we recommend doing it.

9. For ARIES: Take up the red candle from the Altar in your left hand and go clockwise to the Aries symbol. Holding the red band of the Lotus Wand in your right hand, trace a clockwise circle over the Zodiacal symbol followed by the Invoking Pentagram of Spirit Active, vibrating the associated Divine names (**BITOM** and **EHEIEH**).[93] Give the Opening of the Veil, followed by the LVX Signs. Then trace the Invoking Pentagram of Fire, followed by the sigil of Aries in the center, vibrating the names **OIP TEAA PEDOCE** and **ELOHIM.** Give the Sign of Philosophus. (You can place the candle by the Zodiacal symbol in order to hold the script.) Then say:

The Heaven is above and the Earth is beneath. And betwixt the Light and the Darkness, the colors vibrate. I supplicate the Powers and Forces governing the Nature, Place, and Authority of the Sign *Aries*, by the Majesty of the Divine Name, YOD HEH VAV HEH, with which, in Earth life and language, I ascribe the letter *Heh*, to which is allotted the symbolic Tribe of *Gad* and over which is the Angel MELCHIDAEL, to bestow this present day and hour, and confirm their mystic and potent influence upon the *Red Band* of this Lotus Wand, which I hereby dedicate to purity and to Occult Work, and may its grasp strengthen me in the work of the character of *Aries* and its attributes. (Light the Aries candle by using the taper to transfer the flame from the red candle. Replace the red candle on the Altar.)

10. For TAURUS: Take up the salt in your left hand and go clockwise to the Taurus symbol. Holding the red-orange band of the Lotus Wand in your right hand, trace a clockwise circle over the Zodiacal symbol followed by the Invoking Pentagram of Spirit Passive, vibrating the associated Divine names (**NANTA** and **AGLA**). Give the Opening of the Veil, followed by the LVX Signs. Then trace the Invoking Pentagram of Earth, followed by the sigil of Taurus in the center, vibrating the names **EMOR DIAL HECTEGA** and **ADONAI.** Give the Sign of Zelator. (You can place the platter of salt by the Zodiacal symbol in order to hold the script.) Then say:

The Heaven is above and the Earth is beneath. And betwixt the Light and the Darkness, the colors vibrate. I supplicate the Powers and Forces governing the Nature, Place, and Authority of the Sign *Taurus,* by the Majesty of the Divine Name, YOD

93. Complete information on the Spirit Pentagrams and the Elemental Pentagrams can be found in Ciceros, *Golden Dawn Magic*, 226–30.

HEH HEH VAV, with which, in Earth life and language, I ascribe the letter *Vav*, to which is allotted the symbolic Tribe of *Ephraim* and over which is the Angel ASMODEL, to bestow this present day and hour, and confirm their mystic and potent influence upon the *Red-orange Band* of this Lotus Wand, which I hereby dedicate to purity and to Occult Work, and may its grasp strengthen me in the work of the character of *Taurus* and its attributes. (Light the Taurus candle by using the taper to transfer the flame from the Aries candle. Replace the salt.)

11. For GEMINI: Take up the rose in your left hand and go clockwise to the Gemini symbol. Holding the orange band of the Lotus Wand in your right hand, trace a clockwise circle over the Zodiacal symbol, followed by the Invoking Pentagram of Spirit Active, vibrating the associated Divine names (**EXARP** and **EHEIEH**). Give the Opening of the Veil, followed by the LVX Signs. Then trace the Invoking Pentagram of Air, followed by the sigil of Gemini in the center, vibrating the names **ORO IBAH AOZPI** and **YHVH.** Give the Sign of Theoricus. (You can place the rose by the Zodiacal symbol in order to hold the script.) Then say:

The Heaven is above and the Earth is beneath. And betwixt the Light and the Darkness, the colors vibrate. I supplicate the Powers and Forces governing the Nature, Place, and Authority of the Sign *Gemini*, by the Majesty of the Divine Name, YOD VAV HEH HEH, with which, in Earth life and language, I ascribe the letter *Zayin*, to which is allotted the symbolic Tribe of *Manasseh* and over which is the Angel AMBRIEL, to bestow this present day and hour, and confirm their mystic and potent influence upon the *Orange Band* of this Lotus Wand, which I hereby dedicate to purity and to Occult Work, and may its grasp strengthen me in the work of the character of *Gemini* and its attributes. (Light the Gemini candle by using the taper to transfer the flame from the Taurus candle. Replace the rose.)

12. For CANCER: Take up the Cup from the central Altar in your left hand and go clockwise to the Cancer symbol. Holding the yellow-orange band of the Lotus Wand in your right hand, trace a circle over the Zodiacal symbol, followed by the Invoking Pentagram of Spirit Passive, vibrating the associated Divine names (**HCOMA** and **AGLA**). Give the Opening of the Veil, followed by the LVX Signs. Then trace the Invoking Pentagram of Water, followed by the sigil of Taurus in the center, vibrating the names **EMPEH**

ARSEL GAIOL and **Aleph Lamed, EL**. Give the Sign of Practicus. (You can place the Cup by the Zodiacal symbol in order to hold the script.) Then say:

The Heaven is above and the Earth is beneath. And betwixt the Light and the Darkness, the colors vibrate. I supplicate the Powers and Forces governing the Nature, Place, and Authority of the Sign *Cancer*, by the Majesty of the Divine Name, HEH VAV HEH YOD, with which, in Earth life and language, I ascribe the letter *Cheth*, to which is allotted the symbolic Tribe of *Issachar* and over which is the Angel MURIEL, to bestow this present day and hour, and confirm their mystic and potent influence upon the *Yellow-orange Band* of this Lotus Wand, which I hereby dedicate to purity and to Occult Work, and may its grasp strengthen me in the work of the character of *Cancer* and its attributes. (Light the Cancer candle by using the taper to transfer the flame from the Gemini candle. Replace the cup.)

13. For LEO: Take up the red candle from the Altar in your left hand and go clockwise to the Leo symbol. Holding the yellow band of the Lotus Wand in your right hand, trace a circle over the Zodiacal symbol, followed by the Invoking Pentagram of Spirit Active, vibrating the associated Divine names (**BITOM** and **EHEIEH**). Give the Opening of the Veil, followed by the LVX Signs. Then trace the Invoking Pentagram of Fire, followed by the sigil of Leo in the center, vibrating the names **OIP TEAA PEDOCE** and **ELOHIM.** Give the Sign of Philosophus. Then say:

The Heaven is above and the Earth is beneath. And betwixt the Light and the Darkness, the colors vibrate. I supplicate the Powers and Forces governing the Nature, Place, and Authority of the Sign *Leo*, by the Majesty of the Divine Name, HEH VAV YOD HEH, with which, in Earth life and language, I ascribe the letter *Teth*, to which is allotted the symbolic Tribe of *Judah* and over which is the Angel VERCHIEL, to bestow this present day and hour, and confirm their mystic and potent influence upon the *Yellow Band* of this Lotus Wand, which I hereby dedicate to purity and to Occult Work, and may its grasp strengthen me in the work of the character of *Leo* and its attributes. (Light the Leo candle by using the taper to transfer the flame from the Cancer candle. Replace the red candle.)

14. For VIRGO: Take up the salt in your left hand and go clockwise to the Virgo symbol. Holding the yellow-green band of the Lotus Wand in your right hand, trace a circle over

the Zodiacal symbol, followed by the Invoking Pentagram of Spirit Passive, vibrating the associated Divine names (**NANTA** and **AGLA**). Give the Opening of the Veil, followed by the LVX Signs. Then trace the Invoking Pentagram of Earth, followed by the sigil of Virgo in the center, vibrating the names **EMOR DIAL HECTEGA** and **ADONAI.** Give the Sign of Zelator. Then say:

The Heaven is above and the Earth is beneath. And betwixt the Light and the Darkness, the colors vibrate. I supplicate the Powers and Forces governing the Nature, Place, and Authority of the Sign *Virgo,* by the Majesty of the Divine Name, HEH HEH YOD VAV, with which, in Earth life and language, I ascribe the letter *Yod,* to which is allotted the symbolic Tribe of *Naphthali* and over which is the Angel HAMALIEL, to bestow this present day and hour, and confirm their mystic and potent influence upon the *Yellow-green Band* of this Lotus Wand, which I hereby dedicate to purity and to Occult Work, and may its grasp strengthen me in the work of the character of *Virgo* and its attributes. (Transfer the flame to the Virgo candle as before. Replace the salt.)

15. For LIBRA: Take up the rose in your left hand and go clockwise to the Libra symbol. Holding the green band of the Lotus Wand in your right hand, trace a circle over the Zodiacal symbol, followed by the Invoking Pentagram of Spirit Active, vibrating the associated Divine names (**EXARP** and **EHEIEH**). Give the Opening of the Veil, followed by the LVX Signs. Then trace the Invoking Pentagram of Air, followed by the sigil of Libra in the center, vibrating the names **ORO IBAH AOZPI** and **YHVH.** Give the Sign of Theoricus. Then say:

The Heaven is above and the Earth is beneath. And betwixt the Light and the Darkness, the colors vibrate. I supplicate the Powers and Forces governing the Nature, Place, and Authority of the Sign *Libra*, by the Majesty of the Divine Name, VAV HEH YOD HEH, with which, in Earth life and language, I ascribe the letter *Lamed*, to which is allotted the symbolic Tribe of *Asshur* and over which is the Angel ZURIEL, to bestow this present day and hour, and confirm their mystic and potent influence upon the *Green Band* of this Lotus Wand, which I hereby dedicate to purity and to Occult Work, and may its grasp strengthen me in the work of the character of *Libra* and its attributes. (Transfer the flame to the Libra candle as before. Replace the rose.)

16. For SCORPIO: Take up the Cup in your left hand and go clockwise to the Scorpio symbol. Holding the blue-green band of the Lotus Wand in your right hand, trace a circle over the Zodiacal symbol, followed by the Invoking Pentagram of Spirit Passive, vibrating the associated Divine names (**HCOMA** and **AGLA**). Give the Opening of the Veil, followed by the LVX Signs. Then trace the Invoking Pentagram of Water, followed by the sigil of Scorpio in the center, vibrating the names **EMPEH ARSEL GAIOL** and **Aleph Lamed, EL**. Give the Sign of Practicus. Then say:

The Heaven is above and the Earth is beneath. And betwixt the Light and the Darkness, the colors vibrate. I supplicate the Powers and Forces governing the Nature, Place, and Authority of the Sign *Scorpio*, by the Majesty of the Divine Name, VAV HEH HEH YOD, with which, in Earth life and language, I ascribe the letter *Nun*, to which is allotted the symbolic Tribe of *Dan* and over which is the Angel BARCHIEL, to bestow this present day and hour, and confirm their mystic and potent influence upon the *Blue-green Band* of this Lotus Wand, which I hereby dedicate to purity and to Occult Work, and may its grasp strengthen me in the work of the character of *Scorpio* and its attributes. (Transfer the flame as before. Replace the cup.)

17. For SAGITTARIUS: Take up the red candle in your left hand and go clockwise to the Sagittarius symbol. Holding the blue band of the Lotus Wand in your right hand, trace a circle over the Zodiacal symbol, followed by the Invoking Pentagram of Spirit Active, vibrating the associated Divine names (**BITOM** and **EHEIEH**). Give the Opening of the Veil, followed by the LVX Signs. Then trace the Invoking Pentagram of Fire, followed by the sigil of Sagittarius in the center, vibrating the names **OIP TEAA PEDOCE** and **ELOHIM.** Give the Sign of Philosophus. Then say:

The Heaven is above and the Earth is beneath. And betwixt the Light and the Darkness, the colors vibrate. I supplicate the Powers and Forces governing the Nature, Place, and Authority of the Sign *Sagittarius*, by the Majesty of the Divine Name, VAV YOD HEH HEH, with which, in Earth life and language, I ascribe the letter *Samekh,* to which is allotted the symbolic Tribe of *Benjamin* and over which is the Angel ADVACHIEL, to bestow this present day and hour, and confirm their mystic and potent influence upon the *Blue Band* of this Lotus Wand, which I hereby dedicate to purity and to Occult Work, and may its grasp strengthen me in the work of the character of *Sagittarius* and its attributes. (Transfer the flame as before. Replace the candle.)

18. For CAPRICORN: Take up the salt in your left hand and go clockwise to the Capricorn symbol. Holding the blue-violet band of the Lotus Wand in your right hand, trace a circle over the Zodiacal symbol, followed by the Invoking Pentagram of Spirit Passive, vibrating the associated Divine names (**NANTA** and **AGLA**). Give the Opening of the Veil, followed by the LVX Signs. Then trace the Invoking Pentagram of Earth, followed by the sigil of Capricorn in the center, vibrating the names **EMOR DIAL HECTEGA** and **ADONAI.** Give the Sign of Zelator. Then say:

The Heaven is above and the Earth is beneath. And betwixt the Light and the Darkness, the colors vibrate. I supplicate the Powers and Forces governing the Nature, Place, and Authority of the Sign *Capricorn*, by the Majesty of the Divine Name, HEH YOD HEH VAV, with which, in Earth life and language, I ascribe the letter *Ayin*, to which is allotted the symbolic Tribe of *Zebulun* and over which is the Angel HANAEL, to bestow this present day and hour, and confirm their mystic and potent influence upon the *Blue-violet Band* of this Lotus Wand, which I hereby dedicate to purity and to Occult Work, and may its grasp strengthen me in the work of the character of *Capricorn* and its attributes. (Transfer the flame as before. Replace the salt.)

19. For AQUARIUS: Take up the rose in your left hand and go clockwise to the Aquarius symbol. Holding the violet band of the Lotus Wand in your right hand, trace a circle over the Zodiacal symbol, followed by the Invoking Pentagram of Spirit Active, vibrating the associated Divine names (**EXARP** and **EHEIEH**). Give the Opening of the Veil, followed by the LVX Signs. Then trace the Invoking Pentagram of Air, followed by the sigil of Aquarius in the center, vibrating the names **ORO IBAH AOZPI** and **YHVH.** Give the Sign of Theoricus. Then say:

The Heaven is above and the Earth is beneath. And betwixt the Light and the Darkness, the colors vibrate. I supplicate the Powers and Forces governing the Nature, Place, and Authority of the Sign *Aquarius*, by the Majesty of the Divine Name, HEH YOD VAV HEH, with which, in Earth life and language, I ascribe the letter *Tzaddi*, to which is allotted the symbolic Tribe of *Reuben* and over which is the Angel CAMBRIEL, to bestow this present day and hour, and confirm their mystic and potent influence upon the *Violet Band* of this Lotus Wand, which I hereby dedicate to purity and to Occult Work, and may its grasp strengthen me in the work of the character of *Aquarius* and its attributes. (Transfer the flame as before. Replace the rose.)

20. For PISCES: Take up the Cup in your left hand and go clockwise to the Pisces symbol. Holding the red-violet band of the Lotus Wand in your right hand, trace a circle over the Zodiacal symbol, followed by the Invoking Pentagram of Spirit Passive, vibrating the associated Divine names (**HCOMA** and **AGLA**). Give the Opening of the Veil, followed by the LVX Signs. Then trace the Invoking Pentagram of Water, followed by the sigil of Pisces in the center, vibrating the names **EMPEH ARSEL GAIOL** and **Aleph Lamed, EL**. Give the Sign of Practicus. Then say:

The Heaven is above and the Earth is beneath. And betwixt the Light and the Darkness, the colors vibrate. I supplicate the Powers and Forces governing the Nature, Place, and Authority of the sign *Pisces,* by the Majesty of the Divine Name, HEH HEH VAV YOD, with which, in Earth life and language, I ascribe the letter *Qoph*, to which is allotted the symbolic Tribe of *Simeon* and over which is the Angel AMNITZIEL, to bestow this present day and hour, and confirm their mystic and potent influence upon the *Red-violet Band* of this Lotus Wand, which I hereby dedicate to purity and to Occult Work, and may its grasp strengthen me in the work of the character of *Pisces* and its attributes. (Transfer the flame as before. Replace the cup.)

Invocation of Isis

21. Stand west of the Altar and face east. Place the wand on the Altar with the flower end pointed toward the East.

22. Raise both hands and say: **O ISIS! Great Goddess of the Forces of Nature, let Thine Influence descend and consecrate this Wand which I dedicate to Thee for the performance of the works of the Magic of Light!**

Closing

23. Wrap the wand in white silk or linen.

24. Perform the Purification and Consecration.

25. Perform the Reverse Circumambulation.

26. Go west of the Altar and perform the Adoration.

27. Give the License to Depart.

28. Perform the LBRP.

29. Say: **I now declare this Temple duly closed. So mote it be!**

✠ ✠ ✠

The Rose Cross Lamen

The word *lamen* comes from the Latin word for "plate" and indicates a symbolic breastplate that generally signifies the magician's rank, authority, or power. A lamen is a magical pendant worn by the magician in ritual, suspended from a yellow cord, ribbon, or collar so that it hangs over the heart center of Tiphareth.

Lamens come in an endless variety of shapes and symbolism. Golden Dawn Officers wear lamens to indicate their specific station and duties within the Hall. Another type of lamen is talismanic in nature and functions as a storehouse for the particular energy that the magician wishes to attract. Some lamens contain the sigils of angels or spirits that the magician wears only when working with those particular beings.

The Rose Cross Lamen can be described as the key symbol or a magical coat of arms for the adept of the Second Order. Based on the Rosicrucian symbolism of the red rose united to the golden cross, it combines a vast amalgam of ideas and forces that lie at the heart of Hermetic magic, including the elements, planets, Zodiacal signs, Sephiroth, Hebrew alphabet, pentagrams, hexagrams, alchemical principles, etc. The Lamen is a complete synthesis of the King Scale of color attributions. It is the cross in Tiphareth, the receptacle and the center of the forces of the Sephiroth and the paths.

This single emblem is described as "the Key of sigils and Rituals" and represents the Great Work itself, balanced and completed.

The Rose Cross Lamen is to be made by each Adept alone and, once consecrated, should not be touched by any other person. It is wrapped in white silk or linen when not in use.

The four arms of the cross are attributed to the four elements in their proper colors. The white portion belongs to Spirit and the planets embodied in the hexagram. The floriated ends of the arms show the symbols of the three alchemical principles.

The central rose is a symbol of the entire manifest universe. It contains twenty-two petals assigned to the letters of the Hebrew alphabet and the twenty-two Navitoth on the Tree of Life.

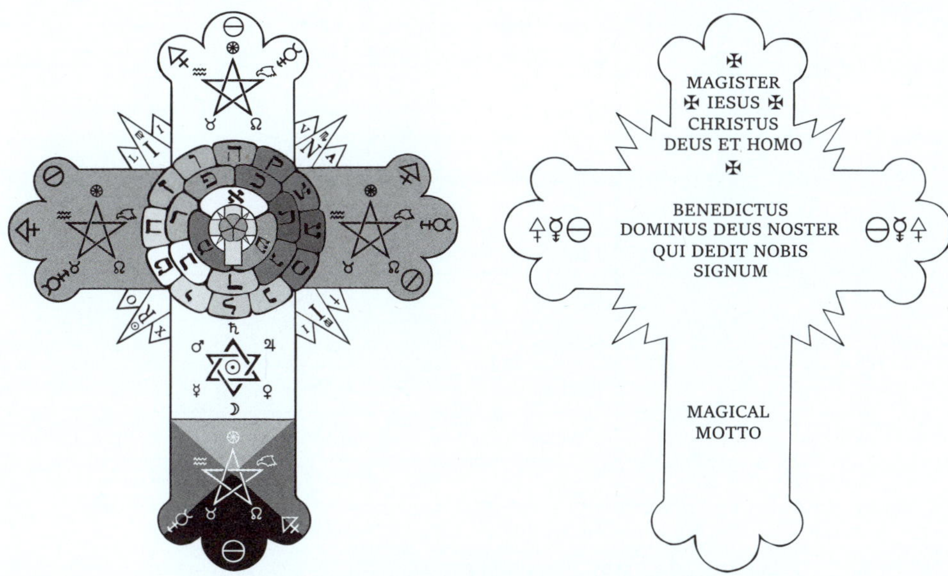

Figure 31: The Rose Cross Lamen (Front and Back)

The petals of the rose are arranged in three rows that divide the Hebrew alphabet into the three Mother Letters (elements), the seven Double Letters (planets), and the twelve Simple Letters (signs). When properly painted, the rows of petals should resemble a perfect artist's color wheel. The colors of the 22 Petals are listed in table 6.

Hebrew Letter	*Petal Color*	*Letter Color*
Aleph	Yellow	Violet
Beth	Yellow	Violet
Gimel	Blue	Orange
Daleth	Green	Red
Heh	Red	Green
Vav	Red-orange	Blue-green
Zayin	Orange	Blue
Cheth	Yellow-orange	Blue-violet
Teth	Yellow	Violet
Yod	Yellow-green	Red-violet
Kaph	Violet	Yellow

Table 6: Colors of the 22 Petals of the Lamen (*continued*)

Hebrew Letter	*Petal Color*	*Letter Color*
Lamed	Green	Red
Mem	Blue	Orange
Nun	Blue-green	Red-orange
Samekh	Blue	Orange
Ayin	Blue-violet	Yellow-orange
Peh	Red	Green
Tzaddi	Violet	Yellow
Qoph	Red-violet	Yellow-green
Resh	Orange	Blue
Shin	Red	Green
Tau	Blue-violet	Yellow-orange

Table 6: Colors of the 22 Petals of the Lamen (*continued*)

At the center of the rose is a white circular portion representing the reflected spiritual brightness of Kether, and within this is a Red Rose of Five Petals and the Golden Cross of Six Squares. Four green rays issue from the angles of the cross. They are the symbols of the Receiving Force.

Large white rays springing from behind the rose at the intersecting arms of the cross are waves of the Divine Light issuing forth, and the letters and symbols on them refer to the Analysis of the Keyword.

Upon the white portion of the lamen below the rose is a hexagram with the planets in the order that is the key of the Supreme Ritual of the Hexagram.

Around the pentagrams, which are shown on each elemental-colored arm, are drawn the symbols of the Spirit and the four elements, in the order that is the key to the Supreme Ritual of the Pentagram (table 7). Upon each of the floriated arms of the cross are symbols of the three alchemical principles of sulfur, salt, and mercury, but arranged in a different order for each elemental arm, showing their different operation within the various elements.

The top arm of the cross is assigned to Air and the yellow color of Tiphareth.

The bottom arm of the cross, attributed to Earth, displays the four colors of Malkuth. The left arm is attributed to Fire and is painted the red color of Geburah. The right arm represents Water and is painted the blue color of Chesed.

Elemental Arms	*Ground Color*	*Color of Symbols*
Right Arm (Water)	Blue	Orange
Left Arm (Fire)	Red	Green
Top Arm (Air)	Yellow	Violet
Center (Spirit)	White	Black
Bottom Arm (Earth)	Citrine, olive, russet, black	White

Table 7: Colors of the Elemental Arms of the Lamen

The white rays issuing from behind the rose at the inner angles between the arms of the cross are rays of the divine light issuing from the reflected light of Kether in its center. The letters and symbols on them refer to the Analysis of the Keyword, I.N.R.I.

The back of the cross bears the Latin inscription "The Master Jesus Christ, God and Man" between four Pyramidal Crosses, which represent the four pyramids of the elements opened out. This inscription is placed at the top to indicate the descent of the Divine Light into Tiphareth.

At the bottom is written the motto or magical name of the magician who has attained the grade of Zelator Adeptus Minor.

In the center of the cross's backside, between the symbols of the alchemical principles, is written in Latin "Blessed be the Lord our God who hath given us the Symbol Signum."

Consecration of the Rose Cross Lamen

The Temple is to be arranged in accordance with the *General Temple Setup for an Adept Working in the Portal Hall,* with the Natural Elemental Symbols, but place the Cup between the Cross and Triangle as in the Neophyte Ritual. Ideally the Lotus Wand should be placed on top of the Altar, with the flower toward the east, but this is not always practical. As an alternative, the wand could be placed in a specially made wand stand at the side of the Altar or wherever is most convenient.

The Opening

1. Place the new Rose Cross Lamen upon the White Triangle.[94]

94. In ritual, the Triangle symbol of the Golden Dawn can act as a Triangle of Art, or a Triangle of Manifestation.

2. Take up the Lotus Wand by the black portion. Go clockwise to the northeast of the temple and say, **Hekas! Hekas! Este Bebeloi!** Return to west of the altar.

3. Perform the LBRP

4. Perform the LBRH.

5. Perform the Purification and the Consecration

6. Hold the wand by the white portion and perform the Mystic Circumambulation.

7. Perform the Adoration.

Proclamation of Intention (Optional)[95]

8. Say: **I, (state your magical motto), a (Frater/Soror) of the Rose of Ruby and the Cross of Gold and a member of the Body of the Christos, do this day undertake the Consecration of this Rose Cross Lamen.**

With the Divine permission, I shall consecrate this Rose Cross Lamen as a labor in the Divine Science, in pursuit of the Great Work, which is to so purify and exalt my spiritual nature that with the Divine aid I may at length become more than human, and thus gradually raise and unite myself to my Higher and Divine Genius. So mote it be!

Preliminary Invocation

9. Perform the SIRP.
(NOTE: When performing the SIRP with the Lotus Wand, follow this format: Grasp the white band of the wand for the QC and the Spirit Pentagrams, and the appropriate Kerubic band when invoking each element—the violet Aquarius band for Air, the yellow Leo band for Fire, the blue-green Scorpio band for Water, and the red-orange Taurus band for Earth.)

---

95. Nontraditional. This our own addition to the rite.

Invoking the Powers of the Rose Cross Lamen

10. Stand west of the altar facing east, holding white band of the Lotus Wand.

11. Trace the symbol of the Circle and Cross (the Rose Cross) over the Lamen.

Figure 32: Tracing the Symbol of the Rose Cross

12. Invoke all the divine and angelic names of Tiphareth with the speech given below or an alternative speech also provided. As you vibrate the names, trace their sigils in the air over the Lamen:

O Thou most sublime Majesty on High, who art at certain seasons worthily represented by the glorious Sun of Tiphareth, I beseech Thee to bestow upon this symbol of the Rose and the Cross, which I have formed to Thy honor, and for the furtherance of the Great Work, in a spirit of purity and love, the most excellent virtues, by the Divine Name of YHVH, and the great name of YHVH ELOAH VE DAATH. Deign I beseech Thee to grant that the Great Archangel RAPHAEL and the Mighty Angel MICHAEL may strengthen this emblem, and through the sphere of the splendid Orb of Shemesh may confer upon it such Power and Virtue as to lead me by it toward the solution of the Great Secret.

(Alternative version): **O Thou Most Glorious Light which lighteneth every being who cometh into the world. Thou who art in due season shadowed forth by Tiphareth, the Sun of Beauty, I implore Thee to direct Thy Light upon this symbol of the Rose and Cross which I have fashioned in Thine Honor and for the furtherance of the Great Work. By the Divine Name YHVH, by Thy Name of Wisdom YHVH ELOAH VE DAATH, permit I beseech Thee Thy shining Archangel RAPHAEL and Thy Strong Angel MICHAEL, so to influence this emblem that it may be mighty for all**

good so that through the glorious sphere of Shemesh they may bestow upon it such power that in wearing it, I may at length lose and so find myself in that Ineffable Light which I most humbly seek.

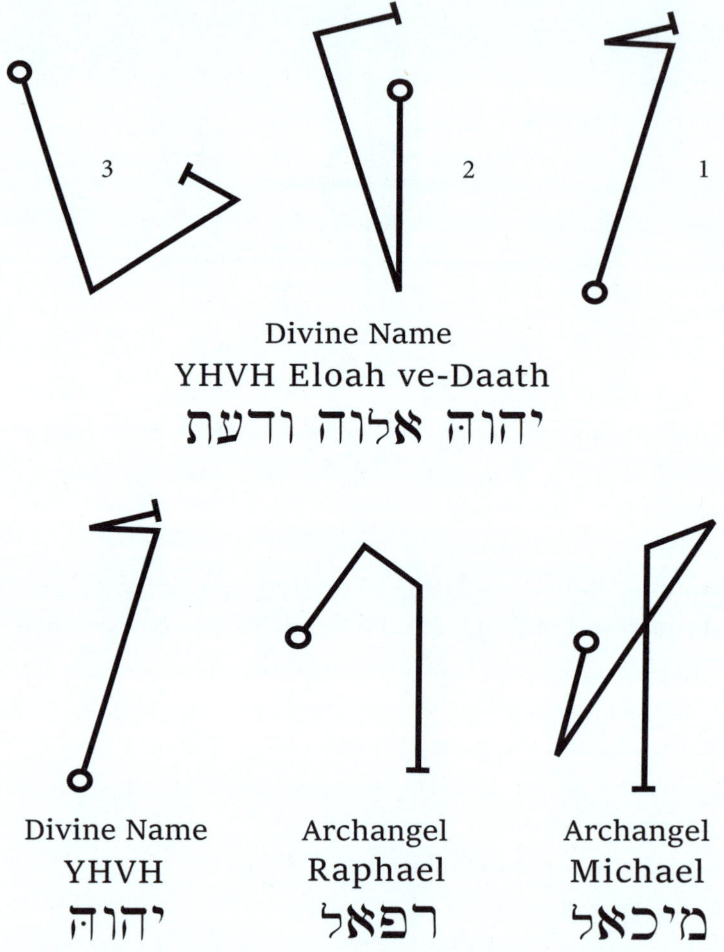

Figure 33: Sigils for the Consecration of the Rose Cross Lamen

13. Raise your hands and eyes skyward during the prayer, lowering them as you finish.

14. Repeat the following passage (from Genesis): **And a River, Nahar, went forth out of Eden to water the Garden, and from thence it was parted and came into four heads.**

15. Trace a clockwise circle over the white portion of the Rose Cross Lamen. Then trace the Greater Invoking Hexagrams of the Planets[96] over the Lamen, repeating the appropriate names and Hebrew letters of *Ararita*, holding the Lotus Wand by the colored band representing either the day or the night house[97] of the planet as follows:

a) *Saturn.* Begin with the Greater Hexagram of Saturn, holding the wand by either violet Aquarius (day house) or blue-violet Capricorn (night house), vibrating **ARARITA**, **YHVH Elohim**, and **ALEPH.**[98] Then follow:

b) *Jupiter.* For the Greater Hexagram of Jupiter, hold the wand by either blue Sagittarius (day house) or red-violet Pisces (night house), vibrating **ARARITA**, **EL**, and **RESH.**

c) *Mars.* For the Greater Hexagram of Mars, hold the wand by either red Aries (day house) or blue-green Scorpio (night house), vibrating **ARARITA**, **ELOHIM GIBOR**, and **ALEPH.**

d) *Venus.* Hold the wand by either green Libra (day house) or red-orange Taurus (night house), vibrating **ARARITA**, **YHVH TZABAOTH**, and **YOD.**

e) *Mercury.* Hold the wand by either orange Gemini (day house) or yellow-green Virgo (night house), vibrating **ARARITA**, **ELOHIM TZABAOTH**, and **TAU.**

f) *Luna.* Hold the wand by the yellow-orange Cancer band only (day or night), vibrating **ARARITA**, **SHADDAI EL CHAI**, and **ALEPH.**

g) *Sol.* Trace the six Invoking Hexagrams as before, but hold the wand by the yellow Leo band only, and draw the Sun symbol in the center of the sixth and final Hexagram.[99] After drawing the last of the six Hexagrams, intone the names **ARARITA**, **YHVH ELOAH VE-DAATH**, and **RESH.**

---

96. For more information on the six invoking forms of the Hexagrams, see Ciceros, *Golden Dawn Magic*, 270.

97. See Table 5: Correspondences of the Lotus Wand on page 250.

98. We find it helpful to trace the Hexagram while vibrating "Ararita," the planet symbol while vibrating the Divine Name, and the Hebrew Letter when vibrating its name.

99. When tracing solar hexagrams, it may be useful to vibrate "Ararita" every time you trace a hexagram (to avoid confusion and not lose your place). But do not trace the various planet symbols and letters of the individual hexagrams. Just trace the symbols of Sol and Resh at the end.

16. Hold the white band of the Lotus Wand. Trace a clockwise circle over the Lamen.

17. Still holding the white band, trace the following equilibrating Pentagrams (with Spirit Wheels) over the Lamen:

a) *Invoking Spirit Active,* vibrating **EXARP** and **EHEIEH**.

b) *Invoking Spirit Passive* and intone **HCOMA** and **AGLA**.

c) *Invoking Spirit Passive* and intone **NANTA** and **AGLA**.

d) *Invoking Spirit Active* and vibrate **BITOM** and **EHEIEH**.

e) Give the Sign of the Rending of the Veil, followed by the LVX Signs.

Consecrating Each Segment of the Lamen

(*NOTE: Stage directions for this section.* Repeat the verses from Genesis II, 13, 14, and 15 as follows, referring to each Element, while holding the Lotus Wand by the Kerubic band of the Element. Then, over the four colored arms of the Lamen, trace the Invoking Pentagrams of each Element in turn, using the proper words and grade signs as shown in the next steps.)

18. RED FIRE ARM: Grasp the wand by the yellow (Leo) band and hold the flower end over the red Fire arm of the cross. Say: **And the Name of the First River is Pison. It is that which compasseth the whole land of Havilah, where there is gold. And the gold of that land is good. There is Bdellium and the Onyx stone.**

Trace a circle over the red arm and draw the *Invoking Pentagram of Spirit Active*, vibrating **BITOM** and **EHEIEH**. Give the Sign of the Rending of the Veil, followed by the LVX Signs. Trace the *Invoking Pentagram of Fire,* vibrating **OIP TEAA PEDOCE** and **ELOHIM**. Give the Philosophus Sign.

19. BLUE WATER ARM: Grasp the wand by the blue-green (Scorpio) band and hold the flower end of the wand over the blue arm of the cross. Say: **And the Name of the Second River is Gihon, the same as that which compasseth the whole land of Ethiopia.**

Trace a circle over the blue arm and draw the *Invoking Pentagram of Spirit Passive*, vibrating **HCOMA** and **AGLA**. Give the Sign of the Rending of the Veil, followed by the LVX Signs. Trace the *Invoking Pentagram of Water*, vibrating the names **EMPEH ARSEL GAIOL** and **AL**. Give the Practicus Sign.

20. YELLOW AIR ARM: Grasp the wand by the violet (Aquarius) band and hold the Lotus flower over the yellow arm of the cross. Say: **And the Name of the Third River is Hiddekel, that which goeth forth to the East of Assyria.**

Trace a circle over the yellow arm and draw the *Invoking Pentagram of Spirit Active*, vibrating the names **EXARP** and **EHEIEH**. Give the Sign of the Rending of the Veil, followed by the LVX Signs. Trace the *Invoking Pentagram of Air*, intoning the names **ORO IBAH AOZPI** and **YHVH**. Give the Theoricus Sign.

21. FOUR-COLORED EARTH ARM: Grasp the wand by the red-orange (Taurus) band and hold the Lotus flower over the dark, Earthy arm of the cross. Say: **And the Fourth River is Euphrates.**

Trace a circle over the arm and draw the *Invoking Pentagram of Spirit Passive*, vibrating the names **NANTA** and **AGLA**. Give the Sign of the Rending of the Veil, followed by the LVX Signs. Trace the *Invoking Pentagram of Earth*, intoning the names **EMOR DIAL HECTEGA** and **ADONAI**. Give the Zelator Sign.

22. Hold the wand by the white part and trace a clockwise circle from left to right over the outermost twelve petals of the rose and vibrate the name **ADONAI**.

23. Trace a circle over the seven middle petals of the rose and intone **ARARITA**.

24. Trace a circle over the three innermost Petals and vibrate **YHVH**.

25. Draw a vertical line from the top to the bottom of the cross and say: **EHEIEH**.

26. Trace a horizontal line from left to right on the cross and say: **ELOHIM**.

The Closing

27. Wrap the Rose Cross Lamen in white silk or linen.

28. Perform the Purification and Consecration.

29. Perform the Reverse Circumambulation.

30. Go west of the Altar and perform the Adoration.

31. Give the License to Depart.

32. Perform the LBRP.

33. Say: **I now declare this Temple duly closed. So mote it be!**

✠✠✠

The Magic Sword

The Magic Sword of the Adeptus Minor is to be used in all cases where great force and strength are required, but principally for banishing and for defense against evil forces. For this reason it is attributed to the Sephirah Geburah. The sword should be used with great respect only for banishings, protection, and certain rituals where the force of Geburah is needed to bar and threaten.

Any convenient sword of medium length and weight may be adapted to this use, but the handle, hilt, and guard should be wide enough to write the necessary inscriptions on. Every part of the handle is to be painted red, although a strip of leather can be wrapped around the grip for added comfort.

The divine and angelic names related to Geburah are then to be added in green, and also their sigils.[100]

---

100. It is also acceptable to include only the sigils of Geburah and not Mars, since the primary symbolism for the Sword comes from the Fifth Sephirah.

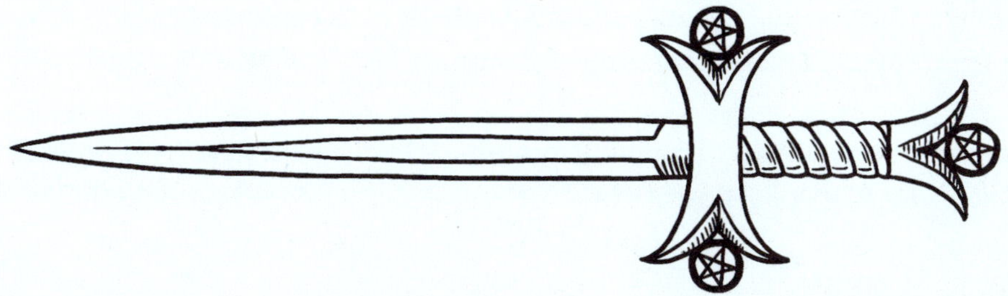

Figure 34: The Magic Sword

In addition to protective pentagrams, divine names and sigils of Geburah written in Hebrew letters are added in green to the hilt:

- Godname: Elohim Gibor (אלהים גבור)
- Sephirotic archangel: Kamael (כמאל)
- Sephirotic angels: Seraphim (שרפים)
- Planet: Madim (Mars) (מדים)
- Planetary angel: Zamael (זמאל)
- Planetary intelligence: Graphiel (גראפיאל)
- Planetary spirit: Bartzabel (ברצבאל)
- Magical Motto: —

Consecration of the Magic Sword

The Temple is to be arranged in accordance with the *General Temple Setup for an Adept Working in the Portal Hall* with the Natural Elemental Symbols. Ideally the Lotus Wand and the Sword should be placed on top of the Altar, north and south, respectively,[101] but depending on space, this is not always convenient or safe. They could be placed in specially made wand stands on either side of the Altar or placed wherever is most convenient.

This ritual should be performed on the day and hour of Mars (or on the day of Sol and the hour of Mars).[102] Have an astrological chart on hand to determine where Mars is at the time of working. It is also advantageous if the planet Mars is in domicile or in

101. Lotus Flower and Sword hilt toward the east.

102. For Planetary Hours, see tables 14 and 15 in Ciceros, *Golden Dawn Magic*, 90–91.

exaltation, and if the Sun, Moon, or Mars is in Aries, Scorpio, the First House, or the Eighth House and not badly aspected.

1. Stand west of the Altar, holding the Lotus Wand by the black portion, and say: **HEKAS! HEKAS! ESTE BEBELOI!**

2. Perform the LBRP.

3. Perform the LBRH.

4. Perform the Purification and Consecration.

5. Take up the wand by the white portion and perform the Mystic Circumambulation.

6. Perform the Adoration.

Proclamation of Intention (Optional)[103]

7. Hold the Lotus Wand by the white band, in line with your Middle Pillar, visualizing all the Sephiroth as energized with the Divine Light. When ready, raise the Wand high and say:

I, (state your magical motto), a (Frater/Soror) of the Rose of Ruby and the Cross of Gold and a member of the Body of the Christos, have opened the temple this day to undertake the Consecration of this Magic Sword of Art.

I swear that with the Divine permission I shall consecrate this Sword as a labor in the Divine Science, in pursuit of the Great Work, which is to so purify and exalt my spiritual nature that with the Divine aid I may at length become more than human, and thus gradually raise and unite myself to my Higher and Divine Genius. So mote it be!

LIRH of Geburah

8. Perform the *Lesser Invoking Ritual of the Hexagram of Geburah* as follows:

103. Nontraditional. This is our own addition to the rite.

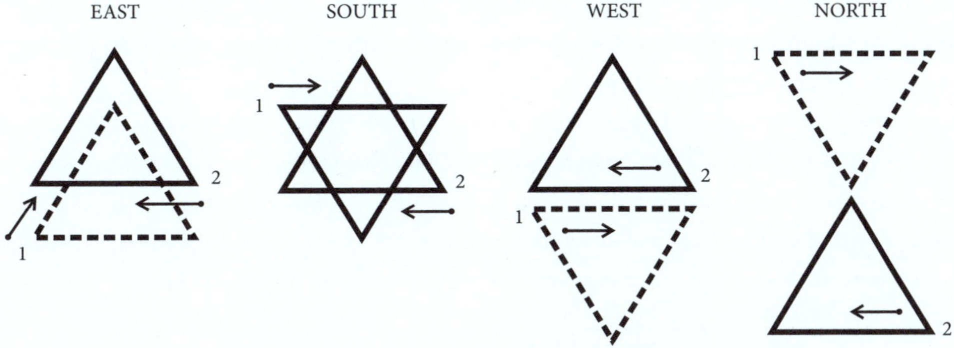

Figure 35: Lesser Invoking Hexagrams of Geburah

(NOTE: Hold the Wand by the white band throughout the ritual.[104])

a) Go to the east (or center) of the temple and perform the Qabalistic Cross.

b) Go to the eastern edge of the temple. Trace the Lesser Invoking Eastern Hexagram of Geburah toward the east. Thrust through the center of the figure and vibrate the word **ARARITA.**[105] Trace the Mars symbol in the center.

c) Walk to the southern boundary of the temple and trace the Lesser Invoking Southern Hexagram of Geburah toward the south. Charge the center of the figure as before and vibrate **ARARITA.** Trace the Mars symbol in the center.

d) Go to the western edge of the temple and draw the Lesser Invoking Western Hexagram of Geburah toward the west. Energize it by thrusting through the center of the figure and vibrate as before, **ARARITA.** Trace the Mars symbol in the center.

e) Walk to the northern boundary of the temple and draw the Lesser Invoking Northern Hexagram of Geburah toward the north. Thrust and intone as before, **ARARITA.** Trace the Mars symbol in the center.

f) Return to the east (or center) and perform the Analysis of the Keyword.

9. Continue to grasp the Lotus Wand by the white band and hold it vertically before you, in alignment with your Middle Pillar. Feel the energy of the Geburic circle you

---

104. All Sephirotic energies are invoked using the white band of the Lotus Wand.

105. Keep your arm extended as you walk around the room, connecting the center of all the hexagrams with a white circle of light.

have created as well as the Divine white Light created by the QC and the AK. Be conscious of the balancing spheres of Kether and Malkuth within you, and focus the Divine Light in your Tiphareth center.

Consecration of the Sword

10. To perform the *Greater Invoking Ritual of the Hexagram of Geburah*, go clockwise around the Altar so that you face the direction in which you have astrologically determined Mars to be—standing so that the Altar is between yourself and Mars.

Figure 36: Greater Invoking Hexagram of Geburah

a) Perform the Qabalistic Cross.

b) Trace the *Greater Invoking Hexagram of Geburah* and vibrate **ARARITA.** Trace the symbol of Mars and vibrate **ELOHIM GIBOR.** Trace and vibrate the letter **ALEPH.**[106]

c) Vibrate **GEBURAH** and trace its sigil.

d) Vibrate **ELOHIM GIBOR** and trace its sigil.

e) Vibrate **MADIM** and trace its sigil.

f) Vibrate **KAMAEL** and trace its sigil.

g) Vibrate **SERAPHIM** and trace its sigil.

h) Go west of the Altar and face east. Perform the *Analysis of the Keyword.*

---

106. This is the second Aleph of ARARITA, assigned to the Mars point of the hexagram.

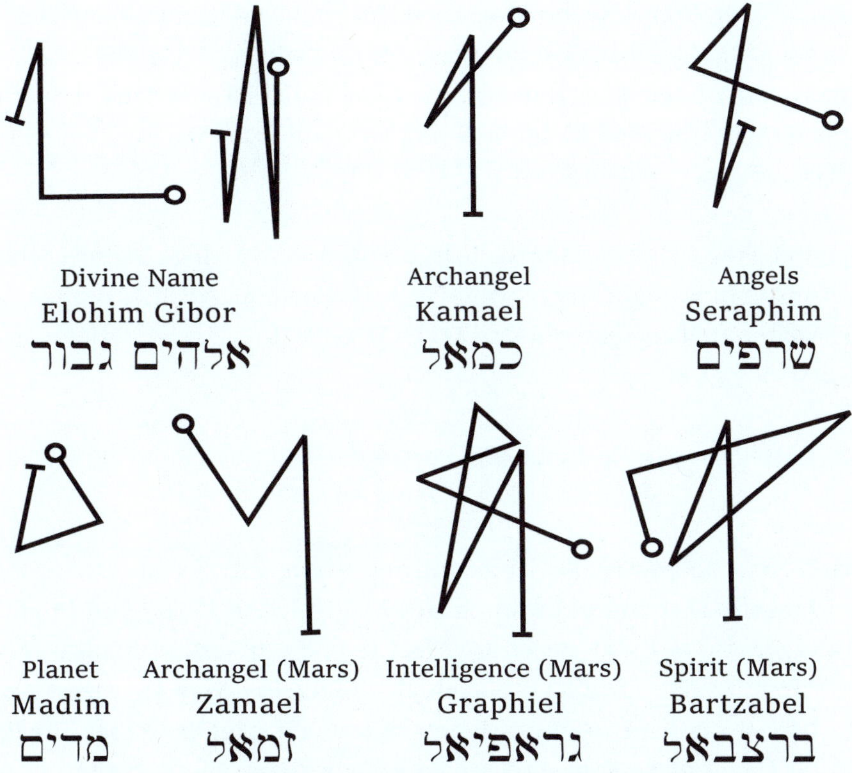

Figure 37: Sigils Traditionally Associated with the Magic Sword

11. Place the Lotus Wand aside. Take the Stolistes Cup of Water from the north and purify the Sword by marking it with water in the figures of the Cross and Water Triangle, saying: **So therefore, first, the Priest who governeth the works of Fire, must sprinkle with the lustral water of the loud resounding sea.** (Replace the Cup.)

12. Take the Incense from the south and consecrate the Sword by marking it with the figures of the Cross and Fire Triangle, saying: **And when after all the Phantoms are banished, thou shalt see that Holy and Formless Fire, that Fire which darts and flashes through the hidden depths of the Universe, hear thou the voice of Fire!** (Replace the Incense and return to the Altar, standing so that the Altar is between yourself and Mars.)

13. Take up the Lotus Wand by the white band and hold it vertically before you, in alignment with your Middle Pillar. Feel the energy of the Geburic circle you have created as well as the Divine white Light created by the QC and the AK. Be conscious of the balancing spheres of Kether and Malkuth within you, and focus the Divine Light in your Tiphareth center.

14. Still grasping the wand with the white band, trace an invoking circle over the Sword. Trace the Greater Invoking Hexagram of Mars and vibrate **ARARITA.** Within the circle, trace the symbol of Mars and vibrate **ELOHIM GIBOR.** Trace and vibrate the letter **ALEPH.**

15. Recite the following Invocation to the Powers of Geburah, tracing the sigil of each as you read it:

O Mighty Power who governeth Geburah, Thou strong and terrible Divine ELOHIM GIBOR, I beseech Thee to bestow upon this Magic Sword Power and Might to slay the evil and weakness I may encounter. In the Fiery Sphere of Madim, may it be welded and tempered to unswerving strength and fidelity. May Thy Great Archangel KAMAEL bestow upon me courage wherewith to use it aright and may The Powerful Angels of the Order of Seraphim scorch with their flames the feebleness of purpose which would hinder my search for the True Light.

16. Return to the west of the Altar facing east. Perform the *Analysis of the Keyword.*

17. Give a single knock on the Altar with the bottom of the Lotus Wand.

18. Take up the newly charged Sword and return to the Altar, standing so that the Altar is between yourself and Mars.

19. Holding the Sword vertically before you, point downward in the form of a cross in alignment with your Middle Pillar. Feel the energy of the Geburic circle you have created as well as the Divine white Light created by the QC and the AK. Be conscious of the balancing spheres of Kether and Malkuth within you, and focus the Divine Light in your Tiphareth center.

GIRH of *Geburah*

20. Perform the *Greater Invoking Ritual of the Hexagram of Geburah* with the Sword:

a) Perform the Qabalistic Cross.

b) Trace the Greater Invoking Hexagram of Mars and vibrate **ARARITA.** Trace the symbol of Mars and vibrate **ELOHIM GIBOR.** Trace and vibrate the letter **ALEPH.**

c) Vibrate **GEBURAH** and trace its sigil.

d) Vibrate **ELOHIM GIBOR** and trace its sigil.

e) Vibrate **MADIM** and trace its sigil.

f) Vibrate **KAMAEL** and trace its sigil.

g) Vibrate **SERAPHIM** and trace its sigil.

h) Go to the west of the Altar and face east. Perform the *Analysis of the Keyword.*

LBRH of *Geburah*

21. Perform the *Lesser Banishing Ritual of the Hexagram of Geburah* as follows: Holding the Sword vertically before you, point downward in the form of a cross in alignment with your Middle Pillar. Feel the energy of the Geburic circle you have created as well as the Divine white Light created by the QC and the AK. Be conscious of the balancing spheres of Kether and Malkuth within you, and focus the Divine Light in your Tiphareth center.

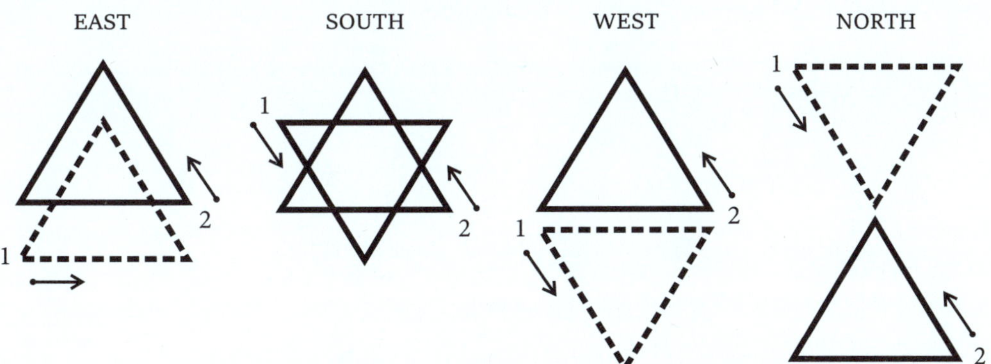

Figure 38: Lesser Banishing Hexagrams of Geburah

a) Go to the east (or center) of the temple and perform the *Qabalistic Cross.*

b) Go to the eastern edge of the temple. Trace the Lesser Banishing Eastern Hexagram of Geburah toward the east. Thrust through the center of the figure and vibrate the word **ARARITA.** Trace the Mars symbol in the center.

c) Walk to the southern boundary of the temple and trace the Lesser Banishing Southern Hexagram of Geburah toward the south. Charge the center of the figure as before and vibrate **ARARITA.** Trace the Mars symbol in the center.

d) Go to the western edge of the temple and draw the Lesser Banishing Western Hexagram of Geburah toward the west. Energize it by thrusting through the center of the figure and vibrate as before, **ARARITA.** Trace the Mars symbol in the center.

e) Walk to the northern boundary of the temple and draw the Lesser Banishing Northern Hexagram of Geburah toward the north. Thrust and intone as before, **ARARITA.** Trace the Mars symbol in the center.

f) Return to the east (or center) and perform the *Analysis of the Keyword.*

22. Secure the Sword in a burse or wrap it in red silk or linen and lay it upon the Altar.

23. Perform the Purification and Consecration.

24. Perform the Reverse Circumambulation.

25. Go west of the Altar and perform the Adoration.

26. Give the License to Depart.

27. Perform the LBRP.

28. Say: **I now declare this Temple duly closed. So mote it be!**

✠ ✠ ✠

The Elemental Tools

There are four basic magical Elements: Fire, Water, Air, and Earth. These four primary Elements are regarded as realms, kingdoms, or divisions of Nature. They are the basic modes of existence and action—the building blocks of everything in the universe. All that exists or has the potential to exist contains one or more of these energies. These Elements are not to be confused with the scientist's table of elements, which are only the most materialized expressions of the Elements in the physical plane.

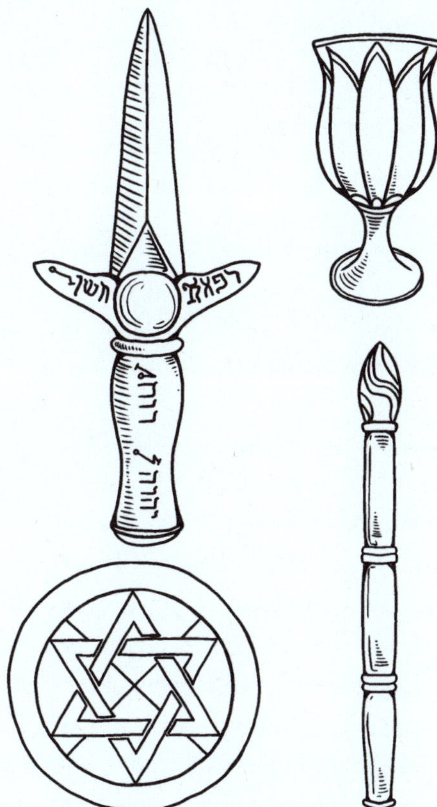

Figure 39: The Elemental Tools

The four Elemental Weapons or tools used by Golden Dawn magicians are the Earth Pentacle, the Air Dagger, the Water Cup, and the Fire Wand. These are the Tarot symbols equating to the divine name YHVH. These implements are used whenever the Adept is working with any of the four elements: They have a certain bond and sympathy between them so that even if only one of these tools is used, the others should also be present.

Preparation for Consecrating the Elemental Tools

For any of the Consecration Rituals that follow in this chapter, the Temple is to be arranged in accordance with the *General Setup for an Adept Working*. The Adept will need the newly consecrated Lotus Wand, Rose Cross Lamen, and Magic Sword. The Four Enochian Elemental Tablets should be placed around the room in their respective quarters. Upon the central black Altar should be:

- Cross and Triangle, Tablet of Union (center)
- Earth Pentacle, platter of salt (north)
- Air Dagger, rose, incense (east)
- Water Cup, separate cup of water (west)
- Fire Wand, red candle (south)

The Adept will also need a cloth bag of linen or silk in the appropriate elemental color for wrapping the newly consecrated elemental tool.

MAGICAL WEAPONS VERSUS TOOLS

Traditionally, the Fire Wand, Water Cup, Air Dagger, and Earth Pentacle are known collectively as the "Elemental Weapons." This title harkens back to a time in the ancient world when one of the primary duties of a magician was to perform magic that drives away evil. However, referring to the Elemental Tools as "weapons" gives an inaccurate portrayal of how these instruments are employed in our tradition and might be an inadvertent remnant of a medieval worldview from a time when almost all spirits were thought to be hostile and adversarial to the magician. Rather than viewing these implements as weapons to "battle" unruly spirits, we should think of them as talismanic badges of authority. Perhaps it is time to de-weaponize the Elemental Tools and recognize them for what they are: consecrated passkeys to the unseen realms.

The Fire Wand

The Fire Wand is used in all magical workings that involve elemental Fire. This wand falls under the Hebrew letter Yod of the Tetragrammaton and is a potent symbol of the magician's willpower. It should not be used in anything other than a ritual that involves the elements.

The shape of the wand marks it as a symbol of masculinity. Like the thyrsus of Dionysus, the shape is that of a cone mounted on a shaft. The symbolism of the cone of the Fire Wand may be derived from the association of the circle with the triangle or pyramid, and may also be a form of the solar glyph. In any event, the flaming Yods painted around the cone firmly establish its masculine fire energy.

The Fire Wand is the most challenging of all the Elemental Weapons to construct. The problem it presents is that a magnetic wire must run through its center, end to end. The Golden Dawn manuscripts suggest making the wand out of bamboo cane, which has a natural hollow running through it, but this is not a very satisfactory way to create the implement.

The wand is traditionally painted red, with three yellow Yods on the cone and four yellow rings on the shaft. One recent innovation is to paint the wand completely in the flashing Fire colors of red and green without any yellow. Divine and angelic names and sigils are painted in green on the red portions of the wand.[107]

- Divine Name: Elohim (אלהים)
- Archangel: Michael (מיכאל)
- Angel: Ariel (אריאל)
- Ruler: Seraph (שרף)
- River of Paradise: Pison (River of Fire) (פישון)
- Cardinal Point: Darom (South) (דרום)
- Element: Ash (Fire) (אש)
- Magical Motto: —

107. See Figure 40: Sigils Associated with the Fire Wand on page 287.

Consecration of the Fire Wand

The Opening

1. Take up the Lotus Wand by the black portion. Go clockwise to the northeast of the temple and say: **Hekas! Hekas! Este Bebeloi!** Return to west of the altar.

2. Put down the Lotus Wand and take up the Magic Sword.

3. Perform the LBRP. Replace the Sword.

4. Perform the Purification and the Consecration.

5. Take up the Lotus Wand by the white portion and perform the Mystic Circumambulation.

6. Perform the Adoration.

Proclamation of Intention (Optional)

7. Hold the Lotus Wand by the white band, in line with your Middle Pillar, visualizing all the Sephiroth as energized with the Divine Light. When ready, raise the Wand high and say:

I, (state your magical motto), a (Frater/Soror) of the Rose of Ruby and the Cross of Gold and a member of the Body of the Christos, have opened the temple this day to undertake the Consecration of this Fire Wand.

I swear that with the Divine permission I shall consecrate this Fire Wand as a labor in the Divine Science, in pursuit of the Great Work, which is to so purify and exalt my spiritual nature that with the Divine aid I may at length become more than human, and thus gradually raise and unite myself to my Higher and Divine Genius. So mote it be!

SIRP of Fire

8. Perform the *Supreme Invoking Ritual of the Pentagram of Fire*[108] as follows:

a) Face east and, holding the white band of the Lotus Wand, perform the Qabalistic Cross.

b) Go to the east and trace a large clockwise circle before the Air Tablet. Then trace the *Invoking Pentagram of Spirit Active* and vibrate **BITOM.** Trace the Spirit wheel in the center and intone **EHEIEH.** Give the Sign of the Opening of the Veil, followed by the LVX Signs.

c) Grasp the Wand by the yellow Leo band. Then trace a smaller circle before the Air quadrant (upper left portion) of the Air Tablet. Within this circle trace the *Invoking Pentagram of Fire* and vibrate **OIP TEAA PEDOCE.** Draw the sigil of Leo in the center and intone **ELOHIM.** Give the Sign of Philosophus.

d) Turn to the south and go to the Fire Tablet. Trace the same figures, vibrate the same words, and give the same gestures. Do the same with the Water Tablet in the west and the Earth Tablet in the north.

e) Give the invocation of the Archangels and end with the Qabalistic Cross.

The Watchtower of the South

9. Stand north of the altar, facing south and the Tablet of Fire, holding the Lotus Wand. (*Optional:* You may place the Fire Wand on top of the white triangle or leave it on the south side of the Altar.)

10. Holding the Lotus Wand by the white band, trace a clockwise circle over the Fire Wand. Trace the I*nvoking Pentagram of Spirit Active* over the Fire Wand while vibrating **BITOM.** Then trace the symbol of the Spirit Wheel in the center while vibrating **EHEIEH.** Give the Sign of the Rending of the Veil, followed by the LVX Signs.

11. Hold the wand by the yellow Leo band and trace a clockwise circle in the air over the Fire Wand. Trace the *Invoking Pentagram of Fire* over the Fire Wand while vibrating **OIP**

108. This is a Single Element Pentagram Ritual. The only pentagrams employed are the *Invoking Pentagram of Spirit Active* and the *Invoking Pentagram of Fire* in all four quarters, toward all four Enochian Tablets. See Ciceros, *Golden Dawn Magic*, 236–38.

TEAA PEDOCE. Then trace the symbol of Leo in the center while vibrating **ELOHIM.** Give the Philosophus Sign.

12. (*NOTE*: In the following speech, invoke the divine and angelic names already painted upon the Fire Wand, making their Hebrew letters and sigils in the air over the Fire Wand with the Lotus Wand. See figure 40.) Say:

O Thou Who art from everlasting, Thou Who hast created all things, and doth clothe Thyself with the Forces of Nature as with a garment, by Thy Holy and Divine Name ELOHIM whereby Thou art known especially in that quarter we name DAROM, the South. I beseech Thee to grant unto me strength and insight for my search after the Hidden Light and Wisdom.

I entreat Thee to cause Thy Wonderful Archangel MICHAEL, who governeth the works of Fire, to guide me in the Pathway: and furthermore to direct Thine Angel ARIEL to watch over my footsteps therein. May the Ruler of Fire, the powerful Prince SERAPH by the gracious permission of the Infinite Supreme, increase and strengthen the hidden forces and occult virtues of this Fire Wand, so that I may be enabled with it to perform aright those magical operations, for which it has been fashioned. For which purpose I now perform this mystic rite of Consecration in the Divine Presence of ELOHIM!

13. Lay the Lotus Wand aside. Take the Fire Wand from the Altar and place it on the elemental altar in front of the Enochian Tablet of Fire in the South.[109]

14. Take up the Sword and go to the Southern Tablet of Fire.

15. With the Sword, trace a clockwise circle around the entire Tablet. Trace the *Invoking Pentagram of Spirit Active* toward the Tablet while vibrating **BITOM.** Then trace the symbol of the Spirit Wheel in the center while vibrating **EHEIEH.** Give the Sign of the Rending of the Veil, followed by the LVX Signs.

---

109. You could leave the Fire Wand on the central Altar and continue. However, we have found it most effective to take it to the South and address the angelic forces directly, to invoke them from their abodes.

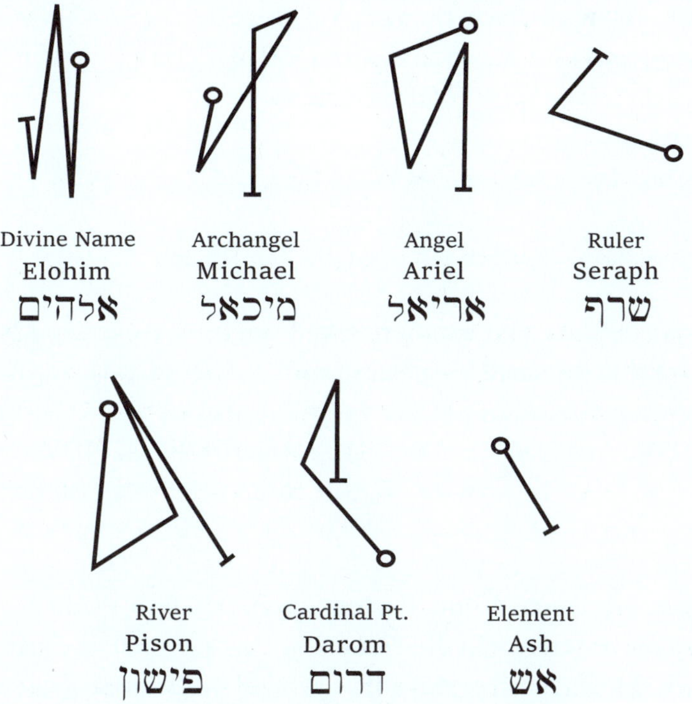

Figure 40: Sigils Associated with the Fire Wand

16. Trace another circle around the entire Fire Tablet with the Sword. Then trace the *Invoking Pentagram of Fire* toward the Tablet while vibrating **OIP TEAA PEDOCE**. Then trace the symbol of Leo in the center while vibrating **ELOHIM**. Give the Philosophus Sign.

17. Read the following Invocation to the Enochian King of Fire:

In the Three Great Secret Holy Names of God borne upon the Banners of the South, OIP TEAA PEDOCE,[110] I summon Thee, Thou Great King of the South, EDELPERNAA,[111] to attend upon this ceremony and by Thy presence increase its effect, whereby I do now consecrate this Magical Fire Wand. Confer upon it the utmost

110. Optional: Trace the Invoking Pentagram of Fire in front of the Tablet while vibrating "OIP TEAA PEDOCE" or simply point to the name on the Tablet.

111. Optional: Trace a clockwise spiral over the letters of the name EDELPERNAA at the center of the Tablet.

occult might and virtue of which Thou mayest judge it to be capable in all works of the nature of Fire so that in it I may find a strong defense and a powerful weapon wherewith to rule and direct the Spirits of the Elements.

18. With the Sword, trace over the Fire Wand the *Greater Invoking Hexagram of Saturn.*

19. Read the Invocation to the Six Seniors of the Fire Tablet:

Ye Mighty Princes of the Great Southern Quadrangle, I invoke you who art known to me by the honorable title, and position of rank, of Seniors. Hear my petition, O ye mighty Princes, the Six Seniors of the Southern quarter of the Earth who bear the names of AAETPIO. AAPDOCE. ADOEOET. ANODOIN. ALNDVOD. ARINNAP.[112] (Pronounced Ah-ah-AY-TAY-pay-ee-oh. Ah-ah-PAY-doh-kay. Ah-doh-AY-oh-ay-tay. Ah-noh-DOH-ee-en. Al-EN-dah-voh-dah. Ah-reh-EE-noo-nah-peh.)

And be this day present with me. Bestow upon this Fire Wand the Strength and purity whereof ye are Masters in the Elemental Forces which ye control; that its outward and material form may remain a true symbol of the inward and spiritual force. (Replace the Sword.)

20. (*NOTE:* In the following speeches, read the invocations of the angels governing the four quadrants, or sub-elements,[113] of the Fire Tablet: Fire of Fire, Water of Fire, Air of Fire, and Earth of Fire.)

For the Sub-Element of Fire

21. Take up the Sword and trace a clockwise circle in front of the Fire quadrant (lower right portion) of the Fire Tablet. Then trace the Invoking Pentagrams of *Spirit Active* (**BITOM, EHEIEH**) and *Invoking Fire* (**OIP TEAA PEDOCE, ELOHIM**) in front of the Fire quadrant and give the proper signs (Opening Veil, LVX, and Philosophus Signs).

---

112. Optional: Trace the Saturn Hexagram over the Enochian Tablet first, to invoke the Seniors from their abode, and intone their names. Then trace the figure and intone the names a second time over the Fire Wand to visualize and direct the current of energy there.

113. These sections are also known as lesser angles, or sub-angles, of a Tablet.

22. Say: **O Thou Mighty Angel, BZIZA** (Beh-ZOAD-ee-zoad-ah),[114] **Thou who art Ruler and President over the Four Angels of the Fiery Lesser Quadrangle of Fire, I invocate Thee to impress into this weapon the force and fiery energy of Thy Kingdom and Servants, that by it I may control them for all just and righteous purposes.**

23. With the Sword, trace a clockwise circle over the Fire Wand. Then trace the Invoking Pentagrams of *Spirit Active* (**EXARP, EHEIEH**) and *Invoking Fire* (**OIP TEAA PEDOCE, ELOHIM**) over the Wand and give the proper signs just as before.[115] Replace the Sword.

For the Sub-Element of Water

24. Take up the Water Cup from the Altar and trace a clockwise circle in front of the Water quadrant (upper right portion) of the Fire Tablet. Then trace the Invoking Pentagrams of *Spirit Active* (**BITOM, EHEIEH**) and *Invoking Fire* (**OIP TEAA PEDOCE, ELOHIM**) in front of the Water quadrant and give the proper signs as before.

25: Say: **O Thou Mighty Angel, BANAA** (Bah-EN-ah-ah), **Thou who art Ruler and President over the Four Angels of Fluid Fire, I beseech Thee to impress into this weapon Thy Magic Power that by it I may control the Spirits who serve Thee for all just and righteous purposes.**

26. With the Water Cup, trace a clockwise circle over the Fire Wand. Then trace the Invoking Pentagrams of *Spirit Active* (**BITOM, EHEIEH**) and *Invoking Fire* (**OIP TEAA PEDOCE, ELOHIM**) over the Wand and give the proper signs. Replace the Water Cup.

For the Sub-Element of Air

27. Take up the Air Dagger and trace a circle in front of the Air quadrant (upper left portion) of the Fire Tablet. Then trace the Invoking Pentagrams of *Spirit Active* (**BITOM, EHEIEH**) and *Invoking Fire* (**OIP TEAA PEDOCE, ELOHIM**) in front of the Air quadrant and give the proper signs.

---

114. In all cases it is helpful to point at these angels on the Tablet while reading these sections.

115. Tracing over the Fire Wand directs the current of energy into it. Strongly visualize the energy from the Tablet entering the Fire Wand.

28. Say: **O Thou Mighty Angel, BDOPA** (Bay-DOH-pah)**, Thou who art Ruler and President over the Four Angels and Governors of the subtle and aspiring Etheric Fire, I beseech Thee to bestow upon this weapon Thy strength and fiery steadfastness, that with it I may control the Spirits of Thy Realm for all just and righteous purposes.**

29. With the Air Dagger, trace a clockwise circle over the Fire Wand. Then trace the Invoking Pentagrams of *Spirit Active* (**BITOM, EHEIEH**) and *Invoking Fire* (**OIP TEAA PEDOCE, ELOHIM**) over the Wand and give the proper signs. Visualize the energy going from the Tablet to the Fire Wand. Replace the Dagger.

For the Sub-Element of Earth

30. Take up the Earth Pentacle and trace a circle in front of the Earth quadrant (lower left portion) of the Fire Tablet. Then trace the Invoking Pentagrams of *Spirit Active* (**BITOM, EHEIEH**) and *Invoking Fire* (**OIP TEAA PEDOCE, ELOHIM**) in front of the Earth quadrant and give the proper signs.

31. Say: **O Thou Mighty angel, BPSAC** (Bay-PAY-sah-cah)**, Thou who art Ruler and President over the Four Angels of the denser Fire of Earth, I beseech Thee to bestow upon this weapon Thy strength and fiery steadfastness that with it I may control the Spirits of Thy Realm for all just and righteous purposes.**

32. With the Earth Pentacle, trace a clockwise circle over the Fire Wand. Then trace the Invoking Pentagrams of *Spirit Active* (**EXARP, EHEIEH**) and *Invoking Fire* (**OIP TEAA PEDOCE, ELOHIM**) over the Wand and give the proper signs. Visualize the transfer of energy from Tablet to Wand. Replace the Pentacle.

SIRP of Fire with Fire Wand

33. Take up the newly consecrated Fire Wand and perform with it the *Supreme Invoking Ritual of the Pentagram of Fire* following the same instructions as given in step 8, simply substituting the Fire Wand in place of the Lotus Wand.

34. *Optional Step:* Go to the south, holding the Fire Wand high, and recite the *Prayer of the Salamanders* from the Philosophus Ceremony:

Immortal, Eternal, Ineffable, and Uncreated Father of All, borne upon the Chariot of Worlds which ever roll in ceaseless motion. Ruler over the Ethereal Vastness where the Throne of Thy Power is raised, from the summit of which Thine Eyes behold all and Thy Pure and Holy Ears hear all—help us, Thy children, whom Thou hast loved since the birth of the Ages of Time! Thy Majesty, Golden, Vast, and Eternal, shineth above the Heaven of Stars. Above them art Thou exalted.

O Thou Flashing Fire, there Thou illuminatest all things with Thine Insupportable Glory, whence flow the Ceaseless Streams of Splendour which nourisheth Thine Infinite Spirit. This Infinite Spirit nourisheth all and maketh that inexhaustible Treasure of Generation which ever encompasseth Thee—replete with the numberless forms wherewith Thou hast filled it from the Beginning. From this Spirit arise those most holy kings who are around Thy Throne and who compose Thy Court.

O Universal Father, One and Alone! Father alike of Immortals and Mortals. Thou hast specially created Powers similar unto Thy Thought Eternal and unto Thy Venerable Essence. Thou hast established them above the Angels who announce Thy Will to the world.

Lastly, Thou hast created us as a third Order in our Elemental Empire. There our continual exercise is to praise and to adore Thy Desires: there we ceaselessly burn with Eternal Aspirations unto Thee, O Father! O Mother of Mothers! O Archetype Eternal of Maternity and Love! O Son, the Flower of all Sons! Form of all Forms! Soul, Spirit, Harmony, and Numeral of all things! Amen![116]

The Closing

35. Wrap the Fire Wand in red silk or linen.

36. Perform the Purification and Consecration.

37. Perform the Reverse Circumambulation.

38. Go west of the Altar and perform the Adoration.

---

116. From the Ceremony of the 4=7 Grade of Philosophus in Regardie, *The Golden Dawn*, 249–50.

39. Give the License to Depart.

40. Perform the LBRP.[117]

41. Say: **I now declare this Temple duly closed. So mote it be!**

✠ ✠ ✠

The Water Cup

The Water Cup is used in all magical workings relating to the nature of elemental Water, under the presidency of the Hebrew letter Heh of YHVH and the Cup of the Tarot. The Water Cup is to be marked with eight raised, etched, or painted lotus petals.

This cup should not be confused with the Stolistes Cup or a separate chalice required for the Repast of the Four Elements. A plain chalice of this sort is symbolic of the heart center of Osiris and of Tiphareth. The more elaborate Water Cup of the Adept is to be used in rituals involving the elements.

This is one implement whose construction seems to vary with the ingenuity of the magician making it. The Golden Dawn instructions suggest that any glass cup with a stem can be used, and paper petals attached. Although this method is the least satisfying and easiest to break, it appears to have been the most common method used to create the Cup in the early days of the Order.

When looking for an appropriate cup, try to find a metal or wood cup with a top edge that flares outward like a crocus flower, a design that was often used in ancient Egyptian cups.

Eight petals cut out of leather or similar crafting material can be attached to a brass or pewter cup with sturdy, general-purpose craft glue. The petals and body of the Cup should be painted blue. The outlines of the petals, as well as all Hebrew letters and sigils, should be painted orange (see figure 41).

- Divine Name: EL (אל)
- Archangel: Gabriel (גבריאל)
- Angel: Taliahad (טליהד)
- Ruler: Tharsis (תרשיס)

117. If you prefer, perform the *Supreme Banishing Ritual of Fire*, but only if all implements have not been consecrated at the same ceremony.

- River of Paradise: Gihon (River of Water) (גיחון)
- Cardinal Point: Maarab (West) (מערב)
- Element: Mayim (Water) (מים)
- Magical Motto: —

Consecration of the Water Cup

The Opening

1. Take up the Lotus Wand by the black portion. Go clockwise to the northeast of the temple and say, **Hekas! Hekas! Este Bebeloi!** Return to west of the altar.

2. Put down the Lotus Wand and take up the Magic Sword.

3. Perform the LBRP. Replace the Sword.

4. Perform the Purification and the Consecration.

5. Take up the Lotus Wand by the white portion and perform the Mystic Circumambulation.

6. Perform the Adoration.

Proclamation of Intention (Optional)

7. Hold the Lotus Wand by the white band, in line with your Middle Pillar, visualizing all the Sephiroth as energized with the Divine Light. When ready, raise the Wand high and say:

I, (state your magical motto), a (Frater/Soror) of the Rose of Ruby and the Cross of Gold and a member of the Body of the Christos, have opened the temple this day to undertake the Consecration of this Water Cup.

I swear that with the Divine permission I shall consecrate this Water Cup as a labor in the Divine Science, in pursuit of the Great Work, which is to so purify and exalt my spiritual nature that with the Divine aid I may at length become more than

human, and thus gradually raise and unite myself to my Higher and Divine Genius. So mote it be!

SIRP of Water

8. Perform the *Supreme Invoking Ritual of the Pentagram of Water*[118] as follows:

a) Face east and, holding the white band of the Lotus Wand, perform the Qabalistic Cross.

b) Go to the east and trace a large clockwise circle before the Air Tablet. Then trace the *Invoking Pentagram of Spirit Passive* and vibrate **HCOMA.** Trace the Spirit wheel in the center and intone **AGLA.** Give the Sign of the Opening of the Veil, followed by the LVX Signs.

c) Grasp the Wand by the blue-green Scorpio band. Then trace a smaller circle before the Water quadrant (upper right portion) of the Air Tablet. Within this circle trace the *Invoking Pentagram of Water* and vibrate **EMPEH ARSEL GAIOL.** Draw the symbol of the Eagle's head in the center and intone **Aleph Lamed, EL.** Give the Sign of Practicus.

d) Turn to the south and go to the Fire Tablet. Trace the same figures, vibrate the same words, and give the same gestures. Do the same with the Water Tablet in the west and the Earth Tablet in the north.

e) Give the invocation of the Archangels and end with the Qabalistic Cross.

The Watchtower of the West

9. Stand east of the altar, facing west and the Tablet of Water, holding the Lotus Wand. (*Optional:* You may place the Water Cup on top of the white triangle or leave it on the west side of the Altar.)

10. Holding the Lotus Wand by the white band, trace a clockwise circle over the Water Cup. Trace the *Invoking Pentagram of Spirit Passive* over the Cup while vibrating **HCOMA.** Then trace the symbol of the Spirit Wheel in the center while vibrating **AGLA.** Give the Sign of the Rending of the Veil, followed by the LVX Signs.

---

118. This is another Single Element Pentagram Ritual. See Ciceros, *Golden Dawn Magic*, 236–38.

11. Hold the wand by the blue-green Scorpio band and trace a clockwise circle in the air over the Cup. Trace the *Invoking Pentagram of Water* over the Cup while vibrating **EMPEH ARSEL GAIOL.** Then trace the symbol of Aquarius in the center while vibrating **Aleph Lamed, EL.** Give the Practicus Sign.

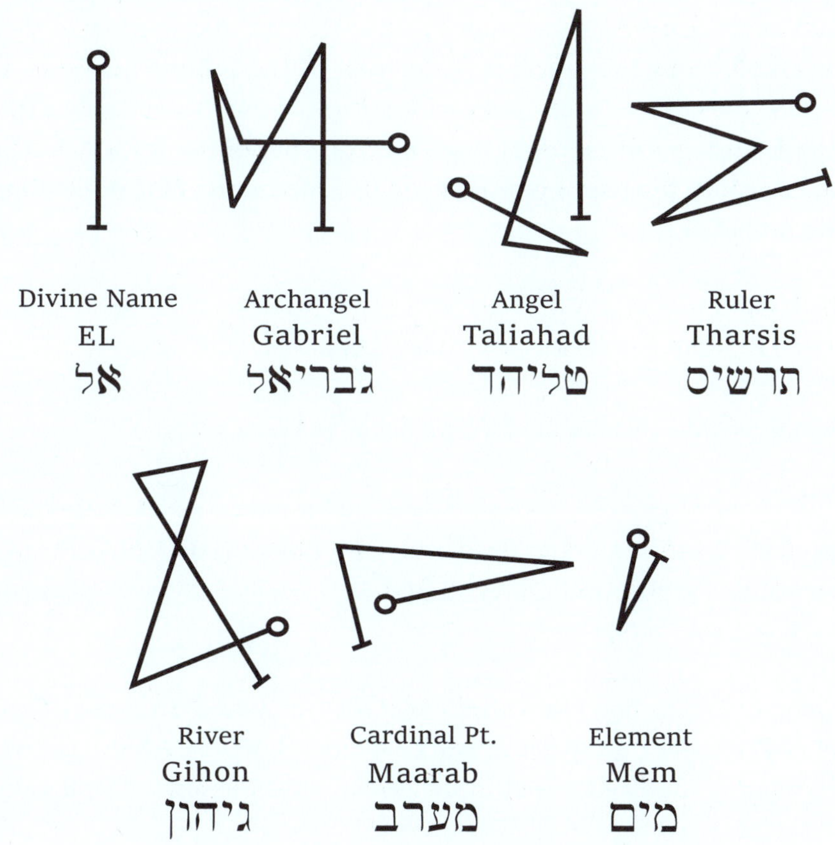

Figure 41: Sigils Associated with the Water Cup

12. (*NOTE*: In the following speech, invoke the divine and angelic names already painted upon the Water Cup, making their Hebrew letters and sigils in the air over the Cup with the Lotus Wand.) Say:

O Thou Who art from everlasting, Thou Who hast created all things, and doth clothe Thyself with the Forces of Nature as with a garment, by Thy Holy and Divine Name EL whereby Thou art known especially in that quarter we name MAARAB, the West.

I beseech Thee to grant unto me strength and insight for my search after the Hidden Light and Wisdom.

I entreat Thee to cause Thy Wonderful Archangel GABRIEL, who governeth the works of Air, to guide me in the Pathway: and furthermore to direct Thine Angel TALIAHAD to watch over my footsteps therein. May the Ruler of Water, the powerful Prince THARSIS by the gracious permission of the Infinite Supreme, increase and strengthen the hidden forces and occult virtues of this Water Cup, so that I may be enabled with it to perform aright those magical operations, for which it has been fashioned. For which purpose I now perform this mystic rite of Consecration in the Divine Presence of EL!

13. Lay the Lotus Wand aside. Take the Water Cup from the Altar and place it on the elemental altar in front of the Enochian Tablet of Water in the West.

14. Take up the Sword and go to the Western Tablet of Water.

15. With the Sword, trace a clockwise circle around the entire Tablet. Trace the *Invoking Pentagram of Spirit Passive* toward the Tablet while vibrating **HCOMA.** Then trace the Spirit Wheel in the center while vibrating **AGLA.** Give the Sign of the Rending of the Veil, followed by the LVX Signs.

16. Trace another circle around the entire Tablet with the Sword. Then trace the *Invoking Pentagram of Water* toward the Tablet while vibrating **EMPEH ARSEL GAIOL.** Then trace the symbol of the Eagle's head in the center while vibrating **Aleph Lamed, EL.** Give the Practicus Sign.

17. Read the following Invocation to the Enochian King of Water:

In the Three Great Secret Holy Names of God borne upon the Banners of the West, EMPEH ARSEL GAIOL,[119] I summon Thee, Thou Great King of the West, RA AGIOSEL,[120] to attend upon this ceremony and by Thy presence increase its effect,

119. Optional: Trace the Invoking Pentagram of Water in front of the Tablet while vibrating "EMPEH ARSEL GAIOL" or simply point to the name on the Tablet.

120. Optional: Trace a clockwise spiral over the letters of the name RAAGIOSEL at the center of the Tablet.

whereby I do now consecrate this Magical Chalice. Confer upon it the utmost occult might and virtue of which Thou mayest judge it to be capable in all works of the nature of Water so that in it I may find a strong defense and a powerful weapon wherewith to rule and direct the Spirits of the Elements.

18. With the Sword, trace over the Cup the *Greater Invoking Hexagram of Saturn.*

19. Read the Invocation to the Six Seniors of the Water Tablet:

Ye Mighty Princes of the Great Western Quadrangle, I invoke you who art known to me by the honorable title, and position of rank, of Seniors. Hear my petition, O ye mighty Princes, the Six Seniors of the Western quarter of the Earth who bear the names of LSRAHPM. SLGAIOL. SAIINOV. SONIZNT. LAOAXRP. LIGDISA. (El-ess-rah-hay-pay-mee. Ess-el-gah-ee-ol. Sah-ee-ee-noh-vah. Soh-nee-zoad-noo-tay. Lah-oh-ahx-ar-pay.)

And be this day present with me. Bestow upon this Water Cup the Strength and purity whereof ye are Masters in the Elemental Forces which ye control; that its outward and material form may remain a true symbol of the inward and spiritual force. (Replace the Sword.)

20. (*NOTE:* In the speeches that follow, read the invocations of the angels governing the four quadrants of the Water Tablet: Fire of Water, Water of Water, Air of Water, and Earth of Water.)

For the Sub-Element of Fire

21. Take up the Fire Wand and trace a clockwise circle in front of the Fire quadrant (lower right portion) of the Water Tablet. Then trace the Invoking Pentagrams of *Spirit Passive* (**HCOMA, AGLA**) and *Invoking Water* (**EMPEH ARSEL GAIOL; Aleph Lamed, EL**) in front of the Fire quadrant and give the proper signs (Opening Veil, LVX, and Practicus Signs).

22. Say: **O Thou Powerful Angel, HNLRX** (Hay-en-el-rex)**, Thou who art Lord and Ruler over the Fiery Waters, I beseech Thee to endow this Cup with the Magic Powers**

of which Thou art Lord, that I may with its aid direct the Spirits who serve Thee in purity and singleness of aim.

23. With the Fire Wand, trace a clockwise circle over the Cup. Then trace the Invoking Pentagrams of *Spirit Passive* (**HCOMA, AGLA**) and *Invoking Water* (**EMPEH ARSEL GAIOL; Aleph Lamed, EL**) over the Cup and give the proper signs just as before. Visualize the flow of energy from Tablet to Cup. Replace the Fire Wand.

For the Sub-Element of Water

24. Take up the Sword and trace a clockwise circle in front of the Water quadrant (upper right portion) of the Water Tablet. Then trace the Invoking Pentagrams of *Spirit Passive* (**HCOMA, AGLA**) and *Invoking Water* (**EMPEH ARSEL GAIOL; Aleph Lamed, EL**) in front of the Water quadrant and give the proper signs as before.

25: Say: **O Thou Powerful Angel, HTDIM** (Hay-tay-dee-may)**, Thou who art Lord and Ruler over the pure and fluid Element of Water, I beseech Thee to endow this Cup with the Magic Powers of which Thou art Lord, that I may with its aid direct the Spirits who serve Thee in purity and singleness of aim.**

26. With the Sword, trace a clockwise circle over the Cup. Then trace the Invoking Pentagrams of *Spirit Passive* (**HCOMA, AGLA**) and *Invoking Water* (**EMPEH ARSEL GAIOL; Aleph Lamed, EL**) over the Cup and give the proper signs. Visualize the flow of energy from Tablet to Cup. Replace the Sword.

For the Sub-Element of Air

27. Take up the Air Dagger and trace a clockwise circle in front of the Air quadrant (upper left portion) of the Water Tablet. Then trace the Invoking Pentagrams of *Spirit Passive* (**HCOMA, AGLA**) and *Invoking Water* (**EMPEH ARSEL GAIOL; Aleph Lamed, EL**) in front of the Air quadrant and give the proper signs.

28. Say: **O Thou Powerful Angel, HTAAD** (Hay-tah-ah-dee)**, Thou who art Lord and Ruler of the Etheric and Airy qualities of Water, I beseech Thee to endow this Cup with the Magic Powers of which Thou art Lord, that I may with its aid direct the Spirits who serve Thee in purity and singleness of aim.**

29. With the Air Dagger, trace a clockwise circle over the Cup. Then trace the Invoking Pentagrams of *Spirit Passive* (**NANTA, AGLA**) and *Invoking Water* (**EMPEH ARSEL GAIOL; Aleph Lamed, EL**) over the Cup and give the proper signs. Replace the Dagger.

For the Sub-Element of Earth

30. Take up the Earth Pentacle and trace a clockwise circle in front of the Earth quadrant (lower left portion) of the Water Tablet. Then trace the Invoking Pentagrams of *Spirit Passive* (**HCOMA, AGLA**) and *Invoking Water* (**EMPEH ARSEL GAIOL; Aleph Lamed, EL**) in front of the Earth quadrant and give the proper signs.

31. Say: **O Thou Powerful angel, HMAGL** (Hay-mah-gee-el)**, Thou who art Lord and Ruler of the more dense and solid qualities of Water, I beseech Thee to endow this Cup with the Magic Powers of which Thou art Lord, that with its aid I may direct the Spirits who serve Thee in purity and singleness of aim.**

32. With the Pentacle, trace a clockwise circle over the Water Cup. Then trace the Invoking Pentagrams of *Spirit Passive* (**HCOMA, AGLA**) and *Invoking Water* (**EMPEH ARSEL GAIOL; Aleph Lamed, EL**) over the Cup and give the proper signs. Replace the Pentacle.

SIRP of Water with Water Cup

33. Take up the newly consecrated Water Cup and perform with it the *Supreme Invoking Ritual of the Pentagram of Water* following the same instructions as given in step 8, simply substituting the Water Cup in place of the Lotus Wand.

34. *Optional Step:* Go to the north holding the Cup high and recite the *Prayer of the Undines* from the Practicus Ceremony:

Terrible King of the Sea, Thou who holdest the Keys of the Cataracts of Heaven, and who enclosest the subterranean Waters in the cavernous hollows of Earth. King of the Deluge and the Rains of Spring. Thou who openest the sources of the rivers and of the fountains; Thou who commandest moisture which is, as it were, the Blood of the Earth, to become the sap of the plants. We adore Thee and we invoke Thee. Speak Thou unto us, Thy mobile and changeful creatures, in the Great Tempests, and we

shall tremble before Thee. Speak to us also in the murmur of the limpid Waters, and we shall desire Thy love.

O Vastness! Wherein all the rivers of Being seek to lose themselves—which renew themselves ever in Thee! O Thou Ocean of Infinite Perfection! O Height which reflectest Thyself in the Depth! O Depth which exhaltest into the Height! Lead us into the true life, through intelligence, through love! Lead us into immortality through sacrifice, that we may be found worthy to offer one day unto Thee, the Water, the Blood and Tears, for Remission of Sins! Amen.

The Closing

35. Wrap the Water Cup in blue silk or linen.

36. Perform the Purification and Consecration.

37. Perform the Reverse Circumambulation.

38. Go west of the Altar and perform the Adoration.

39. Give the License to Depart.

40. Perform the LBRP.[121]

41. Say: **I now declare this Temple duly closed. So mote it be!**

✠ ✠ ✠

121. If you prefer, perform the *Supreme Banishing Ritual of Water*, but only if all implements have not been consecrated at the same ceremony.

The Air Dagger

The Air Dagger is to be used in all magical workings of the element of Air and falls under the Hebrew letter Vav of YHVH and the Sword of the Tarot. It is to be used with the three other Elemental Tools. In symbolism the dagger can be compared to the tip of the spear, cast through the air to hit its target.

There should be no confusion between the Magic Sword and the Air Dagger. The Magic Sword is under Geburah and is for strength and defense. These two implements belong to different planes, and any substitution of one for the other will serve to undermine your magical efforts.

The Air Dagger is not to be used in rituals that call for a plain dagger, such as the Lesser Ritual of the Pentagram. For the LRP, a black-handled dagger of no special design should suffice.

The blade of the dagger should be between 4–6 inches. The hilt of the Air Dagger is yellow, the color assigned to elemental Air, and should be wide enough to add the appropriate divine names and sigils, painted in violet (see figure 42).

- Divine Name: YHVH (יהוה)
- Archangel: Raphael (רפאל)
- Angel: Chassan (חשן)
- Ruler: Arel (אראל)
- River of Paradise: Hiddikel (River of Air) (הדקל)
- Cardinal Point: Mizrach (East) (מזרח)
- Element: Ruach (Air) (רוח)
- Motto: —

Consecration of the Air Dagger

The Opening

1. Take up the Lotus Wand by the black portion. Go clockwise to the northeast of the temple and say, **Hekas! Hekas! Este Bebeloi!** Return to west of the altar.

2. Put down the Lotus Wand and take up the Magic Sword.

3. Perform the LBRP. Replace the Sword.

4. Perform the Purification and the Consecration.

5. Take up the wand by the white portion and perform the Mystic Circumambulation.

6. Perform the Adoration.

Proclamation of Intention (Optional)

7. Hold the Lotus Wand by the white band, in line with your Middle Pillar, visualizing all the Sephiroth as energized with the Divine Light. When ready, raise the Wand high and say:

I, (state your magical motto), a (Frater/Soror) of the Rose of Ruby and the Cross of Gold and a member of the Body of the Christos, have opened the temple this day to undertake the Consecration of this Air Dagger.

I swear that with the Divine permission I shall consecrate this Air Dagger as a labor in the Divine Science, in pursuit of the Great Work, which is to so purify and exalt my spiritual nature that with the Divine aid I may at length become more than human, and thus gradually raise and unite myself to my Higher and Divine Genius. So mote it be!

SIRP of Air

8. Perform the *Supreme Invoking Ritual of the Pentagram of Air*[122] as follows:

a) Face east and, holding the white band of the Lotus Wand, perform the Qabalistic Cross.

b) Go to the east and trace a large clockwise circle before the Air Tablet. Then trace the *Invoking Pentagram of Spirit Active* and vibrate **EXARP.** Trace the Spirit wheel in the center and intone **EHEIEH.** Give the Sign of the Opening of the Veil, followed by the LVX Signs.

---

122. See Ciceros, *Golden Dawn Magic*, 236–38.

c) Grasp the Wand by the violet Aquarius band. Then trace a smaller circle before the Air quadrant (upper left portion) of the Air Tablet. Within this circle trace the *Invoking Pentagram of Air* and vibrate **ORO IBAH AOZPI.** Draw the sigil of Aquarius in the center and intone **YHVH.** Give the Sign of Theoricus.

d) Turn to the south and go to the Fire Tablet. Trace the same figures, vibrate the same words, and give the same gestures. Do the same with the Water Tablet in the west and the Earth Tablet in the north.

e) Give the invocation of the Archangels and end with the Qabalistic Cross.

The Watchtower of the East

9. Stand west of the altar, facing east and the Tablet of Air, holding the Lotus Wand. (*Optional:* You may place the Air Dagger on top of the white triangle or leave it on the east side of the Altar.)

10. Holding the Lotus Wand by the white band, trace a clockwise circle over the Air Dagger. Trace the *Invoking Pentagram of Spirit Active* over the Dagger while vibrating **EXARP.** Then trace the symbol of the Spirit Wheel in the center while vibrating **EHEIEH.** Give the Sign of the Rending of the Veil, followed by the LVX Signs.

11. Hold the wand by the violet Aquarius band and trace a clockwise circle in the air over the Dagger. Trace the *Invoking Pentagram of Air* over the Dagger while vibrating **ORO IBAH AOZPI.** Then trace the symbol of Aquarius in the center while vibrating **YHVH.** Give the Theoricus Sign.

12. (*NOTE*: In the following speech, invoke the divine and angelic names already painted upon the Dagger, making their Hebrew letters and sigils in the air over the Dagger with the Lotus Wand.) Say:

O Thou Who art from everlasting, Thou Who hast created all things, and doth clothe Thyself with the Forces of Nature as with a garment, by Thy Holy and Divine Name YHVH whereby Thou art known especially in that quarter we name MIZRACH, the East. I beseech Thee to grant unto me strength and insight for my search after the Hidden Light and Wisdom.

I entreat Thee to cause Thy Wonderful Archangel RAPHAEL, who governeth the works of Air, to guide me in the Pathway: and furthermore to direct Thine Angel CHASSAN to watch over my footsteps therein. May the Ruler of Air, the powerful Prince EREL by the gracious permission of the Infinite Supreme, increase and strengthen the hidden forces and occult virtues of this Air Dagger, so that I may be enabled with it to perform aright those Magical operations, for which it has been fashioned. For which purpose I now perform this mystic rite of Consecration in the Divine Presence of YHVH!

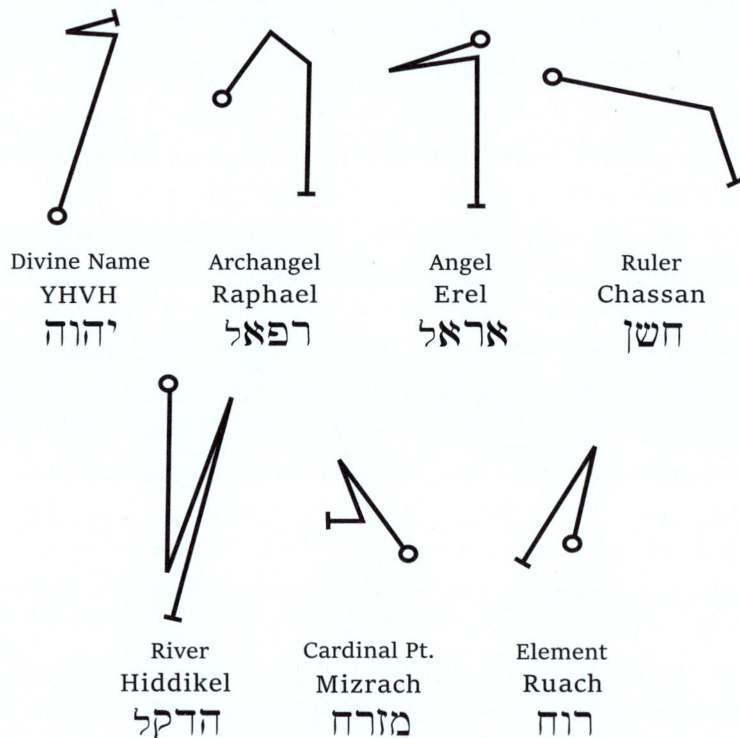

Figure 42: Sigils Associated with the Air Dagger

13. Lay the Lotus Wand aside. Take the Dagger from the Altar and place it on the elemental altar in front of the Enochian Tablet of Air in the East.

14. Take up the Sword and go to the Eastern Tablet of Air.

15. With the Sword, trace a clockwise circle around the entire Tablet. Trace the *Invoking Pentagram of Spirit Active* toward the Tablet while vibrating **EXARP.** Then trace the symbol of the Spirit Wheel in the center while vibrating **EHEIEH.** Give the Sign of the Rending of the Veil, followed by the LVX Signs.

16. Trace another circle around the entire Air Tablet with the Sword. Then trace the *Invoking Pentagram of Air* toward the Tablet while vibrating **ORO IBAH AOZPI.** Then trace the symbol of Aquarius in the center while vibrating **YHVH.** Give the Theoricus Sign.

17. Read the following Invocation to the Enochian King of Air:

In the Three Great Secret Holy Names of God borne upon the Banners of the East, ORO IBAH AOZPI,[123] **I summon Thee, Thou Great King of the East, BATAIVAH,**[124] **to attend upon this ceremony and by Thy presence increase its effect, whereby I do now consecrate this Magical Dagger. Confer upon it the Utmost Occult Might and Virtue of which Thou mayest judge it to be capable in all works of the nature of Air so that in it I may find a strong defense and a powerful weapon wherewith to rule and direct the Spirits of the Elements.**

18. With the Sword, trace over the Dagger the *Greater Invoking Hexagram of Saturn.*

19. Read the Invocation to the Six Seniors of the Air Tablet:

Ye Mighty Princes of the Great Eastern Quadrangle, I invoke you who art known to me by the honorable title, and position of rank, of Seniors. Hear my petition, O ye mighty Princes, the Six Seniors of the Eastern quarter of the Earth who bear the names of HABIORO. AHAOZPI. AAOZAIF. AVTOTAR. HTMORDA. HIPOTGA.[125]

---

123. Optional: Trace the Invoking Pentagram of Air in front of the Tablet while vibrating "ORO IBAH AOZPI" or simply point to the name on the Tablet.

124. Optional: Trace a clockwise spiral over the letters of the name BATAIVAH at the center of the Tablet.

125. Optional: Trace the Saturn Hexagram over the Enochian Tablet first, to invoke the Seniors from their abode, and intone their names. Then trace the figure and intone the names a second time over the Air Dagger to direct the current of energy there.

(Pronounced Hah-BEE-oh-roh. Ah-HAH-oh-zoad-pee. Ah-AH-oh-zah-eef. Ah-VAH-toh-tah-ray. Hay-TAY-mor-dah. Hay-EE-poh-tay-gah.)

And be this day resent with me. Bestow upon this Air Dagger the Strength and Purity whereof ye are Masters in the Elemental Forces which ye control, that its outward and material form may remain a true symbol of the inward and spiritual force. (Replace the Sword.)

20. (*NOTE:* In the following speeches, read the invocations of the angels governing the four quadrants of the Air Tablet: Fire of Air, Water of Air, Air of Air, and Earth of Air.)

For the Sub-Element of Fire

21. Take up the Fire Wand and trace a clockwise circle in front of the Fire quadrant (lower right portion) of the Air Tablet. Then trace the Invoking Pentagrams of *Spirit Active* (**EXARP, EHEIEH**) and *Invoking Air* (**ORO IBAH AOZPI, YHVH**) in front of the Fire quadrant and give the proper signs (Opening Veil, LVX, and Theoricus Signs).

22. Say: **O Thou Resplendent Angel, EXGSD** (Ex-gee-ESS-dah)**, Thou who governest the Fiery Realms of Air, I conjure Thee to confer upon this Dagger, Thy Mysterious and Magical Powers, that I thereby may control the Spirits who serve Thee for such purposes as be pure and upright.**

23. With the Fire Wand, trace a clockwise circle over the Air Dagger. Then trace the Invoking Pentagrams of *Spirit Active* (**EXARP, EHEIEH**) and *Invoking Air* (**ORO IBAH AOZPI, YHVH**) over the Dagger and give the proper signs just as before. Visualize the flow of energy from Tablet to Dagger. Replace the Fire Wand.

For the Sub-Element of Water

24. Take up the Water Cup and trace a clockwise circle in front of the Water quadrant (upper right portion) of the Air Tablet. Then trace the Invoking Pentagrams of *Spirit Active* (**EXARP, EHEIEH**) and *Invoking Air* (**ORO IBAH AOZPI, YHVH**) in front of the Water quadrant and give the proper signs as before.

25: Say: **O Thou Resplendent Angel, EYTPA** (Ay-EE-tay-pay-ah)**, Thou who governest the Realms of fluid Air, I conjure Thee to confer upon this Dagger Thy Mysterious**

Powers, that by its aid I may control the Spirits who serve Thee for such purposes as be pure and upright.

26. With the Water Cup, trace a clockwise circle over the Dagger. Then trace the Invoking Pentagrams of *Spirit Active* (**EXARP, EHEIEH**) and *Invoking Air* (**ORO IBAH AOZPI, YHVH**) over the Dagger and give the proper signs. Visualize the flow of energy from Tablet to Dagger. Replace the Water Cup.

For the Sub-Element of Air

27. Take up the Sword and trace a circle in front of the Air quadrant (upper left portion) of the Air Tablet. Then trace the Invoking Pentagrams of *Spirit Active* (**EXARP, EHEIEH**) and *Invoking Air* (**ORO IBAH AOZPI, YHVH**) in front of the Air quadrant and give the proper signs.

28. Say: **O Thou Resplendent Angel, ERZLA** (Ay-ray-ZOAD-lah)**, Thou who rulest the Realms of Pure and Permeating Air, I conjure Thee to confer upon this Dagger the Magic Powers of which Thou art Master, whereby I may control the Spirits who serve Thee, for such purposes as be pure and upright.**

29. With the Sword, trace a clockwise circle over the Air Dagger. Then trace the Invoking Pentagrams of *Spirit Active* (**EXARP, EHEIEH**) and *Invoking Air* (**ORO IBAH AOZPI, YHVH**) over the Dagger and give the proper signs. Replace the Sword.

For the Sub-Element of Earth

30. Take up the Earth Pentacle and trace a circle in front of the Earth quadrant (lower left portion) of the Air Tablet. Then trace the Invoking Pentagrams of *Spirit Active* (**EXARP, EHEIEH**) and *Invoking Air* (**ORO IBAH AOZPI, YHVH**) in front of the Earth quadrant and give the proper signs.

31. Say: **O Thou Resplendent angel, ETNBR** (Ay-tay-EN-bay-ray)**, Thou who rulest the Denser Realms of Air symbolized by the Lesser Angle of Earth, I conjure Thee to confer upon this Dagger the Magic Powers of which Thou art Master, whereby I may control the spirits who serve Thee, for such purposes as be pure and upright.**

32. With the Earth Pentacle, trace a clockwise circle over the Air Dagger. Then trace the Invoking Pentagrams of *Spirit Active* (**EXARP, EHEIEH**) and *Invoking Air* (**ORO IBAH AOZPI, YHVH**) over the Dagger and give the proper signs. Replace the Pentacle.

SIRP of Air with Dagger

33. Take up the newly consecrated Air Dagger and perform with it the *Supreme Invoking Ritual of the Pentagram of Air* following the same instructions as given in step 8, simply substituting the Air Dagger in place of the Lotus Wand.

34. *Optional Step:* Go to the east, holding the Dagger high, and recite the *Prayer of the Sylphs* from the Theoricus Ceremony:

Spirit of Life! Spirit of Wisdom! Whose breath giveth forth and withdraweth the form of all things. Thou before Whom the life of beings is but a shadow which changeth, and a vapor which passeth. Thou who mountest upon the clouds, and who walkest upon the Wings of the Wind. Thou who breathest forth Thy Breath, and endless space is peopled.

Thou drawest in Thy Breath, and all that cometh from Thee returneth unto Thee! Ceaseless Motion, in Eternal stability, be Thou eternally blessed! We praise Thee and we bless Thee in the Changeless Empire of Created Light, of Shades, of Reflections, and of Images.

And we aspire without cessation unto Thy Immutable and Imperishable Brilliance. Let the Ray of Thy Intelligence and the warmth of Thy Love penetrate even unto us! Then that which is volatile shall be fixed; the Shadow shall be a Body; the Spirit of Air shall be a soul; the Dream shall be a Thought. And no more shall we be swept away by the Tempest, but we shall hold the bridles of the Winged Steeds of Dawn. And we shall direct the course of the Evening Breeze to fly before Thee!

O Spirit of Spirits! O Eternal Soul of Souls! O Imperishable Breath of Life! O Creative Sigh! O Mouth which breathest forth and withdrawest the life of all beings, in the flux and reflux of Thine Eternal Word, which is the Divine Ocean of Movement and of Truth!

The Closing

35. Wrap the Air Dagger in yellow silk or linen.

36. Perform the Purification and Consecration.

37. Perform the Reverse Circumambulation.

38. Go west of the Altar and perform the Adoration.

39. Give the License to Depart.

40. Perform the LBRP.[126]

41. Say: **I now declare this Temple duly closed. So mote it be!**

✠ ✠ ✠

The Earth Pentacle

A pentacle is a circular disk that serves as a container for the magical forces inscribed on it. The Earth Pentacle of the Golden Dawn is used in all workings pertaining to the nature of Earth, and is under the presidency of the Hebrew letter Heh Final of the Tetragrammaton and the Pentacle of the Tarot.

One or both sides of the pentacle are inscribed with a white hexagram superimposed over a circle that is divided into the colors of Malkuth. A white border along the edge contains the divine names and sigils of elemental Earth.

The four quarters of the pentacle are painted in the Queen Scale colors of Malkuth to indicate the sub-elements that exist within the makeup of the tenth Sephirah. The citrine quarter is the airy part of Earth, formed from the mixture of orange and green (Hod and Netzach). Russet is the fiery part of Earth, formed from the mixture of orange and violet (Hod and Yesod). Olive is the watery part of Earth, created from combining green and violet (Netzach and Yesod). Black is Earth of Earth, a combination of all the colors grounding in Malkuth.

---

126. If you prefer, perform the *Supreme Banishing Ritual of Air*, but only if all implements have not been consecrated at the same ceremony.

The white hexagram is a symbol of the divine union of opposites, the marriage of Fire and Water. It represents perfect harmony and reconciliation. The white border symbolizes the Divine Spirit surrounding and binding together all four sub-elements of Malkuth.

Circular disks around 5 inches in diameter and between ½ and ¾ of an inch in thickness can be purchased at craft stores and inscribed with the necessary symbolism on one or both sides, including the divine names of Earth (see figure 43):

- God Name: Adonai (אדני)
- Archangel: Uriel (אוריאל)
- Angel: Phorlakh (פורלאך)
- Ruler: Kerub (כרוב)
- River Of Paradise: Phrath (River of Earth) (פרת)
- Cardinal Point: Tzaphon (North) (צפון)
- Element: Aretz (Earth) (ארץ)
- Magical Motto —

Consecration of the Earth Pentacle

The Opening

1. Take up the Lotus Wand by the black portion. Go clockwise to the northeast of the temple and say, **Hekas! Hekas! Este Bebeloi!** Return to west of the altar.

2. Put down the Lotus Wand and take up the Magic Sword.

3. Perform the LBRP. Replace the Sword.

4. Perform the Purification and the Consecration.

5. Take up the Lotus Wand by the white portion and perform the Mystic Circumambulation.

6. Perform the Adoration.

Proclamation of Intention (Optional)

7. Hold the Lotus Wand by the white band, in line with your Middle Pillar, visualizing all the Sephiroth as energized with the Divine Light. When ready, raise the Wand high and say:

I, (state your magical motto), a (Frater/Soror) of the Rose of Ruby and the Cross of Gold and a member of the Body of the Christos, have opened the temple this day to undertake the Consecration of this Earth Pentacle.

I swear that with the Divine permission I shall consecrate this Earth Pentacle as a labor in the Divine Science, in pursuit of the Great Work, which is to so purify and exalt my spiritual nature that with the Divine aid I may at length become more than human, and thus gradually raise and unite myself to my Higher and Divine Genius. So mote it be!

SIRP of Earth

8. Perform the *Supreme Invoking Ritual of the Pentagram of Earth*[127] as follows:

a) Face east and, holding the white band of the Lotus Wand, perform the Qabalistic Cross.

b) Go to the east and trace a large clockwise circle before the Air Tablet. Then trace the *Invoking Pentagram of Spirit Passive* and vibrate **NANTA.** Trace the Spirit wheel in the center and intone **AGLA.** Give the Sign of the Opening of the Veil, followed by the LVX Signs.

c) Grasp the Wand by the red-orange Taurus band. Then trace a smaller circle before the Earth quadrant (lower left portion) of the Air Tablet. Within this circle trace the *Invoking Pentagram of Earth* and vibrate **EMOR DIAL HECTEGA.** Draw the sigil of Taurus in the center and intone **ADONAI.** Give the Sign of Zelator.

d) Turn to the south and go to the Fire Tablet. Trace the same figures, vibrate the same words, and give the same gestures. Do the same with the Water Tablet in the west and the Earth Tablet in the north.

e) Give the invocation of the Archangels and end with the Qabalistic Cross.

---

127. See Ciceros, *Golden Dawn Magic*, 236–38.

The Watchtower of the North

9. Stand south of the altar facing north and the Tablet of Earth, holding the Lotus Wand. (*Optional:* You may place the Earth Pentacle on top of the white triangle or leave it on the north side of the Altar.)

10. Holding the Lotus Wand by the white band, trace a clockwise circle over the Earth Pentacle. Trace the *Invoking Pentagram of Spirit Passive* over the Pentacle while vibrating **NANTA.** Then trace the symbol of the Spirit Wheel in the center while vibrating **AGLA.** Give the Sign of the Rending of the Veil, followed by the LVX Signs.

11. Hold the wand by the red-orange Taurus band and trace a clockwise circle in the air over the Pentacle. Trace the *Invoking Pentagram of Earth* over the Pentacle while vibrating **EMOR DIAL HECTEGA.** Then trace the symbol of Taurus in the center while vibrating **ADONAI.** Give the Zelator Sign.

12. (*NOTE*: In the following speech, invoke the divine and angelic names already painted upon the Pentacle, making their Hebrew letters and sigils in the air over the Pentacle with the Lotus Wand.) Say:

O Thou Who art from everlasting, Thou Who hast created all things, and doth clothe Thyself with the Forces of Nature as with a garment, by Thy Holy and Divine Name ADONAI whereby Thou art known especially in that quarter we name TZAPHON, the North. I beseech Thee to grant unto me strength and insight for my search after the Hidden Light and Wisdom.

I entreat Thee to cause Thy Wonderful Archangel URIEL, who governeth the works of Earth, to guide me in the Pathway: and furthermore to direct Thine Angel PHORLAKH to watch over my footsteps therein. May the Ruler of Earth, the powerful Prince KERUB by the gracious permission of the Infinite Supreme, increase and strengthen the hidden forces and occult virtues of this Earth Pentacle, so that I may be enabled with it to perform aright those Magical operations, for which it has been fashioned. For which purpose I now perform this mystic rite of Consecration in the Divine Presence of ADONAI!

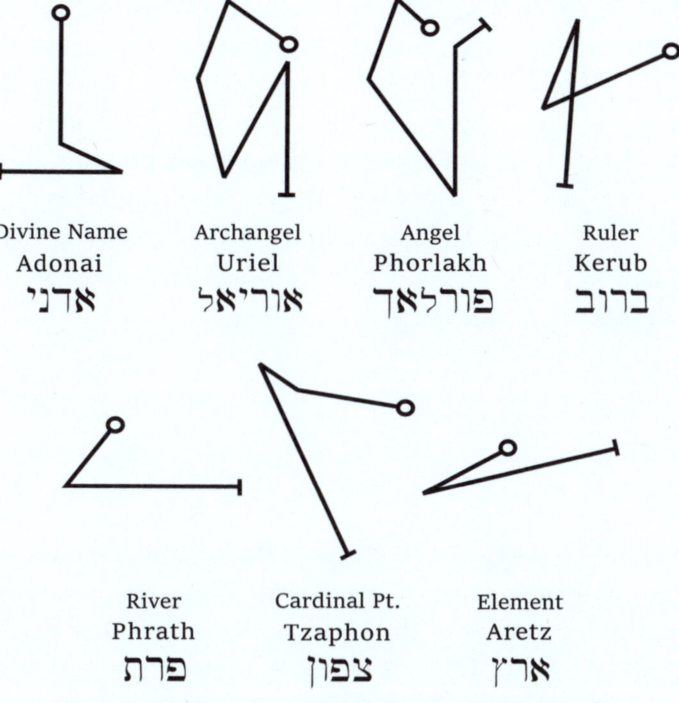

Figure 43: Sigils Associated with the Earth Pentacle

13. Lay the Lotus Wand aside. Take the Pentacle from the Altar and place it on the elemental altar in front of the Enochian Tablet of Earth in the North.

14. Take up the Sword and go to the Northern Tablet of Earth.

15. With the Sword, trace a clockwise circle around the entire Tablet. Trace the *Invoking Pentagram of Spirit Passive* toward the Tablet while vibrating **NANTA.** Then trace the symbol of the Spirit Wheel in the center while vibrating **AGLA.** Give the Sign of the Rending of the Veil, followed by the LVX Signs.

16. Trace another circle around the entire Earth Tablet with the Sword. Then trace the *Invoking Pentagram of Earth* toward the Tablet while vibrating **EMOR DIAL HECTEGA.** Then trace the symbol of Taurus in the center while vibrating **AGLA.** Give the Zelator Sign.

17. Read the following Invocation to the Enochian King of Earth:

In the Three Great Secret Holy Names of God borne upon the Banners of the North, EMOR DIAL HECTEGA,[128] I summon Thee, Thou Great King of the North, IC ZOD HEH HAL,[129] to attend upon this ceremony and by Thy presence increase its effect, whereby I do now consecrate this Magical Pentacle. Confer upon it the Utmost Occult Might and Virtue of which Thou mayest judge it to be capable in all works of the nature of Earth so that in it I may find a strong defense and a powerful weapon wherewith to rule and direct the Spirits of the Elements.

18. With the Sword, trace over the Pentacle the *Greater Invoking Hexagram of Saturn.*

19. Read the Invocation to the Six Seniors of the Earth Tablet:

Ye Mighty Princes of the Great Northern Quadrangle, I invoke you who art known to me by the honorable title, and position of rank, of Seniors. Hear my petition, O ye mighty Princes, the Six Seniors of the Northern quarter of the Earth who bear the names of LAIDROM. ALHCTGA. ACZINOR. AHMLICV. LZINOPO. LIIANSA. (Pronounced: Lah-EE-dah-roh-mee. Al-HECK-tay-gah. Ah-kah-ZOD-ee-noh-ray. Ah-hay-meh-LEE-coh-vah. El-ZOD-ee-noh-poh. Lee-EE-ah-en-sah.)

And be this day present with me. Bestow upon this Earth Pentacle the Strength and Purity whereof ye are Masters in the Elemental Forces which ye control, that its outward and material form may remain a true symbol of the inward and spiritual force. (Replace the Sword.)

20. (*NOTE:* In the following speeches, read the invocations of the angels governing the four quadrants, or sub-elements, of the Earth Tablet. The four sub-elements of the Earth Tablet are Fire of Earth, Water of Earth, Air of Earth, and Earth of Earth.)

128. Optional: Trace the Invoking Pentagram of Earth in front of the Tablet while vibrating "EMOR DIAL HECTAGA" or simply point to the name on the Tablet.

129. Optional: Trace a clockwise spiral over the letters of the name IC ZOD HEH HAL at the center of the Tablet.

For the Sub-Element of Fire

21. Take up the Fire Wand and trace a clockwise circle in front of the Fire quadrant (lower right portion) of the Earth Tablet. Then trace the Invoking Pentagrams of *Spirit Passive* (**NANTA, AGLA**) and *Invoking Earth* (**EMOR DIAL HECTEGA, ADONAI**) in front of the Fire quadrant and give the proper signs (Opening Veil, LVX, and Zelator Signs).

22. Say: **O Thou Resplendent Angel, NASMT**[130] (En-ah-ESS-em-tay)**, Thou who governest the Fiery essences of Earth, I invocate to Thee to bestow upon this Pentacle the Magic Powers of which thou art Sovereign, that by its help I may govern the Spirits of Whom Thou art Lord, in all seriousness and steadfastness.**

23. With the Fire Wand, trace a clockwise circle over the russet quarter of the Pentacle. Then trace the Invoking Pentagrams of *Spirit Passive* (**NANTA, AGLA**) and *Invoking Earth* (**EMOR DIAL HECTEGA, ADONAI**) over the Pentacle and give the proper signs just as before. Visualize the flow of energy from Tablet to Pentacle. Replace the Fire Wand.

For the Sub-Element of Water

24. Take up the Water Cup and trace a clockwise circle in front of the Water quadrant (upper right portion) of the Earth Tablet. Then trace the Invoking Pentagrams of *Spirit Passive* (**NANTA, AGLA**) and *Invoking Earth* (**EMOR DIAL HECTEGA, ADONAI**) in front of the Water quadrant and give the proper signs as before.

25: Say: **O Thou Glorious Angel, NPHRA** (En-pay-HAY-rah)**, Thou who governest the moist and fluid essences of Earth, I invocate Thee to bestow upon this Pentacle the Magic Powers of which Thou art Sovereign that by its help I may govern the Spirits, of whom Thou art Lord, in all seriousness and steadfastness.**

26. With the Water Cup, trace a clockwise circle over the olive portion of the Pentacle. Then trace the Invoking Pentagrams of *Spirit Passive* (**NANTA, AGLA**) and *Invoking Earth* (**EMOR DIAL HECTEGA, ADONAI**) over the Pentacle and give the proper signs. Visualize the flow of energy from Tablet to Pentacle. Replace the Water Cup.

---

130. Optional: Point to this Archangel on the Tablet. And do the same for all angels of the Subelements.

For the Sub-Element of Air

27. Take up the Air Dagger and trace a clockwise circle in front of the Air quadrant (upper left portion) of the Earth Tablet. Then trace the Invoking Pentagrams of *Spirit Passive* (**NANTA, AGLA**) and *Invoking Earth* (**EMOR DIAL HECTEGA, ADONAI**) in front of the Air quadrant and give the proper signs.

28. Say: **O Thou Glorious Angel, NBOZA** (En-boh-ZOAD-ah)**, Thou who governest the Airy and Delicate Essence of the Earth, I invocate Thee to bestow upon this Pentacle the Magic Powers of which Thou art Master, that with its help I may govern the spirits of whom Thou art Lord, in all seriousness and steadfastness.**

29. With the Air Dagger, trace a clockwise circle over the citrine part of the Pentacle. Then trace the Invoking Pentagrams of *Spirit Passive* (**NANTA, AGLA**) and *Invoking Earth* (**EMOR DIAL HECTEGA, ADONAI**) over the Pentacle and give the proper signs. Replace the Dagger.

For the Sub-Element of Earth

30. Take up the Magic Sword and trace a clockwise circle in front of the Earth quadrant (lower left portion) of the Earth Tablet. Then trace the Invoking Pentagrams of *Spirit Passive* (**NANTA, AGLA**) and *Invoking Earth* (**EMOR DIAL HECTEGA, ADONAI**) in front of the Earth quadrant and give the proper signs.

31. Say: **O Thou Glorious angel, NOCNC** (En-oh-CAH-en-cah)**, Thou who governest the dense and solid Earth, I invocate Thee to bestow upon this Pentacle the Magic Powers of which Thou art Master, that with its help I may govern the spirits of whom Thou art Lord, in all seriousness and steadfastness.**

32. With the Sword, trace a clockwise circle over the black portion of the Pentacle. Then trace the Invoking Pentagrams of *Spirit Passive* (**NANTA, AGLA**) and *Invoking Earth* (**EMOR DIAL HECTEGA, ADONAI**) over the Pentacle and give the proper signs. Visualize the flow of energy from Tablet to Pentacle. Replace the Sword.

SIRP of Earth with Pentacle

33. Take up the newly consecrated Earth Pentacle and perform with it the *Supreme Invoking Ritual of the Pentagram of Earth* following the same instructions as given in step 8, simply substituting the Earth Pentacle in place of the Lotus Wand.

34. *Optional Step:* Go to the north, holding the Pentacle high, and recite the *Prayer of the Gnomes:*

O Invisible King, Who, taking the Earth for Foundation, didst hollow its depths to fill them with Thy Almighty Power. Thou whose Name shaketh the Arches of the World. Thou who causest the Seven Metals to flow in the veins of the rocks, King of the Seven Lights, Rewarder of the subterranean Workers, lead us into the desirable Air and into the Realm of Splendor. We watch and we labor unceasingly, we seek and we hope, by the twelve stones of the Holy City, by the buried talismans, by the Axis of the Lodestone which passes through the center of the Earth—O Lord, O Lord, O Lord! Have pity upon those who suffer. Expand our hearts, unbind and upraise our minds, enlarge our natures.

O Stability and Motion! O Darkness veiled in Brilliance! O Day clothed in Night! O Master who never dost withhold the wages of Thy Workmen! O Silver Whiteness—O Golden Splendor! O Crown of Living and Harmonious Diamond! Thou Who wearest the Heavens on Thy Finger like a ring of Sapphire! Thou Who hidest beneath the Earth in the Kingdom of Gems, the marvelous Seed of the Stars! Live, reign, and be Thou the Eternal Dispenser of the Treasures whereof Thou hast made us the Wardens.[131]

The Closing

35. Wrap the Earth Pentacle in dark silk or linen.

36. Perform the Purification and Consecration.

37. Perform the Reverse Circumambulation.

---

131. From the Ceremony of the 1=10 Grade of Zelator in Regardie, *The Golden Dawn*, 184.

38. Go west of the Altar and perform the Adoration.

39. Give the License to Depart.

40. Perform the LBRP.[132]

41. Say: **I now declare this Temple duly closed. So mote it be!**

✠ ✠ ✠

132. If you prefer, perform the *Supreme Banishing Ritual of Earth*, but only if all implements have not been consecrated at the same ceremony.

chapter 5

SOLO RITUALS FOR THE ADEPT

In chapter 3 we discussed the importance of healing in magic and provided group healing rituals for the Outer Order. Healing is no less important to the rituals of the Inner Order. Adepts of the Second Order embrace the title of "Rosicrucian," and the first principle of a Rosicrucian is "to cure the sick, and that freely."[133]

Of course healing in magic does not require complex rituals. For an individual who is in need of health and convalescence, the best course of action is a holistic embrace of a healthy lifestyle, a reduction of stress, a positive outlook, and a daily regimen of meditation, invocation, and visualization methods that focus on the elimination of illness from the body.

Nevertheless, a trained magician working to effect a healing on someone who is in need of it can bring all their energy and skills to bear on the goal of restoring good health.

133. From *The Fama Fraternitatis*. See Waite, *The Real History of the Rosicrucians*, 64–84.

Rose Cross Lamen Rite of Healing

This ritual uses the Adept's Rose Cross Lamen described in the previous chapter as a tool for projecting healing energies to another individual. The healing qualities of Tiphareth embodied in the Lamen are used to restore the health and vitality of another person.

The rite also employs a variation on a technique described by Israel Regardie in his book *The Art of True Healing*.[134] Regardie suggested using the negative or Queen Scale colors[135] in visualizations that involve healing the person who is actually performing the exercise. In Regardie's words, "I employ the negative color because it tends to make the sphere of sensation open, passive and receptive." Conversely, if the practitioner is performing the exercise for someone else's benefit, they would employ the positive or King Scale color when visualizing energy, because the act of *projecting energy* to another is a positive, stimulating act. The person receiving the benefit of the exercise can aid the process by remaining receptive and open.

Synopsis: After opening and purifying the temple, the Adept performs the Rose Cross Ritual.[136] Then they build up an astral image of the person in need of healing. The Adept projects a red ray from their Geburah and Tiphareth centers to eliminate the source of illness. Then, using the energies represented on the petals of the Rose Cross Lamen, the Adept projects healing rays in the King Scale Colors to the Middle Pillar centers of the sick person: The petals chosen represent the initial letters of the names of the Sephiroth (K—Kether, B—Binah,[137] Tau—Tiphareth, Yod—Yesod, Mem—Malkuth), which, once they reach the person, are turned to the receptive colors of the Queen Scale in order to allow the sick person to receive the healing. Brilliant white light is projected over the astral form, which is then sent to the person, before the rite is closed.

Preparation: The Temple should be arranged in accordance with the General Temple Setup for the Adept in the Portal Hall. Have either the Natural Elemental Symbols or the Elemental Tools on top of the Altar. Water and incense should be placed in the North and South. The Adept should be dressed in the regalia of the Second Order, have their Lotus Wand, and wear their consecrated Rose Cross Lamen.

1) Be seated and close your eyes. Spend some time performing the Four-fold Breath.

134. Reprinted in *Gold: Israel Regardie's Lost Book of Alchemy*, 167–91.

135. The color scales are described in Ciceros, *Golden Dawn Magic*, pages 73–74, 91, and 98.

136. See Ciceros, *Golden Dawn Magic*, 277–81.

137. The forces and divine names of Binah are extended to Daath in the Middle Pillar.

2) When ready to begin, give five knocks (וווו-ו).

3) Take up the Lotus Wand by the black end. Go to the Northeast and proclaim: **HEKAS, HEKAS, ESTE BEBELOI! Far from this sacred place be the profane!**

4) Go to the East. Grasp the Lotus Wand by the white portion and point with the black. Perform the LBRP.

5) Take up the cup. Purify the Temple with Water in all quarters, starting in the East, by drawing the Cross and Invoking Water Triangle. Say: **The Rivers have raised, O Tetragrammaton! The Rivers have raised their sound. The Rivers keep raising their pounding. Above the sounds of vast waters, the majestic breaking waves of the sea, AL is majestic in the Height!**

6) Replace the cup. Take up the incense. Consecrate the Temple with Fire in all quarters by tracing the Cross and the Invoking Fire Triangle. Say: **Adonai hath built his chambers with beams in the very Waters. Making the clouds his chariot, walking upon the wings of the Wind. Making his angels spirits, His ministers a devouring Fire!**

7) Replace incense. Circumambulate the Temple three times with Sol, saluting with the Neophyte Signs when passing the East.

8) Stand west of the Altar and face east. Perform the Adoration to the Lord of the Universe.

Proclamation of Intention

9) Say: **I, (state your magical motto), a Frater/Soror of the Rose of Ruby and the Cross of Gold and a member of the Body of the Christos, do this day undertake the Rite of Healing for (person's name). With the Divine permission, I shall fulfill the first Rule of a Rosicrucian, which is to heal the sick and that freely. So mote it be!**

10) Perform the *Ritual of the Rose Cross.*

11) After you have established the six crosses in the room, do not immediately perform the Analysis of the Keyword, but instead project an astral image of the person you intend to heal in the center of the room. Send a healing, rose-colored thought ray from

your Tiphareth Center, through the Rose Cross Lamen, to the astral image of the person. Bring forth a red ray from your Geburah to Tiphareth through the Lamen, and project it at the source of ailment or infection. Visualize this ray purging the illness from the body of the sick individual. When this is accomplished, project a healing rose pink ray from Tiphareth itself, to mend and restore the person to good health.

12) Give the Projection Sign at the Astral figure and intone **EHEIEH**, employing the Vibratory Formula of the Middle Pillar. As you do so, imagine the petal of the Hebrew Letter Kaph being sent forth from the Rose on your lamen. Empowered by the rose ray of your Tiphareth, it ascends to the Kether Center of the Astral form of the person. Once this happens, the Kether sphere turns brilliant white. Give the Sign of Silence.

13) Again give the Sign of the Enterer at the figure and intone **YHVH ELOHIM**, using the Vibratory Formula. Visualize the petal of the Hebrew letter Beth going forth from your lamen on the rose pink ray of Tiphareth. See it enter the Daath center of the person's astral form. Once this occurs, the Daath sphere becomes white-gray. Give the Sign of Silence.

14) Project again at the figure and intone the name **YHVH ELOAH VE-DAATH.** See the petal of the Hebrew letter Tau rise from the lamen and travel along the rose pink ray. Imagine it being absorbed into the Tiphareth center of the person. Once this happens, the Tiphareth sphere becomes golden-yellow. Give the Sign of Silence.

15) Project again at the figure and vibrate the name **SHADDAI EL CHAI.** See the Yod-petal lift off your lamen to journey along the rose pink ray until it is absorbed into the Yesod Center of the person's astral form. When this occurs, the Yesod sphere changes to bright violet. Give the Sign of Silence.

16) Project for the last time and intone the name **ADONAI HA-ARETZ.** Visualize the petal of the letter Mem traversing the rose ray to the Malkuth Center of the Astral form. When this happens, the sphere takes on the four colors of Malkuth. Give the Sign of Silence.

17) Imagine the astral form of the person completely cured and revitalized by the healing energies of the Reconciling Pillar you have invoked. See the person as strong, active, and full of life. Visualize the shining Archangel Raphael standing over them, holding the Caduceus Wand over the crown of the individual's head. At this point, withdraw the rose pink ray back into your Tiphareth center.

18) Finally, perform the Analysis of the Keyword as given at the end of the Rose Cross Ritual. At the words "Let the Divine Light Descend!," visualize the brilliant white Supernal Light bathing the astral form of the person, providing a spiritual healing as well as a physical one.

19) Repeat the invocation: **Come, Thou, in the Power of Light! Come, Thou, in the Light of Wisdom! Come, Thou, in the Mercy of the Light! The Light hath Healing in its Wings!**

20) Contemplate the healing Light about the astral form for some time, circulating the pure energy in ribbons and spiral bands which serve to strengthen the aura of the person.

21) When finished, say to the figure: **Go, thou, to the living being of whom thou art a reflection. Take with thee strength, vitality, and health. Return with the blessings of YEHESHUAH YEHOVASHAH!**

22) Trace the Rose Cross before the figure and send it to the individual. End the visualization.

23) Perform the Qabalistic Cross.

24) Purify and consecrate the Temple as before.

25) Perform the reverse circumambulation.

26) Say: **In the name of YEHESHUAH, I now set free any spirits that may have been imprisoned by this ceremony.**

27) Perform the LBRP.

28) Give five knocks, as in the beginning (ו-וווו).

29) Say, **I now declare this Temple duly closed.**

✠ ✠ ✠

Charging the Guardians of the Temple

At all stages of the system, the Golden Dawn employs built-in safeguards to protect the Initiate from imbalance and harmful influences from within as well as without. The whole system is geared toward gradual dispensing of magical knowledge and experience, so that students are neither overwhelmed by overstimulation of psychic senses nor meddling with forces that they are not ready for. For example, the Neophyte is given the Lesser Ritual of the Pentagram for invoking desirable forces and banishing unwanted ones. As students progress to the higher grades, they use a variety of other techniques and symbols for protection and to avoid the pitfalls of egotism and delusion in the astral realms.

If we wish to explore the heavens, we must maintain a firm foothold in the earthly realm and be prepared to face any obstacles that cross our path. Rites of protection serve as both our shield and our sword, safeguarding us from harmful forces while allowing us secure passage through the shifting currents of the astral plane.

Besides defending the magician's physical and psychic well-being, rituals of protection teach us that defensive magic is not marked by aggression, but rather wisdom, humility, duty, and sound judgment. Ultimately these rites are not merely tools; they embody our quest for spiritual growth and connection with the Divine.

This ritual requires the making of a Kerubic plaque (or a series of four such plaques) to represent four angels known as the Kerubim. These symbols are charged to act as the protectors of the temple space.

The Kerubim, "the Strong Ones," are the living Powers of Tetragrammaton on the Material Plane and the Presidents of the four Elements. They operate through the Fixed or Kerubic Signs of the Zodiac:

Kerub of Fire: ARYEH, the Lion, attributed to the Sign LEO
Kerub of Water: NESHER, the Eagle, attributed to the Sign SCORPIO
Kerub of Air: ADAM, the Man, attributed to the Sign AQUARIUS
Kerub of Earth: SHOR, the Bull, attributed to the Sign TAURUS

The Kerubim are the guardians of the four Cardinal points and the four rivers that flow down the Tree of Life from the Creator. In Genesis, the Kerubim were the angels who shielded the Garden of Eden from the sight of a fallen humanity. They were also the four creatures seen in Ezekiel's vision.

The plaques can be carved from wood or simply printed on paper and laminated. After the ritual, hooks or Velcro can be used to hang them on the walls of your personal temple in the directions of the four winds. (If you decide to make the single compound plaque, hang it in the west or on the outer door of your temple.)

Synopsis: After purifying the temple and building a magic circle by performing the Supreme Invoking Ritual of the Pentagram, the magician consecrates each Kerub in the order of the four Qabalistic Worlds (Fire, Water, Air, Earth), invoking each Kerub by name and sigil, and charges them to protect the temple. This is accompanied by strong visualizations of the Kerubim. The plaque (or plaques) are then hung on the door (or walls) of the temple, and the ritual is closed down.

Preparation: Follow the General Setup for the Adept in the Portal Hall. Upon the Altar should be the Cross and Triangle and the four Elemental Tools. The Lotus Wand and a sword or dagger for Banishing should be close at hand. Place the Kerubic plaque (or plaques) on the center of the Altar. Give the LVX Signs upon entering the Temple.

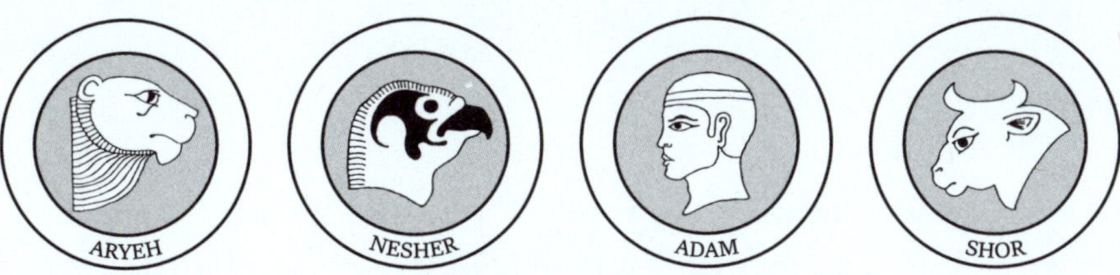

Figure 44: Kerubic Plaques

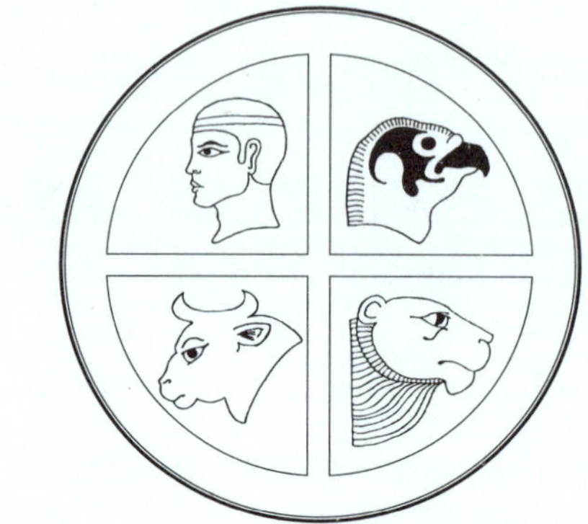

Figure 45: A Compound Kerubic Plaque

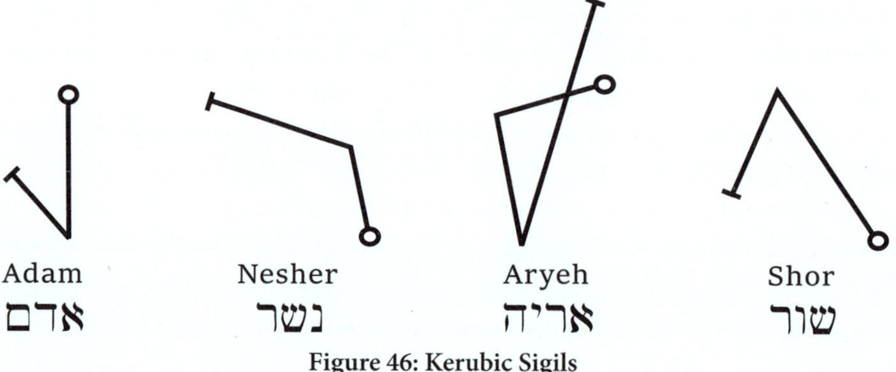

Figure 46: Kerubic Sigils

1) Be seated and close your eyes. Spend some time performing the Four-fold Breath.

2) When ready to begin, give five knocks (ו-וווו).

3) Take up the Lotus Wand by the black end. Go to the Northeast and proclaim, **HEKAS, HEKAS, ESTE BEBELOI! Far from this sacred place be the profane!**

4) Perform the LBRP.

5) Take up the cup of water and go to the East. Trace with it the Cross and the Invoking Triangle of Water in all quarters. Then say, **And I heard the sound of their wings, a sound like that of the vast waters, like the sound of the Almighty One.** Replace the cup.

6) Take up the incense and go to the East. Trace with it the Cross and the Invoking Triangle of Fire in all quarters. Then say: **And as for the likeness of the living creatures, their appearance was like burning coals of Fire. Something appearing like torches was moving back and forth between the living creatures, and the fire was bright, and out of the fire there was lightning going forth.** Replace the incense.

7) Perform the Mystic Circumambulation.

8) Perform the Adoration to the Lord of the Universe.

Proclamation of Intention

9) Say: **I, (state your magical motto), a Frater/Soror of the Rose of Ruby and the Cross of Gold and a member of the Body of the Christos, do this day undertake a ritual of protection for this temple.**

With the Divine permission, I shall charge the mighty Kerubim who are the living powers of Tetragrammaton and presidents of the four elements to guard this sacred temple and keep far removed the evil and the unbalanced. Thus may I be enabled to pursue the Great Work, which is to so purify and exalt my spiritual nature that with the Divine aid I may at length become more than human, and thus gradually raise and unite myself to my Higher and Divine Genius. So mote it be!

10) Perform with the Lotus Wand the SIRP.

11) Return to the west of the Altar and face east. Take up the Fire Wand in the left hand and the Lotus Wand in the right. Trace a circle over the Lion Kerub. Hold the Lotus Wand by the yellow band of Leo and trace the Invoking Pentagram of Spirit Active over the lion, intoning the words **BITOM** and **EHEIEH.** Give the Sign of the Rending of the Veil, followed by the LVX Signs. Then trace the Invoking Pentagram of Fire over the Lion. Vibrate **OIP TEAA PEDOCE.** Draw the sigil of Leo and intone **ELOHIM.** Give the Philosophus Sign.

12) Vibrate the Kerubic name of **ARYEH** and trace its sigil over the Lion. Say: **Strong and formidable Lord of Fire! ARYEH! Thou who ruleth the Sickle of Stars! Sole house of the Sun! ARYEH! Judah, thou art he whom thy brethren shall praise: thy**

hand shall be in the neck of thine enemies. Judah is a Lion's whelp! ARYEH! The Lion flames. There the Sun's course runs hottest. Empty of grain the arid fields appear when first the Sun into the Lion enters.

13) Trace a Cross over the Lion and say: **In the name of the head of the Lion and the powers of ASH, I charge thee to guard this Temple and the mystic sphere contained within from all mundane and profane forces. Keep far removed the evil and the unbalanced. PROTEGE HOC TEMPLUM!**

14) Strongly visualize the mighty Lion Kerub in the south of the temple, with wings that stretch from corner to corner over the full length of the wall.

15) Replace the Fire Wand and take up the Water Cup in the left hand. Hold the Lotus Wand by the blue-green band of Scorpio. Trace a circle over the Eagle Kerub. Then trace the Invoking Pentagram of Spirit Passive over the eagle, intoning the words **HCOMA** and **AGLA.** Give the Sign of the Rending of the Veil, followed by the LVX Signs. Draw the Invoking Pentagram of Water over the Eagle. Vibrate **EMPEH ARSEL GAIOL.** Then trace the sigil of the Eagle and intone **Aleph Lamed, EL.** Give the Sign of Practicus.

16) Vibrate the Kerubic name of **NESHER** and trace its sigil over the Eagle. Say: **There is a place above where Scorpio bent, in tail and arms surrounds a vast extent. In a wide circuit of the heavens he shines, and fills the place of two celestial signs. NESHER! Lofty Eagle born from the sting of the scorpion. Dan shall be a serpent by the way, an adder in the path. NESHER! Lord of the Waters of transformation! Only when Sol is in your house can the iron be turned to gold!**

17) Trace a Cross over the Eagle and say: **In the name of the head of the Eagle and the powers of MAYIM, I charge thee to guard this Temple and the mystic sphere contained within from all mundane and profane forces. Keep far removed the evil and the unbalanced. PROTEGE HOC TEMPLUM!**

18) Strongly visualize the mighty Eagle Kerub in the west of the temple, with wings that stretch the full length of the wall.

19) Replace the Water Cup and take up the Air Dagger in the left hand. Hold the Lotus Wand by the violet band of Aquarius. Trace a circle over the Man Kerub. Then trace the Invoking Pentagram of Spirit Active over the Man, intoning the names **EXARP** and **EHEIEH.** Give the Sign of the Rending of the Veil, followed by the LVX Signs. Draw the Invoking Pentagram of Air over the Man. Vibrate **ORO IBAH AOZPI.** Then trace the sigil of Aquarius and intone **YOD HEH VAV HEH.** Give the Sign of Theoricus.

20) Vibrate the Kerubic name of **ADAM** and trace its sigil over the Man. Say: **While by the Horse's head the Water-Pourer spreads his right hand. Thou ridest upon the winged steeds of Dawn. ADAM! Brilliant Lord of Air! Mighty One of the Eastern Wind! Reuben, thou art the firstborn, the might, and the beginning of strength, the excellency of dignity and the excellency of power. Emblem of the tribe of Reuben! ADAM! Great indeed are thy powers of thought.**

21) Trace a Cross over the Man and say: **In the name of the head of the Man and the powers of RUACH, I charge thee to guard this Temple and the mystic sphere contained within from all mundane and profane forces. Keep far removed the evil and the unbalanced. PROTEGE HOC TEMPLUM!**

22) Strongly visualize the great Kerub of the Man in the east of the temple, with wings that fill the height and breadth of the wall.

23) Replace the Air Dagger and take up the Earth Pentacle in the left hand. Hold the Lotus Wand by the red-orange band of Taurus. Trace a circle over the Bull Kerub. Then trace the Invoking Pentagram of Spirit Passive over the Bull, intoning the names **NANTA** and **AGLA.** Give the Sign of the Rending of the Veil followed by the LVX Signs. Draw the Invoking Pentagram of Earth over the Bull. Vibrate **EMOR DIAL HECTEGA.** Then trace the sigil of Taurus and intone **ADONAI.** Give the Sign of Zelator.

24) Vibrate the Kerubic name of **SHOR** and trace its sigil over the Bull. Say: **Zephyr is wandering here with gentle sound, the first fresh fragrance of the Spring to seek: The milk-white steer, whose budding horns are crowned with flowery garlands, is kneeling on the ground. SHOR! Mighty Bull of Light! Sturdy Lord of Earth! Thou art Apis, Bull of the Nile. Ephraim, his glory is like the firstling of a bullock, and his**

horns are like the horns of unicorns. SHOR! Thou who plows the Furrow of Heaven! Thy hoof-prints are embedded in the earth!

25) Trace a Cross over the Bull and say: **In the name of the head of the Bull and the powers of ARETZ, I charge thee to guard this Temple and the mystic sphere contained within from all mundane and profane forces. Keep far removed the evil and the unbalanced. PROTEGE HOC TEMPLUM!**

26) Strongly visualize the great Bull Kerub in the north of the temple, with wings that fill the entire wall.

27) Replace the Earth Pentacle. Grasp the Lotus Wand by the white portion and trace a circle over the outer rim of the Kerubic plaque (or plaques). Trace the Invoking Pentagrams of Spirit Active and Spirit Passive, vibrating the appropriate words: **EXARP—EHEIEH. HCOMA—AGLA. NANTA—AGLA. BITOM—EHEIEH.** Give the Sign of the Rending of the Veil, followed by the LVX Signs.[138]

28) Say: **I, (give magical name), charge ye wardens of the Four Elements under the presidency of Spirit to act as sentinels of this sacred Temple. Be ye watchful guardians against all hostile and unwanted forces or beings. PROTEGITE HOC TEMPLUM! Mighty Kerubim! Keep this sphere pure and holy, so that I may enter in, undisturbed, and perform aright the works of the Magic of Light.**

29) Strongly visualize the four mighty Kerubim surrounding you on all sides, ringing the entire temple with their protective presence.

30) Give the Projection Sign at the plaque (or plaques) five times. At the end, give the Sign of Silence for Protection.

31) Give five knocks (ו-וווו) against the side of the Altar to seal the charge and announce that the Guardians have been appointed to their task.

---

138. If you have created four plaques, then trace the Fire Pentagrams over the Fire Plaque, Water Pentagrams over the Water Plaque, etc.

32) Take up the Kerubic plaques from the Altar and attach them to the four walls of the Temple room. (If you decide to make the single compound plaque, hang it in the west or on the outer door of your temple.)

33) Return to the east of the Temple and perform the Adoration to the Lord of the Universe.

34) Purify the Temple with Water and Fire, as in the beginning.

35) Perform the Reverse Circumambulation.

36) Say: **I now release any spirits that may have been imprisoned by this ceremony. Depart in peace to your abodes and habitations. Go with the blessings of YEHESHUAH YEHOVA-SHAH!**

37) Perform the LBRP.

38) Give five knocks (ו-וווו).

39) Say: **I now declare this Temple duly closed.**

✠ ✠ ✠

Assumption of Godforms

Within the Golden Dawn system of magic, there is a particular set of teachings collectively known as the "Z-Documents," the "Z-Docs," or simply the "Zeds." These manuscripts explain how the various sections and aspects of the Order's Neophyte Ritual can be used in the Second Order as practical ritual formulae for endless varieties of high magical procedures. The creation of rituals based on these formulae is discussed in the manuscript known as "Z.2: The Formulae of the Magic of Light."[139] Within the Magic of Light, five categories of practical magic are classified under the five letters of the Pentagrammaton, the "five-lettered name"—YHShVH (יהשוה), or *Yesheshuah*—wherein each letter is assigned to one of the five elements.

139. See Regardie, *The Golden Dawn,* 479–509, and Ciceros, *Golden Dawn Magic,* 333–80.

Golden Dawn Adepts are expected to study the ritual outlines of magical rites provided in the Z.2 document and create their own unique versions of the same in fully expanded rituals.

All works of spiritual development and transformation fall under the letter Shin and the element of Spirit. This category is further divided into three types of magic that correspond to the three Yods or flames of the Shin. These three flames are further assigned to the three Mother Letters: Aleph (א) "Invisibility," Mem (מ) "Transformations," and Shin (ש) "Spiritual Development."

Godform Assumption, which was briefly introduced in chapter 2, falls under the letter Mem, transformation, which some have called "shapeshifting." Within our tradition this does not mean physical shapeshifting, but rather the creation of an astral form that is worn over the physical body like a mask or garment. Transformation rituals are performed to obtain spiritual insight, wisdom, and hidden knowledge. In a well-performed transformation ritual, a sensitive person should be able to see the astral form worn by the magician within the mind's eye.

DON'T BLAME HORUS

In the Neophyte Obligation, the candidate swears "not to suffer myself to be placed in such a state of passivity that any uninitiated person or power may cause me to lose control of my words or actions." The inclusion of this clause was in part due to concern over the loss of will that was thought to accompany the practice of hypnosis at the time. But it is also a good reminder that the magician should never become an unwitting tool for incorporeal beings. Remember, spirits may not be who they say they are.

On one occasion we observed the problems that arose when a student who was not properly trained in godform assumption was said to have taken on the godform of Horus. When problems arose as a result, the excuse was "Horus made me do it."

This is why Golden Dawn Magicians are taught to always be in control of our own magic. We assume the form of a high deity or angel, rather than letting such deities subsume us. Adepts are taught to test "all things of doubtful or fictitious seeming with sure knowledge and sound judgment." As always, this is good advice.

The Rite of Assumption to the Godform of Osiris

This ritual is specifically designed for an Adept who wishes to explore a more formalized ritual experience in assuming a godform that is fundamental to the Hall of the Neophytes. The skills gained through practicing this more elaborate version of godform assumption will, via muscle memory, help the magician achieve the same results whenever a more shortened version of godform assumption is called for.

The rite utilizes the godform of Ousiri (Ou-see-ree), which is the Coptic name of the god Osiris, who is associated with the Office of the Hierophant in the Outer Order.

In the Neophyte Hall, the throne of the Hierophant and the godform of Osiris are stationed on the center of the Dais in the East, the place of the dawning light.

Figure 47: The God Osiris

Osiris, or *Asar*, was originally an Egyptian god who died with the harvest only to be reborn in the spring. Because of this, Osiris became the god of the dead and of resurrection. In early legend, he was also a water god who represented the fertility brought by the Nile. Legend has it that Osiris instituted the cult of the gods, built the first towns and temples, and laid down the laws governing religious worship. He was given the title "unnefer" (*onnophris* in Greek), which is said to mean "the good one." As the story goes, his evil brother Set plotted to kill his brother. Set entombed the body of Osiris in a chest and flung it into the waters of the Nile. The chest later ended up on a shore, where a tree trunk grew around it. This tree was eventually cut down and used as a column in a king's house. The chest containing the body of Osiris was later recovered by his wife, Isis, but Set found it and dismembered the body into fourteen pieces, which he then scattered. Isis patiently searched for the remnants and reconstituted the body, all except for the phallus. Isis, aided by Thoth, Anubis, and Horus, was able to restore the dead god back to life.

Osiris represented a being who was both a man and a god; someone who, by virtue of his suffering and death, humans could identify with—more so than the other gods. However, he also offered the hope of resurrection after death; the idea that humans, too, triumph over death and attain everlasting life. Thus Osiris became the god of the underworld, with the power to bestow eternal life upon the dead, who, successfully passing the ordeal of the "Weighing of the Soul," were allowed to live in the underworld. Osiris became known as *Osiris Khenti Amenti*, or "lord of the westerners," because the dead were thought to go into the west, the direction of the setting sun.

Eventually Osiris was thought to be even more powerful than Ra, the sun god, taking on the powers of a cosmic being and the creator of all. He governed initiation, eternal life, judgment, water, agriculture, religion, discipline, order, and law. Osiris is represented standing or sitting on a throne and dressed in mummy wrappings. He wears the Atef crown, a high white miter or cone flanked by two ostrich feathers. His hands, which are folded across his breast, hold a crook and a scourge.

The Rite of Assumption to the Godform of Osiris can be performed in either the Neophyte Hall or the General Setup for the Adept in the Portal Hall. If utilizing the Neophyte Hall, place the wand and regalia of the Hierophant on the throne in the East and enter with the Neophyte Signs. If the ritual is performed in the Portal Hall, then the Adept may dress in the regalia of the Second Order, give the Portal Signs upon entering the Temple, and utilize the Lotus Wand. In either case, the Adept is initially seated in the West.

Synopsis: The Adept performs the Four-Fold Breath. When ready, he gives a battery of five knocks to signify the four elements crowned by Spirit. After proclaiming the commencement of the ritual, the Adept performs the LBRP to cleanse the space, the Adoration to invoke the Highest, the AK to reaffirm the regenerative and harmonizing essence of Tiphareth to aid the Working, and the MP to activate the Pillar of Balance within the Adept's aura. Next, the Adept performs the Vibratory formula of Middle Pillar, intoning the name *Ousiri* six times, once for each letter of the name. At the end of the sixth vibration, the Adept projects a white ray of light from their Tiphareth center to the throne in the East, and begins to visualize the godform of Osiris there. When the image is well-formulated on the Astral, the Adept steps into the godform and continues to activate it.

The Adept is seated on the throne of the Hierophant. When the godform is fully activated, the Adept performs a godform invocation.

When all visualizations and meditations are complete, the Adept steps out of the godform before closing down the temple.

1) Take a few moments to relax and practice the Four-fold Breath technique.

2) Give five knocks (וווו-ו) and go the Northeast to proclaim, **Astu! Pu tebu-na bet em khut!** ("Behold, I have endowed a place with power!")

3) Perform the LBRP.

4) Perform the Adoration to the Lord of the Universe.

5) Perform the Analysis of the Keyword.

6) Perform the Exercise of the Middle Pillar.

Figure 48: Sigil of Ousiri

7) Once the Middle Pillar is completely formulated within your sphere of sensation, trace within your heart the Coptic letters of the name OUSIRI (ⲟⲩⲥⲓⲣⲓ) in pure white. Then trace with the wand the letters and sigil of the name[140] toward the East.

8) Bring the Divine Light down from your Kether center to your Tiphareth center, and as you do so, give the Sign of the Enterer, at the same time vibrating the name **OUSIRI** for as long as your exhalation of breath will last. At the end of the vibration, give the Sign of Silence. Repeat this procedure of vibration a total of six times, once for every Coptic letter of the name.

9) After the sixth vibration of the name, project a white ray of light from your Tiphareth toward the throne in the east and formulate the godform of Osiris there: The figure wears a yellow-and-white-striped nemyss surmounted by the white Stenu Crown of the Upper Regions. His skin is reddish brown. From his chin hangs the royal beard of authority and judgment. He is wrapped entirely in white mummy cloth, except for his head and hands. His collar is banded white, red, blue, yellow, and black. His wristbands are banded yellow and white. He holds in his right hand a white Djed Wand. His throne is white decorated with yellow, which stands upon a white pavement. The lower part of his body is mummified, alluding to the material body of man, but the upper half is liberated, referring to the living spirit of humanity.

10) Continue projecting the white ray until the astral figure is well formulated. Then step into the godform of Osiris that you have built up in the East, facing west. Feel your mind and reasoning faculties (Ruach) empowering the shell of the astral godform, breathing life into it. When you have felt this happen, proclaim, **Nuk Asar Un-nefer!** ("I am Osiris Onnophris!")

11) Be seated, but remain in this godform, contemplating its attributes and spiritual qualities, identifying them as your own.

12) After a pause, repeat the following: **I am the Prince in the field. My soul doth breathe forever and ever and my form is made anew with life upon earth. I am the**

140. The Coptic letters of Ousiri are transliterated into Hebrew letters and then traced on the rose of the Golden Dawn's Rose Cross Lamen (עושירי) to create the sigil.

lord of everlastingness, passing through millions of years in the course of mine existence. My name is made to endure. In the tomb I have lain only to again draw forth breath. I am renewed. The God Ptah hast opened my mouth. My word is Maat. Those who have lain in death rise up to look upon me, and their hearts are at peace. I maketh mortals to be born again, renewed in their youth. I have received the Crook and the Whip. When I turn my face upon Amentet, the earth shinest as with refined copper. I am crowned even as Ra himself. His disk is my disk. His rays of light are my rays of light. His risings are my risings. His throne is my throne. His knowledge is my knowledge. Behold, my face shineth before Ra and my soul liveth before Amoun.

13) Pause and contemplate. Then say the following: **I am the Resurrection and the Life. He that believeth in Me, though he were dead, yet shall he live. And whosoever liveth and believeth in me shall never die. I am the first and I am the last. I am he that liveth but was dead, and behold I am alive forever more, and hold the Keys of Hell and Death. For I know that my Redeemer liveth and that he shall stand at the latter day upon the earth. I am the Way, the Truth and the Life. No one cometh unto the Creator but by me. I am purified. I have passed through the Gates of Darkness unto Light. I have fought upon earth for good. I have finished my work. I have entered into the invisible. I am the Sun in his rising. I have passed through the hour of Cloud and Night. I am Amoun, the Concealed One, the Opener of the Day. I am Osiris Onnophris, the Justified One. I am the Lord of Life, triumphant over Death. There is no part of me that is not of the Gods. I am the Preparer of the Pathway, the Rescuer unto the Light! Out of the Darkness, let the light arise!**[141]

14) Then say: **I am the Reconciler with the Ineffable. I am the Dweller of the Invisible. Let the White Brilliance of the Divine Spirit descend.**[142]

15) Once again, see the Divine Light descend through the Middle Pillar, from your Kether center to your Malkuth center.

16) Continue to meditate for a short length of time. When finished, step out of the god-form of Osiris, which once again becomes inanimate. Withdraw the white ray from the

---

141. From the Ceremony of the 5=6 Grade of Adeptus Minor in Regardie's *The Golden Dawn*, 312–13.

142. From the Ceremony of the 5=6 Grade of Adeptus Minor in Regardie's *The Golden Dawn*, 312–13.

godform back into your Tiphareth center. Imagine the figure of Osiris slowly begin to fade until it vanishes entirely.

17) Perform the Adoration to the Lord of the Universe.

18) Give the LVX Signs.

19) Perform the LBRP.

20) Give five knocks (ו-וווו) and declare the Temple duly closed.

✠ ✠ ✠

chapter 6

GROUP WORK FOR THE INNER ORDER

The Golden Dawn's Second Order is essentially rooted in the principles of Rosicrucianism, a spiritual philosophy founded on the life of Christian Rosenkreutz, also known as C.R.C., the allegorical founder of the Brotherhood of the Rose Cross. The myth of Christian Rosenkreutz is itself an allegory of the life of Christ, and this is the primary ritual drama of the Second Order. The Rosicrucian brotherhood was rumored to be a secretive order of Initiates who studied alchemy, Qabalah, astrology, magic, and Christian mysticism. Stories of the brotherhood began to surface in Europe around 1614.

The Vault of the Adepti

S. L. MacGregor Mathers firmly established the ideals of Rosicrucianism in the Golden Dawn's Second Order when he finished the elaborate initiation ceremony into the grade of Adeptus Minor. Based on the legend of Christian Rosenkreutz, this ritual involves the discovery of C.R.C.'s tomb, known as the Vault of the Adepti. An account of this chamber, along with its contents, make up some of the most vital portions of the *Fama Fraternitatis*, one of the three famous Rosicrucian Manifestos. In the allegory of the *Fama*, the life and works of Christian Rosenkreutz are recounted, as well as a description of his burial chamber. It was this description that MacGregor Mathers drew upon in his spectacular creation of the Vault of the Adepti, a seven-sided chamber filled with symbolism.

A complete description of the Vault can be found elsewhere, but in brief, the vault has:

- Seven walls, each of which is assigned to one of the seven planets of the ancients.
- Each wall is comprised of 40 squares depicting the Divine Spirit, the four Kerubim, the three Alchemical Principles, the three most ancient of the Elements, the ten Sephiroth of the Tree of Life, the seven planets, and the twelve signs of the Zodiac. (These 40 squares represent these particular forces operating throughout the planet.[143])
- A white ceiling embellished with an upright triangle within a heptagram, with the angles assigned to the ten Sephiroth. In the center is a white rose of 22 petals assigned to the 22 Hebrew letters.
- A black floor embellished with an inverted triangle within a heptagram, with the angles assigned to the ten Qlippoth. In the center is a red rose of 49 petals united to a golden cross.
- A *pastos*, or sarcophagus, of C.R.C., covered with symbolism.
- A white circular tripod Altar placed over the pastos.
- On the Altar are four Kerubic elemental plaques along with the symbols of the elements (Fire—black Calvary cross with a rose of 25 petals; Water—chalice; Air—a dagger; Earth—a chain).[144] A white letter Shin at the center of the Altar, along with the crossed crook and scourge.

The Mystical Vault is the primary temple and ritual chamber of the Second Order, and all grade initiations performed by the R.R. et A.C. require it. This seven-sided temple is re-consecrated once every year on or around the feast day of Corpus Christi.

143. These forces also exist within each planetary force (i.e., Fire of Jupiter, Mercury of Luna, Chesed of Saturn, etc.). All these symbols can be explored through skrying and Spirit Vision work.

144. Within the Vault, the directions assigned to the elements follow those of the cardinal signs of a Zodiacal chart: East–Fire, North–Water, West–Air, South–Earth.

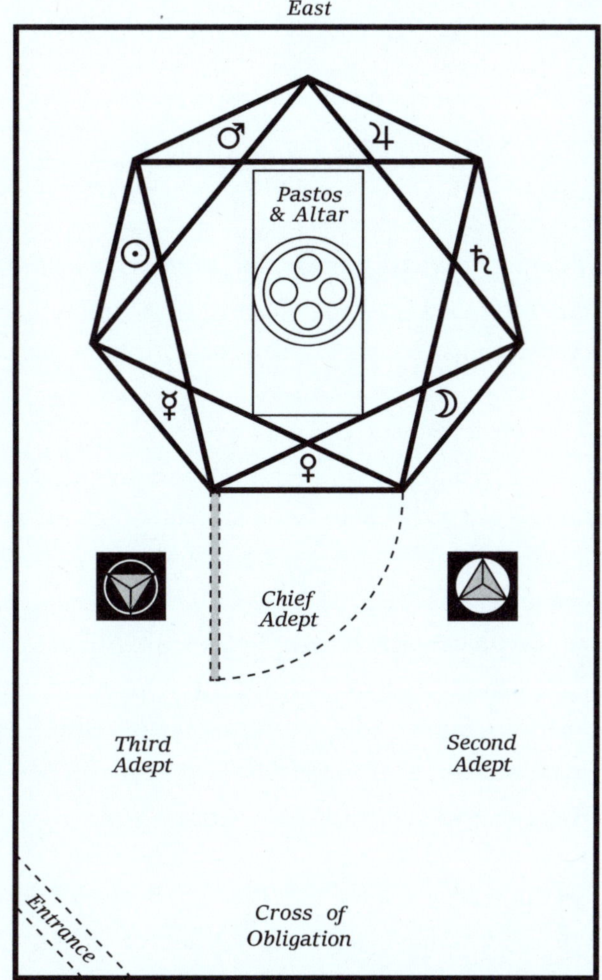

Figure 49: The Seven-Sided Vault of the Adepti

Outside of initiation ceremonies, one of the most common uses of the Vault is as a chamber for meditation and reflection. Additionally, every symbol within the Vault offers an opportunity for skrying and spirit vision work, whether you are working solo or in a group. This chapter offers a small selection of group workings that can be performed in this amazing chamber.[145]

145. Note: Banishing is never done inside the Vault.

General Second Order Opening

Just as the Opening of the Neophyte Hall provides a structured ceremony for beginning a group ritual of the Outer Order, the General Second Order Opening is an *optional* way to begin a group Second Order Working within the Vault.[146] While a group of experienced Adepts can simply skip this opening, enter the Vault, and begin the main ritual at hand, there are times when performing the General Opening can provide a powerful and balanced transition from one plane of Working to the next.

Items needed: All are dressed in the white robes of an Adept, Rose Cross Lamens, yellow socks or slippers.

Ritual Officers:

- Adeptus Primus (Chief Adept): Dressed in blue-and-violet-striped nemyss,[147] blue mantle trimmed with violet, Phoenix Collar, Chief Adept's Wand, Crux Ansata.
- Adeptus Secundus (Second Adept): Dressed in red-and-orange-striped nemyss, red mantle trimmed with orange, Phoenix Wand, Crux Ansata.
- Adeptus Tertius (Third Adept): Dressed in yellow-and-rose-pink-striped nemyss, yellow mantle trimmed with rose-pink, Lotus Wand, Crux Ansata.
- A fourth participant may act as Hodos.
- There may be a few other participants.

All enter Portal by giving the Sign of the Rending of the Veil before them, followed by the Sign of the Closing of the Veil behind them. All are seated in the Portal of the Vault as in the 5=6 ceremony. All are equipped with the usual implements. Additional participants may carry Lotus Wands.

146. Adapted from the Ceremony of the 5=6 Grade of Adeptus Minor in Regardie's *The Golden Dawn*, 288–345.

147. The colors of the three Adepts are, respectively, the King and Queen Scale colors of Chesed, Geburah, and Tiphareth.

Part 1: Opening

(Adeptus Primus leads a brief meditation such as the Middle Pillar Exercise.)

Adeptus Primus gives a knock ו. All rise.
Adeptus Primus: (knocks ו)
Adeptus Secundus: (knocks ו)
Adeptus Tertius: (knocks ו)
Adeptus Primus: (knocks ו)
Adeptus Third: (knocks ו)
Adeptus Secundus: (knocks ו)
Adeptus Primus: **Avete, Fratres et Sorores.**
Adeptus Secundus: **Roseae Rubeae.**
Adeptus Tertius: **Et Aureae Crucis.**

Adeptus Primus: **Very Honoured Fratres et Sorores, assist me to open the Tomb of the Adepti. Associate Adeptus Minor, see that the Portal is closed and guarded.**

Adeptus Tertius goes to the door, checks it, and gives the Sign of the Closing of the Veil.

Adeptus Tertius: **Merciful Exempt Adept, the Portal of the Vault is closed and guarded.**

Adeptus Primus: **Mighty Adeptus Major, by what Sign hast thou entered the Portal?**

Adeptus Secundus: **By the Sign of the Rending Asunder of the Veil.** (Gives sign.)

Adeptus Primus: **Associate Adeptus Minor, by what sign hast thou closed the Portal?**

Adeptus Tertius: **By the Sign of the Closing of the Veil.** (Gives sign.)

Adeptus Secundus: **PEH.**
Adeptus Tertius: **RESH.**
Adeptus Secundus: **KAPH.**
Adeptus Tertius: **TAU.**

Adeptus Tertius: **Which is the Veil of the Sanctum Sanctorum.**

Adeptus Secundus: **The Mystic Number of this Grade is 21.**

Adeptus Primus: **Associate Adeptus Minor, what is the Password formed therefrom?**

Adeptus Tertius: **ALEPH.**
Adeptus Primus: **HEH.**
Adeptus Tertius: **YOD.**
Adeptus Primus: **HEH.**
Adeptus Tertius: **Eheieh.**

Adeptus Secundus: **The Tomb of the Adepti is the symbolic Burying Place of Christian Rosenkreutz, which he made to represent the Universe.**

Adeptus Tertius: **He is buried in the Center of the Heptagonal Sides and beneath the Altar, his head being toward the East.**

Adeptus Secundus: **He is buried in the Center because that is the point of balanced forces.**

Adeptus Tertius: **The Mystic Name of Christian Rosenkreutz signifies the Rose and Cross of Christ; the Fadeless Rose of Creation, the Immortal Cross of Light.**

Adeptus Secundus: **This place was entitled by our still more ancient Fratres and Sorores, the Tomb of Osiris Onnophris, the Justified One.**

Adeptus Tertius: **The shape of the Tomb is that of an equilateral Heptagon, a figure of Seven sides.**

Adeptus Secundus: **The Seven Sides allude to the Seven Lower Sephiroth, the seven Palaces, and the Seven days of Creation. Seven is the height above. Seven is the depth beneath.**

Adeptus Tertius: **The Tomb is symbolically situated in the Center of the Earth, in the Mountain of the Caverns, the Mystic Mountain of Abiegnus. The meaning**

of this title of Abiegnus . . . Abiagnus, Lamb of the Father. It is by metathesis . . . Abi-Genos, born of the Father. Bia-Genos, Strength of our race, and the four words make the sentence: ABIEGNUS ABIAGNUS ABIGENOS BIAGENOS. "Mountain of the Lamb of the Father, and the Strength of our Race." I.A.O. YEHESHUAH. Such are the words.

All salute with LVX Signs.

Adeptus Primus: **Mighty Adeptus Major, what is the Key to this tomb?**

Adeptus Secundus: **The Rose and the Cross, which resume the Life of Nature, and the powers hidden in the word I.N.R.I.**

Adeptus Tertius steps forward, extends Crux, and says: **The Emblem which we bear in our left hands is a form of the Rose and the Cross, the ancient Crux Ansata, or Egyptian symbol of Life.**

Adeptus Secundus: **It represents the force of the Ten Sephiroth in Nature, divided into a Hexad and a Tetrad. The oval embraces the first Six Sephiroth, and the Tau Cross the lower Four answering to the Four Elements.**

Adeptus Primus: **Associate Adeptus Minor, what is the Emblem which I bear upon my breast?**

Adeptus Tertius: **The complete symbol of the Rose and Cross.**

Adeptus Primus: **Mighty Adeptus Major, what is its meaning?**

Adeptus Secundus: **It is the Key of Sigils and Rituals, and represents the force of the Twenty-Two Letters in Nature, as divided into a Three, a Seven, and a Twelve. Many and great are its Mysteries.**

Adeptus Tertius steps forward, holds up Wand, and says: **I bear a simple Wand, having the colors of the Twelve Signs of the Zodiac between Light and Darkness, and surmounted by the Lotus Flower of Isis. It symbolizes the development of creation.** (Steps back.)

ADEPTUS SECUNDUS steps forward, holds up Wand, and says: **Mine is a Wand terminating in the Symbol of the Binary, and surmounted by the Tau Cross of Life, or the head of the Phoenix, sacred to Osiris. The Seven colors of the Rainbow between Light and Darkness are attributed to the Planets. It symbolizes Rebirth and Resurrection from Death.** (Steps back.)

ADEPTUS PRIMUS steps forward, holds up Wand, and says: **My Wand is surmounted by the Winged Globe, around which the twin Serpents of Egypt twine. It symbolizes the equilibrated force of the Spirit and the Four Elements beneath the everlasting wings of the Holy One.** (Steps back.) **Associate Adeptus Minor, what are the words inscribed upon the Door of the Tomb? And how is it guarded?**

ADEPTUS TERTIUS: **Post Centum Viginti Annos Patebo. After one hundred and twenty years I shall open. The door is guarded by the Elemental Tablets and the Kerubic Emblems.**

ADEPTUS PRIMUS: **To the 120 years are referred symbolically the five grades of the First Order, and to the revolution of the powers of the Pentagram. Also the five preparatory examinations for this grade. It is written "His days shall be 120 years." And 120 divided by 5 equals 24, the number of hours in a day, and of the thrones of the Elders in the Apocalypse. Further, 120 equals the number of the Ten Sephiroth multiplied by that of the Zodiac, whose Key is the working of the Spirit and the Four Elements, typified in the Wand which I bear.**

PART 2: ENTERING THE VAULT

ADEPTUS PRIMUS opens the Door to the Vault, enters, and passes to East. ADEPTUS SECUNDUS enters and passes to the South, facing North. ADEPTUS TERTIUS enters and passes to North, facing South. HODOS may enter Vault to form a fourth side in the West. The THREE OFFICERS raise and cross their Wands to form a pyramid above the Altar, and join Cruces below the Wands.

ADEPTUS PRIMUS: **Let us analyze the Keyword. I.**
ADEPTUS SECUNDUS: **N.**

Adeptus Tertius: **R.**
All: **I.**

Adeptus Primus: **YOD.**
Adeptus Secundus: **NUN.**
Adeptus Tertius: **RESH.**
All: **YOD.**

Adeptus Primus: **Virgo, Isis, Mighty Mother.**
Adeptus Secundus: **Scorpio, Apophis, Destroyer.**
Adeptus Tertius: **Sol, Osiris, Slain and Risen.**
All: **Isis, Apophis, Osiris. IAO.**

All separate Wands and Cruces and give Sign of the Tau Cross.

All: **The Sign of Osiris Slain.**

Adeptus Primus: **L. The Sign of the Mourning of Isis.** (Gives Sign while speaking.)

Adeptus Secundus: **V. The Sign of Apophis and Typhon.** (Gives Sign while speaking.)

Adeptus Tertius: **X. The Sign of Osiris Risen.** (Gives Sign while speaking.)

All: **L.V.X. Lux, the Light, of the Cross.** (All give Signs while speaking.)

Adeptus Primus raises Wand and says: **In the Grand Word YEHESHUAH, by the Keyword, I.N.R.I. and through the concealed word LVX, I have opened the tomb of the Adepti.**

Adeptus Tertius: **Ex Deo Nascimur.**
Adeptus Secundus: **In Yeheshua Morimur.**
Adeptus Primus: **Per Spiritum Sanctum Reviviscimus.**
All give LVX Signs in silence.

✠ ✠ ✠

The Work

The Middle point of the ritual will be the main magical Working. This could be any ritual that is required to be performed in the Vault. When the Work is completed, proceed with the Closing.

General Second Order Closing

(Adeptus Primus gives a knock ˺. All rise.)

Adeptus Primus: (Knocks ˺)

Adeptus Secundus: (Knocks ˺)

Adeptus Tertius: (Knocks ˺)

Adeptus Primus: (Knocks ˺)

Adeptus Third: (Knocks ˺)

Adeptus Secundus: (Knocks ˺)

Adeptus Secundus: **Roseae Rubeae.**

Adeptus Tertius: **Et Aureae Crucis.**

Adeptus Primus: **Very Honoured Fratres et Sorores, assist me to close the Tomb of the Adepti. Associate Adeptus Minor, what is the number of the 15th letter of the Hebrew alphabet spelled out in its entirety?**[148]

Adeptus Tertius: **The complete spelling of Samekh, the Letter of the Path which leads from Yesod to Tiphareth through the Veil of Paroketh, is One Hundred and Twenty.**

Adeptus Primus: **Mighty Adeptus Major, how is that number formed?**

Adeptus Secundus: **By the continued multiplication of the first five numbers of the decimal scale.**

Adeptus Primus: **Post Centum Viginti Annos Patebo. Thus have I closed the Tomb of the Adepti in the Mystic Mountain of Abiegnus.**

148. In the original, the question is "How many Princes did Darius set over his Kingdom?" We opted for a more meaningful esoteric question to arrive at the number 120.

ADEPTUS PRIMUS closes the Door of the Vault and draws Curtains.

ADEPTUS TERTIUS: **Ex Deo Nascimur.**
ADEPTUS SECUNDUS: **In Yesheshua Morimur.**
ADEPTUS SECUNDUS: **Per Spiritum Sanctum Reviviscimus.**

ALL give the LVX Signs in silence.

✠ ✠ ✠

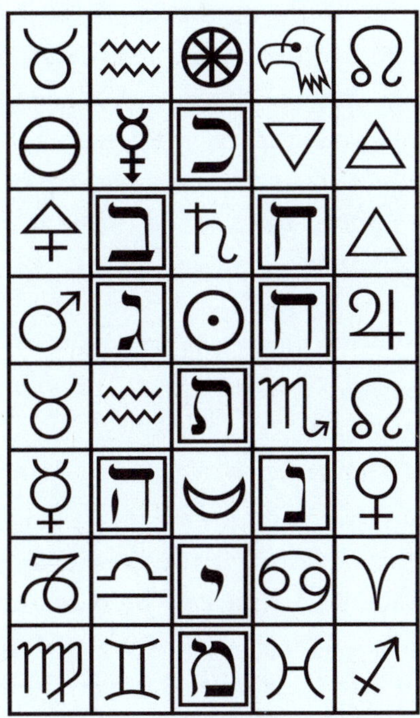

Figure 50: A Single Vault Wall

AN INVOCATION OF ISIS AND A SKRYING ON THE SATURN WALL

This group ritual is a combination of an invocation and skrying. Skrying or spirit vision work in our tradition involves inducing astral images and information with the help of symbols.[149] In this case, the symbol employed is the planetary square of Saturn on the Saturn Wall of the Vault.

149. For more information on spirit vision work, see Ciceros, *Golden Dawn Magic*, 297–316.

While the ceremony calls for the three primary officers of the Second Order (Adeptus Primus, Adeptus Secundus, and Adeptus Tertius), participants may choose to commence with the General Second Order Opening, or not. Ideally, the ritual should take place on a Saturday during the hour of Saturn.

Preparation: Upon the Circular Altar should be placed a statue of Isis on a blue-violet cloth, Qamea of Saturn, appropriate Saturnian incense,[150] and other symbols. The Elements for the Mystic Repast will also be needed (Rose, Red Candle, Chalice of Wine, and Platten of bread and salt). You will also need a small bowl for offerings.

Synopsis: The Adepts enter the Vault and begin the invocation of Isis, calling upon the goddess to aid the work of skrying on the Saturn Wall. Adeptus Primus opens the Saturn Square on the Saturn Wall by tracing the appropriate Hexagrams and then begins to lead all participants in a Skrying into the Square. When the skrying is finished, there is a Thank Offering to Isis, followed by a Mystic Repast.

(NOTE: During the skrying part of the ritual, participants can sit on the floor or on chairs, so long as there is room to maneuver and the floor is protected from the feet of the chairs by a cloth.)

Optional: Open with the General Second Order Opening.
Enter the Vault and close the door.

Part 1: Invocation of Isis

Adeptus Primus in the East raises wand toward the Rose in the ceiling and says: **In the Name and Power of the Divine Spirit, I invoke ye, ye Angels of the Celestial Spheres. Guard this Sacred Chamber so we may pursue the ancient and Holy rites unhindered by the profane. Keep far removed the evil and the uninitiated, that they penetrate not into the abode of our mysteries. Inspire and sanctify all who enter this place with the illimitable Wisdom of the Divine Light. IAO. IAO. IAO.** (Lowers wand.)

Adeptus Primus: **Very Honoured Fratres et Sorores, I invite you to join with me now in this Work of Art, as we call upon the forces of Saturn in this Mystical Vault. We invoke the forces of Saturn, as did the Priests and Priestesses of long**

150. Use powdered incense sparingly in the enclosed Vault. Otherwise use stick incense.

ago. Our ancient Fratres and Sorores knew this Planetary power in its masculine form as Ea, as Heru-Ka-Pet, as Shabbathai, as Cronos, as Saturnus, and in its feminine form as Ishtar, as Isis, as Hera, as Rhea, as Juno, and many other names both known and unknown.

In this time and in this place, we call upon this power under the Mighty Name of ISIS, the Queen of Heaven, Mother of the Gods! Isis the beneficent! Isis the Creator! Holy art Thou! We invoke Thee, O Isis! Bestow upon us your gift of magical words and powers! We invoke Thee, O Isis! Grant unto us the understanding of your ancient Wisdom as we perform this Work of Sacred Sight!

Adeptus Secundus in the South: **Holy art Thou, O Isis! Giver of Life! Sister of Osiris! Mother of Horus! Isis the magician! We invoke Thee, O Isis, winged goddess of the solar disk and the lunar crescent!**

Adeptus Tertius in the North: **Holy art Thou, Blessed Isis, celestial mother. Thou who nurtures us in times of affliction. Help us to seek out the lost fragments of our spiritual selves, as you sought and found the divided parts of your beloved Osiris.**

Adeptus Primus: **We invoke thee, O Isis, by the Mystic names of IAO Sabaoth, Adonios, Agathos Daimon, Akrammachamarei** (Ak-ram-mach-am-ar-ray-ee), **Sesengenbarpharanges** (Say-sen-gen-bar-ran-ges), **Ablanathanalba** (Ah-Blah-nath-an-al-ba!). **We invoke thee!** (Traces the sigil of Ese,[151] the Coptic name of Isis, over the Altar.)

151. Ese is the Coptic name of Isis. For the sigil, it is transliterated into Hebrew as Aleph Shin Heh.

Êse

ⲎⲤⲈ

אשה

Figure 51: Sigil of Isis

All raise Wands on High and point Cruxes toward the statue of Isis.

Adeptus Primus: **Holy art Thou!**

Adeptus Secundus: **ISET**

Adeptus Tertius: **ISIS**

Adeptus Primus: **ESE**

Adeptus Secundus: **Great Goddess of the disk and crescent!**

Adeptus Tertius: **Isis, the Throne of Power!**

Adeptus Primus: **We invoke thee!**

Adeptus Secundus: **ISET**

Adeptus Tertius: **ISIS**

Adeptus Primus: **ESE**

Adeptus Secundus: **Great Goddess of the disk and crescent!**

Adeptus Tertius: **Isis, the Throne of Power!**

Adeptus Primus: **Holy art Thou!**

Adeptus Secundus: **ISET**

Adeptus Tertius: **ISIS**

Adeptus Primus: **ESE**

Adeptus Secundus: **Great Goddess of the disk and crescent!**

Adeptus Tertius: **Isis, the Throne of Power!**

Adeptus Primus: **We invoke thee!**

ALL lower their implements and vibrate the name of **ESE! ESE! ESE!** three times slowly, giving the Projection Sign at the altar with each vibration. At the end, give the Sign of Silence. All visualize the Goddess strongly for a few moments.

ADEPTUS PRIMUS: **We invoke Thee, O Isis, that Thou mayst bestow a ray of Thy perfect knowledge upon us in this Saturnian Working. Grant Thy magical power to our rites and aid us to understand clearly things both visible and invisible that appertain unto the sphere of Shabbathai. To the glory of the Ineffable Name. Amen.**

ALL give the LVX Signs.

Part 2: Skrying

This particular working is for the Saturn Square of the Saturn Wall.
ALL face Saturn Wall.
ALL perform the Qabalistic Cross.

ADEPTUS PRIMUS moves to the Saturn wall, traces a circle in front of the Spirit Wheel square, and says: **Unto the Highest First.** ADEPTUS PRIMUS traces the Spirit Sigil and vibrates: **EHEIEH! AGLA!**

ALL give the LVX Signs.

ADEPTUS PRIMUS: **Before you is the Portal of Saturn on the Wall of Shabbathai. Observe its Flashing Colors of Blue-Violet and Yellow-Orange. Burn its image into your mind. See the interplay of the colors in the edges where these colors meet. See the apparent "flatness" of the square disappear as the square becomes three-dimensional. It acquires depth and space. It is a doorway into an inner world. The meaning of the Hebrew name of Saturn, Shabbathai, is "the Seventh." The number seven is a gateway to the higher realms. This Portal is a gateway which permits the powers of Shabbathai to be known.**

ADEPTUS SECUNDUS traces a large circle in front of the Saturn Wall, followed by the *Greater Invoking Hexagram of Saturn*. After the Hexagram is drawn, ALL vibrate:

ARARITA. Adeptus Secundus then traces the sigil of Saturn in the center, and All vibrate: **YHVH ELOHIM.**

Adeptus Tertius traces a smaller circle in front of the Saturn Square of the Saturn Wall, followed by the *Greater Invoking Hexagram of Saturn*. After the Hexagram is drawn, All vibrate: **ARARITA.** Adeptus Tertius then traces the sigil of Saturn in the center, and All vibrate: **YHVH ELOHIM.**

Adeptus Primus traces the Hebrew letter Aleph before the square. All vibrate: **ALEPH.** Adeptus Primus may then remain standing or be seated along with the rest of the Officers as the skrying continues.

Adeptus Primus leads the beginning part of the Work: **The square before you loses its edged solidity and becomes a long blue-violet Portal into Etheric World. A long blue-violet tunnel that you can see stretches backward beyond the confines of this small room, beyond space and time. See it clearly, the hardness of the edges becoming elastic, almost fluid, as if you could put your hand right through the symbol. Stare at it without blinking your eyes, taking it in. At last, when you have implanted this symbol in your mind, close your physical eyes and with your mind's eye, see the blue-violet background color transmute into brilliant yellow-orange. Likewise, see the yellow-orange color of the Saturn symbol turn to blue-violet. When the colors have reversed themselves, step through the Portal with your astral self. Step through.** (Pause.)

The Saturn symbol parts before you like a curtain, and you find yourself on the other side. You find yourself within a misty, cool, high landscape of mountains that are so old that they have been worn down by wind and rain from many thousands of centuries. Beyond the mountains is the emerald sea, a deep indigo expanse of water which was ancient when the gods were young.

We ask for a guide to lead us on this journey. So with one voice we shall vibrate three times the name of an appropriate guide, Kassiel, the archangel of Saturn. We will do so now.

All: **KASSIEL. KASSIEL. KASSIEL.** (Pause.)

ADEPTUS PRIMUS: **Kassiel appears, a great grey-haired, winged Archangel in indigo robes. The symbol of Saturn is upon his chest and he holds in his hand an hourglass. His wings are black, indigo, and yellow-orange.**

We greet the figure by vibrating the name of YHVH ELOHIM. We also salute him astrally by giving the L.V.X. Signs. The Archangel returns them. (Pause.)

Kassiel may show you many things on this journey. He will show each one of us a vision filled with important symbolism. I, as Chief Adept, will no longer guide you on this journey for the next few minutes. Kassiel will do that for us. Feel free to speak out and share any visual images that you are shown, or if you wish, keep them to yourself until after the skrying is completed. Take note of what you see. Ask questions of your guide. Test them if need be. Always act with respect and confidence. Seek and ye shall find.

ADEPTUS PRIMUS lets the skrying continue silently with only occasional commentary.[152] When a reasonable amount for the skrying has passed, ADEPTUS PRIMUS ends it as follows:

ADEPTUS PRIMUS: **Our skrying into the Saturn Square is completed. Gaze upon the brilliant countenance of the Archangel Kassiel once more. We thank him for the guidance that he has provided us on this journey, each in our own way. Take a few moments now to thank the Archangel and possibly receive any further communications.** (Pause.)

We thank Kassiel for leading us into the Saturn Square of the wall of Shabbathai. Be there peace between us and you. Go with the blessings of YHVH ELOHIM.

ADEPTUS PRIMUS makes the Sign of the Circled Cross toward the Saturn Square. The Skrying is ended.

ALL give the LVX Signs, then return to their former stations around the Altar.

152. When each participant is finished with the vision, they can indicate this by softly saying, "So mote it be."

Part 3: Thank Offering to Isis

Adeptus Primus: **We thank Thee, O Isis, for gracing this Holy Chamber with thy Divine Presence and lending Thy illuminating strength to our ceremony. Thou art ever welcome in this temple, especially during those rites when Thy Saturnian energies are called upon. We ask that Thou accept the thanks of Thy humble Fratres and Sorores with an offering made pleasing unto Thee. The offerings made unto Isis are given to us by the great God Osiris. Osiris, who was resurrected by the power and love of Isis. It is Osiris, Onnophris, the justified One, who has given us these Offerings to please Isis; that Great Goddess of Life may nurture us on our continual quest for the Light and the hiding place of the true Lapis Philosophorum.**

Adeptus Secundus: **Holy art Thou, O Isis! Giver of Life! Sister of Osiris! Mother of Horus! Isis the magician! O Isis, winged goddess of the solar disk and the lunar crescent! Lady of the solid earth.** (Places Bread and Salt into Isis's Bowl of Offerings.)

Adeptus Tertius: **Holy art Thou, Blessed Isis, celestial mother. Goddess of the swift Air.** (Places a few Rose petals into Isis's Bowl of Offerings.)

Adeptus Secundus: **O thou Great Goddess of Life, thou Lady of Love, Thou art crowned Queen of the Gods. Solace of mankind. Goddess of the emerald Sea.** (Places some drops of wine into Isis's Bowl of Offerings.)

Adeptus Tertius: **Lady of Heaven, Goddess of warmth and Fire, Creatrix and Divine One.** (Sprinkles incense into Isis's Bowl of Offerings.)

Adeptus Primus: **Thou art the visible representative of the Invisible, Eternal, and Immortal One who is both Many and One. We hail Thee in all Thy multifarious forms! Thou who nurtures us in times of affliction. Help us to seek out the lost fragments of our spiritual selves, as you sought and found the divided parts of your beloved Osiris.** (Sprinkles incense into Isis's candle.)

All raise Wands on High. Point Cruxes toward the statue of Isis and say: **We thank Thee, Isis of the Solar Disk, Isis of the Lunar Crescent. Isis of the Throne of Power. We thank Thee!**

All give the LVX Signs.

Part 4: Mystic Repast

The lid of the pastos is removed. In the East, Adeptus Primus hands their wand to Adeptus Secundus and steps inside the pastos, facing west.

Adeptus Primus: **Nothing now remains but to partake together of the Mystic Repast of Osiris, and to remember the Tiphareth clause of our solemn Obligation. For our Victory is in the Rose of Ruby and Cross of Gold.**

Adeptus Primus takes on the Godform of Osiris and says the Prayer of Osiris:

For Osiris Onnophris, who is found perfect before the Gods, hath said:
These are the Elements of my Body,
Perfected through Suffering, Glorified through Trial.
For the scent of the Dying Rose is as the repressed Sigh of my suffering:
And the flame red Fire as the Energy of mine Undaunted Will:
And the Cup of Wine is the pouring out of the Blood of my Heart:
Sacrificed unto Regeneration, unto the Newer Life:
And the Bread and Salt are as the Foundations of my Body,
Which I destroy in order that they may be renewed.
For I am Osiris Triumphant, even Osiris Onnophris, the Justified.
I am He who is clothed with the Body of Flesh,
Yet in whom is the Spirit of the Great Gods.
I am the Lord of Life, triumphant over Death.
Those who partaketh with me shall arise with me.
I am the Manifestor in matter of Those Whose Abode is in the Invisible.
I am purified. I stand upon the Universe.
I am its Reconciler with the Eternal Gods.
I am the Perfector of Matter,
And without me, the Universe is not.

ADEPTUS PRIMUS continues from the East: **I invite you to inhale with me the perfume of the Rose, as a symbol of Air.** (Smells rose.) **To feel with me the warmth of this sacred Fire.** (Spreads hands over candle.) **To eat with me this Bread and Salt as types of Earth.** (Eats bread.) **And finally to drink with me this sacramental Wine, the consecrated symbol of Elemental Water.** (Makes a Cross in the Air with the Cup and drinks.)

ADEPTUS PRIMUS passes the rose to ADEPTUS SECUNDUS in the South, who smells the rose and passes it on to the person at their left. The rose is passed around the circle until it comes back to ADEPTUS PRIMUS, who replaces it on the Altar.

ADEPTUS PRIMUS passes the candle to ADEPTUS SECUNDUS, who feels its warmth. The candle is passed around until it comes back to ADEPTUS PRIMUS, who replaces it on the Altar.

ADEPTUS PRIMUS serves ADEPTUS SECUNDUS the Bread and Salt, which is passed around the Altar until it is replaced by ADEPTUS PRIMUS.

ADEPTUS PRIMUS serves ADEPTUS SECUNDUS the Cup of Wine, which is passed around the Altar until it is replaced by ADEPTUS PRIMUS. If any wine is left in the Cup, ADEPTUS PRIMUS finishes it and inverts it and says: **Tetelestai!**

ADEPTUS PRIMUS takes back their wand and points it toward the Rose in the ceiling: **Unto Thee, Sole Wise, Sole Mighty, and Sole Eternal One, be the praise and Glory forever, who has permitted us to penetrate thus far into the Sanctuary of Thy Mysteries. Not unto us, but unto Thy Name be the Glory. Let the influence of Thy Divine Ones descend upon our heads and teach us the value of self-sacrifice, so that we shrink not in the hour of trial, but thus our names may be written on high, and our Genius may stand in the presence of the Holy Ones, in that hour when the Son of Man is invoked before the Lord of Spirits, and His Name in the presence of the Ancient of Days.**

ADEPTUS SECUNDUS: **Be our minds opened unto the Higher.**
ADEPTUS TERTIUS: **Be our hearts as centers of Light.**
ADEPTUS PRIMUS: **Be our bodies as Temples of the Rosy Cross.**

Before exiting the Vault, ALL give the LVX Signs.

Optional: Proceed to the General Second Order Closing.

✠ ✠ ✠

An Invocation of Ra and a Skrying on the Sun Wall

This group ritual is similar to the previous one. Ideally, the ritual should take place on a Sunday.

Figure 52: The Sun God Ra

Preparation: Upon the Circular Altar should be placed a statue of Ra on an orange cloth, Qamea of Sol, appropriate Solar incense and other symbols. The Elements for the Mystic Repast will also be needed. You will also need a small bowl for offerings.

Synopsis: The Adepts enter the Vault and begin the invocation of Ra, calling upon the God to aid the work of skrying on the Sun Wall. Adeptus Primus opens the Sun Square on the Sun Wall by tracing the appropriate Hexagrams and then begins to lead all participants on a Skrying into the Square. When the skrying is finished, there is a Thank Offering to Ra, followed by a Mystic Repast.

(NOTE: During the skrying part of the ritual, participants can sit on the floor or on chairs, so long as there is room to maneuver and the floor is protected from the feet of the chairs by a cloth.)

Optional: Open with the General Second Order Opening.

Part 1: Invocation of Ra

Adeptus Primus raises Wand toward the Rose in the Ceiling: **In the Name and Power of the Divine Spirit, I invoke ye, ye Angels of the Celestial Spheres. Guard this Sacred Chamber so we may pursue the ancient and Holy rites unhindered by the profane. Keep far removed the evil and the uninitiated, that they penetrate not into the abode of our mysteries. Inspire and sanctify all who enter this place with the illimitable Wisdom of the Divine Light. IAO. IAO. IAO.** (Lowers Wand.)

Very Honoured Fratres et Sorores, I invite you to join with me now in this Work of Art, as we call upon the forces of Sol in this Mystical Vault. We invoke the forces of Sol, as did the Priests and Priestess of long ago. Our ancient Fratres and Sorores knew this Solar power as Aten, as Shemesh, as Helios, as Apollo, as Balsames, as Phre, as Sol Invictus, as Mithras, and many other names both known and unknown.

In this time and in this place, we call upon this power under the Mighty Name of RA, the Creator, Father of the Gods! Thou Golden Hawk of the Sun! We invoke Thee, O Ra! Bestow upon us your gift of radiant Light! We invoke Thee,

O Ra! Grant unto us your illuminating Wisdom as we perform this Work of Sacred Sight!

Adeptus Secundus: **Homage to thee, O Ra, at thy glorious Rising. Thou Risest, thou shinest at the Dawn. The company of the Gods praise Thee at Sunrise and at Sunset, when as thy morning boat meeteth thy Evening boat with fair winds, thou sailest over the heights of Heaven with a gladdened Heart.**[153]

Adeptus Tertius: **O thou Only One, Thou Perfect One. O thou who art eternal. Who art never weak, whom no power can abase. O thou splendour of the noonday Sun, Over the things which appertain to thy sphere, none hath domination at all.**

Adeptus Primus: **And therefore we honor thee.**

Adeptus Secundus: **Thou great Hawk, who by thy luminous face makest all humanity to rejoice, thou renewest thy youth, and dost set thy self in Yesterday's place. O Divine One, self-created, self-anointed, thou art the Lord of Heaven and Earth, and didst create beings Celestial and beings Terrestrial.**

Adeptus Tertius: **O thou heir of Eternity, everlasting Ruler, self-sustained, as thou risest thy gracious rays are upon all faces and abide in every heart. Live thou in us, as we shall live in Thee, O thou Golden Hawk of the Sun!**[154]

Adeptus Secundus: **O thou God of Life, thou Lord of Love, Thou art crowned King of the Gods. Banisher of Apep! Brightener of Amenti! Exalted Sekhem!**

Adeptus Tertius: **Isis and Nephthys salute thee, singing unto thee songs of joy at thy rising in the Matet boat. The souls of the East follow thee, the souls of the West praise thee. Thou hast the heart of joy within thy shrine!**

153. From the "Hymn to Ra" in Regardie, *The Tree of Life*, 259.

154. From the "Hymn to Ra" in Regardie, *The Tree of Life*, 259.

Adeptus Primus: **We invoke thee, O Ra, by the Mystic names of IAO Sabaoth, Adonios, Agathos Daimon, Akrammachamarei** (Ak-ram-mach-am-ar-ray-ee)**, Sesengenbarpharanges** (Say-sen-gen-bar-ran-ges), **Ablanathanalba** (Ah-Blah-nath-an-al-ba!)**. We invoke thee!** (Traces the sigil of Ra over the Altar.)

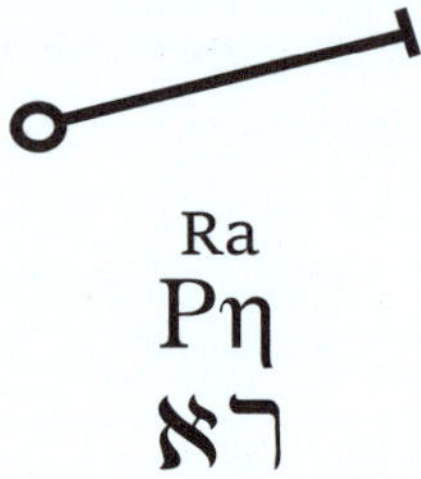

Figure 53: Sigil of Ra

All raise Wands on High. Point Cruxes toward the statue of Ra.

Adeptus Primus: **We invoke thee!**
Adeptus Secundus: **Ra-Asar!**
Adeptus Tertius: **Ra-Temu!**
Adeptus Primus: **Ra-Harmachis!**
Adeptus Secundus: **Ra of the Solar Disk!**
Adeptus Tertius: **Thou Golden Hawk of the Sun!**
Adeptus Primus: **We invoke thee!**
Adeptus Secundus: **Ra-Asar!**
Adeptus Tertius: **Ra-Temu!**
Adeptus Primus: **Ra-Harmachis!**
Adeptus Secundus: **Ra of the Solar Disk!**
Adeptus Tertius: **Thou Golden Hawk of the Sun!**
Adeptus Primus: **We invoke thee!**
Adeptus Secundus: **Ra-Asar!**
Adeptus Tertius: **Ra-Temu!**
Adeptus Primus: **Ra-Harmachis!**
Adeptus Secundus: **Ra of the Solar Disk!**
Adeptus Tertius: **Thou Golden Hawk of the Sun!**

ALL lower implements and vibrate the name of Ra six times slowly, giving the Projection Sign at the altar with each vibration: **RA! RA! RA! RA! RA! RA!** (At the end, ALL give the Sign of Silence and visualize Ra strongly for a few moments.)

ADEPTUS PRIMUS: **We invoke Thee, O Ra, that Thou mayst bestow Thy radiating strength upon us in this Solar Working. Grant Thine illuminating rays of Wisdom to our rites and aid us to see clearly things both visible and invisible that appertain unto your Solar sphere. To the glory of the Ineffable Name. Amen.**

ALL give the LVX Signs.

PART 2: SKRYING

(This particular working is for the Sun Square of the Sun Wall.)

ALL face Sun Wall. ALL OFFICERS except for ADEPTUS PRIMUS may stand or be seated comfortably, so long as they can see the square.

ALL perform the Qabalistic Cross.

ADEPTUS PRIMUS moves to the Sun wall, traces a circle in front of the Spirit Wheel, and says: **Unto the Highest First.** ADEPTUS PRIMUS charges the square with the Spirit Sigil and vibrates: **EHEIEH! AGLA!**

ALL give the LVX Signs.

ADEPTUS PRIMUS: **Before you is the Portal of Sol on the Wall of Shemesh. Observe its Flashing Colors of Orange and Blue. Burn its image into your mind. See the interplay of the colors in the edges where these colors meet. See the apparent "flatness" of the square disappear as the square becomes three-dimensional. It acquires depth and space. It is a doorway into an inner world. The Visible Sun is the dispenser of Light to the Earth. This Portal is a gateway which permits the Invisible Sun of Spirit to shine in from Above.**

ADEPTUS PRIMUS traces a large circle in front of the Sun Wall, followed by the six forms of the *Greater Invoking Hexagrams of Sol.* After the sixth Hexagram is drawn, ALL vibrate: **ARARITA.** Adeptus Primus then traces the sigil of Sol in the center, and All vibrate: **YHVH ELOAH VE-DAATH.**

Adeptus Primus repeats the last step and traces all six forms again (much smaller this time) for the Sun Square of the Sun Wall and vibrates the same words.

Adeptus Primus traces the Hebrew letter Resh before the square and vibrates its name: **RESH.** Adeptus Primus may then remain standing or be seated along with the rest of the Officers as the skrying continues.

Adeptus Primus leads the beginning part of the Skrying Work: **The square before you loses its hardness and becomes a long orange Portal into Etheric World. A long orange tunnel that you can see stretches backward beyond the confines of this small room, beyond space and time. See it clearly, the hardness of the edges becoming elastic, almost fluid, as if you could put your hand right through the symbol. Stare at it without blinking your eyes, taking it in. At last, when you have implanted this symbol in your mind, close your physical eyes and with your mind's eye, see the orange background color transmute into brilliant blue. Likewise, see the blue color of the sun symbol turn to orange. When the colors have reversed themselves, step through the Portal with your Astral self. Step through.** (Pause.)

The Sun symbol parts before you like a curtain, and you find yourself on the other side. The warm rays of the Sun caress your face and the bright Light of day greets you. There is hot sand under your sandaled feet. Palm trees and rocky outcroppings dot the landscape before you. (Pause.)

You wish for a guide to lead you in this journey. So with one voice we shall vibrate three times the name of an appropriate guide. *Michael Shemeshel*. We will do so now.

All vibrate: **MICHAEL SHEMESHEL. MICHAEL SHEMESHEL. MICHAEL SHEMESHEL.** (Pause.)

ADEPTUS PRIMUS continues: **Michael appears—a great fair-haired, winged Archangel in a Golden armored breastplate with a cape of orange attached by a slender chain around his neck. Upon his breast is the figure of a Hexagram. His wings are of orange and blue feathers. He carries a long golden staff surmounted by a Solar disk.**

We greet the figure by vibrating the name of YHVH ELOAH VE-DAATH. We also astrally salute him by giving the L.V.X. Signs. The Archangel returns them. (Pause.)

Michael will show us many things on this journey. He will show each one of us a vision filled with important symbolism. I, as Chief Adept, will no longer guide you on this journey for the next few minutes. Michael will do that for us. Feel free to speak out and share any visual images that you are shown, or if you wish, keep them to yourself until after the skrying is completed. Ask questions of your guide. Test them if need be. Always act with respect and confidence. Seek and ye shall find.

ADEPTUS PRIMUS lets the skrying continue on with only occasional commentary. When a reasonable amount for the skrying has passed, ADEPTUS PRIMUS ends it as follows:

ADEPTUS PRIMUS: **Our skrying into the Sun Square is completed. Gaze upon the brilliant countenance of the Archangel Michael once more. We thank him for the guidance that he has provided us on this journey, each in our own way. Take a few moments now to thank the Archangel and possibly receive any further communications.**

(Pause.)

We thank Michael for leading us into the Sun Square of the wall of Shemesh. Be there peace between us and you. Go with the blessings of YHVH ELOAH VE-DAATH.

ADEPTUS PRIMUS makes the Sign of the Circled Cross toward the Sun Square. The Skrying is ended.

ALL give the LVX Signs, then return to their former stations around the Altar.

PART 3: THANK OFFERING TO RA

ADEPTUS PRIMUS: **We thank Thee, O Ra, for gracing this Holy Chamber with thy Divine Presence and lending Thy illuminating strength to our ceremony. Thou art ever welcome in this temple, especially during those rites when Thy Solar energies are called upon. We ask that Thou accept the thanks of Thy humble Fratres and Sorores with an offering made pleasing unto Thee. The offerings made unto Ra are given to us by the great God Osiris. Osiris, whose shrine in the heart of Amentet is visited every night by the Sektet boat of Ra, which stops to pay homage to the Lord of Life, triumphant over death. It is Osiris, Onnophris, the justified One, who has given us these Offerings to please Ra; that the Sektet boat of Night may again become the Matet boat of Day, and the Hawk of Sun may continue to rise and Light our Path to the true Lapis Philosophorum.**

ADEPTUS SECUNDUS: **Thou great Hawk, who by thy luminous face makest all humanity to rejoice, thou renewest thy youth, and dost set thy self in Yesterday's place. O Divine One, self-created, self-anointed, thou art the Lord of Heaven and Earth, and didst create beings Celestial and beings Terrestrial.** (Places Bread and Salt into Ra's Bowl of Offerings.)

ADEPTUS TERTIUS: **O thou heir of Eternity, everlasting Ruler, self-sustained, as thou risest thy gracious rays are upon all faces and abide in every heart. Live thou in us, as we shall live in Thee, O thou Golden Hawk of the Sun!** (Places a few Rose petals into Ra's Bowl of Offerings.)

ADEPTUS SECUNDUS: **O thou God of Life, thou Lord of Love, Thou art crowned King of the Gods. Banisher of Apep! Brightener of Amenti! Exalted Sekhem!** (Places some drops of wine into Ra's Bowl of Offerings.)

ADEPTUS TERTIUS: **Isis and Nephthys salute thee, singing unto thee songs of joy at thy rising in the Matet boat. The souls of the East follow thee, the souls of the West**

praise thee. Thou hast the heart of joy within thy shrine! (Sprinkles incense into Ra's Bowl of Offerings.)

ADEPTUS PRIMUS: **Thou art the visible representative of the Invisible, Eternal and Immortal One who is both Many and One. We hail Thee in all Thy multifarious forms!** (Sprinkles incense into Ra's candle.)

ALL raise wands and point Cruxes toward the statue of Ra and say: **We thank Thee, Ra-Asar! Ra-Temu! Ra-Harmachis! Ra of the Solar Disk. Thou Golden Hawk of the Sun! We thank Thee!**

ALL give the LVX Signs.

PART 4: MYSTIC REPAST

Perform the Mystic Repast with the Prayer of Osiris as given in the previous ritual.

CLOSING

Optional: Proceed to the General Second Order Closing.

✠✠✠

The Higher and Divine Genius

At the heart of the Golden Dawn tradition lies the ultimate goal of the Great Work: union with the Divine. All the rituals, study work, exercises, and meditations that Initiates undertake are geared toward this end, which is summed up perfectly in the Tiphareth clause of the Adeptus Minor obligation: "I further promise and swear that with the Divine Permission I will, from this day forward, apply myself to the Great Work—which is, to purify and exalt my Spiritual Nature so that with the Divine Aid I may at length attain to be more than human, and thus gradually raise and unite myself to my Higher and Divine Genius, and that in this event I will not abuse the great power entrusted to me."

The Higher and Divine Genius, sometimes referred to as the True Self or the *Augoeides,* represents the core of one's being, the unadulterated essence that transcends the limitations of the personal ego. The Golden Dawn uses various terms to describe different aspects of the True Self, including the Higher and Divine Genius, the Higher Genius, the Higher Self, the Augoeides, the Lower Genius, and the Lower Self. Many Golden Dawn magicians also refer to the Higher Self as the Holy Guardian Angel, or HGA. The often subtle differences between these terms has already been covered elsewhere.[155] The Higher Self is the Divine Spark that exists at the center of every individual, the connecting link between human and Deity.

How important is the Higher Self to our work? We can turn to Regardie for the answer:

> Thus the supreme object of all magical ritual is the building of the pyramidal apex, and the installation of the battlements on the intellectual tower; in other words, the communion with the Higher Self. For every man is that the most important step, and no other compares with it in importance and validity until this one union has been accomplished. It brings with it new powers, new extensions of consciousness, and a new vision of life. It throws a brilliant ray of illumination on the hitherto dark phases of life, removing from the mind the clouds which inhibit the glory of the spiritual light.[156]

The Higher Self is the guiding light along the spiritual path of the adept, illuminating the way toward self-realization and divine communion. It is the ferryman who alone can carry us across the erratic currents of the underworld river of the unconscious mind, to land safely on the Elysian shore beyond. Yet we must always remember that so long as we live, this is not a one-time trip. It is an ongoing voyage that takes effort and dedication. And on every journey taken to the astral realms and back again, we must constantly rely on our ethereal companion in order to avoid the rocks and rip currents.

The pursuit of the Higher Self is a sacred quest, for in recognizing and aligning with this inner source of divine truth, the adept unveils their unique spiritual purpose and experiences a profound sense of inner harmony. It is through disciplined ritual work and introspection that the adept comes to recognize the whispers of the Higher Self, guiding them toward the path of self-fulfillment.

With practice, connecting with the Higher Self can take place at any point within the magician's work, and sometimes unexpectedly so, such as at the crescendo of a complex ritual, or while sitting quietly on the Dais in the middle of a Neophyte Ceremony, or

155. See Ciceros, *Golden Dawn Magic*, 289–92.

156. Regardie, *The Tree of Life*, 110.

even during the performance of a simple Qabalistic Cross or Middle Pillar Exercise. Communications can also happen while meditating within the Vault of the Adepti, a perfect chamber for such occurrences.

Sometimes the key is not to expect communion with the Higher Self at the time and place of *our* choosing, but rather to put in the work and wait for the Angel to make their presence known on *their* timeline.

Overview of the Ritual of Greeting the Angel

By M. Isidora Forrest

An Adept ritual working to initiate contact with the Higher and Divine Genius or Holy Guardian Angel using the magical formulae of the Neophyte Ritual of the Golden Dawn

Introduction

Part of the work of the Zelator Minor Adept of the Second Order of the R.R. et A.C. is to create an original ritual using the formulae of the Neophyte Ritual of the Golden Dawn.

The purpose of this particular piece of grade work is to ensure that the Adept, preparing to take the Hierophantic Throne of the East for the first time, fully understands the magical formulae and mechanisms of the ritual that they will soon be called upon to lead. There is no better way to make sure one fully understands than to apply the same formulae in an entirely different situation.

The Ritual of Greeting the Angel is the Adept rite I created using the Neophyte formulae to fulfill that part of my own grade work.

Purpose of the Rite

The magical transformation undertaken in this rite is the movement of the Aspirant—the Fourth Adept—from Asiyah to Yetzirah (specifically to Malkhuth of Yetzirah) in order to greet their Higher and Divine Genius or Holy Guardian Angel. By "leveling up" in this way, the natural distance between the Adept and the Angel is decreased and contact with the Angel is easier. With the Fourth Adept operating in Malkhuth of Yetzirah, the Angel may reach down from Yesod and Tiphereth of Yetzirah to more easily connect with the Aspirant. Of course, a ritual like this is just *one* way to facilitate this important contact. Contact between the Adept and their Higher and Divine Genius is always an ongoing journey.

Ritual Formulae and Magical Structure

As noted, the formulae of the rite are those from the Neophyte Ritual. But since this is an Adept rite, instead of taking place before and on the threshold of Malkhuth in Asiyah on the Tree of Life, this ritual takes advantage of the Qabbalistic Four Worlds structure. Most of the ritual symbolically takes place in Malkhuth, Yesod, and Tiphereth of Asiyah. At its climax, the Aspirant will rise in vision to pass through the station of Daath of Asiyah, then through Kether of Asiyah and into Malkhuth of Yetzirah.

Temple Layout and Ritual Stations of the Officers

The Pillars and Altar are arranged as in the Neophyte Ritual. Thrones for the Officers are placed in a triangle with the First Adept's Throne in the East, beyond the Pillars (as in the Neophyte Ritual), Second Adept in the South, and Third Adept in the North.

The First Adept is stationed in the East of the temple, symbolically in Tiphereth of Asiyah, and channeling the influences of Kether of Asiyah and of the Yetziratic Tree beyond.

The Second Adept is stationed in the North of the temple, opposite the Third Adept in the South of the temple. The Second Adept represents the powers of the Dark Pillar of Severity, while the Third Adept represents the powers of the Bright Pillar of Mercy. The Second Adept's additional station in the West of the temple is symbolically situated in Malkhuth of Asiyah, receiving the influences of all the Trees in all the Worlds. The Third Adept's additional station is in the center of the temple, West of the Double Cube Altar, and is situated on the Middle Pillar, symbolically in Yesod of Asiyah.

The Fourth Adept is the Aspirant in this ritual. The Fourth Adept is guided through various stations during the rite. At the culmination of the rite, the Fourth Adept takes their place between the temple Pillars in order to rise up the Middle Pillar, through Kether of Asiyah and into Malkhuth of Yetzirah.

By rotating ritual roles, all Adepts taking part may also have the opportunity to greet their own Angels during the course of the rite. This role switching is optional; if your Adept College wishes to do this, the ritual script shows how to do so.

Deityforms of the Officers

The Fourth Adept/Aspirant's Archetypal or Adamic Form is the Adam, representing Humanity in our search for the Divine. At the point in the rite where the Fourth Adept rises to contact their personal Genius, they leave the Archetypal Form of the Adam seated on the Throne between the Pillars and ascend in spirit as their individual self, using their Inner Order motto.

The Third Adept's Godform is the Archangel Raphael, the Reconciler between Heaven and Earth and the Healer of God.

The Second Adept's Goddessform is the Great Kerubic Archangel Sandalphon, the Completion of All Things and the Power of Creation and Form.

The First Adept's Godform is the Great Kerubic Archangel Metatron, the Initiation of All Things and the Power of Creation and Force.

Overview of the Ritual Actions

The temple is opened by Watchtower, with the Second and Third Adepts sharing ritual duties (as noted in the script). The Aspirant is brought into the temple and receives the first purification and consecration from the Third Adept. The Third Adept guides the Aspirant to the West of the Altar, facing East, as the Officers and Aspirant assume their Deity and Archetypal Forms. Since all ritualists are Adepts, no hoodwink or cord is used in this ritual.

With the Aspirant admitted, all join together to repeat the Tiphereth clause of the Obligation of the Minor Adept, setting the tone for the ritual. Next, the Aspirant is called forth from the darkness by the Voice of their Higher and Divine Genius or Angel.

As in the Neophyte ritual, the guiding Officer circumambulates with the Aspirant, conducting purifications and consecrations in the East and West. The first two circumambulations raise the temple from Malkhuth of Asiyah to Yesod of Asiyah.

All Adepts face East and give the Sign of the Rending of the Veil. The First Adept descends to the East of the Altar, facing East, and traces the invoking Solar Hexagrams between the Pillars. The First Adept returns to the East of the temple, then descends the Middle Pillar "in the Power of the Light." Taking the Aspirant by the hand, the First Adept draws them between the Pillars, facing East. A Throne is placed behind the Aspirant for future use.

The fourth and final purification and consecration takes place. The Aspirant, using their Inner Order motto, invokes their Higher and Divine Genius. The Officers form a triangle around the Aspirant and join wands above their head. Using the Khabs-am-Pekht formula, all Adepts visualize the words of the formula as the Bow of Qesheth, "launching" the Aspirant up the Middle Pillar, passing Daath and Kether, and into the citrine quarter of Malkhuth of Yetzirah.

Time is now allowed for the Aspirant to greet and commune with their Genius. If each of the Officers also wish to greet their own Genius, the rite is repeated for each person, starting from the Aspirant's invocation.

When all who wish have completed their communion, the Adepts proceed to the circulation of the Divine Light in the Path of Light. The rite is closed by the tracing of the banishing Solar Hexagrams, making the Sign of the Closing of the Veil, and by Watchtower, as it was opened.

The Ritual of Greeting the Angel

By M. Isidora Forrest

Temple Arrangement: Pillars and Altar are placed as in the Neophyte Ritual. First Adept's Throne is in the East. Second Adept's Throne is in the North; Second Adept also takes a station in the West. Third Adept's Throne is in the South; Third Adept also moves about in the Temple as the Hegemon does in the Neophyte Ritual. The Temple space symbolically encompasses Malkhuth, Yesod, and Tiphereth of Asiyah.

First Adept's Godform is Metatron. The First Adept wears the white robe of an Adept with white tabard and wields the Yellow Hexagram Wand of the Cancellarius.

Second Adept's Goddessform is Sandalphon. The Second Adept wears the white robe of an Adept with black tabard and wields the Lotus Wand of the Isis of Nature.

Third Adept's Godform is Raphael. The Third Adept wears the white robe of an Adept with yellow tabard and wields the Silver Pentagram Wand of Yesod. (NOTE: This is not a standard GD wand; it is particular to this rite and features a silver pentagram on a shaft of violet.)

Fourth Adept's Archetypal Form is the Adam, the Human. The Fourth Adept represents Humanity as a whole until ready to contact their Angel as an individual, and wears the white robe of an Adept.

All Adepts also wear the five-petaled Rose Cross Lamen.

Opening

The Ritual is opened by Watchtower. Second Adept performs the Rite up to the point that Spirit is invoked. Third Adept invokes Spirit and leads Hermetic Adoration.

Reception of the Adam into the Temple

First Adept in East. Second Adept in West. Third Adept by doorway. Fourth Adept in Pronaos.

First Adept: **Avete, Fratres and Sorores of the Rose of Ruby and the Cross of Gold. We are gathered for this Rite for the purpose of increasing our knowledge of the Higher and Divine Genius, sometimes also known as the Holy Guardian Angel. Therefore, we join together in Word and Will to ascend the Tree of Life seeking that Light of the Hidden Wisdom that lies within each of us and within all human beings and within all things.**

Very Honored Third Adept, I charge you to admit the Aspirant and administer the first purification and consecration upon the Threshold of the Temple.

Third Adept: *(To Aspirant)* **Ave, Soror/Frater Rosae Rubeae…**

Fourth Adept/Aspirant: **et Aureae Crucis.**

Third grips Fourth with LVX grip and draws them into the Temple.

Third Adept: **Unpurified and unconsecrated, thou canst not enter the company of the Angels, thou who art yet human.**

Third performs cross and triangle purification and consecration, then leads the Fourth Adept to West of Altar, facing East. Third Adept returns to Throne.

Assumption of Godforms

First Adept: *(Making Projecting Sign)* **Let the Name and Number of the Officers in this Rite be proclaimed that the Powers whose Images they are may be awakened**

in the sphere of the Adepts, the College, and the Order. For by Names and Images are all Powers awakened and reawakened. *(Makes Sign of Silence.)*

FOURTH ADEPT: **I am the Adam, the Human Being. I am all of us. I am Humanity. Both Beast and Angel, I seek balance between the two. I have seen the Beast; I have known it. Now I would see the Angel, and know it, too. I stretch out my hand to the Divine, for I am Human, and this I may do.**

SECOND ADEPT: **I am the Great Kerubic Archangel, Sandalphon. Beneath the shadow of my wings existeth the Life of the Universe. Mine is the Completion of All Things for Mine is the manifestation of the Elements. My stations in the Temple are two; in the West of the Temple in Malkhuth receiving the influences of all the Trees in all the Worlds, and beside the Dark Pillar of Severity, for my Name is Understanding and I am the Great Divine Power of Creation and Form.**

FIRST ADEPT: **I am the Great Kerubic Archangel, Metatron. The Crown of Creation is upon My Brow. Mine is the Initiation of All Things for Eheieh is with Me. My station is in the East of the Temple in Tiphereth channeling the influences of the Yetziratic Tree and of Kether of Asiyah into the Temple. I am called Wisdom and I am the Great Divine Power of Creation and Force.**

THIRD ADEPT: **I am the Mighty Archangel, Raphael. I am the Reconciler between Heaven and Earth, receiving the Light of Kether and Tiphereth and reflecting it into Malkhuth. My stations are two; the first is on the Middle Pillar of the Temple in Yesod, bringing the Life of Spirit to the Elements. The second is beside the Bright Pillar of Mercy for I am the Purifier and Consecrator and the Healer of God. It is I who lead the Adam upon their journey toward Beauty.**

The Obligation

FIRST ADEPT: **We have received the Adam into the company of the Angels. Now, my Fratres et Sorores, I ask you to stand, facing East, in the sign of Osiris Slain and together repeat the Tiphereth clause of the Obligation of the Adeptus Minor.**

ALL: **In the Divine Name of Beauty, Yod Heh Vav Heh Eloah Va-Daath, I vow that I will strive to the utmost to lead a pure and unselfish life. I further promise and swear that with the Divine permission, I will, from this day forward, apply myself to the Great Work; which is to so purify and exalt my Spiritual Nature that with the Divine Aid, I may at length attain to be more than human, and thus gradually raise and unite myself to my Higher and Divine Genius. On this day and in this place, I die to the old life and am reborn to the new.**

THE CALLING

FIRST ADEPT turns to face West. ALL except FIRST and FOURTH ADEPTS are seated.

FIRST ADEPT: **The Voice of my Self said unto me:** *(assumes Sign of the Enterer)* **"Let me enter the Path of Return and peradventure thus shall I find the Light of my Higher Soul. I am the only being in an Abyss of Darkness. From the Darkness and from the Silence of a Primal Sleep, now come I forth at my birth."** *(Ceases sign.)*

And the Voice of the Angel answered unto my Self: *(assumes Sign of Silence)*

"I am the One who formulates in the Light reaching even unto the Darkness of a Primal Sleep. I call unto thee. Arise and be born, O Adam!" *(Ceases sign.)*

RAISING THE TEMPLE

FIRST ADEPT: **Let the Mystic Circumambulation take place in the Path of Light as we elevate this Temple from Sephirah to Sephirah.**

FIRST and SECOND ADEPTS are in their places in East and West. THIRD and FOURTH ADEPTS circumambulate. As FOURTH ADEPT passes East, FIRST ADEPT knocks. As FOURTH ADEPT passes West, SECOND ADEPT knocks. As FOURTH ADEPT passes East for second time, FIRST ADEPT knocks. Upon reaching the Southwest for the second time, THIRD ADEPT halts and bars the FOURTH ADEPT.

THIRD ADEPT: **Unpurified and unconsecrated, thou canst not enter the Kingdom of Malkhuth, O human being.**

THIRD ADEPT purifies and consecrates the ADAM.

Third Adept: **Twice purified, twice consecrated, thou mayest approach the Guardian of Malkhuth.**

The circumambulation continues until SECOND ADEPT bars the FOURTH ADEPT in West. ALL halt.

SECOND ADEPT: **Thou canst not pass by Me, saith the Guardian of Malkhuth, unless thou canst tell Me My Name.**

FOURTH ADEPT: **Malkah the Queen is Thy Name. The Great One, Mother of the Universe art Thou.**

SECOND ADEPT: **The Divine is all about thee, O Humanity, in every stone and in the breath of every holy living thing. The Great Goddess of Nature is One with the Great Goddess of Atziluth. What thou seekest is already within thy possession and yet thou hast it not.**

SECOND ADEPT ceases barring: **Thou hast known Me, so pass thou on.**

THIRD and FOURTH ADEPTS circumambulate. As FOURTH ADEPT passes East, FIRST ADEPT knocks. As FOURTH ADEPT passes West, SECOND ADEPT knocks. Upon reaching the Northeast for the second time, THIRD ADEPT halts and bars the FOURTH ADEPT.

THIRD ADEPT: **Unpurified and unconsecrated thou canst not enter the Astral Light of the Foundation, O human being.**

THIRD ADEPT purifies and consecrates the FOURTH ADEPT.

THIRD ADEPT: **Thrice purified and thrice consecrated, thou mayest approach the Guardian of the Foundation.**

The circumambulation continues. THIRD ADEPT moves directly in front of FIRST ADEPT and FOURTH ADEPT and bars the FOURTH ADEPT in East. ALL halt.

THIRD ADEPT: **Thou canst not pass by Me, saith the Guardian of the Foundation, unless thou canst tell Me My Name.**

FOURTH ADEPT: **Opener of the Pathways is Thy Name. Reflector of the Light and Its Mediator to the Earth art Thou.**

THIRD ADEPT: **There is more in Heaven and Earth than thou hast ever dreamed, O Humanity. Before thou canst open thy heart to the Divine, thou must open thy mind. Dream what thou hast not dared to dream and thou shalt see whether or not it is Illusion.**

THIRD ADEPT ceases barring: **Thou hast known Me, so pass thou on to the Cubical Altar of the Universe.**

As the FOURTH ADEPT passes the East, FIRST ADEPT knocks. FOURTH ADEPT goes to West of Altar, facing East. SECOND ADEPT moves to left of the FOURTH ADEPT and THIRD ADEPT to right. With FIRST ADEPT, they form the Supernal Triad about the FOURTH ADEPT.

THIRD ADEPT: **Let us open the Pathways to the Admirable Light.**

ALL make Sign of the Rending of the Veil toward the East.

FIRST ADEPT moves to East of Altar, turns, and traces Invoking Solar Hexagrams between the Pillars. ALL vibrate appropriate Names. FIRST ADEPT returns to Throne in East and prepares to descend the Middle Pillar bringing the Light.

FIRST ADEPT: *(While descending)*

I come in the Power of the Light.
I come in the Light of Wisdom.
I come in the Mercy of the Light.
The Light hath healing in its wings.

First Adept grasps the Fourth Adept by the hand, leads them around the Altar, and places them between the Pillars, facing East. Third Adept places a Throne behind the Fourth Adept. The Fourth Adept will be seated on this Throne later in the rite. First Adept returns to Throne.

First Adept: **Let the fourth purification and consecration take place.**

Third Adept does this.

Third Adept: (*Tracing Cross and Triangle on the* Aspirant) **I purify thee with Water.** (*Tracing Cross and Triangle on the* Aspirant) **I consecrate thee with Fire.**

Four times purified and four times consecrated, I charge thee, Very Honored (Soror/Frater Motto of the Adept), to make thy invocation.

Individual Invocation of the Angel

Fourth Adept: **In the Name of the Ruler of the Universe, Whom Nature hath not formed, the vast and the mighty One, Ruler of the Light and of the Darkness, I, (Motto of the Adept), now invoke my Higher Genius to grant aid unto the higher aspirations of my soul.**

Upon a Golden Cross, I am a Red Rose opening to the Dawning Light. Opening to the Touch of my Deeper Soul, my Higher and Divine Genius, my Holy Guardian Angel. Opening my sphere of sensation. Opening my mind. Opening my heart. I raise up my hand to Thee, Shining Angel, Thou Holy and Divine Self. Come and take my hand. Let me know Thee. Let me journey across even the Abyss to see Thee, and to know Thee in my mind and to know Thee in my heart. Come, Bright Angel, come, I invoke Thee, I call Thee, I ask Thee.

Ascent of the Tree

Adepts form Triangle around the Aspirant as before and join implements over Aspirant's head. All are now operating in Tiphereth. In a moment, the Khabs-Am-Pekht formula will be used as the Bow of Qesheth and the Arrow of Samech to "launch" the

ASPIRANT up the Middle Pillar, through Daath, Kether, and finally into the citrine part of Malkhuth of Yetzirah.

SECOND ADEPT: **We call thee to the Living Beauty.**

THIRD ADEPT: **We call thee to the Living Light.**

FIRST ADEPT: **Long hast thou dwelt without the Knowledge of thine Higher and Divine Genius, yet like the Lamp of the Keryx, unseen by the Child of Earth, the Light of thy Holy Guardian Angel ever went before thee. Now shall that Light be revealed.**

Let the ASPIRANT visualize the ascent as the OFFICERS speak the formula.

FIRST ADEPT: **Soror/Frater, we charge thee: quit the Night, and seek the Day!**

FIRST ADEPT: **Khabs—**
SECOND ADEPT: **Am—**
THIRD ADEPT: **Pekht!**
SECOND ADEPT: **Konx—**
THIRD ADEPT: **Om—**
FIRST ADEPT: **Pax!**
THIRD ADEPT: **Light—**
FIRST ADEPT: **In—**
SECOND ADEPT: **Extension!**

ALL uncross implements, but continue to hold them upright in line with their Middle Pillars. With the vibration of IAO, the ASPIRANT ascends the Middle Pillar.

ALL: *(Vibrate very strongly)* **IAO.**

The ASPIRANT is seated on the Throne between the Pillars, facing East. ALL OFFICERS resume their Thrones.

In vision, upon reaching Malkhuth of Yetzirah, ASPIRANT gives LVX Signs and silently makes any additional personal invocation of the Genius desired. Time is now allowed for the individual visionary experience of the Aspirant, including greeting the Angel, communing with It, trying to learn Its Name, etc.

In the meantime, Officers should concentrate strongly on their Deityforms since they will leave the Deityform to make their own ascent to the Angel next.

When the Fourth Adept has completed their communion, they descend to Tiphereth of Asiyah in vision, then physically stand.

If other Officers wish to experience their own ascent to the Genius, the Aspirant takes the place of each Officer in turn: Second Adept, then Third Adept, then First Adept. The Deityform of each Officer is left at the station to be taken up by the Fourth Adept as each Officer takes their turn.

Ritual is repeated from the Aspirant's invocation, through the vibration of IAO, as well as the ascent and return for each participant.

Upon completion, All return to Thrones. The Fourth Adept is seated on a Throne in the West.

Circulation of the Light of the Angel

First Adept: **Let the Mystic Circumambulation take place in the Path of Light.**

First Adept remains in the East. All others line up in the Northeast of the temple in this order: Second Adept, Third Adept, and Fourth Adept. First Adept raises Wand to signal start of circumambulation. Each Adept makes the Saluting Sign as they pass the East. After passing the East once, the Second Adept drops out in the West and raises Wand. After passing the East twice, Third Adept spirals into the center of the Temple, between the Pillars, and raises Wand. Fourth Adept passes the East thrice and stops at their Throne in the West. Then All give the Sign of Silence and are reseated on their Thrones.

The Closing

Third Adept: **May that which we have touched this day remain with us and within our hearts. May the pathways to each of our Higher Souls be ever opened unto us.** (*To all Adepts*) **Let us stand and face East.** *(Done.)*

ALL: **Not unto our names, but unto Thine be the glory, Thou who hast allowed us to see even a glimpse of our Shining Selves.**

FIRST ADEPT descends to East of Altar, facing East, and performs the Banishing Solar Hexagrams between the Pillars. ALL vibrate appropriate Names. ALL give the Sign of the Closing of the Veil.

FIRST ADEPT is seated. SECOND ADEPT stands and performs first part of Closing by Watchtower (the Elemental Pentagrams), then is reseated. ALL vibrate appropriate Names with the Adept.

THIRD ADEPT stands and performs the conclusion of the Closing by Watchtower (the Spirit Pentagrams). All join in the vibrations. THIRD ADEPT is reseated.

FIRST ADEPT: **Tetelestai (*knocks*)! It is finished.**

ALL exit Temple.

✠ ✠ ✠

Enochian Work

Enochian, also called Angelic, is both a language with its own alphabet and a system of magic that was discovered by Elizabethan magician Dr. John Dee and his assistant Edward Kelly. Beginning in 1582, Dee and his seer continued to uncover the Enochian system over a period of seven years. This language, known as the "Secret Angelic Language," became known as Enochian because it was said to be the angelic language revealed to the prophet Enoch by the angel Ave.

The Enochian system has been a part of the Golden Dawn curriculum since the bare-bones outlines of the initiation rituals were first set down in the folios of the Cipher Manuscript. Divine Enochian names, as well as the Watchtower Tablets from which they were taken, are introduced to the student in the grades from Zelator through Portal. However, the Enochian system is not studied at length by the student until they enter the Second Order. Different aspects of the Enochian system are studied in every grade and sub-grade of the Second Order.

Several Second Order rituals contain Enochian material in varying degrees. The Adeptus Minor studies the Enochian alphabet, learns to perform divinations through Enochian

Chess, invokes Enochian entities and angels in ritual magic, and creates Enochian talismans. The Golden Dawn's knowledge of Enochian is not limited to what MacGregor Mathers compiled over a century ago, nor even to the Enochian documents included in the Zelator Adeptus Minor curriculum as printed in Regardie's *The Golden Dawn*. Nevertheless, skrying into the various Enochian Squares on the Elemental Tablets is a major focus of the Enochian work of an Adeptus Minor.

Readers were briefly introduced to the Golden Dawn's Enochian Elemental Tablets in our previous book *Golden Dawn Magic*. Each Tablet is essentially a magic square of Enochian letters set within a grid of twelve columns and thirteen rows (often called ranks). The names of several elemental powers, angels, and divine entities are derived from the various letters on these four tablets, along with the fifth Tablet of Union assigned to Spirit.

Every square of the Enochian Tablets actually represents a three-dimensional truncated pyramid with a square base and a letter written on its flat summit. The four triangles that comprise the sides of the figure are each attributed to various elemental, Sephirotic, Zodiacal, and planetary forces. The truncated pyramids not only act as perfect aids for skrying into the Enochian squares but also clearly depict the cosmic elements that are combined in each Watchtower square—elements that hold the keys to the forces powering the universe.

The pyramid is sometimes said to represent a hollow mountain or earthen mound from which the world was created. The square base and the four sides of the pyramid represents the earth and the four directions in space. The apex of the structure rises to the sky, piercing the heavens and joining Heaven and Earth. It is therefore a symbol of the point of connection between the worldly and the heavenly—a pathway to heaven. The truncated pyramid does not have a capstone. Capstones represent a finished work of great importance. Thus the truncated pyramid is a symbol of "unfinished work." It is the duty of the magician to equilibrate the four elements of the pyramid within the soul through spiritual alchemy, and replace the capstone of the psychic structure through magical practice.

Golden Dawn Enochian Magic is a multifaceted system of angelic hierarchies, pictographic script, powerful invocations, and compelling skrying symbols. Many consider it the pinnacle of our system.

An Evocation of the Enochian Archangel Aabai

Servient Square Abai in the Fire Angle of the Earth Tablet

This ceremony is designed for five Adepts. Its purpose is to evoke and communicate with *Aabai*, the Enochian Archangel of the servient square *Abai* in the Fire subangle of the Earth Tablet.[157] To accomplish this, the elemental sides of the truncated pyramid square are invoked by their respective officers. The Enochian letter assigned to this square is *Una* (equivalent to the letter *A*.)

The Abai Square is further described as an Osiris Square, because the four pyramidal sides are completely balanced between the elements of Fire, Water, Air, and Earth. The Abai Square has the added advantage of having these four elements in the order of the Four Winds: Air on the eastern side, Fire on the South, Water on the Western side, and Earth on the North.

Figure 54: Abai Pyramid Square

Officers Needed:
ADEPTUS SPIRITUS: Adept of Spirit, seated in the East or Northeast
ADEPTUS IGNIS: Adept of Fire, seated in the South
ADEPTUS AQUAE: Adept of Water, seated in the West
ADEPTUS AERIS: Adept of Air, seated in the East
ADEPTUS TERRAE: Adept of Earth, seated in the North[158]
The officers should be dressed in white robes with robes and nemyses in flashing elemental colors.

Preparation: The temple is set up in accordance with the General Setup for the Adept in the Portal Hall. Pillars are in the East. Enochian Tablets are in their respective quarters,

157. Located in the Air column of the Water row.

158. In this instance, the four officers align perfectly with their quarter or elemental direction according to the Four Winds, but this is not always the case depending on the square chosen.

preferably on side altars with glassed pillar candles in the appropriate elemental colors. Incense sticks are in the South, and a Stolistes Cup of water is in the West.

There is a White central Altar, upon which are placed:

- Elemental Tools (Dagger, Wand, Cup, and Pentacle) and incense
- Tablet of Union
- Three-dimensional Abai pyramid in color[159]

Each officer will need a flat, laminated diagram of the Abai pyramid in color. Adeptus Spiritus will need a Lotus Wand. A large white triangle should be placed on the floor between the pillars in the East.

Synopsis: Adepts open with the LBRP, consecration and purification. This is followed by a three-center Middle Pillar, vibrating the Three Holy Secret Names of God associated with Earth.

Adeptus Terrae opens the Tablet of Earth, and all Officers trace invoking pentagrams of Spirit passive and Earth over the central Altar. All five Officers assume the godform of Osiris.

Next comes the Yeheshuah Formula and the Watchtower invocations, beginning with Establishment of Yod:

1. Adeptus Ignis traces the invoking Pentagram of Earth (for the Earth Tablet) and the Invoking Pentagram of Fire for the establishment of Yod-Fire and then invokes Tasame, the Kerubic Angel of Fire, for the Subangle.
2. Adeptus Aquae traces the invoking Pentagram of Earth (for the Earth Tablet) and the Invoking Pentagram of Water for the establishment of Heh-Water and then invokes Metas, the Kerubic Angel of Water, for the Subangle.
3. Adeptus Aeris traces the invoking Pentagram of Earth (for the Earth Tablet) and the Invoking Pentagram of Air for the establishment of Vav-Air, and then invokes Sameta, the Kerubic Angel of Air, for the Subangle.
4. Adeptus Terrae traces the invoking Pentagram of Earth (for the Earth Tablet) and the Invoking Pentagram of Earth for the establishment of Heh-Final-Earth, and then invokes Asamet, the Kerubic Angel of Earth, for the Subangle.

159. This can be created out of paper, folded and taped.

5. Adeptus Spiritus invokes Spirit Passive over the Tablet of Union and invokes the Divine Names of Invocation and Obligation from the Sephirotic Cross of the Subangle.

The evocation of Aabai takes place, commencing with the Adepts circumambulating to build the energy, followed by the Hermetic Adoration. Two Enochian Keys are read, one for Earth and one for Fire of Earth. Individually, the Adepts trace the Enochian letters of the name Aabai toward the space between the pillars above the triangle. They vibrate the name of the Angel several times. When the angel appears, Adeptus Spiritus leads the working. When finished, the pyramid of Aabai is closed.

Opening Formula

Adeptus Spiritus: Battery of Knocks 4-1.

Adeptus Spiritus: **Hekas, Hekas, este Bebeloi. Far, far from this Sacred Place be the profane.**

Adeptus Aeris performs the LBRP.

Adeptus Aquae and Adeptus Ignis perform Purification and Consecration with water and incense as follows:

Adeptus Aquae purifies with Water by tracing the Cross and Water Triangle in all Quarters. When returning to the east, says: **I purify with Water.**

Adeptus Ignis consecrates with Fire by tracing the Cross and Fire Triangle in all Quarters. When returning to the east, says: **I consecrate with Fire.**

Adeptus Aquae and Adeptus Ignis return to place. All perform the Qabalistic Cross.

All perform a Three-center Middle Pillar, vibrating **EMOR** at Kether, **DIAL** at Malkuth, **HECTEGA** for Tiphareth.

Adeptus Spiritus goes to the Earth Tablet in the North and traces the Invoking Spirit Passive Pentagram with Spirit Wheel.[160] All vibrate **NANTA** as Adeptus Spiritus

160. Except for the LBRP at the beginning, vibrate only Enochian names for the pentagrams, not Hebrew.

charges the center of the figure. Adeptus Spiritus gives the Sign of the Rending of the Veil.

Adeptus Terrae goes to the Earth Tablet in the North and traces the Invoking Earth Pentagram with Taurus symbol ♉. All vibrate **EMOR, DIAL, HECTEGA** as Adeptus Terrae charges the center of the figure. Adeptus Spiritus gives the Zelator Sign.

All come to the Altar at the center, Adeptus Aeris in East, Adeptus Ignus in South, Adeptus Aquae in West, Adeptus Terrae in North, Adeptus Spiritus east or northeast of Adeptus Aeris. All trace Invoking Spirit Passive Pentagram over Altar with Spirit Wheel in center ⊛. All charge figure in center by vibrating **NANTA.** All give the Sign of the Rending of the Veil.

All trace Invoking Earth Pentagram over Altar with Taurus ♉ symbol in center. All charge figure in center by vibrating **EMOR, DIAL, HECTEGA.** All give the Zelator Sign.

Adeptus Spiritus: **Now let us assume the Divine form of the God who governs the Square of Abai—Osiris, God of the Four Elements in Equilibrium under the uniting influence of Spirit.** *(All give Sign of Osiris Slain.)*

All: **OUSIRI.** *(Vibrate five times while assuming godform.)*

Adeptus Spiritus: *(Folding arms in Sign of Osiris Risen)* **Anok Ousiri.**[161]
Adeptus Ignus: *(Folding arms in Sign of Osiris Risen)* **Anok Ousiri.**
Adeptus Aquae: *(Folding arms in Sign of Osiris Risen)* **Anok Ousiri.**
Adeptus Aeris: *(Folding arms in Sign of Osiris Risen)* **Anok Ousiri.**
Adeptus Terrae: *(Folding arms in Sign of Osiris Risen)* **Anok Ousiri.**

---

161. Coptic for "I am Osiris."

Yeheshuah Formula and Watchtower Invocations: THE ESTABLISHMENT OF YOD

י

Adeptus Ignus goes sunwise to East of Altar and takes up Fire Wand. Adeptus Ignus then goes to South of the Temple and stands facing South.[162] Adeptus Ignus uses the Fire Wand to mark the three points of the Fire Triangle in the South. Elevating the Implement, the Adeptus Ignus then circumambulates the Hall once and says:

Adeptus Ignus: *(Circumambulating)* **And when after all the phantoms have been banished, thou shalt see that Holy and formless fire, that Fire which darts and flashes through the hidden depths of the Universe.** *(Completing circumambulation in the South.)* **Hear thou the voice of Fire!**

Using the Fire Wand, Adeptus Ignus traces Invoking Pentagram of Earth (for Earth Tablet) and then traces within the Pentagram the triangle symbol of Earth 🜃.

Adeptus Ignus: *(Pointing the Implement at the center of Pentagram)* **EMOR, DIAL, HECTEGA.** *(Gives the Zelator Sign.)* **In the Names and Letters of the Great Northern Quadrangle, I invoke ye, ye Angels of the Watchtower of the North!**

Using the Fire Wand, Adeptus Ignus traces Invoking Pentagram of Fire (for the establishment of Yod) and then traces within the Pentagram the Kerubic symbol of Fire—Leo ♌.

Adeptus Ignus: *(Pointing the Fire Wand at the center of Pentagram)* **TASAME.**[163] *(Gives the Sign of Philosophus.)* **In the Names and Letters of the Fire Angle of the Tablet of Earth, I invoke Thee, Tasame, Fire Kerub of Opemnire.**[164]

Adeptus Ignus replaces Fire Wand and returns sunwise to their station.

162. This is because the southern side of the pyramid of Abai is Fiery.

163. Pronounced "Tah-sah-may," the name of the Kerubic angel of Fire for the Subangle.

164. Pronounced "Ohpem-nee-ray," Divine Name of Invocation (formerly known as the Angel of Call) for the quadrant of Fire of Earth.

THE ESTABLISHMENT OF HEH

Adeptus Aquae goes sunwise to West of Altar and takes up Water Cup. Adeptus Aquae then comes to West of the Temple and stands facing West.[165] Adeptus Aquae uses the Water Cup to mark the three points of the Water Triangle in the West. Elevating the Cup, the Adeptus Aquae then circumambulates the Hall once and says:

Adeptus Ignus: *(Circumambulating)* **So therefore first, the Priest who governeth the works of Fire must sprinkle with the lustral Waters of the Loud, resounding Sea.** *(Completing circumambulation in the South.)* **Hear thou the voice of Water!**

Using the Water Cup, Adeptus Aquae traces Invoking Pentagram of Earth (for Earth Tablet) and then traces within the Pentagram the triangle symbol of Earth 🜃.

Adeptus Aquae: *(Pointing the Implement at the center of Pentagram)* **EMOR, DIAL, HECTEGA.** *(Gives the Zelator Sign.)* **In the Names and Letters of the Great Northern Quadrangle, I invoke ye, ye Angels of the Watchtower of the North!**

Using the Water Cup, Adeptus Aquae traces Invoking Pentagram of Water (for the establishment of Heh) and then traces within the Pentagram the Kerubic symbol of Water, the eagle head.

Adeptus Aquae: *(Pointing the Cup at the center of Pentagram)* **METAS.**[166] *(Gives the Sign of Practicus.)* **In the Names and Letters of the Fire Angle of the Tablet of Earth, I invoke Thee, Metas, Water Kerub of Opemnire.**

Adeptus Aquae replaces Cup and returns sunwise to his station (his station may be in the west).

---

165. This is because the western side of the pyramid of Abai is Watery.

166. Pronounced "May-tas," the name of the Kerubic angel of Water for the Subangle.

THE ESTABLISHMENT OF VAV

ו

Adeptus Aeris comes sunwise to East of Altar and takes up Air Dagger. Adeptus Aeris then comes to East of the Temple and stands facing East.[167] Adeptus Aeris uses the Air Dagger to mark the three points of the Air Triangle in the East. Elevating the Dagger, the Adeptus Aeris then circumambulates the Hall once and says:

Adeptus Aeris: *(Circumambulating)* **Such a Fire existeth, extending through the rushings of Air, or even a Fire formless, whence cometh the image of a voice. Or even a flashing light, abounding, revolving, whirling forth, crying aloud.** *(Completing circumambulation in the East.)* **Hear thou the voice of Air!**

Using the Air Dagger, Adeptus Aeris traces Invoking Pentagram of Earth (for Earth Tablet) and then traces within the Pentagram the triangle symbol of Earth 🜃.

Adeptus Aeris: *(Pointing the Implement at the center of Pentagram)* **EMOR, DIAL, HECTEGA.** *(Gives the Zelator Sign.)* **In the Names and Letters of the Great Northern Quadrangle, I invoke ye, ye Angels of the Watchtower of the North!**

Using the Air Implement, Adeptus Aeris traces Invoking Pentagram of Air (for the establishment of Vav) and then traces within the Pentagram the Kerubic symbol of Air—Aquarius ♒).

Adeptus Aeris: *(Pointing the Dagger at the center of Pentagram, then Gives the Sign of Theoricus)* **SAMETA.**[168] **In the Names and Letters of the Fire Angle of the Tablet of Earth, I invoke Thee, Sameta, Air Kerub of Opemnire.**

Adeptus Aeris replaces Air Dagger and returns sunwise to his station.

---

167. This is because the eastern side of the pyramid of Abai is Airy.

168. Pronounced "Sah-may-tah," the Kerubic Angel of Air for the Subangle.

THE ESTABLISHMENT OF HEH SOPHITH

Adeptus Terrae comes sunwise to North of Altar and takes up Earth Pentacle. Adeptus Terrae then comes to East of the Temple and stands facing East.[169] Adeptus Terrae uses the Earth Pentacle to mark the three points of the Earth Triangle in the East. Elevating the Implement, the Adeptus Terrae then circumambulates the Hall once and says:

Adeptus Terrae: *(Circumambulating)* **Stoop not down into that darkly splendid world, where continually Heth a faithless depth and Hades wrapped in gloom, delighting in unintelligible images, precipitous, winding, a black ever-rolling abyss, ever espousing a body unluminous, formless and void.** *(Completing circumambulation in the North.)* **Hear thou the voice of Earth!**

Using the Earth Pentacle, Adeptus Terrae traces Invoking Pentagram of Earth (for Earth Tablet) and then traces within the Pentagram the triangle symbol of Earth ∇.

Adeptus Terrae: *(Pointing the Implement at the center of Pentagram)* **EMOR, DIAL, HECTEGA.** *(Gives the Zelator Sign.)* **In the Names and Letters of the Great Northern Quadrangle, I invoke ye, ye Angels of the Watchtower of the North!**

Using the Earth Pentacle, Adeptus Terrae traces Invoking Pentagram of Earth (for the establishment of Heh Sophith) and then traces within the Pentagram the Kerubic symbol of Earth—Taurus ♉.

Adeptus Terrae: *(Pointing the Implement at the center of Pentagram)* **ASAMET.**[170] *(Gives the Sign of Zelator.)* **In the Names and Letters of the Fire Angle of the Tablet of Earth, I invoke Thee, Asamet, Earth Kerub of Opemnire.**

Adeptus Terrae replaces Implement and returns sunwise to his station.

---

169. This is because the northern side of the pyramid of Abai is Earthy.

170. Pronounced "Ah-sah-met," the Kerubic Angel of Earth for the Subangle.

THE DESCENT OF SHIN

Adeptus Spiritus, West of the Altar, takes up Incense from the center of the Altar. Adeptus Spiritus then uses the Incense to mark the three points of the Supernal Triangle above the Altar (centered above the Tablet of Union).

Adeptus Spiritus: *(Tracing a clockwise Circle in the horizontal plane above the Tablet)* **There is a fifth in the Middle, another Channel of Light, where the life-bearing Light descends as far as the Material Channels.** *(Completing Circle.)* **Hear thou the Voice of Spirit.**

Using the Incense, the Adeptus Spiritus traces in the vertical plane over the Tablet of Union the Invoking Pentagram of Spirit Passive, and then traces within the Pentagram the Sigil of Eth, the Spirit Wheel ⊛.

Adeptus Spiritus: *(Pointing Incense at center of Pentagram)* **NANTA.** *(Gives the Sign of the Rending of the Veil.)* **In the Names and Letters of the Mystical Tablet of Union, which binds together the Four Tablets into One under the presidency of the Spirit, I invoke ye, ye Divine Forces of the Spirit of Life!**

Using the Incense, the Adeptus Spiritus traces in the vertical plane over the Tablet of Union the Calvary Cross while vibrating the Divine Names of Fire of Earth[171] as follows:

Adeptus Spiritus: *(Tracing vertical shaft of the Cross)* **OPEMNIRE.** *(For horizontal arm of the Cross, vibrate)* **ILPIZODA.**[172] **I invoke ye also in the Holy Names and Letters of the Sephirotic Calvary Cross governing the Fire Angle of the Watchtower of Earth, ye Divine Forces of the Spirit of Life!**

---

171. These names represent the Sephirotic Cross of the Lesser Angle of Fire of Earth.

172. Pronounced "Ee-el-pee-zod-ah," Divine Name of Obligation (formerly known as the Angel of Command).

ADEPTUS SPIRITUS makes the Sign of the Rending of the Veil, followed by the LVX Signs in Silence, then replaces the incense upon the Altar.

ADEPTUS SPIRITUS: **Ol sonuf vaoresagi, goho Jada Balata. ELEXARPEH. COMANANU, TABITOM. Zodacareme eca, od zodameranu! Odo Cicale Qaa, Piape Piamoel od Vaoan.**

I invoke ye, ye angels of the Celestial Spheres whose dwelling is in the Invisible. Ye are the guardians of the Gates of the Universe. Be ye also the guardians of this mystic sphere. Keep far removed the evil and the unbalanced. Strengthen and inspire us, so that we may preserve unsullied this abode of Mysteries of the Eternal Gods. Let this place be pure and holy, so that we may enter in and become a partaker of the secrets of the Light Divine.

ADEPTUS SPIRITUS takes his Lotus Wand and goes sunwise to the Northeast.

ADEPTUS SPIRITUS: **The visible sun in the dispenser of light to the Earth. Let us therefore form a vortex in this chamber that the invisible sun of Spirit may shine therein from above.**

ALL circumambulate thrice then return to place.

ALL perform the Adoration to the Lord of the Universe:

Holy art Thou, Lord of the Universe,
Holy art Thou, Whom Nature hath not formed.
Holy art Thou, the Vast and the Mighty One.
Lord of the Light, and of the Darkness.

ALL assume the Sign of Osiris Risen.

The Evocation of Aabai

Adeptus Terrae: **Hear ye the Fifth Angelic Key revealed unto Enoch, which calleth the Powers of Earth.** *(Recite the Fifth Key in Enochian.)*

Sapah Zimmi DU-I-V Od Noas Ta Qanis Adroch Dorphal Caosg Od Faonts Piripsol Ta Blior. Casarm A-M-Ipzi Nazarth AF Od Dlugar Zizpo Zlida Caosgi Tol Torgi: Od Z Chis E Siasch L Ta-Vi-U Od Iaod Thild Ds Hubar P E O A L Soba Cormfa Chis Ta La Vls Od Q Cocasb. Eca Niis Od Darbs Qaas F Etharzi Od Biliora. Ia-Ial Ed-Nas Cicles. Bagle? Ge-Iad I L.

(Others may chant **Emor, Dial,** *and* **Hectega** *under this Calling of the Key softly in the background.)*

After reading the Key, Adeptus Terrae assumes the Sign of Zelator.

Adeptus Ignus: **Hear ye the Fifteenth Angelic Key revealed unto Enoch, which calleth the Powers of Fire of Earth.** *(Recite the Fifteenth Key in Enochian.)*

Ilasa! tabaanu li-El pereta, casaremanu upaahi cahisa dareji; das oado caosaji oresacore: das omaxa monasaci Baeouibe od emetajisa Iaiadix. Zodacare od Zodameranu! Odo cicale Qaa. Zodoreje, lape zodiredo Noco Mada, hoathahe I-A-I-D-A.

(Others may chant **OPEMNIRE** *and* **ILPIZODA** *under this Calling of the Key softly in the background.)*

After reading the Key, Adeptus Ignus assumes the Sign of Philosophus.

Adeptus Spiritus: **O thou mighty Archangel who governeth the plane of this Square, we as Adepts of the Rose of Ruby and the Cross of Gold call thee forth in respect, in friendship, and in service to the Great Work. We call thee in the Divine Names which govern the Earth Tablet and the Watchtower of the North:**

All: **EMOR. DIAL. HECTEGA.**

ADEPTUS SPIRITUS: **And in the Divine Names which govern the Fiery Lesser Angle of the Tablet of the North—**

ALL: **OPEMNIRE. ILPIZODA.**

ADEPTUS SPIRITUS: **And in Thine own true Archangelic Name of Light—**

Figure 55: Una

ADEPTUS SPIRITUS: *(Standing, traces the letter Una [the Enochian letter for A] toward the space between the Pillars above the Triangle)* Vibrates: **UNA.** *(Makes the Sign of the Rending of the Veil and remains in the Sign of the Cross.)*

ADEPTUS AERIS: *(Standing, traces the letter Una [the Enochian letter for A] toward the space between the Pillars above the Triangle)* Vibrates: **UNA.** *(Assumes the Sign of Theoricus.)*

Figure 56: Pa

ADEPTUS AQUAE: *(Standing, traces the letter Pa [the Enochian letter for B] toward the space between the Pillars above the Triangle)* Vibrates: **PA.** *(Assumes the Sign of Practicus.)*

ADEPTUS IGNUS: *(Standing, traces the letter Una [the Enochian letter for A] toward the space between the Pillars above the Triangle)* Vibrates: **UNA.** *(Assumes the Sign of Philosophus.)*

Figure 57: Gonu

Adeptus Terrae: *(Standing, traces the letter Gonu [the Enochian letter for I] toward the space between the Pillars above the Triangle)* Vibrates: **GONU.** *(Assumes the Sign of Zelator.)*

Adeptus Spiritus: *(Making the Sign of the Rending of the Veil)* **AABAI.** *(Remains in the Sign of the Cross.)*

Adeptus Aeris: *(Making the Sign of the Rending of the Veil)* **AABAI.** *(Remains in the Sign of the Cross.)*

Adeptus Aquae: *(Making the Sign of the Rending of the Veil)* **AABAI.** *(Remains in the Sign of the Cross.)*

Adeptus Ignis: *(Making the Sign of the Rending of the Veil)* **AABAI.** *(Remains in the Sign of the Cross.)*

Adeptus Terrae: *(Making the Sign of the Rending of the Veil)* **AABAI.** *(Remains in the Sign of the Cross.)*

All: *(Using the Vibratory Formula of the Middle Pillar with the Projection Sign)* **AABAI. AABAI. AABAI.**

Aabai appears between the Pillars and the Five Adepti give the Sign of Silence. Five Adepti then give the LVX Signs and Aabai responds with the same.

Adeptus Spiritus leads Working with Aabai.

Closing the Pyramid of Abai

When All are ready, Adeptus Spiritus gives a single Knock. All rise.

ADEPTUS SPIRITUS takes up his Lotus Wand and goes to the Southeast and says: **The Sun, daily setting, is the Bringer of Repose to the Earth. Let us devolve the Whorl by thrice completing the Circle of this Place, the Abode of the Invisible Sun.**

ALL perform the Mystic Reverse Circumambulation (thrice) and then return to place.

ALL perform the Adoration to the Lord of the Universe:

Holy art Thou, Lord of the Universe,
Holy art Thou, Whom Nature hath not formed.
Holy art Thou, the Vast and the Mighty One.
Lord of the Light, and of the Darkness.

ADEPTUS SPIRITUS goes sunwise to the north of the Altar and takes up the Earth Pentacle. He goes sunwise to the north and stands facing the Tablet of Earth. Using the Earth Pentacle, he traces a counterclockwise Circle around the Tablet. He then traces within the circle the Banishing Pentagram of Earth. He traces the Kerubic symbol of Earth (Taurus ♉) in the center.

ADEPTUS SPIRITUS: *(Pointing Implement at center of Pentagram)* **EMOR, DIAL, HECTEGA.** *(All give the sign of Zelator.)* **In the names and letters of the Great Northern Quadrangle, I now free any Spirits that may have been imprisoned by this Ceremony.**

ADEPTUS SPIRITUS traces the Banishing Spirit Passive Pentagram with Spirit Wheel. ADEPTUS SPIRITUS vibrates **NANTA** as he charges the center of the figure. ADEPTUS SPIRITUS gives the Sign of the Closing of the Veil. He returns the Earth Element to the Altar.

OTHER ADEPTI (IGNUS, AQUAE, AERIS, and TERRAE) all take up their Elemental Implement and go sunwise to their respective Quarters. In unison and in silence, they each trace the Banishing Earth Pentagram toward the Quarter and give the Zelator Sign. They then trace the Banishing Pentagram of their respective element and give the appropriate Sign.

ADEPTUS SPIRITUS goes sunwise to West of the Altar and takes up Incense from the center of the Altar. ADEPTUS SPIRITUS then uses the Incense to trace a counterclockwise Circle above the Altar (centered above the Tablet of Union). Using the Incense, the

ADEPTUS SPIRITUS traces in the vertical plane over the Tablet of Union the Banishing Pentagram of Spirit Passive and then traces within the Pentagram the Sigil of Eth, the Spirit Wheel.

ADEPTUS SPIRITUS: *(Pointing Incense at center of Pentagram)* **NANTA.** *(Gives the Sign of the Closing of the Veil.)*

ADEPTUS SPIRITUS replaces Incense upon the Altar and takes up his Lotus Wand.

ADEPTUS SPIRITUS: **Depart ye all in peace unto your appointed Abodes. May the blessings of Iada**[173] **be with you now and forevermore. Be there always peace between us and you, and be ye ready to come when ye are called.**

ADEPTUS SPIRITUS traces a Circled Cross in the Air toward the East and says: **IADA.**

ALL: **Not unto us but unto Thy Name be the glory, Who has allowed us to enter thus far into Thy Sacred Mysteries.** Vibrate: **AMEN.**

ADEPTUS SPIRITUS: **Tetelstai. It is finished. I now declare this temple duly closed. So mote it be.**

✠✠✠

Consecration of an Enochian Talisman

This ceremony is designed for two Adepts. Its purpose is to consecrate a pair of Enochian talismans created from one of the Kerubic squares of the Enochian Tablet of Earth—specifically the square of Kerubic Fire, symbolized by the Sign of Leo ♌ in the Subangle of Fire of the Earth Tablet, to which is assigned the Enochian letter Gisagi (equivalent to the letter *T*). The design of the talismans is based upon the truncated pyramid design of the Enochian square Tasame, which is also the name of the Kerubic Angel of the square.

Figure 58: Gisagi

173. "God."

This particular working has three main sections. First, the ceremony is opened in the Grade of Zelator, which resonates with the Earthy nature of the talisman. Second, the talismans are created from and charged with forces from the Subangle of Fire of Earth. Third, each Adept charges their own talisman not only for the purpose of magical inspiration but also for use as a skrying symbol though which the Adept can explore the energies of the square's Enochian realm.

Synopsis: The Adepts open the Zelator Hall and invoke the energies of elemental Earth and the Sephirah Malkuth. This is followed by the *Enochian Invoking Ritual of the Pentagram*, beginning with the *Enochian Cross*. The Archangels invoked after the Enochian Cross is performed (Nusameta, Enasameta, Entasame, and Numetasa) are the Kerubic archangels of the Fire quadrant of the Earth Tablet.

The Tablet of the north is invoked with the Zelator Earth invocation, followed by the reading of the 5th Enochian Key (or Call) of Earth and the 15th Key of Fire of Earth. The Adepts invoke Opemnire and Ilpezda, the Divine names of Invocation and Obligation for the Fire quadrant of the Earth Tablet. Then they invoke the Kerubic Archangel and the Kerubic Angel of the square (Entasame and Tasame) while tracing the initial Enochian letters of their names.

The talismans are purified, consecrated, and anointed, and pentagrams are traced over them before the Adepts begin to skry the square. When finished, the rite is closed down.

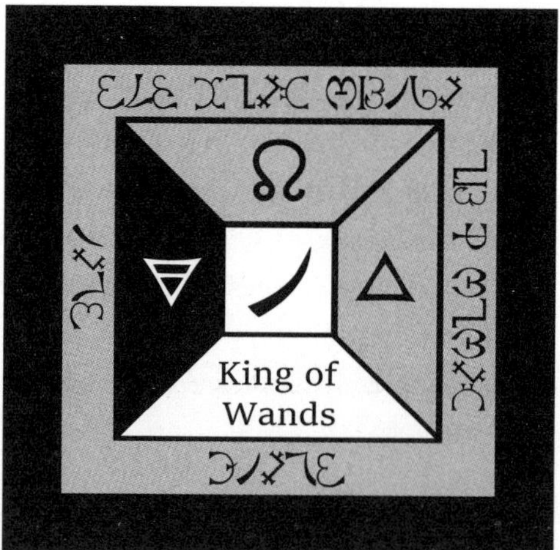

Figure 59: Talisman for Enochian Square of Tasame

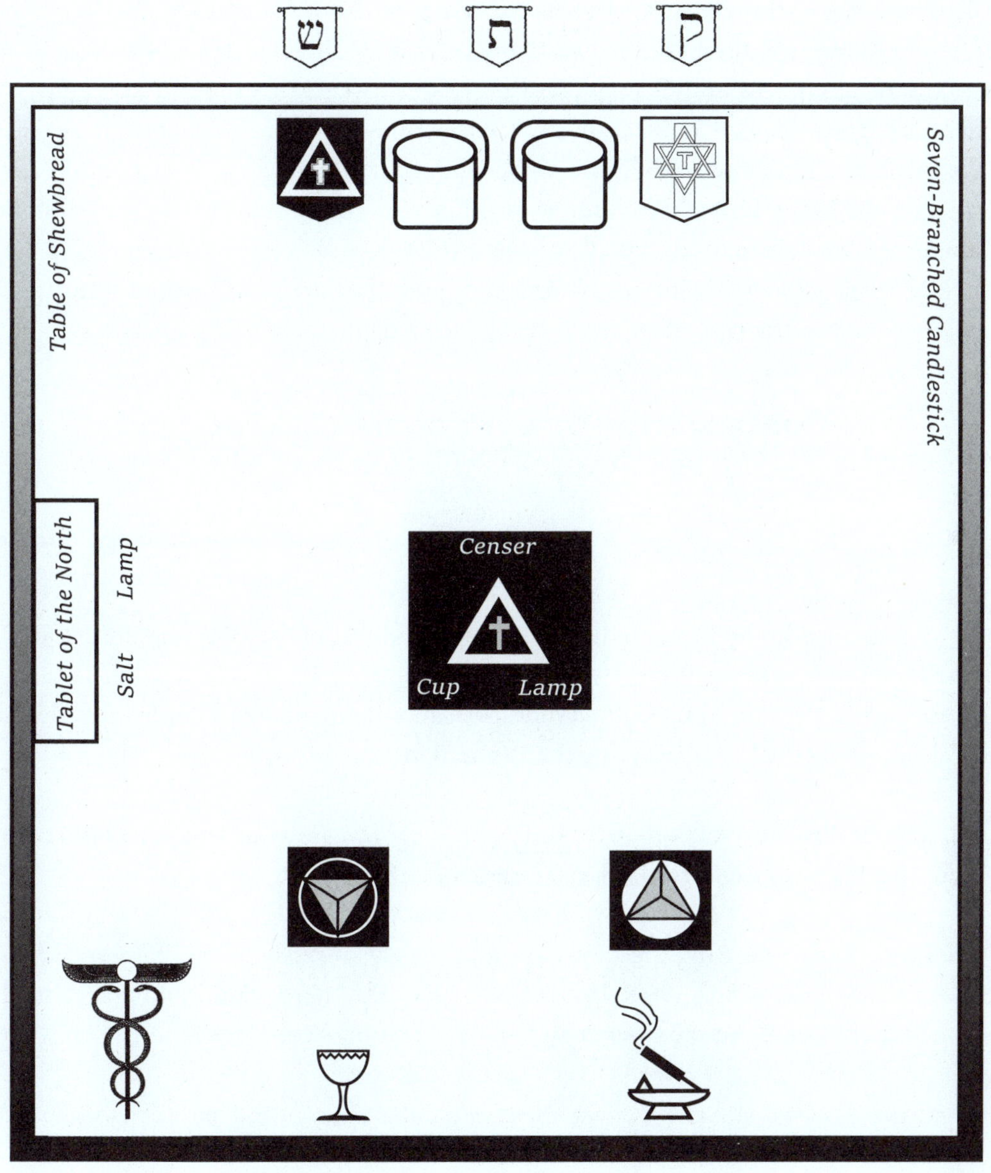

Figure 60: The Zelator Hall Setup for Two Adepts

Temple Setup: Arranged as for the Second Point of the Zelator Ceremony (see figure 60).[174] Two thrones in the East, the two Banners, and the three Portals of Qesheth in the East. The Zelator Cross and Triangle on the Altar, with an Air Censer, Fire Lamp, and Water Cup. The Stolistic Cup, Dadouchic Censer, and Kerykeion[175] should be available in the West. The Emblems of the Table of Shewbread and the Seven-Branched Menorah may be on the Walls, and the Flaming Sword Between the Kerubayim on the West face of the Altar. Two Talismans designed as in figure 59.

(NOTE: Have the following ready for a later point in the ritual: a cup of water, a vial of oil, incense, and the two talismans, one for each Adept.)

Consecration of an Enochian Talisman for Magical Inspiration

By Jayne Gibson

General Opening

Adepts are seated in the East, meditating upon the object of the Working until ready to begin. The First Adept gives one single Knock and rises to stand before the Throne of the East, facing West, holding Lotus Wand by White Band. Second Adept stands, facing West, holding the Lotus Wand by the White Band.

First Adept: **Unseen Watchers over our Sacred Order, assist us to open this Temple of the Magic of Light in the 1=10 Grade of Zelator.**

The Second Adept, bearing the Lotus Wand, proceeds directly to the West and stands between the Pillars, facing West. Holds Lotus Wand by Black Band and traces to the West with the Black Band the Cherev Sigil of the Flaming Sword (see figure 4).

The Second Adept again grips the White Band of the Lotus Wand and turns sunwise to face the Altar and salute with the Step and Sign of the Zelator.

174. In addition to the Tablet of the North, the Tablet of Union could be present, either in the north, on the central Altar, or above the eastern throne. (The other three Tablets should also be present but hidden under veils.)

175. Keryx Wand.

First Adept returns the Sign to the Altar.

First Adept sets aside the Lotus Wand in the East and then goes sunwise to the West of the Hall and takes up the Dadouchos Censer. Second Adept takes up the Stolistes Cup. Both proceed to their proper Pillars.

First Adept *(elevating Lamp in both hands)*: **When, after all the phantoms are banished, thou shalt see that holy and formless Fire, that Fire which darts and flashes through the hidden depths of the Universe, hear thou the voice of Fire!**

First Adept consecrates toward the East, tracing the Cross and touching the three vertices of the Fire Triangle.

First Adept *(elevating Censer)*: **I consecrate with Fire.**

Second Adept *(elevating Cup)*: **First, the Priest/ess, who governeth the Works of Fire, must sprinkle with the lustral Waters of the Loud and Resounding Sea. Hear thou the Voice of Water!**

Second Adept purifies toward the East, tracing the Cross and lustrating the three vertices of the Water Triangle.

Second Adept *(raising Cup on high)*: **I purify with Water.**

First Adept then takes up the Kerykeion and walks directly Eastward between the Pillars until East of the Pillars.

First Adept *(elevating Wand of Keryx in both hands)*: **The Temple is cleansed.**

First Adept returns to the West and replaces the Keryx Wand. First Adept then proceeds sunwise to the East and retrieves the Lotus Wand. Second Adept returns to the West and replaces the Cup.

First Adept is standing in the East, facing West in the Sign of Osiris Slain. Second Adept assumes this same pose.

First Adept: **By Names and Images are all Powers awakened and reawakened. The Name of the Element to which this Grade is attributed, that it may be reawakened within my Sphere and in the Sphere of this Order.** *(Holding Lotus Wand by Red-Orange Band of Taurus, the Adept traces the Kerubic Shor Sigil ♉ with the White Floral Head of the Lotus Wand.)* **ADONAI HA-ARETZ** *(still holding the Lotus Wand by the Red-Orange Band of Taurus, let the Adept trace the Alchemic Terra Sigil 🜃 with the White Floral Head of the Lotus Wand)***, the Element of Earth.**

And I name the Sephirah to which this Grade corresponds, that it may be reawakened in the Spheres of those present and in the Sphere of this Order. *(Holding Lotus Wand by the White Band, let the Adept trace a Circle with the White Floral Head of the Wand.)* **Malkuth, the Kingdom, being the tenth Sephirah of the Tree of Life.**

First Adept knocks once.

First Adept *(facing West with both arms raised)*: **We shall adore the Lord and King of Earth.**

Both Adepts face the East.

Second Adept *(elevating the Lotus Wand in both hands by White Band)*: **ADONAI HA-ARETZ. ADONAI MELEKH.** *(Tracing Qabalistic Cross over self)* **Unto Thee be the Kingdom, the Power and the Glory. Atah, Malkuth, ve-Geburah, ve-Gedulah.** *(Traces Qabalistic Cross to East. Traces circle in Cross to create Rose Cross.)* **Chavatzeleth ha-Sharon, Shoshanath ha-Amaqim—The Rose of Sharon and the Lilly of the Valley.** *(Gives Projecting Sign to the East.)* **Amen!** *(Assumes the Sign of Silence, remaining in contemplation of the Divine Glory beyond the Veil in the East.)*

First Adept *(with Lotus Wand)* comes sunwise to the West and takes up Keryx Wand. Second Adept *(with Lotus Wand)* follows the First to the North, both standing in front of the Tablet.

First Adept *(holding Keryx Wand)* takes up the Paten of Salt and stands facing North.

First Adept: **Let the Earth adore Adonai!**
(Casts a pinch of Salt to the North.) Both Adepts vibrate: **ADONAI**
(Casts a second pinch of Salt to the North.) Both Adepts vibrate: **ADONAI**
(Casts a third pinch of Salt to the North.) Both Adepts vibrate: **ADONAI**

First Adept puts aside Keryx Wand and takes up Lotus Wand, then goes to sit in the East.

Second Adept goes to East of Altar to begin the Enochian Invoking Ritual of the Pentagram for the Kerubic square beginning with the *Enochian Cross.*

The Enochian Invoking Ritual of the Pentagram

Second Adept: *(Making Cross.)*

GEH *("thou art")*
LONUDOHA *("kingdom")*
MICAOLZODA *("power")*
BUSADA *("glory")*
GOHED *("everlasting")*[176]

Second Adept makes Invoking Pentagrams of Earth in all Quarters.

Second Adept: *(Standing in Sign of Cross.)*

Before me, NUSAMETA.
Behind me, ENASAMETA.
On my right hand, ENTASAME.
On my left hand, NUMETASA.[177]

---

176. Using only Enochian letters, these words are Geh, Londoh, Micaolz, Busd, Gohed. Vowels are added to make the words more pronounceable.

177. In Enochian letters, the names are transliterated as NSMTA, NASMT, NTSAM, NMTAS.

For about me flame the Pentagrams, and within the Column shines the Six-rayed Star.

SECOND ADEPT: *(Making Cross.)*
GEH *("thou art")*
LONUDOHA *("kingdom")*
MICAOLZODA *("power")*
BUSADA *("glory")*
GOHED *("everlasting")*

BOTH ADEPTS go the North. Both face the Northern Watchtower Tablet.

FIRST ADEPT: **And the Elohim said, "Let us make ADAM in our Image, after Our likeness, and let them have dominion over the fish of the sea and over the fowl of the air and over the cattle and over all of the Earth, and over every creeping thing that creepeth over the Earth."** *(Holding Lotus Wand by Red-Orange Band, traces an invoking Circle before the Tablet with the White Floral head of the Wand.)* **And the Elohim created *Eth-ha-Adam* in Their own Image, in the Image of the Elohim created They them. In the name of Adonai Melekh and of the Bride, Malkah, Queen of the Kingdom ...**

BOTH ADEPTS *(give Zelator Sign)*: **Spirits of Earth adore Adonai!**

FIRST ADEPT *(traces Kerubic Shor Sigil ♉ within the Pentagram)*: **In the name of Uriel, the Great Archangel of the Earth, and the Kerubic Sigil of Shor, the Ox.** *(Gives Zelator Sign.)* **Spirits of Earth, adore Adonai!**

FIRST ADEPT *(traces Vertical Line of the Great Cross before the Watchtower)*: **In the Names and Letters of the Great Northern Quadrangle revealed unto Enoch by the Great Angel Ave.** *(Gives Zelator Sign.)* **Spirits of Earth, adore Adonai!**

FIRST ADEPT *(traces Horizontal Line of the Great Cross before the Watchtower)*: **In the Three Great Secret Names of God, borne upon the Banners of the North—MOR DIAL HECTEGA.** *(Gives Zelator Sign.)* **Spirits of Earth, adore Adonai!**

First Adept *(traces Invoking Royal Spiral at the Center of the Great Cross before the Watchtower)*: **In the Name of IC ZOD HEH HAL, Great Queen of the North.** *(Gives Zelator Sign.)* **Spirits of Earth, adore Adonai!**

First Adept: **In and by these Divine and Angelic Names, most potent in the Northern Quarter and in the Element of Earth.** *(Both Adepts make the Sign of Rending the Veil, and remain in Cross.)* **We open the Gates of the North, that the Holy Powers of Earth may indwell this Temple and illumine our Work herein as an Adept of the Rose of Ruby and the Cross of Gold.** *(Both Adepts stand in Osiris Risen and open Clairvoyant awareness in the Spirit Vision to the influx of the Holy Powers of Earth into the Sanctuary.)*

First Adept then lights the Elemental Lamp before the Watchtower of the North.

Opening the Tablet and Square

First Adept reads the Enochian Key of Earth (5th Key) as follows:

> **Sapah Zimmi DU-I-V Od Noas Ta Qanis Adroch Dorphal Caosg Od Faonts Piripsol Ta Blior. Casarm A-M-Ipzi Nazarth AF Od Dlugar Zizpo Zlida Caosgi Tol Torgi: Od Z Chis E Siasch L Ta-Vi-U Od Iaod Thild Ds Hubar P E O A L Soba Cormfa Chis Ta La Vls Od Q Cocasb. Eca Niis Od Darbs Qaas F Etharzi Od Biliora. Ia-Ial Ed-Nas Cicles. Bagle? Ge-Iad I L.**

First Adept traces the Invoking Spirit Passive Pentagram and gives the Sign of the Rending of Veil over entire Tablet.

Second Adept *(traces Invoking Earth Pentagram over the entire Tablet, tracing the Bull ♉ sigil, vibrating)*: **EMOR DIAL HECTAGA** (including **IC ZOD HE HAL**, if desired). Both Adepts give Zelator Sign.

First Adept reads the Key of Fire of Earth (15th Key) as follows:

> **Ilasa! tabaanu li-El pereta, casaremanu upaahi cahisa dareji; das oado caosaji oresacore: das omaxa monasaci Baeouibe od emetajisa Iaiadix. Zodacare od**

Zodameranu! Odo cicale Qaa. Zodoreje, lape zodiredo Noco Mada, hoathahe I-A-I-D-A.

First Adept traces Invoking Fire Pentagram (including Leo ♌ Kerubic sigil) over the subangle, vibrating **OPEMNIRE** and **ILPEZODA.**[178]

Figure 61: Daruxa

Second Adept traces Invoking Fire Pentagram, vibrating **OPEMNIRE.**
Second Adept *(traces the Enochian letter Daruxa while vibrating)*: **ENTASAME.**
Second Adept *(traces the Enochian letter Gisagi [see figure 58] while vibrating)*: **TASAME.**[179]

First Adept goes to the East; Second Adept to the West.

Both Adepts elevate their Lotus Wand by the White Band.

First Adept: **In the Divine Names of ADONAI HA-ARETZ, ADONAI MELEKH, I declare that we have opened the Gate of the Gods and entered the Immeasurable Region and proclaim this Temple of Magic of Light duly open in the 1=10 Grade of Zelator of the Hermetic Order of the Golden Dawn.**

First Adept: (Knocks וווו - ווו - ווו)

Second Adept: (Knocks וווו - ווו - ווו)

Consecration of the Talismans

A Cup of Water, a Vial of Oil, and Incense are on the Altar. The Incense is to the apex of the Triangle; the Cup of Water is to the left basal angle; the Vial of Oil is to the right basal angle.

---

178. In Enochian lettering, these transliterated names are spelled OPMNIR and ILPIZ.

179. Transliterated as NTASM and TASM.

Both Adepts are in the East.

First Adept (with Talisman) goes to the West of the Altar, facing East.

First Adept: **O ADONAI, ADONAI, open for me the Gates of Wisdom and Righteousness, that I may enter in this sacred place, for without are darkness and sorrow, and the eyes open in vain. Thou Vast and the Mighty One! How precious, Lord, Thy Love! Hence the children of Earth take refuge in the Shadow of Thy Wings.**

First Adept anoints Talisman with Oil.

First Adept: **When my earthly part has burnt to ashes, my spirit shall arise and my soul shall seek the Lord.**

First Adept replaces the Oil on the Altar. Takes up the Cup of Water and purifies Talisman.

First Adept: **I shall draw Water from the Living Spring, because it has been opened to me, and I shall take the Water of Life freely and be cleansed, for fair it is and pure, and gives rest to the Soul. Purify my earthly parts, O Lord, purge away the old leaven; for it is through the Fires and Waters of this earthly life that I am prepared for the things that are of Heaven.**

First Adept replaces the Cup on the Altar and takes up the Incense. Censes the Talisman.

First Adept: **O ADONAI, ADONAI, Indwelling One, Mystic God of Love, who dwellest in the hearts of Humanity and in the secret soul of the Universe, I lay my heart upon Thy shrine. I beseech Thee in the Name of EMR DIAL HECTGA, and in the tremendous Name of Strength ENTASAME, hear my prayer: May Thy holy word be understood and adored in the world and may the kingdom of Thy Holy Spirit come unto me. Permeate this Talisman with Thy Holy Fire that it may infuse my soul with passion and inspiration for the Great Work and imbue my mind with ceaseless wonder and joy in all magical endeavors.**

First Adept returns to the East. Second Adept comes to the West of the Altar, facing East, and repeats the same procedure as above.

First Adept comes (with Talisman) and stands between the Pillars. Advances to the Black Pillar, raises Lotus Wand, and touches Talisman with Black End.

First Adept: **And the Great Angel Samael spake and said: I am the Prince of Darkness and of Night. The foolish and rebellious gaze upon the face of the created World, and find therein nothing but terror and obscurity. It is to them the Terror of Darkness and they are as drunken men stumbling in the Darkness. Return, for thou canst not pass by.**

First Adept retreats back to between the Pillars. First Adept advances to the White Pillar, raises the Lotus Wand, and touches the Talisman with the Black End.

First Adept: **The Great Angel Metatron answered and said: I am the Angel of the Presence Divine. The Wise gaze upon the created World and behold there the dazzling image of the Creator. Not yet can thine eyes bear that dazzling Image. Return, for thou canst not pass by.**

First Adept retreats back to between the Pillars. First Adept now advances up the Middle Pillar to the West of the Altar, facing East.

First Adept: **The Great Angel Sandalphon said, I am the reconciler for Earth, and the Celestial Soul therein. Form is invisible alike in Darkness and in blinding Light. I am the left hand Kerub of the Ark and the Feminine Power, as Metatron is the right hand Kerub and the Masculine Power, and I prepare the way to the Celestial Light.**

First Adept traces the Invoking Spirit Passive Pentagram over the Talisman and Rending of Veil.

First Adept traces the invoking Earth Pentagram over the Talisman, vibrating: **EMOR DIAL HECTEGA** and **IC ZOD HEH HAL.**

First Adept draws the letter Daruxa over Talisman, vibrating: **ENTASAME.**
First Adept draws Gisagi over Talisman, vibrating: **TASAME.**
First Adept makes Zelator Sign over the Talisman and goes to sit in the East.

Second Adept comes to between the Pillars and repeats this procedure.

Both Talismans are on the altar. Spirit Passive Earth, Earth and Fire Pentagrams drawn over altar. Incense is lit.

Both Adepts vibrate:

EMOR DIAL HECTEGA
ENTASAME
TASAME

Both Adepts now skry the Square.

Closing

When finished with the skrying, both Adepts go and stand to the West of the Altar, facing East.

First Adept: **In the Divine Name of MOR DIAL HECTGA, we declare that the Work for which we have assumed this temple of Fiery Earth has been accomplished faithfully. These Talismans shall be pathways for magical inspiration directed by Divine Spirit and manifesting within our souls and minds that we may ever advance in the Great Work.**

Second Adept: **Through the use of these talismans for magical inspiration, we shall be enflamed with passion and strengthened by the Powers that come through this channel, which shall be a true communication from the Divine to our human souls. This we do declare through the Powers of the Realm of Fiery Earth and by all of the Divine Names of that most lofty realm.**

First Adept: **All ye Spirits who have participated in this ceremony, depart ye in peace into your abodes. May the blessing of MOR DIAL HECTGA be upon you.**

Be there peace between us, and be ye ready to come when ye are called. *(Both Adepts make the LVX Signs.)*

The talismans are wrapped and put away.

Tablet is closed by the proper reverse Pentagrams.
Hall is closed by *SBRP of Earth*, reverse circumambulation, and adoration.

✠ ✠ ✠

Overview of the Angelic Rite of Healing

By M. Isidora Forrest

An Adept Healing Ritual employing
the Formulae of the Enochian Angelic Tablets

Introduction

This is a ritual that I created for our Adept College as part of our College's regular ritual Work. The person seeking healing need not be an Adept, but the ritual Officers should be.

This ritual employs the formulae of the Enochian or Angelic Tablets—and thus the five Elements—as well as the Pentagram, the Spiral, and information that the Angel Nalvage imparted to John Dee and Edward Kelley. Nalvage told them that, among the things that the Enochian Tablets contain, is knowledge of "the conjoining and knitting together of natures." This information is the key to the method of healing used in this ritual.

Purpose of the Rite

The purpose of this rite is, of course, healing. This may be healing of a physical nature, a mental nature, or a soul—or psychic—nature.

Ritual Formulae and Magical Structure

The overall structure of the ritual is a modified version of the Opening/Closing of the Watchtowers. Thus, the five elements (Earth, Air, Water, Fire, Spirit), represented by the Elemental Tablets and the Tablet of Union, and the Enochian Elemental Monarchs are strongly present in this rite.

The ritual features a number of five-fold patterns and spirals, as these are most often found in living things—and this rite is entirely concerned with the promotion of life and health. As an example of this five-fold formula in the rite, the Adept of Earth uses a cut apple, which reveals the five-fold seed pattern in the fruit, as one of the ritual implements of Earth.

The mechanism of the healing itself is "the conjoining and knitting together of natures" noted to Dee and Kelley by the Angel Nalvage. The Nature of the disease, ruled by an Archangel of one of the Servient Squares of one of the Enochian Tablets, is "conjoined and knit together" with the Nature of its cure, which is necessarily ruled by the same Archangel. Conjoining the disease with its cure recreates the original state of balance in the subject of the healing, enabling them to return to health.

Temple Layout and Ritual Stations of the Officers

The temple is arranged as the Portal of the Vault of the Adepts, except that there is no central Altar. In place of the Altar, the Tablet of Union is painted on a cloth, approximately 2 by 3 feet, and set on the floor in the center of the temple. The subject of the healing will eventually sit upon this cloth Tablet of Union. A sturdy canvas or other heavy cloth and acrylic paints are appropriate materials for creating this Tablet.

In the East: The Enochian Tablet of Air is placed on the Eastern wall of the temple; a small Altar is set before it. Upon the Eastern Altar is the Air Dagger and a bird's wing or large feather. This is the station of the Adept of Air, and a Throne is placed in the East for this Adept.

In the South: The Enochian Tablet of Fire is placed on the Southern wall of the temple; a small Altar is set before it. Upon the Southern Altar is the Fire Wand and a ceramic vessel filled with sand into which is sunk a container of chafing fuel (such as Sterno®). This is the station of the Adept of Fire, and a Throne is placed in the South for this Adept.

In the West: the Enochian Tablet of Water is placed on the Western wall of the temple; a small Altar is set before it. Upon the Western Altar is the Water Cup, full of pure water, a nautilus shell (cut in half to show the spiral if possible), and a libation bowl. This is the station of the Adept of Water, and a Throne is placed in the West for this Adept.

In the North: The Enochian Tablet of Earth is placed on the Northern wall of the temple; a small Altar is set before it. Upon the Northern Altar is the Pentacle, a bowl of apples, a small knife for cutting an apple, and a deep-voiced drum. This is the station of the Adept of Earth, and a Throne is placed in the North for this Adept.

In the Center: The Enochian Tablet of Union, painted on cloth as noted above, is placed on the floor. This is the station of the Adept of Spirit. If the temple space is sufficiently large, a small Throne may be placed to the East of the Tablet of Union for the Adept of Spirit. If not, the Adept of Spirit may take a Throne in the South, to the East of the Adept of Fire. The Adept of Spirit shall also have a white over-robe ready for the subject of the healing, which will be used later in the ritual.

In the Northeast: A Throne is placed for the Pola Vaoan, the subject of the healing. The Pola Vaoan's second station is in the center upon the cloth Tablet of Union. The Pola Vaoan also has a third station, in the Southeast after the healing.

In addition, the temple is decorated with living plants and small living creatures in containers (birds, fish, lizards, snakes, and so on). Larger pets may also be present if they can be still and not distract participants. All living creatures may be omitted if none are available or if the creatures would be endangered in any way. Crystals, stones, flowers, incense with a green-plant or floral scent, and a decorative censer in which to burn the incense are also recommended.

The temple is illuminated by candlelight or natural daylight only.

Roles and Deityforms of the Officers

The Adept of Air invokes the powers of Air, takes on the Godform of the Enochian King of Air, Bataivah, and assists the other Elemental Adepts in Assuming their Deityforms. The Adept of Air wears the white robe of the Adept, a yellow tabard, and the Rose Cross lamen.

The Adept of Fire invokes the powers of Fire, takes on the Godform of the Enochian King of Fire, Edelpernaa, and assists the other Elemental Adepts in Assuming their Deityforms. The Adept of Fire wears the white robe of the Adept, a red tabard, and the Rose Cross lamen.

The Adept of Water invokes the powers of Water, takes on the Goddessform of the Enochian Queen of Water, Raagiosel, and assists the other Elemental Adepts in Assuming their Deityforms. The Adept of Water wears the white robe of the Adept, a blue tabard, and the Rose Cross lamen.

The Adept of Earth invokes the powers of Earth, takes on the Goddessform of the Enochian Queen of Earth, Iczodhihal, and assists the other Elemental Adepts in Assuming their Deityforms. The Adept of Earth wears the white robe of the Adept, a black tabard, and the Rose Cross lamen.

The Adept of Spirit invokes the powers of Spirit, gives the initial invocation of the Enochian Kings and Queens, invokes the Archangel of the appropriate Servient Square, and oversees the "conjoining and knitting together of natures" of the disease and its cure. The Adept of Spirit wears the white robe of the Adept, a white tabard, and the Rose Cross lamen.

The Pola Vaoan is the subject of the healing. Pola Vaoan is Enochian for "Dual Truth," and the subject is so-named because of the two states in which they exist: the current imbalanced state and the coming balanced state. The Pola Vaoan wears a white robe only, unless they are an Adept, in which case they also wear the Rose Cross lamen.

Overview of the Ritual Actions

The ritual is opened with the Analysis of Paroketh, the Kerygma, and the Qabbalistic Cross—in Enochian. This is followed by the Analysis of the Keyword LVX (in English).

The temple is opened using a modification of the Opening by Watchtower, here called Opening the Watchtowers to Healing. Each of the Elemental Adepts invokes their specific Watchtower, and the Pola Vaoan requests healing after each invocation. Note that the Elemental Powers of the Watchtowers are invoked in Winds order (not Tetragrammaton or Cardinal order as in some other rites), because this ritual is intended to have effect in the physical world.

Next, the Elemental Monarchs are invoked and the Elemental Adepts take on the Deityform of the Monarch of their Element. All the Elemental Adepts assist each other in taking on the Deityform, but the lead in each case is the Adept opposite the Element of the Adept taking on Deityform; for example, Air is led by Water, Fire by Earth, and so on. The Elemental Adepts, with the power of their Deityform, then formulate the Seat of Mercy, a sphere of healing surrounding the Tablet of Union, which is symbolically in the Holy of Holies of the Temple.

Following this, the Archangel of the Servient Square is invoked by the Adept of Spirit and the Adept in the Deityform of the Elemental Monarch ruling the Element of the

Square; in this example, Queen Raagiosel and the Adept of Water. In the presence of the Archangel, the four Elemental Monarchs add their power to the Seat of Mercy.

The Adept of Spirit brings the Pola Vaoan to the Seat of Mercy and gives the sign of the Rending of the Veil to open the sphere of healing magic to the Pola Vaoan. The Adept of Spirit leads the Pola Vaoan in a visualization of the "conjoining and knitting together of Natures" as the Elemental Adepts assist with this magic.

The Pola Vaoan remains in meditation for as long as they wish. When ready, the Pola Vaoan rises and speaks as a signal that they have completed their meditation. With the Work complete, the Archangel is thanked and the power released. The Watchtowers are closed with the Elemental Adepts thanking the Monarchs and releasing their Deity-forms and powers. Finally, the Adepts devolve the Whorl, give praise to the Ruler of the Universe, analyze the Keyword and Paroketh, Close the Veil, and perform the Qabalistic Cross.

Preparation Required Before Working the Rite

Based on their Adept knowledge, the Adepts confer to choose a Servient Square that will represent the illness of the Pola Vaoan and its cure. The Adepts will also select the appropriate Enochian Keys to invoke that Square.

For example, in this ritual script, the Square Hedadanu was chosen. It is the Servient Square of Zodiacal Cancer.[180] Thus this Square could literally represent the disease cancer; as Air of Water, perhaps lung cancer. Or, less literally, it could represent a mental issue that is "eating away" at the Pola Vaoan. There are a WIDE range of choices Adepts could make in this matter. The Adepts will invoke the Archangel Who rules the Servient Square. Since the Archangel's name includes a letter from the Tablet of Union that is added to the name of the Angel of the Servient Square, in this case the Archangel is Cahedadanu. The Adepts will also need to ascertain the Angelic Names of Invocation and Obligation for the Square.

In preparation for the rite, the Pola Vaoan should perform a personal purification sometime prior to arriving for the ritual. If the Pola Vaoan is an Adept, let them also spend some time chanting the name of the Archangel of the Servient Square.

---

180. The servient square of Hedadanu is located in the Air quadrant of the Water Tablet (in the Water column of the Fire row).

ANGELIC RITE OF HEALING

By M. Isidora Forrest

OPENING

ADEPTS enter the temple and take their places in the appropriate quarters; ADEPT OF SPIRIT at center; East of Tablet of Union. POLA VAOAN is in the Northwest. ALL rise and face East.

ADEPT OF WATER: *(Giving Practicus sign)* **Malasa!**
ADEPT OF AIR: *(Giving Theoricus sign)* **Donu!**
ADEPT OF FIRE: *(Giving Philosophus sign)* **Gere!**
ADEPT OF EARTH: *(Giving Zelator sign)* **Emeta!**
ADEPT OF SPIRIT: **The whole word is Paroketh, which is the Veil of the Sanctum Sanctorum.**

ALL give sign of the Rending of the Veil.

ADEPT OF SPIRIT: *(Spiraling counterclockwise from the center to circumambulate the Portal, ending in the Northwest beside the POLA VAOAN, and vibrating the Enochian)* **PAREMU, PAREMU, GOSAA! Far, far from this sacred place be the profane!**

ADEPT OF SPIRIT returns to center. ALL perform Angelic Cross in Enochian, then analyze the Keyword in English. If POLA VAOAN is an Adept, they join in; if not, they stand facing East in an attitude of openness.

ANGELIC CROSS

Adepts: *(Touching crown and vibrating)* **ENONUCA I**
(Touching heart and vibrating) **ELONUDOHEH,**
(Touching right shoulder and vibrating) **MICALAZODA,**
(Touching left shoulder and vibrating) **BUSIDIRE.**
(Tracing circle) **PAEMBETA A HOMINU.**
(Folding hands) **KARESTATEOS.**

ALL Analyze the Keyword.

Opening the Watchtowers of Healing

(NOTE: Powers of the Watchtowers are invoked in Winds order because the rite is intended to have effect in the physical world.)

Adept of Air takes up Air Dagger, marks points of the Air triangle centered on the Tablet of Air. Adept of Air touches the Dagger to the Wing or Feather, then circumambulates the temple with Wing/Feather elevated.

Adept of Air: **Such a Fire existeth, extending through the rushings of Air, or even a Fire formless whence cometh the image of a Voice, or even a flashing Light, abounding, revolving, whirling forth, crying aloud:** *(facing Tablet)* **Hear thou the Voice of Air!**

With Wing, Adept of Air traces a circle around the Tablet and within it, the invoking pentagram of Air and the sigil of Adam.

Adept of Air: *(Vibrating)* **ORO, IBAH, AOZODAPI.** *(Giving Theoricus sign)* **In the Names and Letters of the Great Eastern Quadrangle, I invoke Ye, Ye Angels of the Watchtower of the East!** *(Ceasing sign)* **Come to us under the wise rulership of Bataivah, Thy King.** *(Tracing spiral of the Monarch's name on Tablet of Air and vibrating)* **BATAIVAH.**

(Assuming orant posture) **I ask Ye to bring with Ye into this temple the Living Air with its blessings of balance and knowledge of the truth. O bright-voiced Angels of the Watchtower of the East, bring with Ye the Words of Power and the healing of Air.**

Adept of Air turns to temple center.

Pola Vaoan: *(Speaking from their place in the Northeast, facing East)* **O Angels of the Watchtower of the East, breathe over me the Words of Power and bring me the healing of Air.**

Adept of Fire takes up Fire Wand, marks points of the Fire triangle centered on the Tablet of Fire. Adept of Fire touches the Wand to vessel, lights the chafing fuel, then circumambulates the temple with vessel of Fire elevated.

Adept of Fire: **And when, after all the phantoms have been banished, thou shalt see that holy and formless Fire, that Fire which darts and flashes through the hidden depths of the Universe:** *(facing Tablet of Fire)* **Hear thou the Voice of Fire!**

With Fire, Adept of Fire traces a circle around the Tablet and within it, the invoking pentagram of Fire and the sigil of Aryeh.

Adept of Fire: *(Vibrating)* **OIPE, TEAA, PEDOCE.** *(Giving Philosophus sign)* **In the Names and Letters of the Great Southern Quadrangle, I invoke Ye, Ye Angels of the Watchtower of the South!** *(Ceasing sign)* **Come to us under the powerful rulership of Edelpernaa, Thy King.** *(Tracing spiral of the Monarch's name on Tablet and vibrating)* **EDELPERNAA.** *(Assuming orant posture)* **I ask Ye to bring with Ye into this temple the Living Fire with its blessings of transformation and energy. O fiery-voiced Angels of the Watchtower of the South, bring with Ye the power to make change and the healing of Fire.**

Adept of Fire turns to temple center.

Pola Vaoan: *(Speaking from their place in the Northeast, facing South)* **O Angels of the Watchtower of the South, temper me in the alembic of change and bring me the healing of Fire** *(turning to face center)***.**

Adept of Water takes up Water Cup, marks points of the Water triangle centered on the Tablet of Water. Adept of Water touches the Cup to nautilus Shell, then circumambulates the temple with Shell elevated.

Adept of Water: **Therefore first the Priestess who governeth the works of Fire must sprinkle with the lustral water of the loud, resounding sea:** *(facing Tablet)* **Hear thou the Voice of Water!**

With Shell, Adept of Water traces a circle around the Tablet and within it, the invoking pentagram of Water and the sigil of Nesher.

Adept of Water: *(Vibrating)* **EMPEH, ARSEL, GAIOL.** *(Giving Practicus sign)* **In the Names and Letters of the Great Western Quadrangle, I invoke Ye, Ye Angels of the Watchtower of the West!** *(Ceasing sign)* **Come to us under the loving rulership of Raagiosel, Thy Queen.** *(Tracing spiral of the Monarch's name on Tablet and vibrating)* **RAAGIOSEL.**

(Assuming orant posture) **I ask Ye to bring with Ye into this temple the Living Water with its blessings of purity and rebirth. O moon-voiced Angels of the Watchtower of the West, bring with Ye soul-nourishing Magic and the healing of Water.**

Adept of Water turns to temple center.

Pola Vaoan: *(Speaking from their place in the Northeast, facing West)* **O Angels of the Watchtower of the West, feed me upon your Magic and bring me the healing of Water** *(turning to face center)*.

Adept of Earth takes up Pentacle, marks points of the Earth triangle centered on the Tablet of Earth. Adept of Earth touches the Pentacle to Apples, then cuts open one Apple crosswise to reveal the five-fold pentagram pattern within. Adept of Earth circumambulates the temple with cut Apple elevated.

Adept of Earth: **For the Creator worked the All with Her own hands so that the World-Body might be fully completed, and the world might become visible and not seem ethereal:** *(facing Tablet of Earth)* **Hear thou the Voice of Earth!**

With Apple, Adept of Earth traces a circle around the Tablet and within it, the invoking pentagram of Earth and the sigil of Shor.

Adept of Earth: *(Vibrating)* **EMOR, DIAL, HECTEGA.** *(Giving Zelator sign)* **In the Names and Letters of the Great Northern Quadrangle, I invoke Ye, Ye Angels of**

the Watchtower of the North! *(Ceasing sign)* **Come to us under the renewing rulership of Iczodhihal, Thy Queen.** *(Tracing spiral of the Monarch's name on Tablet and vibrating)* **ICZODHIHAL.**

(Assuming orant posture) **I ask Ye to bring with Ye into this temple the Living Earth with its blessings of stillness and depth. O dark-voiced Angels of the Watchtower of the North, bring with Ye Divine joyfulness and the healing of Earth.**

Adept of Earth turns to temple center.

Pola Vaoan: *(Speaking from their place in the Northeast, facing North)* **O Angels of the Watchtower of the North, support me in joy and bring me the healing of Earth** *(turning to face center)*.

The Descent of Spirit

Adept of Spirit marks points of the Spirit triangle in the air above the Tablet of Union. Adept of Spirit circumambulates the Tablet on the floor with arms upraised.

Adept of Spirit: **And there is a fifth in the middle, another channel of the Light, whence the Life-Bearing Light descends even as far as the Material Channels:** *(facing East)* **Hear thou the Voice of Spirit!**

Adept of Spirit traces a circle around the Tablet and within it, the invoking pentagram of Spirit Active and the sigil of Eth.

Adept of Spirit: *(Vibrating)* **EXARP. BITOM.**

Adept of Spirit traces the invoking pentagram of Spirit Passive and the sigil of Eth.
Adept of Spirit: *(Vibrating)* **HCOMA. NANTA.**

(Giving the sign of the Rending of the Veil) **In the Names and Letters of the mystical Tablet of Union which binds together the Four Tablets into one under the presidence of Spirit, I invoke Ye, Ye Divine Forces of the Spirit of Life!**

(Speaking) **"Ol sonuph vaorsa gi," goho Iada Balata.** *(Vibrating)* **ELEXARPEH. COMANANU. TABITOM.** *(Speaking)* **Zodacare, ca, od zodameranu! Odo Cicale Qaa, Piape Piamoel od Vaoan!**

I invoke Ye, Ye Angels of the Celestial Spheres whose dwelling is in the Invisible. Ye are the guardians of the Gates of the Universe; be Ye also the Watchers of our Mystic Temple and the Divine Agents of Healing. Keep far removed the evil. Strengthen and inspire the initiates so that we may preserve unsullied this abode of the Mysteries of the Eternal Gods. Let this place be pure and holy so that we may enter in and become partakers of the secrets of the Divine Light.

(Assuming orant posture) **I ask Ye to bring with Ye into this temple the Living Spirit with its blessings of Sacred Light and Life. O life-breathing Angels of the Tablet of Union, bring with Ye sweet ecstasy and the healing of Spirit.**

Pola Vaoan: *(Speaking from their place in the Northeast and facing center)* **O Angels of the Tablet of Union, illuminate me with the Divine Life and bring me the healing of Spirit.**

Adept of Spirit moves to the Northeast.

Adept of Spirit: **The Sun daily returning is the dispenser of Light to the Earth. Let us initiate the Whorl, by thrice completing the circle of this place, the abode of the Invisible Sun.**

All line up in Northeast of the temple for circumambulation in this order: Spirit, Air, Fire, Water, Earth, Pola Vaoan. Upon completion, All return to stations.

Next, on a signal from Adept of Spirit, Elemental Adepts step forward to encircle the Tablet of Union. As they circumambulate the Tablet of Union thrice, Adept of Spirit stands in the sign of Osiris Slain. Upon completion, Adept of Spirit assumes Osiris Risen. All return to stations.

All Adepts face East and assume Osiris Slain.

ADEPTS: *(Together)* **Holy Art Thou, Ruler of the Universe. Holy Art Thou, Whom Nature hath not formed. Holy Art Thou, the vast and the mighty one, Ruler of the Light and of the Darkness.**

ALL ADEPTS assume Osiris Risen.

Assumption of the Deityforms of the Monarchs

ADEPT OF SPIRIT: **From out of the Primordial Darkness of No-Thing-Ness emerged the Primordial Light! And four Great Beings gathered around that Light—Four Holy Living Things, Themselves Primordial Powers. By our Art, we know Their Names: BATAIVAH, the King of Air; EDELPERNAA, the King of Fire; RAAGIOSEL, the Queen of Water; ICZODHIHAL, the Queen of Earth!**

When They *have* an image, They may be seen as great, six-winged Beings, full of eyes before and behind Them. They flash with a Divine incandescence and we must shield our eyes from Their beauty. They sing continually …

ELEMENTAL ADEPTS: *(Chanting together)* **Holy, Holy, Holy, Divine One, Pantokrator! The One Who Was, the One Who Is, and the One Who Is To Come!**

ADEPT OF SPIRIT: **O Holy, Living Ones, we sing with Ye …**

ADEPT OF SPIRIT AND POLA VAOAN: *(Chanting together)* **Holy, Holy, Holy, Divine One, Pantokrator! The One Who Was, the One Who Is, and the One Who Is To Come!**

ADEPT OF SPIRIT: **… and we call upon Ye to move, descend, and fill these Adepts with Thy graceful powers of healing!**

Bataivah Descends

ADEPT OF AIR turns to face Air Tablet and traces cross before Tablet.

ADEPT OF AIR: **In the three Great, Secret Names of God the Father, God the Mother, and God the Child borne upon the Banner of the East:** *(vibrating)* **ORO, IBAH,**

AOZODAPI, we invoke the Holy, Living King of Air . . . *(tracing spiral and vibrating)* **BATAIVAH!**

Adept of Air turns to center with Air Tablet at their back and opens self to assume Godform. Adept of Fire comes to their left to speak into their left ear. Adept of Earth comes to right to speak into their right ear. Adept of Water stands before Adept of Air.

Adepts of Fire and Earth: *(Choral speaking very softly into Adept's ears)* **Zodacare od zodameranu, Bataivah! Zodacare od zodameranu, Bataivah! Zodacare od zodameranu, Bataivah!**

Adept of Air: **Zodimeii ol, Bataivah!** ["Enter me, Bataivah!"] *(Vibrating alone using simple Vibratory formula)* **BATAIVAH!**

Adept of Fire: **BA—**
Adept of Earth: **TAI—**
Adept of Air: **VAH!**
Adept of Fire: **BA—**
Adept of Earth: **TAI—**
Adept of Air: **VAH!**
Adept of Fire: **BA—**
Adept of Earth: **TAI—**
Adept of Air: **VAH!**

Adept of Air: **Zodacare od zodameranu** *(vibrating with simple Vibratory formula)* **BATAIVAH! BATAIVAH! BATAIVAH! BATAIVAH! Odo cicale Qaa!**

Adept of Water begins to repeatedly trace the Infinity symbol over the Adept of Air, as if tracing two great wings.

ADEPT OF WATER: **Bataivah knows the Truth of what must be healed. Bataivah spreads out His great wings, full of eyes, and enwraps the Two Truths to heal, to heal. Open the channels of the healing Air, O Bataivah, speak Thou the Words of Power.**

ADEPT OF WATER ceases making symbol.

ADEPT OF AIR: *(Speaking as Bataivah)* **I am the Knowledge of the Aions and the cool, bright breath of Dawn. I am the sun-quickened air of early spring and the life-cry of a child being born from its mother's womb. I am the whirling radiance of the healer's hands. I am the Perfect Idea. I am the freedom that begets trust, the knowledge that dispels fear. I am the riddle that fosters creativity and the intelligence that continually discovers the Many Truths. Awaken—and understand Bataivah!**

ALL: *(Vibrating)* **BATAIVAH!**

ADEPT OF AIR allows a few moments to assimilate the energy of the King. When this feels complete, ALL return to their stations. ADEPT OF AIR begins to silently build up a reservoir of Air energy in the Tablet of Air to be released later.

Edelpernaa Descends

ADEPT OF FIRE turns to face Fire Tablet and traces cross before Tablet.

ADEPT OF FIRE: **In the three Great, Secret Names of God the Father, God the Mother, and God the Child borne upon the Banner of the South:** *(vibrating)* **OIP, TEAA, PEDOCE, we invoke the Holy, Living King of Fire ...** *(tracing spiral and vibrating)* **EDELPERNAA!**

ADEPT OF FIRE turns to center with Tablet at their back and opens self to assume Godform.

ADEPTS OF AIR, WATER, EARTH: **Zodacare od zodameranu, Edelpernaa! Zodacare od zodameranu, Edelpernaa! Zodacare od zodameranu, Edelpernaa!**

ADEPT OF FIRE: **Zodimeii ol, Edelpernaa!** ["Enter me, Edelpernaa!"] (*Forcefully speaking and giving sign of Osiris Slain*) **Malapiregi!** ["Fire!"]

ADEPT OF WATER forcefully, but in silence, gives sign of Osiris Risen.

ADEPT OF EARTH: *(Forcefully speaking and giving sign of Osiris Slain)* **Malapiregi!**

ADEPT OF AIR forcefully, but in silence, gives sign of Osiris Risen.

(NOTE: This sequence is repeated three more times, for a total of four times.)

ALL OTHER ADEPTS: *(Chanting softly but with fiery intensity under* ADEPT OF FIRE'S *vibration)* **Edelpernaa! Edelpernaa! Edelpernaa! Edelpernaa!, etc.**

ADEPT OF FIRE: **Zodacare od zodameranu** *(vibrating with simple Vibratory formula)* **EDELPERNAA! EDELPERNAA! EDELPERNAA! EDELPERNAA! Odo cicale Qaa!**

ADEPT OF EARTH: **Edelpernaa empowers the healing. Edelpernaa spreads out His fiery wings, full of eyes, and fans the sacred Fire of the Divine Physician. Open the channels of the healing Fire, O Edelpernaa, radiate Thou the Energy of Transformation.**

ADEPT OF FIRE: *(Speaking as Edelpernaa)* **I am the Energy of All Creation. I am the power of the Red Lion, rushing forward into the Light. I am Passion, the first-born Power, engenderer of all things. I am Desire. I am directed Will. I am loud-shouting Ecstasy, rushing wild in His Divinity. I am your blood. I am the burning that transmutes one thing to another. I am the consummation that obliterates false pride. I am the transformation that releases anger and the courage that sublimates fear. Arise—and feel the power of Edelpernaa!**

ALL: *(Vibrating)* **EDELPERNAA!**

Adept of Fire allows a few moments to assimilate the energy of the King. Adept of Fire begins to silently build up a reservoir of Fire energy in the Tablet of Fire to be released later.

Raagiosel Descends

Adept of Water turns to face Water Tablet and traces cross before Tablet.

Adept of Water: **In the three Great, Secret Names of God the Father, God the Mother, and God the Child borne upon the Banner of the West:** *(vibrating)* **EMPEH, ARSEL, GAIOL, we invoke the Holy, Living Queen of Water . . .** *(tracing spiral and vibrating)* **RAAGIOSEL!**

Adept of Water turns to center with Tablet at their back and opens self to assume Goddessform. Adept of Water takes up and elevates Water Cup, then begins to spin in place slowly.

Adepts of Air, Fire, Earth: *(Hypnotically and softly)* **Zodacare od zodameranu, Raagiosel! Zodacare od zodameranu, Raagiosel! Zodacare od zodameranu, Raagiosel!**

Adept of Water slowly sinks down onto throne and, in vision, turns within.

Adept of Air: **Enter into the Water. A zodelida, arepeheh** ["in the water, descend"].

Adept of Water: **Ol arepeheh a zodelida** ["I descend in the water"]. *(Vibrating)* **RAAGIOSEL!**

Adept of Fire: **Enter into the Water, deeper. A zodelida, arepeheh.**

Adept of Water: **Ol arepeheh a zodelida.** *(Vibrating)* **RAAGIOSEL!**

Adept of Earth: **Enter into the Water, deeper still. A zodelida, arepeheh.**

Adept of Water: **Ol arepeheh a zodelida.** *(Vibrating)* **RAAGIOSEL!**

ADEPT OF WATER: *(Rising and elevating the Water Cup)* **I have entered into Thy Water, O Raagiosel. I am open to Thy flow. I am open to Thy Magic. Zodimeii ol, Raagiosel!** ["Enter me, Raagiosel!"] *(Vibrating and pouring libation from Water Cup into bowl on Water altar)* **RAAGIOSEL! RAAGIOSEL! RAAGIOSEL! RAAGIOSEL! Odo cicale Qaa!**

ADEPT OF AIR: **Raagiosel holds up the mirror of healing vision. Raagiosel's shimmering wings, full of eyes, flow about Her, bright with Magic. Open the channels of the healing Waters, O Raagiosel, pour forth purity and the waters of rebirth.**

ADEPT OF WATER: *(Speaking as Raagiosel)* **I am the Living Soul of All Things. I am the pearl that encircles a single grain of sand in beauty. I am the mysterious depths of the undying ocean. I am Dream, the oblique revealer. I am the nourisher of Spirit. Magic am I. I am the flow that releases jealousy. I am the love that soothes pain. I am the changes that promote growth, the wholeness that allows you to let go. I am the knowing depths of your own holy soul. I am the blessings bestowed. Flow—and be dissolved in the cleansing love of Raagiosel!**

ALL: *(Vibrating)* **RAAGIOSEL!**

ADEPT OF WATER allows a few moments to assimilate the energy of the Queen. ADEPT OF WATER begins to silently build up a reservoir of Water energy in the Tablet of Water to be released later.

Iczodhihal Descends

ADEPT OF EARTH turns to face Earth Tablet and traces cross before Tablet.

ADEPT OF EARTH: **In the three Great, Secret Names of God the Father, God the Mother, and God the Child borne upon the Banner of the North:** *(vibrating)* **EMOR, DIAL, HECTEGA, we invoke the Holy, Living Queen of Earth…** *(tracing spiral and vibrating)* **ICZODHIHAL!**

ADEPT OF EARTH takes up drum and gives it to ADEPT OF FIRE. Then ADEPT OF EARTH turns to center with Tablet at their back and opens self to assume Goddessform. ADEPT OF FIRE gives a rapid battery of ten beats on the drum, rests, then gives ten more.

ADEPT OF EARTH: **We make an earthquake for Thy appearance, O Mighty Queen! The joy of Thy coming is ours, O Iczodhihal. We rejoice in the Life that is Thine. We rejoice in the healing that Thou dost bring.**

ADEPTS AIR, FIRE, WATER: *(Vibrating as low and "thunderously" as possible; by intuition, ADEPT OF FIRE punctuates vibration with slow drum beats at will)* **Ohhhhhhhhhhhhhhhhhhhhhhhhh.**

ADEPT OF EARTH: *(Over their continuing vibration)* **Zodacare od zodameranu, Iczodhihal! Zodacare od zodameranu, Iczodhihal! Zodacare od zodameranu, Iczodhihal!**

I stand upon the mound, the most ancient Earth rising from the Primordial. I open myself to Old Earth as I lay upon Her breast, listening to the deep beating of Her heart. I sink down into the breast of my Mother. I come from my Mother. I am one with my Mother, the Holy, Living Earth—*(vibrating)* **ICZODHIHAL! ICZODHIHAL! ICZODHIHAL! ICZODHIHAL!**

ADEPT OF FIRE: **Iczodhihal provides the foundation of healing. Iczodhihal unfurls Hers wings, full of eyes, and thunder rolls, the Earth quakes. Open the channels to the healing Earth, O Iczodhihal, provide the womb of stillness and the living joy of healing.**

ADEPT OF FIRE gives a drum battery of ten beats, pauses, and gives ten more.

ADEPT OF EARTH: **Zodimeii ol, Iczodhihal!** ["Enter me, Iczodhihal!"] **Odo cicale Qaa! Let the Divine silence of Earth descend!**

ALL are still. ADEPT OF EARTH visualizes returning to the Primordial and assuming the Goddessform of Iczodhihal. When ready, the ADEPT OF EARTH speaks.

ADEPT OF EARTH: *(Speaking as Iczodhihal)* **I am the Mother of all the Living. I am a grain of wheat. I am the soft mud in which you stand, wakeful, alive with anticipation at what waits beneath. I am the mountain where the holy women dance**

and at whose beauty they weep honeyed tears. I am the silence in which you hear the truth. I am the rest that brings strength. I am the abundance that dissolves greed. I am the end to which all must come at last. Be silent—and know the strength of Iczodhihal!

ALL make sign of Silence while silently vibrating **ICZODHIHAL.**

ADEPT OF EARTH allows a few moments to assimilate the energy of the Queen. ADEPT OF EARTH begins to silently build up a reservoir of Earth energy in the Tablet of Earth.

Formulating the Seat of Mercy

ADEPT OF SPIRIT steps to the center and traces a circle around the Tablet of Union. As the ADEPT OF SPIRIT steps back, all four ELEMENTAL ADEPTS step forward to encircle the Tablet of Union. Using grapevine steps, they make one circumambulation of the Tablet.

ALL ADEPTS: *(Vibrating while circumambulating)* **IADA.**

ADEPT OF SPIRIT: **We charge the Living Air, the Living Fire, the Living Water, and the Living Earth to enter in. Breathe, burn, flow, and support our Work, O Holy Living Elements, O Holy Living Creatures! In beauty and in grace, we invoke the Whorl; we create a fit place for the influx of the Living Spirit. We now formulate the Mercy Seat, the place of Divine Life and Light, the place of healing.**

In the Name of *(vibrating)* **NANTA, let Iczodhihal bring the Living Earth!**

ADEPT OF EARTH: *(Using simple Vibratory formula and gestures as desired to channel the reservoir of Earth energy from the Tablet of Earth into the sphere around the Tablet of Union)* **ICZODHIHAL! The Holy Living One of Earth is the womb of healing.**

ADEPT OF EARTH continues using sound, gestures, or other methods to continue to move the energy of Living Elemental Earth into the Sphere.

ADEPT OF SPIRIT: **In the Name of HCOMA, let Raagiosel bring the Living Water!**

ADEPT OF WATER: *(Using simple Vibratory formula and gestures as desired to channel the reservoir of Water energy from the Tablet of Water into the sphere around the Tablet of Union)* **RAAGIOSEL! The Holy Living One of Water fills the womb with the waters of rebirth.**

ADEPT OF WATER continues using sound, gestures, or other methods to continue to move the energy of Living Elemental Water into the Sphere.

ADEPT OF SPIRIT: **In the Name of BITOM, let Edelpernaa bring the Living Fire!**

ADEPT OF FIRE: *(Using simple Vibratory formula and gestures as desired to channel the reservoir of Fire energy from the Tablet of Fire into the sphere around the Tablet of Union)* **EDELPERNAA! The Holy Living One of Fire brings the transforming energy of healing.**

ADEPT OF FIRE continues using sound, gestures, or other methods to continue to move the energy of Living Elemental Fire into the Sphere.

ADEPT OF SPIRIT: **In the Name of EXARP, let Bataivah bring the Living Air!**

ADEPT OF AIR: *(Using simple Vibratory formula and gestures as desired to channel the reservoir of Air energy from the Tablet of Air into the sphere around the Tablet of Union)* **BATAIVAH! The Holy Living One of Air fans the flame of healing truth.**

ADEPT OF AIR continues using sound, gestures, or other methods to continue to move the energy of Living Elemental Air into the Sphere.

ADEPTS continue this flow of energy until they feel that the sphere is fully charged and pulsing with Life.

The Invocation of the Archangel

(NOTE: the following invocation is an example only. Adepts should choose an appropriate Servient Square to represent the nature of the disease and its cure. The Enochian Keys used must also be adjusted to the Servient Square used.)

Adept of Spirit: **Let the Living Elements be joined with the Living Spirit!**

Adepts: *(Vibrating very softly under invocation)* **EXARP. BITOM. HCOMA. NANTA.**

Adept of Spirit: **"Ol sonuph vaorsa gi," goho Iada Balata, "elanusah Caelazoda Vonupeh, Soba zodeol Rore i ta nazodapesada, od Giraa ta malapiregi, das holaqo qaa notahoa zodimedoda, od comemah ta nobeloh zodienu; soba tahila ginonupe Piregi Aladai, das varebesa oboleh giresame, casareme ohorela caba Pire, ol zodonurenusagi Cabe Erem Iadanah."**

Pilah pharezodem od zodenurezoda adana old gono Iadapiel Das home od tohe, Soba iaoda ipam od vala ipamis, Das eloholo vepe zodomeda poamael, od sonuph aai ta Piape Piamoel old Vaoan!

Zodacare, ca, od zodameranu! Odo Cicale Qaa! Zodorege, elape zodiredo Noco Mada, hoath Iaida!

Over the Tablet of Union, Adept of Spirit traces pentagram of Spirit Active and the Eth sigil.

All Adepts: *(Vibrating)* **EXARP. BITOM.**

Adept of Spirit traces pentagram of Spirit Passive and the Eth sigil.

All Adepts: *(Vibrating)* **HCOMA. NANTA.**

Adept of Spirit gives sign of the Rending of the Veil.

ADEPT OF SPIRIT: **I call upon the Holy Living One of Water, Raagiosel** (NOTE: This will vary depending upon the Servient Square chosen), **to aid me to call forth the Powers of Water and the Archangel Cahedadanu.**

ADEPT OF WATER: *(Opening to channel the Powers of Water and chanting softly under reading of the Key)* **EMPEH, ARSEL, GAIOL.**

ADEPT OF SPIRIT: **Otahila elasadi Babage, od dorepaha, gohol: "Gi chisa ge avavago coremepe Malasa-Gala, das sonuph Viva Diva? Casaremi oali Tala-Unu-Malasa-Tala sobam agi coremepo carepe El; casaremegi caroodazodi chisa od vagegi; das ta capimali chisa capimaon: od elonusahinu chisa ta elo Veh-Vare-Unu.**

"Torezodu, Nore Qasahi, od phe Caosaga: Bagile zodire Enai Iada: das i od apila!"

Dooaipe Qaal, zodacare! zodameranu obelisonugi resat-el aai Nore Emoelapi!

ADEPT OF SPIRIT and ADEPT OF WATER face West, trace invoking pentagram of Water and the sigil of Nesher.

ADEPTS OF SPIRIT AND WATER: *(Vibrating)* **EMPEH, ARSEL, GAIOL. RAAGIOSEL.** Both give the Practicus sign.

ADEPT OF WATER: *(Turning to center and continuing to channel the powers of Water while softly chanting under reading of the Key)* **ABEGOTA, AABECAO.**

ADEPT OF SPIRIT: **Coriaxo chisa coremepe od belanusa Lucala, azodiazodore paebe, soba lilononu chisa vireqo Meda-Malasa copehanu od racalire maasi Caosagi, das ialponu dosigi od basagime; od ox ex dazodisa siatarisa od salberoxa cinuxire phaboanu. Vanala chisa Conusata das, Gala-Unu-Meda-Pala cocasabe Meda-Vare oanio, iore eoresa vohime gizodiaxa od cocasaii pelosi molui das pageipe, laragi same darolanu matorebe coacasabe emena. El pataralaxa iolacai matabe nomigi mononusa olora ginai anugelarda.**

Ohio, ohio, ohio, ohio, ohio, ohio!! Noibe ohio Caosagon! Bagile madarida i, zodirepe, chiso darisapa! Niiso, caripe ipe nidali!

Adept of Spirit and Adept of Water face West, trace invoking pentagram of Air and Air sigil.

Adept of Spirit: **In the Name of Invocation …**
Adepts of Spirit and Water: *(Vibrating)* **ABEGOTA!**
Adept of Spirit: **We call Thee!**
And in the Name of Obligation …
Adepts of Spirit and Water: *(Vibrating)* **AABECAO!**
Adept of Spirit: **We ask for Thine aid!**

Adepts of Spirit and Water trace invoking pentagram of Water and Cancer sigil.

Adept of Spirit: **In the Name of Abegota, we invoke the Mighty Archangel** *(vibrating)* **CAHEDADANU!**

Cahedadanu, Who rules over the disease which plagues the Pola Vaoan, *(adding the person's name on earth or, if an Adept, their motto)***, we ask Thee to lend us Thine aid and bring balance to the disease—bring the cure, O Cahedadanu! Bring Thy powers to Kaporeth which now stands revealed behind Paroketh.**

Cahedadanu, we invite Thee to the Mercy Seat.

Adept of Spirit traces Calvary Cross and Veh.

All Adepts: *(Vibrating and using gestures to draw energy from the Water Tablet into the Mercy Seat)* **CAHEDADANU! CAHEDADANU! CAHEDADANU! CAHEDADANU! CAHEDADANU!**

Taking the Mercy Seat

Adept of Spirit: **Let the Pola Vaoan come forth.**

Pola Vaoan comes to stand beside the Adept of Spirit. All Adepts become aware once more of their connections with the Elemental powers and the Archangel. Let the Elemental Adepts once more take up their implements (Feather, Fire, Shell, Apple) and return with them to the center. All should visualize the energy of the Mercy Seat as a great, dynamic Whorl of healing power.

Adept of Air: *(Using simple Vibratory formula and Projecting sign to once more charge the Mercy Seat)* **BATAIVAH!**

Adept of Fire: (*Using simple Vibratory formula and Projecting sign to once more charge the Mercy Seat*) **EDELPERNAA!**

Adept of Water: *(Using simple Vibratory formula and Projecting sign to once more charge the Mercy Seat)* **RAAGIOSEL!**

Adept of Earth: *(Using simple Vibratory formula and Projecting sign to once more charge the Mercy Seat)* **IC ZOD HI HAL!**

Adept of Spirit: *(Using simple Vibratory formula and Projecting sign to once more charge the Mercy Seat)* **CAHEDADANU!**

All Adepts continue channeling the healing powers of their Elements to the Mercy Seat.

With Pola Vaoan standing beside them, Adept of Spirit comes to the East, facing West, and gives the sign of the Rending of the Veil to open the Whorl to the Vaoan. Adept of Spirit directs Pola Vaoan to stand before them, facing East.

Adept of Spirit: *(To Pola Vaoan)* **Open yourself to the healing of the Seat of Mercy.**

Adept of Spirit and Pola Vaoan mirror each other giving the sign of the Rending of the Veil to open the Pola Vaoan's aura to the healing. When Pola Vaoan is ready, Pola Vaoan steps into the center and stands on the Tablet of Union, facing East. The

Pola Vaoan should feel a distinct change in the "atmospheric pressure" inside and outside of the Whorl of the Mercy Seat.

Adept of Spirit gives sign of the Closing of the Veil behind Pola Vaoan.

The Conjoining and Knitting Together of Natures

Adept of Spirit: *(To Pola Vaoan)* **Aspire to the Highest now and be aware of Kether above you. And let us vibrate together the Name Iada.**

All: *(Vibrating)* **IADA.**

Adept of Spirit: **Be aware of Malkuth below you. And let us vibrate together the Name Iada.**

All: *(Vibrating)* **IADA.**

Adept of Spirit: **Be aware of Tiphereth at your heart. And once more let us vibrate Iada.**

All: *(Vibrating)* **IADA.**

All Adepts assist in the visualizations that follow.

Adept of Spirit: **See the Light above, below, within, about you. Let yourself soak in that Light. Call upon your Holy Guardian Angel to aid you.**

Now let yourself be aware of the imbalance that makes you ill. Visualize that imbalance in any way that it comes to you, but find an image, a way to "see" it in vision.

Hold that image and also become aware of the Whorl around you, the healing energy that pulses and lives for you as you stand here in the chamber of the Mercy Seat, the place of the Healing of God. This is the energy of the Archangel Cahedadanu, who rules over the disease and its cure.

(To the Archangel) **We call upon Thee, Cahedadanu, to conjoin and knit together the disease with its cure. Restore the balance!**

Elemental Adepts: *(Chanting softly and continuing to move energy to the Mercy Seat)* **Restore the balance, O Cahedadanu, restore the balance, restore the balance, etc.**

Adept of Spirit: *(To Pola Vaoan)* **Now see the image of the disease reaching out to its opposite which is in the hands of the Archangel. See the balancing energy of the Archangel reaching out toward the disease as you have seen it. They come together. They interweave like threads of a cloth, like long, graceful fingers. They blend like water and wine … and are brought into harmony and balance once more.**

Accept the healing of Cahedadanu.

Adept of Air: **Accept the healing of Bataivah.**
Adept of Water: **Accept the healing of Raagiosel.**
Adept of Fire: **Accept the healing of Edelpernaa.**
Adept of Earth: **Accept the healing of Iczodhihal.**

Adept of Spirit: **Accept the healing of Cahedadanu. Cahedadanu rights the imbalance. Cahedadanu knits together the disease with its opposite, restoring, restoring, restoring the balance within you.**

Adept of Spirit guides Pola Vaoan to be seated on the Tablet of Union for meditation. If desired, a seat may be placed upon the Tablet of Union for the Pola Vaoan. All Adepts return to their stations and are seated for meditation.

Incubation

All remain in silent meditation until the Pola Vaoan is ready to close. When ready, the Pola Vaoan stands and faces East.

POLA VAOAN: **Cool wine from the hands of angels pours through me. The Living Elements and the Living Spirit enter. I hear Their voices. I feel Their healing touch. I am a point of Light emanating from my own heart. All else falls away. All is dissolved in Light. I am whole. I am purified. I am balanced. I am being reborn every day.**

ADEPT OF SPIRIT gives sign of the Rending of the Veil, then takes up the white over-robe and helps POLA VAOAN into it to retain the charge during devocation. POLA VAOAN returns to the Northeast, then moves their throne to the Southeast, taking their new station in the Southeast. The POLA VAOAN may be seated. ALL ADEPTS stand at their stations. ADEPT OF SPIRIt turns to face Tablet of Water.

Closing

ADEPT OF SPIRIT: **O Mighty Archangel Cahedadanu, we thank Thee for Thine assistance in the conjoining the knitting together of Natures. Unhealthy becomes healthy. The imbalance is brought into balance. Cahedadanu, beautiful Archangel, we thank Thee and for now, we bid Thee farewell.**

ADEPT OF SPIRIT traces banishing pentagram of Water and sigil of Cancer toward Tablet of Water.

ALL: *(Vibrating)* **CAHEDADANU.**

ADEPT OF SPIRIT traces banishing pentagram of Air and Air sigil toward Tablet of Water.

ADEPT OF SPIRIT: **In the Name of Invocation, Abegota, and the Name of Obligation, Aabecao, we give thanks for this healing—and we release the power.**

ALL: *(Vibrating)* **ABEGOTA. AABECAO.**

ADEPT OF SPIRIT traces banishing pentagram of Water.

ADEPT OF SPIRIT: **In the three Great Secret Names borne upon the Banner of the West, we give thanks for this healing—and we release the power.**

All: *(Vibrating)* **EMPEH, ARSEL, GAIOL.**

Adept of Spirit: **The shining path of the Archangel Cahedadanu is closed. Let us now Close the Watchtowers and release all the Elemental and Spiritual Beings and Powers that we have invoked during this rite.**

Closing the Watchtowers of Healing

Adept of Air takes up Air Dagger, faces East, and bows in respect.

Adept of Air: **I thank the Holy Living One of Air, King Bataivah, and I release His form from myself** *(doing so)*.

Replacing Dagger and taking up the Wing, Adept of Air traces the reverse circle, the banishing pentagram of Air, and the sigil of Adam.

Adept of Air: *(Vibrating)* **ORO, IBAH, AOZODAPI.** *(Giving Theoricus sign)* **In the Names and Letters of the Great Eastern Quadrangle, I release Ye, Ye Angels of the Watchtower of the East!** *(Ceasing sign and tracing reverse spiral of the Monarch's name on Tablet)* **Be in peace, wise** *(vibrating)* **BATAIVAH.**

O bright-voiced Angels of the Watchtower of the East, I thank Ye for the Words of Power and the healing of Air. May there ever be peace between us *(kissing their hand and extending it toward the Tablet of Air)*.

Adept of Air turns to temple center.

Adept of Fire takes up Fire Wand, faces South, and bows in respect.

Adept of Fire: **I thank the Holy Living One of Fire, King Edelpernaa, and I release His form from myself** *(doing so)*.

Replacing Wand and taking up the vessel of Fire, Adept of Fire traces reverse circle, the banishing pentagram of Fire, and the sigil of Aryeh.

ADEPT OF FIRE: *(Vibrating)* **OIPE, TEAA, PEDOCE.** *(Giving Philosophus sign)* **In the Names and Letters of the Great Southern Quadrangle, I release Ye, Ye Angels of the Watchtower of the South!** *(Ceasing sign and tracing reverse spiral of the Monarch's name on Tablet)* **Be in peace, powerful** *(vibrating)* **EDELPERNAA.**

O fiery-voiced Angels of the Watchtower of the South, I thank Ye for the power to make change and the healing of Fire. May there ever be peace between us *(kissing their hand and extending it toward the Tablet of Fire)*.

ADEPT OF AIR turns to temple center.

ADEPT OF WATER takes up Water Cup, faces West, and bows in respect.

ADEPT OF WATER: **I thank the Holy Living One of Water, Queen Raagiosel, and I release Her form from myself** *(doing so)*.

Replacing Cup and taking up the Shell, ADEPT OF WATER traces reverse circle, the banishing pentagram of Water, and the sigil of Nesher.

ADEPT OF WATER: *(Vibrating)* **EMPEH, ARSEL, GAIOL.** *(Giving Practicus sign)* **In the Names and Letters of the Great Western Quadrangle, I release Ye, Ye Angels of the Watchtower of the West!** *(Ceasing sign and tracing reverse spiral of the Monarch's name on Tablet)* **Be in peace, deep** *(vibrating)* **RAAGIOSEL.**

O moon-voiced Angels of the Watchtower of the West, I thank Ye for the soul-nourishing Magic and the healing of Water. May there ever be peace between us *(kissing their hand and extending it toward the Tablet of Water)*.

ADEPT OF WATER turns to temple center.

ADEPT OF EARTH takes up Pentacle, faces North, and bows in respect.

ADEPT OF EARTH: **I thank the Holy Living One of Earth, Queen Iczodhihal, and I release Her form from myself** *(doing so)*.

Replacing Pentacle and taking up cut Apple, ADEPT OF EARTH traces the reverse circle, the banishing pentagram of Earth, and the sigil of Shor.

ADEPT OF EARTH: *(Vibrating)* **EMOR, DIAL, HECTEGA.** *(Giving Zelator sign)* **In the Names and Letters of the Great Northern Quadrangle, I release Ye, Ye Angels of the Watchtower of the North!** *(Ceasing sign and tracing reverse spiral of the Monarch's name on Tablet)* **Be in peace, strong** *(vibrating)* **ICZODHIHAL.**

O dark-voiced Angels of the Watchtower of the North, I thank Ye for the Divine joyfulness and the healing of Earth. May there ever be peace between us *(kissing their hand and extending it toward the Tablet of Earth)***.**

ADEPT OF EARTH turns to temple center.

Over the Tablet of Union, ADEPT OF SPIRIT traces reverse circle, banishing pentagram of Spirit Active, and the Eth sigil.

ADEPT OF SPIRIT: *(Vibrating)* **EXARP. BITOM.**

ADEPT OF SPIRIT traces banishing pentagram of Spirit Passive and the Eth sigil.

ADEPT OF SPIRIT: *(Vibrating)* **HCOMA. NANTA.**

ADEPT OF SPIRIT gives sign of the Closing of the Veil.

In the Names and Letters of the mystical Tablet of Union which binds together the Four Tablets into one under the presidence of Spirit, I release Ye, Ye Divine Forces of the Spirit of Life!

O life-breathing Angels of the Tablet of Union, I thank Ye for the sweet ecstasy and the healing of Spirit. May there ever be peace between us *(kissing their hand and extending it toward the Tablet of Union)***.**

ADEPT OF SPIRIT spirals out from the center to the Southeast beside POLA VAOAN.

ADEPT OF SPIRIT: **The Sun daily setting is the bringer of repose to the Earth. Let us devolve the Whorl, by thrice completing the circle of the place, the abode of the invisible Sun.**

ALL line up in Southeast corner of the temple for reverse circumambulation: SPIRIT, FIRE, WATER, AIR, EARTH, POLA VAOAN. Upon completion, ALL return to stations. ALL ADEPTS face East and assume Osiris Slain. POLA VAOAN faces East.

ADEPTS: *(Together)* **Holy Art Thou, Ruler of the Universe. Holy Art Thou, Whom Nature hath not formed. Holy Art Thou, the vast and the mighty one, Ruler of the Light and of the Darkness.**

ALL ADEPTS assume Osiris Risen and analyze the Keyword in English, then Paroketh in Enochian:

ADEPT OF WATER: *(Giving Practicus sign)* **Malasa!**
ADEPT OF AIR: *(Giving Theoricus sign)* **Donu!**
ADEPT OF FIRE: *(Giving Philosophus sign)* **Gere!**
ADEPT OF EARTH: *(Giving Zelator sign)* **Emeta!**

ADEPT OF SPIRIT: **The whole word is Paroketh, which is the veil of the Sanctum Sanctorum.**

ALL ADEPTS give sign of the Closing of the Veil.

ALL: **Not unto us, not unto us, but unto Thy name be the glory, Thou Who hast allowed us to penetrate thus far into the Sanctuary of Thy Mysteries. Zodorege, elape zodiredo Noco Mada, hoath Iaida!**

ALL perform Angelic Cross in Enochian:

ANGELIC CROSS

ADEPTS: *(Touching crown and vibrating)* **ENONUCA I**
(Touching heart and vibrating) **ELONUDOHEH,**

(Touching right shoulder and vibrating) **MICALAZODA,**
(Touching left shoulder and vibrating) **BUSIDIRE.**
(Tracing circle) **PAEMBETA A HOMINU.**
(Folding hands) **KARESTATEOS.**

✠ ✠ ✠

Epilogue

CREATING GOLDEN DAWN RITUALS

Within the previous chapters, we have provided many different examples of Golden Dawn rituals. However, these are only a fraction of the type of rites that can be produced for modern students while still following the philosophy and ethos of our practice. By now you should know how ritual magic in our tradition is structured and how it functions. The following information will prove useful should you wish to craft your own Golden Dawn–style rituals.

Remember First Principles

The Golden Dawn was founded to teach its students the fundamentals and practical applications of the Western Esoteric Tradition in order to better align themselves with the Divine. As stated in the Portal Ceremony, this knowledge is bestowed on the student as a trust "not for your selfish advantage, but for the service of all mankind, that the ancient tradition of Initiation be kept pure and undefiled, and the Light be not lost for those that seek it in this Path." (Refer to pages 25–28 of our book *Golden Dawn Magic* for more on this.)

Basic Components of Golden Dawn Ritual

In *The Essential Golden Dawn*, we outlined fourteen different steps common to many Golden Dawn Rituals.[181] In brief, these are:

181. See Ciceros, *The Essential Golden Dawn*, 154–61.

The Opening

1. Declaration of a Commencement of a Ritual
2. A Banishing Ritual
3. Initial Purification and Consecration
4. Circumambulation
5. Adoration

The Middle Point

6. An Invocation Ritual
7. An Invocation to the Highest
8. The Main Working

The Closing

9. Final Purification and Consecration
10. Reverse Circumambulation
11. Adoration
12. License to Depart
13. Banishing Ritual
14. Declare Temple Closed

Not all rituals will follow this exact formula. And we do not expect people to, as Regardie put it, "slavishly follow" our instructions. For example, in step 2, some will prefer to perform a basic invoking ritual rather than a banishing. We prefer to do a banishing in order to clear out any mundane energy or "astral cobwebs" that may have accumulated in the temple prior to ritual work. At step 13, we often forgo the banishing at the end, allowing the effects of the ritual to linger a while, so long as the energy does not interfere with other people who may share the space or with the normal functioning of a household. Nevertheless, this outline is a good formula to follow, particularly for magicians who are just starting to compose rituals.

Keep the Ego in Check

Magic is designed to stimulate the mind, and this can sometimes cause problems in the form of an overinflated ego. Infantile megalomania and delusions of grandeur directly contradict the first principles. They will put an end to your spiritual growth. Be vigilant and watch out for them.

Never Bite Off More Than You Can Chew

Although this should be obvious, it deserves mentioning that it would be a great idea to wait until you have spent some time as an Adept before writing rituals for the Outer Order. Students in the First Order are still learning the basics of magic and don't have the experience or perspective to see the system as a whole. That does not mean you cannot design simple exercises and meditations based on your gradework. Be mindful of how the system is structured and how the various levels fit together.

Writing Group Rituals for the Outer Order

Adepts writing rituals for use in the First Order must keep in mind that many participants will *not* be Adepts. Today, many of the teachings and rituals of the Golden Dawn are readily available to the general public, and a good many Outer Order students may already be completely familiar with them. Nevertheless, it is important that members of both the First and the Second Order stay in their lanes.

It is simply not wise (or fair!) to expect Neophytes, Zelators, and other Outer Order students to be able to perform Adept-level work, such as the Lesser Invoking Ritual of the Hexagram of the Sun, with its twenty-four associated hexagrams! This is not a part of their gradework; it may confuse and discourage them. It may keep them from focusing on their own important work of equilibration. And without a firm foundation, it may hinder their later progress as an Adept if they develop bad habits early on.

The best practice for writing Outer Order Rituals is to concentrate on using symbolism that already exists in the Neophyte Hall and in the gradework given to Neophytes, such as the Lesser Ritual of the Pentagram. Divine forces can be invoked using symbols that every student learns in the First Knowledge Lecture, including the elemental triangles, the symbols of the planets, the symbols of the Zodiacal signs, the emblem of the Tree of Life, the symbols on the Officers' lamens, and the like.

And if it is important that some Adept-level work be done in the ritual, try to limit it as much as possible and ensure that such work is only ever performed by a skilled Adept, usually the Hierophant or Dais Officers.

Writing Group Rituals for the Inner Order

Second Order Initiates have a lot of latitude when it comes to designing ceremonies for other Adepts. They are free to incorporate many of the ritual methods, exercises, and materials covered in the Adeptus Minor curriculum. This opens up a huge amount of source material that the magician can draw from, including virtually everything found in Regardie's *The Golden Dawn* and other sourcebooks.[182] Nevertheless, it is important to understand that even in the Second Order, some material will be limited by grade level. For example, rituals based on Adeptus Major materials would not be appropriate in a ritual designed for Adeptus Minors.

And while the Adept is free to use materials from the Second Order curriculum, that is no excuse to go hog wild and stuff a ceremony with every type of pentagram, hexagram, heptagram, and dodekagram known to humankind. Golden Dawn magicians often have a reputation for wanting to make everything complicated. Remember, not all Adepts have the same skill level, and more layers of complication mean more things can go sideways. When it comes to crafting group ceremonies, try to opt for the "less is more" approach. The Second Order curriculum is extensive. Therefore, Adept-level rites are by their very nature more advanced than First Order rituals. But this should allow you to refine your rituals rather than cram them with unnecessary symbolism.

If you like elaborate, detailed rituals, make sure the Adepts you work with are all on the same page. Otherwise, save the complexity for your own personal solo work.

Writing Solo Rituals for the Adept

Writing solo rituals[183] is actually an essential part of the Adept's gradework as defined in the Order's document entitled "Z.2: The Formulae of the Magic of Light" mentioned in chapter 5. Not only is the magician required to write rituals based on the Z.2 formulas, but they are also required to submit their rituals for approval and be tested on them by performing them in front of their instructor(s), who will determine the effectiveness of the rite, whether the exam requirements are fulfilled, and offer helpful suggestions if need be. The rituals written by Regardie in book 6 of *The Golden Dawn* are great examples of this.[184]

---

182. Regardie's *The Golden Dawn* contains a good deal of the original curriculum through Zelator Adeptus Minor.

183. And sometimes group rituals.

184. Regardie, *The Golden Dawn*, 511–70.

However, writing and performing a few rituals just to satisfy the requirements of an exam is not enough. Solo rituals are the mainstay of the Golden Dawn magician's personal work of self-transformation. Writing effective rituals takes practice. You need to write a series of them. Some may work and others may not. Keep a ritual journal to determine which is which.

Some Final Advice

Poorly designed rituals are those that tend to meander with no real purpose at their core. Their intended goal may be poorly defined or badly executed. They may have all the right speeches and gestures but lack real creative and emotive power. They may be written in such a way that glosses over important magical techniques, such as visualization, vibration, and the movement of energy. However, many unsatisfactory rituals can be improved by reworking them. A well-written Golden Dawn ritual is reminiscent of a well-crafted piece of music, with ebbs and flows, crescendos and decrescendos. It is formulated on chords of logic and focus. It repeats melodies yet changes octaves to build and release energy.

Pay attention to devising stage directions, especially when writing for a group. Read the ritual out loud and do a complete walk-through before performing any ritual you've written. In doing so, you will discover where stage directions might not make sense or need clarification, or where better instructions for visualization may be needed.

The rituals we've supplied here may be worked as is or used as blueprints to create other ceremonies and rites. However you employ them, may their use aid you in the accomplishment of the Great Work, the creation of the Philosopher's Stone, and the quest for the Light Divine.

BIBLIOGRAPHY

Barrabbas, Frater. *Mastering the Art of Ritual Magic: Volume One: Foundation.* Stafford, England: Megalithica Books, 1996.

Beck, Renee, and Sydney Barbara Metrick. *The Art of Ritual: Creating and Performing Ceremonies for Growth and Change.* 1990. Reprint, Berkeley, CA: Apocryphile Press, 2012.

Brier, Bob. *Ancient Egyptian Magic.* New York: Quill, 1981.

Budge, E. A. Wallis. *The Book of the Dead: An English Translation of the Chapters, Hymns, Etc. of the Theban Recension, with Introduction, Notes, Etc.* London: Routledge & Kegan Paul, 1949.

Budge, E. A. Wallis. *The Book of the Dead, with Twenty-Five Illustrations.* London: British Museum Board of Trustees, 1920.

Budge, E. A. Wallis. *Egyptian Magic.* London: Kegan Paul, Trench, Trübner & Co., 1901.

Churchill, Winston. *The Unrelenting Struggle: War Speeches by the Right Hon. Winston S. Churchill.* Boston: Little, Brown and Company, 1942.

Cicero, Chic, and Sandra Tabatha Cicero. *The Essential Golden Dawn.* Woodbury, MN: Llewellyn, 2009.

Cicero, Chic, and Sandra Tabatha Cicero, eds. *Gold: Israel Regardie's Lost Book of Alchemy.* Woodbury, MN: Llewellyn, 2015.

Cicero, Chic, and Sandra Tabatha Cicero. *Golden Dawn Magic: A Complete Guide to the High Magical Arts.* Woodbury, MN: Llewellyn, 2019.

Cicero, Chic, and Sandra Tabatha Cicero. *Ritual Use of Magical Tools: The Magician's Art*. St. Paul, MN: Llewellyn, 2000.

Cicero, Chic, and Sandra Tabatha Cicero. *Secrets of a Golden Dawn Temple: Book 1: Creating Magical Tools.* Loughborough, UK: Thoth, 2004.

Cicero, Chic, and Sandra Tabatha Cicero. *Self-Initiation into the Golden Dawn Tradition.* St. Paul, MN: Llewellyn, 1998.

Cicero, Sandra Tabatha. *The Book of the Concourse of the Watchtowers*. Elfers, FL: H.O.G.D. Books, 2012.

Christian, Paul. *The History and Practice of Magic.* Secaucus, NJ: The Citadel Press, 1972.

Clark, R. T. Rundle. *Myth and Symbol in Ancient Egypt.* New York: Thames and Hudson, 1991.

Denning, Melita, and Osborne Phillips. *Planetary Magick*. St. Paul, MN: Llewellyn, 1989.

DeVore, Nicholas. *Encyclopedia of Astrology.* New York: Philosophical Library, 1947.

Dykes, Benjamin, and Jayne Gibson. *Astrological Magic*. Minneapolis, MN: Cazimi Press, 2012.

Ellis, Normandi. *Awakening Osiris: The Spiritual Keys to the Egyptian Book of the Dead.* Newburyport, MA: New Page Books, 2023.

Everard, Dr. John, trans. *The Divine Pymander of Hermes Trismegistus*. 1650. Reprint, Preston Hollow, NY: Societas Rosicruciana in America, 1991.

Forrest, M. Isidora. *Isis Magic: Cultivating a Relationship with the Goddess of 10,000 Names.* Portland, OR: Abiegnus House, 2013.

Forrest, M. Isidora. "What Is the Isia? 'Samhain' for Isis Devotees?" Isiopolis. October 19, 2012. https://isiopolis.com/2012/10/19/what-is-the-isia-samhain-for-isis-devotees.

Graf, Fritz. *Magic in the Ancient World*. Cambridge, MA: Harvard University Press, 1997.

Gray, William G. *Inner Traditions of Magic.* New York: Samuel Weiser, 1978.

Greer, John Michael. *Circles of Power: Ritual Magic in the Western Tradition.* St. Paul, MN: Llewellyn, 1997.

Greer, John Michael. *The New Encyclopedia of the Occult.* St. Paul, MN: Llewellyn, 2003.

Halevi, Z'ev ben Shimon. *School of Kabbalah.* York Beach, ME: Samuel Weiser, 1985.

Hall, Manly P. *The Secret Teachings of All Ages*. Los Angeles, CA: Philosophical Research Society, 1988.

Hoeller, Stephan A. *Ecclesia Gnostica: Collects, Lessons, and Gospels to Be Used Throughout the Church Year,* 2010. http://gnosis.org/ecclesia/Ecclesia-Gnostica-Lectionary.pdf.

Hope, Murry. *Practical Egyptian Magic.* Wellingborough, Northhamptonshire, UK: Aquarian Press, 1984.

Hope, Murry. *The Psychology of Ritual.* Dorset, UK: Element Books, 1988.

Knight, Gareth. *The Practice of Ritual Magic.* Albuquerque, NM: Sun Chalice Books, 1996.

Levi, Eliphas. *The Magical Ritual of the Sanctum Regnum*. London: George Redway, 1896.

Regardie, Israel. *The Golden Dawn: The Original Account of the Teachings, Rites, and Ceremonies of the Hermetic Order.* Revised and corrected by John Michael Greer. 1937. Reprint, Woodbury, MN: Llewellyn, 2015.

Regardie, Israel. *The Tree of Life: An Illustrated Study in Magic.* 1932. Reprint, St. Paul, MN: Llewellyn, 2001.

Regardie, Israel. *What You Should Know About the Golden Dawn.* 1936. Reprint, Phoenix, AZ: Falcon Press, 1987.

Robinson, James M., ed. *The Nag Hammadi Library in English*. San Francisco, CA: Harper & Row, 1977.

Spence, Lewis. *Ancient Egyptian Myths and Legends*. New York: Dover, 1990.

Stavish, Mark. *Egregores: The Occult Entities That Watch Over Human Destiny*. Rochester, VT: Inner Traditions, 2018.

Stephenson, Barry. *Ritual: A Very Short Introduction.* New York: Oxford University Press, 2015.

Turner, Victor. *The Ritual Process: Structure and Anti-Structure.* Ithaca, NY: Cornell University Press, 1969.

Tyson, Donald. *Ritual Magic: What It Is and How to Do It.* St. Paul, MN: Llewellyn, 2000.

Vaspra, Woody. "Prayer for the Healing and Care of Our Mother Earth." Native American Olympic Team Foundation. Accessed April 2025. https://www.naotf.org/articles/2007/woody.htm.

Waite, A. E. *The Real History of the Rosicrucians*. London: George Redway, 1887.

Watson, Lindsay C. *Magic in Ancient Greece and Rome.* London: Bloomsbury Academic, 2019.

Weschcke, Carl Llewellyn, and Joe H. Slate. *Clairvoyance for Psychic Empowerment.* Woodbury, MN: Llewellyn, 2013.

Westcott, William Wynn. *Collectanea Hermetica.* London: Theosophical Publishing Society, 1895.

PERMISSIONS

Certain brief passages in the rituals "Invocation of Thoth," "Invocation of Iophiel," and "The Flame of the Sacred Heart" have been inspired by or adapted from (and are reproduced with permission from) *Awakening Osiris: The Spiritual Keys to the Egyptian Book of the Dead,* Copyright © 1988, 2023 by Normandi Ellis. All rights reserved. No part of this publication may be reproduced or transmitted in any form or by any means, electronic or mechanical, including photocopying, recording, or by any information storage and retrieval system, without permission in writing from Red Wheel/Weiser, LLC. Reviewers may quote brief passages. Originally published as *Awakening Osiris: A New Translation of the Egyptian Book of the Dead* in 1988 by Phanes Press. This new edition includes a new introduction and an instructional appendix.

The "Invocation of Thoth" and "The Flame of the Sacred Heart" include brief sections inspired by or adapted from *Isis Magic*, Copyright © 2001–2024 by M. Isidora Forrest ("Invoking Star of the Gods," and "Invoking the Four Pillars of the Earth"). Printed with permission.

Portions of the Zodiacal invocations in the "Invocation of the Mazzoloth" were adapted from *Astrological Magic*, Copyright © 2012 by Dr. Benjamin Dykes and Jayne Gibson. Printed with permission.

Original artwork of "The Table of Shewbread" and adapted artwork for "The Seal of Universal Unity" Copyright © 2024 by Adam P. Forrest. Printed with permission.

"The Ceremony of the Rising of the Light: A Summer Solstice Ritual" Copyright © 2024 by Eric V. Sisco. Printed with permission.

"A Requiem Rite" Copyright © 2005–2024 by Jayne Gibson, OZ, and Chic and Tabatha Cicero.

"A Ritual of Honor and Remembrance" Copyright © 2017–2024 by Chic and Tabatha Cicero and Jayne Gibson.

"The Ceremony of the Seven Wanderers: A Winter Solstice Ritual" Copyright © 2013–2023 by Jayne Gibson and Chic and Sandra Tabatha Cicero.

Rituals in chapter 5 were originally published in *Secrets of a Golden Dawn Temple* by Chic and Sandra Tabatha Cicero (St. Paul, MN: Llewellyn Publications, 2000).

"An Evocation of the Enochian Archangel Aabai" was adapted by the authors from "The Astral Evocation of the Enochian Servient Archangel Arbenuhe" by Adam P. Forrest, Copyright © 1995 by Adam P. Forrest. Printed with permission.

The "Invocation of Thoth," the "Invocation of Iophiel," and "Archangelic Rite of Healing" include brief sections adapted from *The Divine Pymander of Hermes Trismegistus,* translated from the original Arabic by Dr. John Everard and published by the Societas Rosicruciana in America. Printed with permission.

Several rituals include material from Israel Regardie's *The Golden Dawn: The Original Account of the Teachings, Rites, and Ceremonies of the Hermetic Order*. Copyright © 2015. Printed with permission from Llewellyn Publications.

Quoted material from Israel Regardie's *The Tree of Life: An Illustrated Study in Magic* Copyright © 2001. Printed with permission from Llewellyn Publications.

ILLUSTRATION CREDITS

All interior illustrations are by Sandra Tabatha Cicero except the following:

Figure 7: The God Thoth on page 75 is from E. A. Wallis Budge, *The Gods of the Egyptians, or Studies in Egyptian Mythology, Vol. 1.*, pages 400–1. (Originally published in 1904 by the Open Court Publishing Company, Chicago, and Methuen & Company, London.) New York: Dover Publications, 1969. No copyright indicated. Public domain.

Figure 10: Iophiel on page 89 was recreated by the Llewellyn Art Department based on a drawing by Sandra Tabatha Cicero.

Figure 15: The Table of Shewbread on page 106 was created by Adam P. Forrest and used with permission.

Figure 22: The Goddess Isis on page 162 is from E. A. Wallis Budge, *The Gods of the Egyptians, or Studies in Egyptian Mythology, Vol. 1.*, pages 202–3. (Originally published in 1904 by the Open Court Publishing Company, Chicago, and Methuen & Company, London.) New York: Dover Publications, 1969. No copyright indicated.

Figure 23: The Seal of Universal Unity on page 164 was created by Sandra Tabatha Cicero, adapted from artwork by Adam P. Forrest and used with permission.

Figure 29: The Lotus Wand on page 248 was recreated by the Llewellyn Art Department based on a drawing by Sandra Tabatha Cicero.

Figure 34: The Magic Sword on page 273 was recreated by the Llewellyn Art Department based on a drawing by Sandra Tabatha Cicero.

Figure 39: The Elemental Tools on page 281 was recreated by the Llewellyn Art Department.

Figure 44: Kerubic Plaques on page 325 was created by Sandra Tabatha Cicero, adapted from artwork by Adam P. Forrest and used with permission.

Figure 45: A Compound Kerubic Plaque on page 326 was created by Adam P. Forrest and used with permission.

Figure 47: The God Osiris on page 333 is from E. A. Wallis Budge, *The Gods of the Egyptians, or Studies in Egyptian Mythology, Vol. 1.*, pages 114–15. (Originally published in 1904 by the Open Court Publishing Company, Chicago, and Methuen & Company, London.) New York: Dover Publications, 1969. No copyright indicated. Public domain.

Figure 50: A Single Vault Wall on page 349 recreated by the Llewellyn Art Department.

Figure 52: The Sun God Ra on page 359 is from *Egyptian Designs* by Carol Belanger Grafton. New York: Dover Publications, 1993.

To Write to the Authors

If you wish to contact the author or would like more information about this book, please write to the author in care of Llewellyn Worldwide Ltd. and we will forward your request. Both the author and the publisher appreciate hearing from you and learning of your enjoyment of this book and how it has helped you. Llewellyn Worldwide Ltd. cannot guarantee that every letter written to the author can be answered, but all will be forwarded. Please write to:

Chic Cicero and Sandra Tabatha Cicero
℅ Llewellyn Worldwide
2143 Wooddale Drive
Woodbury, MN 55125-2989

Please enclose a self-addressed stamped envelope for reply, or $1.00 to cover costs. If outside the U.S.A., enclose an international postal reply coupon.

Many of Llewellyn's authors have websites with additional information and resources. For more information, please visit our website at http://www.llewellyn.com.